The Beverage Book

D0001974

Jean Paré

companyscoming.com
visit our website

Divider Photo

1. Melon Lemonade, page 124
2. Pineapple Mango Smoothie, page 10
3. Christmas Spirit, page 140
4. Purple Cow, page 57
5. Raspberry Spritzer, page 97
6. Orange Almond Cocktail, page 92
7. Cranberry Champagne, page 132

Props Courtesy Of:
Linens 'N Things
Stokes
Winners Stores

We gratefully acknowledge the following suppliers for their generous support of our Test Kitchen and Photo Studio:

Broil King Barbecues
Corelle®
Hamilton Beach® Canada
Lagostina®
Proctor Silex® Canada
Tupperware®

Need dinner solutions?

Find plenty of
valuable advice
and **cooking**
information
on our **website**.

Visit us at
www.companyscoming.com

Table of Contents

Cocktails

Nightcaps

Punches

Pitchers

Holiday

Foreword

We start and end our days with beverages, beginning with that first cup of steaming coffee or tea in the morning and ending with a soothing after-dinner drink or nightcap before bed. We celebrate memorable times with toasts and drink to good health! Beverages of all descriptions are an inseparable part of our daily lives. Finally, they are getting the attention they deserve.

Beverages have become much more than lunch or dinner accompaniments. They help create ambiance at elegant dinner parties or family get-togethers; they add comfort and warmth when you want to feel cozy; and they sparkle and bubble when you're laughing and celebrating.

In *The Beverage Book*, we've compiled more than 170 ways to quench your thirst, including long-time favourites you'll recognize, plus many special creations developed and tested in our own kitchen. Choose something hot or cold, sweet or savoury, with or without alcohol.

Get the energy and nutrition you need for breakfast with a satisfying smoothie or yummy shake. Spice up your coffee break with the taste of cinnamon, almond or vanilla, or try a sweet or tangy tea perfectly steeped. Add a fruity or extracted juice to your child's lunch, or make a vibrantly coloured, refreshing punch for your next birthday party or other special occasion. Put your feet up with a specialty coffee or a deliciously drowsy cocktail. Anything you could thirst for, we've provided—and more!

Hosting a party or family get-together? Try your hand at ice rings and fruit garnishes to add simple elegance, or serve your punch in a beautifully delicate or fantastically fun punch bowl. Need to know what glass is used with what drink? Check page 8 and your presentation will always complement the delicious drink you've made. Wish you could make the perfect cup of coffee or tea? You can! We share our tips with you on page 9.

We've also added 24 ways to say, "Cheers!" in different languages, so you'll always have the right toast for that special moment with family and friends.

Whether you're preparing something steamy and sweet, or cool and quenching, *The Beverage Book* is a resource you won't want to be without.

Cheers!

Jean Paré

Each recipe has been analyzed using the most up-to-date version of the Canadian Nutrient File from Health Canada, which is based on the United States Department of Agriculture (USDA) Nutrient Data Base. If more than one ingredient is listed (such as "hard margarine or butter"), or a range is given (1 – 2 tsp., 5 – 10 mL), then the first ingredient or amount is used in the analysis. Where an ingredient reads "sprinkle," "optional," or "for garnish," it is not included as part of the nutrition information. Milk, unless stated otherwise, is 1% and cooking oil, unless stated otherwise, is canola.

Margaret Ng, B.Sc. (Hon), M.A.
Registered Dietitian

Serving Beverages

Alcoholic Beverages

When preparing cocktails with fruit juice, squeeze and strain the juice just before serving, then add the liquor. This keeps the taste of the juice vibrant and the taste of the alcohol strong. The suggested amount of alcohol per serving is 1 1/4 to 1 1/2 oz. (35 to 50 mL). For punches, keep all ingredients chilled, including the alcohol, until just before serving. This will keep the ice cubes or ice ring from melting too fast and keep the punch chilled longer.

Glasses

There are many different glass shapes and sizes to choose from when serving a beverage—and no glass is right or wrong. But in some cases there is a definite benefit to having a certain glass, as with a red wine glass where the deeper bowl shape captures the bouquet, or the fluted champagne glass that concentrates the effervescence at the top. We've identified five shapes that are reflected in the recipes in this book:

Champagne Flute: A tall, stemmed glass used for champagne and sparkling wine drinks. Holds 3/4 to 1 cup (175 to 250 mL).

Margarita Glass: A wide-rimmed, stemmed glass used for sipping slushy drinks. Rim is often dampened and dipped into salt or sugar. Holds 1 1/2 to 2 cups (375 to 500 mL).

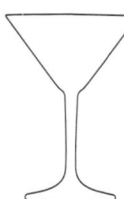

Martini Glass: A wide-rimmed, stemmed glass with a triangular bowl used for martinis and other cocktails. Holds 1/2 to 3/4 cup (125 to 175 mL).

Red Wine and White Wine Glasses: The red wine glass has a slightly larger, deeper bowl. Holds 1 to 1 1/4 cups (250 to 300 mL). The white wine glass has a slightly smaller bowl. Holds 3/4 to 1 cup (175 to 250 mL).

The Perfect Cup Of...

Coffee

1. Use cold water (filtered water is best).

2. Use clean or well-rinsed equipment. If possible, wash your coffee maker after each use and store unassembled.

3. Buy small portions of coffee for immediate use or store unused coffee in a resealable container in the refrigerator. Do not mix old and new coffee.

4. Grind whole beans before brewing and always use the correct size of grind for your coffee maker.

5. Use 1 tbsp. (15 mL) ground coffee for each 8 oz. (1 cup, 250 mL) cold water for fairly weak strength, adding more to suit taste.

6. Serve coffee immediately after brewing and store in an insulated carafe for up to an hour. Do not keep coffee on stove element or base of coffee machine. Do not boil or it will become bitter; do not reheat because it will taste stale.

Tea

1. Heat water (filtered is best) to just boiling.

2. Rinse teapot with hot water to minimize cooling of hot water when added.

3. Use 1 tea bag (or 1 tbsp., 15 mL, loose tea) for each cup.

4. Steep tea for 3 to 6 minutes, depending on type (green tea should steep for 2 to 3 minutes; black for 4 to 5 minutes).

5. Remove tea bag or strain loose tea.

6. For a stronger tea, add more tea bags rather than steeping tea longer than the recommended time. Steeping for too long causes bitterness. For a weaker tea, add more hot water.

7. Loose tea is best for flavour because the leaves can expand. Tea bags restrict the expansion of the leaves necessary for achieving full flavour.

8. Store tea in an airtight, opaque container in a cool, dry place or in tightly closing metal tins. Clear glass jars are acceptable if kept in a closed cupboard away from light. Do not refrigerate.

Glass & Mug sizes used in this book:

Small glass	4 to 8 oz.	125 to 250 mL
Medium glass	8 to 12 oz.	250 to 375 mL
Large glass	12 to 16 oz.	375 to 500 mL
Small mug	6 to 8 oz.	175 to 250 mL
Large mug	8 to 12 oz.	250 to 375 mL

Cantaloupe Smoothie

Have you ever had a melon smoothie? Here's a great one to try, with just a hint of cinnamon!

Ripe medium banana, cut up	1	1
Cantaloupe, seeds removed, chopped	1/2	1/2
Plain yogurt	1 1/2 cups	375 mL
Liquid honey	2 tbsp.	30 mL
Ground cinnamon	1/4 tsp.	1 mL
Ice cubes	6	6

Process all 6 ingredients in blender until smooth. Makes about 4 1/2 cups (1.1 L). Pour into 4 medium glasses. Serves 4.

1 serving: 144 Calories; 1.8 g Total Fat (0.4 g Mono, 0.1 g Poly, 1 g Sat); 6 mg Cholesterol; 28 g Carbohydrate; 1 g Fibre; 6 g Protein; 75 mg Sodium

Pineapple Mango Smoothie

Flavour of the tropics. Thick and refreshing.

Chopped fresh pineapple (or can of pineapple tidbits, 8 oz., 227 mL, drained)	1 cup	250 mL
Ripe medium mango, diced	1	1
Orange juice	1 cup	250 mL
Ice cubes	6	6
Coconut flavouring	1/16 tsp.	0.5 mL

Process all 5 ingredients in blender until smooth. Makes about 3 1/3 cups (825 mL). Pour into 2 large glasses. Serves 2.

1 serving: 166 Calories; 0.9 g Total Fat (0.2 g Mono, 0.2 g Poly, 0.1 g Sat); 0 mg Cholesterol; 41 g Carbohydrate; 3 g Fibre; 2 g Protein; 4 mg Sodium

Raspberry Energizer

Thick, pink drink bursting with raspberry flavour.

Frozen whole raspberries	1 cup	250 mL
Raspberry yogurt	1 cup	250 mL
Soy milk (or milk)	1 cup	250 mL
Raspberry jam	2 tbsp.	30 mL
Large egg (see Note)	1	1

Process all 5 ingredients in blender until smooth. Makes about 3 cups (750 mL). Pour into 2 large glasses. Serves 2.

1 serving: 291 Calories; 7.3 g Total Fat (2 g Mono, 1.7 g Poly, 2.3 g Sat); 116 mg Cholesterol; 46 g Carbohydrate; 4 g Fibre; 12 g Protein; 119 mg Sodium

Pictured on page 17.

Note: Eggs used in beverages should be cold. Remove egg from refrigerator just before adding. Beverages containing uncooked egg should be served immediately.

Yogurt Fruit Smoothie

Very sweet, very pretty beverage with a whisper of cinnamon.

Fresh strawberries	8	8
Ripe medium banana, cut up	1	1
Vanilla yogurt	1 1/2 cups	375 mL
Frozen blueberries	1/2 cup	125 mL
Frozen concentrated orange juice	2 tbsp.	30 mL
Ground cinnamon	1/8 tsp.	0.5 mL
Ice cubes	3	3

Process all 7 ingredients in blender until smooth. Makes about 3 3/4 cups (925 mL). Pour into 4 small glasses. Serves 4.

1 serving: 149 Calories; 2.3 g Total Fat (0.5 g Mono, 0.1 g Poly, 1.3 g Sat); 5 mg Cholesterol; 30 g Carbohydrate; 2 g Fibre; 5 g Protein; 57 mg Sodium

Energy Burst

Tart cranberry, creamy strawberry and nutty wheat germ.
Tastes good—and is good for you!

Cranberry cocktail	2 cups	500 mL
Fresh (or frozen whole) strawberries, chopped	1 cup	250 mL
Strawberry frozen yogurt	1/2 cup	125 mL
Wheat germ, toasted (see Tip, page 13)	2 tbsp.	30 mL

Process all 4 ingredients in blender until smooth. Makes about 3 cups (750 mL). Pour into 2 large glasses. Serves 2.

1 serving: 286 Calories; 4.1 g Total Fat (0.9 g Mono, 0.7 g Poly, 2 g Sat); 5 mg Cholesterol; 61 g Carbohydrate; 3 g Fibre; 4 g Protein; 38 mg Sodium

PB And Banana Toast

The taste of a peanut butter and banana sandwich—in a glass!
For the kid in all of us!

Frozen ripe medium bananas (see Tip, page 21)	2	2
Milk	2 cups	500 mL
Smooth peanut butter	1/4 cup	60 mL
Wheat germ, toasted (see Tip, page 13)	3 tbsp.	50 mL
Liquid honey	2 tbsp.	30 mL
Vanilla	1/8 tsp.	0.5 mL

Process all 6 ingredients in blender until smooth. Makes about 4 cups (1 L). Pour into 4 medium glasses. Serves 4.

1 serving: 269 Calories; 10.9 g Total Fat (4.7 g Mono, 2.8 g Poly, 2.8 g Sat); 5 mg Cholesterol; 35 g Carbohydrate; 3 g Fibre; 10 g Protein; 147 mg Sodium

Breakfast Drinks

Kiwi Yogurt Smoothie

Creamy, tangy smoothie with a touch of sweetness.

Ripe kiwifruit, peeled and chopped	2	2
Vanilla frozen yogurt	1 cup	250 mL
Orange juice	1 cup	250 mL
Liquid honey	1 tbsp.	15 mL

Process all 4 ingredients in blender until smooth. Makes about 2 1/4 cups (550 mL). Pour into 2 medium glasses. Serves 2.

1 serving: 259 Calories; 4.9 g Total Fat (1.3 g Mono, 0.2 g Poly, 2.6 g Sat); 2 mg Cholesterol; 52 g Carbohydrate; 3 g Fibre; 5 g Protein; 72 mg Sodium

Pictured on page 17.

Sunshine Cup

A bright-coloured, fruit-flavoured breakfast delight.
Good morning, sunshine!

Apricot nectar	4 cups	1 L
Can of pineapple tidbits (with juice)	14 oz.	398 mL
Frozen concentrated orange juice	1/4 cup	60 mL

Measure 2 cups (500 mL) apricot nectar, 1/2 can of pineapple tidbits and 2 tbsp. (30 mL) frozen concentrated orange juice into blender. Process until smooth. Transfer to large pitcher. Repeat with remaining apricot nectar, pineapple and concentrated orange juice. Makes about 7 cups (1.75 L). Pour into 6 medium glasses. Serves 6.

1 serving: 161 Calories; 0.2 g Total Fat (0.1 g Mono, 0.1 g Poly, 0 g Sat); 0 mg Cholesterol; 41 g Carbohydrate; 2 g Fibre; 1 g Protein; 6 mg Sodium

 *To toast wheat germ, spread evenly in ungreased shallow pan. Bake in 350°F (175°C) oven for about 3 minutes, stirring or shaking often until golden, or heat and stir in small frying pan on medium. Let stand until cooled completely.*

Apricot Pick-Me-Up

Buttermilk with apricot and pineapple in a light, foamy drink.
A great way to start your day! Store leftover apricot halves in light syrup
in an airtight container in the fridge and use in other beverages.

Apricot nectar	1/2 cup	125 mL
Pineapple juice	1/2 cup	125 mL
Buttermilk	1/3 cup	75 mL
Canned apricot halves (about 4 halves)	1/4 cup	60 mL
Milk	1/4 cup	60 mL

Process all 5 ingredients in blender until smooth and frothy. Makes about 2 cups (500 mL). Pour into 2 medium glasses. Serve immediately. Serves 2.

1 serving: 120 Calories; 0.9 g Total Fat (0.3 g Mono, 0.1 g Poly, 0.5 g Sat); 3 mg Cholesterol; 26 g Carbohydrate; 1 g Fibre; 3 g Protein; 66 mg Sodium

Razzmatazz

Apricot nectar adds an unexpected, delightful flavour
to this thick raspberry smoothie.

Frozen whole raspberries	1 cup	250 mL
Apricot nectar	1 cup	250 mL
Vanilla yogurt	1/2 cup	125 mL
Liquid honey	2 tbsp.	30 mL
Ice cubes	6	6

Process all 5 ingredients in blender until smooth. Makes about 2 3/4 cups (675 mL). Pour into 2 medium glasses. Serves 2.

1 serving: 230 Calories; 1.7 g Total Fat (0.4 g Mono, 0.3 g Poly, 0.8 g Sat); 3 mg Cholesterol; 54 g Carbohydrate; 4 g Fibre; 4 g Protein; 42 mg Sodium

Breakfast Drinks

Banana Shake

Banana and maple make a pleasantly sweet and creamy shake.

Ripe medium banana, cut up	1	1
Milk	1 1/2 cups	375 mL
Vanilla ice cream	1 cup	250 mL
Maple (or maple-flavoured) syrup	2 tbsp.	30 mL

Process all 4 ingredients in blender until smooth. Makes about 2 3/4 cups (675 mL). Pour into 2 medium glasses. Serves 2.

1 serving: 326 Calories; 10 g Total Fat (2.8 g Mono, 0.4 g Poly, 6.1 g Sat); 38 mg Cholesterol; 53 g Carbohydrate; 1 g Fibre; 9 g Protein; 155 mg Sodium

Soy Delicious

Enjoyable because it's sweet, thick and frothy.

Frozen ripe medium banana (see Tip, page 21)	1	1
Soy milk (or milk)	1 1/2 cups	375 mL
Vanilla yogurt	1/2 cup	125 mL
Wheat germ	2 tbsp.	30 mL
Maple (or maple-flavoured) syrup	1 tbsp.	15 mL

Process all 5 ingredients in blender until smooth. Makes about 3 cups (750 mL). Pour into 4 small glasses. Serves 4.

1 serving: 114 Calories; 2.9 g Total Fat (0.5 g Mono, 1.1 g Poly, 0.7 g Sat); 2 mg Cholesterol; 19 g Carbohydrate; 2 g Fibre; 5 g Protein; 31 mg Sodium

Paré Pointer
Say cheers in Austrian: "Prosit!" (PROH-sit)

Citrus Shake

Silky papaya with the tang of grapefruit and orange.
Great citrus combo.

Ruby red grapefruit juice	1 cup	250 mL
Chopped papaya	1 cup	250 mL
Vanilla frozen yogurt	1 cup	250 mL
Frozen concentrated orange juice	2 tbsp.	30 mL

Process all 4 ingredients in blender until smooth. Makes about 2 1/2 cups (625 mL). Pour into 2 medium glasses. Serves 2.

1 serving: 239 Calories; 4.5 g Total Fat (1.3 g Mono, 0.2 g Poly, 2.7 g Sat); 2 mg Cholesterol; 47 g Carbohydrate; 2 g Fibre; 5 g Protein; 72 mg Sodium

Pictured on page 17.

1. Kiwi Yogurt Smoothie, page 13
2. Raspberry Energizer, page 11
3. Citrus Shake, above

Props Courtesy Of: Danesco Inc.

Apple-A-Day

A quick, tasty way to get your "apple a day." Tart and creamy.
Add more honey if you like a sweeter taste.

Apple juice	2 cups	500 mL
Unsweetened applesauce	1 cup	250 mL
Plain (or soy) yogurt	1/2 cup	125 mL
Frozen concentrated apple juice	2 tbsp.	30 mL
Liquid honey	1 tbsp.	15 mL

Ground cinnamon, sprinkle (optional)

Process first 5 ingredients in blender until smooth and frothy. Makes about 3 1/2 cups (875 mL). Pour into 2 large glasses.

Sprinkle each with cinnamon. Serves 2.

1 serving: 281 Calories; 1.4 g Total Fat (0.3 g Mono, 0.2 g Poly, 0.7 g Sat); 4 mg Cholesterol; 66 g Carbohydrate; 2 g Fibre; 4 g Protein; 61 mg Sodium

1. Almond Coffee, page 22
2. Sweet Dreams, page 103
3. Eggnog Cappuccino, page 28

Props Courtesy Of: Canhome Global
Klass Works
Linens 'N Things
Stokes
The Bay
The Paderno Factory Store

Orchard Shake Up

Loads of natural sweetness in this creamy shake.

Can of pear halves (with juice)	14 oz.	398 mL
Chopped pitted dates	1/2 cup	125 mL
Frozen concentrated apple juice	2 tbsp.	30 mL
Vanilla frozen yogurt	1 cup	250 mL
Milk	1 cup	250 mL

Process first 3 ingredients in blender until fruit is finely chopped.

Add frozen yogurt and milk. Process until smooth. Makes about 4 cups (1 L). Pour into 4 medium glasses. Serves 4.

1 serving: 219 Calories; 3 g Total Fat (0.8 g Mono, 0.1 g Poly, 1.7 g Sat); 3 mg Cholesterol; 47 g Carbohydrate; 4 g Fibre; 5 g Protein; 72 mg Sodium

Very Berry Frappé

Very berry cold and refreshing. A zesty drink to wake up to.

Frozen mixed berries	2 cups	500 mL
Milk (or soy milk)	1 cup	250 mL
Dessert tofu (such as Pete's Tofu	3/4 cup	175 mL
Very Berry-flavoured dessert), or		
plain soft tofu		
Cranberry cocktail	1/2 cup	125 mL
Liquid honey	1 tbsp.	15 mL

Process all 5 ingredients in blender until smooth. Makes about 3 1/4 cups (800 mL). Pour into 2 large glasses. Serves 2.

1 serving: 277 Calories; 6.5 g Total Fat (1.4 g Mono, 2.7 g Poly, 1.5 g Sat); 5 mg Cholesterol; 47 g Carbohydrate; 7 g Fibre; 13 g Protein; 75 mg Sodium

Wake-Up Call

Peach and honey with the subtle taste of soy.
A light beverage with just a bit of tang.

Can of sliced peaches in light syrup (with juice)	14 oz.	398 mL
Soy milk (or milk)	1 cup	250 mL
Lite silken firm tofu, chopped	3/4 cup	175 mL
Liquid honey	2 tbsp.	30 mL
Vanilla	1/2 tsp.	2 mL

Process all 5 ingredients in blender until smooth. Makes about 3 cups (750 mL). Pour into 2 large glasses. Serves 2.

1 serving: 342 Calories; 11.4 g Total Fat (2.4 g Mono, 6.1 g Poly, 1.6 g Sat); 0 mg Cholesterol; 47 g Carbohydrate; 2 g Fibre; 20 g Protein; 41 mg Sodium

 *To use overripe bananas, peel and cut them into 2 inch (5 cm) pieces. Arrange in single layer in ungreased 9 x 13 inch (22 x 33 cm) pan. Freeze until firm. Store in resealable freezer bag. Substitute 4 pieces for 1 medium banana. Overripe bananas provide rich flavour to beverages.*

Almond Coffee

A rich, dark, fragrant coffee. Perfect for after dinner.

Hot strong prepared coffee (see Note)	2 cups	500 mL
Almond-flavoured liqueur (such as Amaretto), 2 oz.	1/4 cup	60 mL
Half-and-half cream (or milk)	2 tbsp.	30 mL
Brown sugar, packed	2 tsp.	10 mL
Whipped cream (or frozen whipped topping, thawed)	1/4 cup	60 mL
Sliced almonds, toasted (see Tip, page 23)	1 tbsp.	15 mL
Cocoa, sifted if lumpy (sprinkle)		

Combine first 4 ingredients in 4 cup (1 L) liquid measure or small heatproof pitcher. Makes about 2 1/4 cups (550 mL). Pour into 2 large mugs.

Top each with whipped cream. Sprinkle almonds and cocoa over top. Serves 2.

1 serving: 246 Calories; 8.5 g Total Fat (3.1 g Mono, 0.6 g Poly, 4.3 g Sat); 23 mg Cholesterol; 23 g Carbohydrate; trace Fibre; 2 g Protein; 26 mg Sodium

Pictured on page 18 and on back cover.

Note: For extra-strong flavour, use espresso.

Variation (without alcohol): Omit liqueur. Use same amount of almond-flavoured syrup (such as Torani's).

Paré Pointer

Say cheers in Japanese: "Kampai!" (KAM-pay)

Coffee Drinks

Spiced Iced Coffee

Sweet, smooth, dark coffee—cool and refreshing.

Hot strong prepared coffee (see Note)	4 cups	1 L
Granulated sugar	1/3 cup	75 mL
Cinnamon sticks (4 inches, 10 cm, each)	4	4
Whole cloves	6	6
Coffee-flavoured liqueur (such as Kahlúa), 2 oz.	1/4 cup	60 mL

Ice

Measure first 4 ingredients into medium bowl. Stir until sugar is dissolved. Chill for 1 1/2 to 2 hours until cold.

Strain coffee mixture through sieve into pitcher. Discard solids. Add liqueur. Stir. Makes about 4 cups (1 L).

Pour over ice in 4 medium glasses. Serves 4.

1 serving: 140 Calories; 0.1 g Total Fat (0 g Mono, 0 g Poly, 0 g Sat); 0 mg Cholesterol; 28 g Carbohydrate; 0 g Fibre; 1 g Protein; 12 mg Sodium

Note: For extra-strong flavour, use espresso.

Variation (without alcohol): Omit liqueur. Use same amount of coffee-flavoured syrup (such as Torani's).

Serving Suggestion: Garnish with fresh cinnamon sticks.

 *To toast seeds, nuts and coconut, spread evenly in ungreased shallow pan. Bake in 350°F (175°C) oven for 5 to 10 minutes, stirring or shaking often, until desired doneness.*

Café Olé

Coffee with a sweet, Mexican twist.

ORANGE DREAM TOPPING

Whipping cream	1/2 cup	125 mL
Orange Dream Liqueur, page 139	1/4 cup	60 mL
(or brandy), 2 oz.		
Icing (confectioner's) sugar	1 tbsp.	15 mL
Hot strong prepared coffee (see Note)	4 cups	1 L
Whipping cream	1/2 cup	125 mL
Coffee-flavoured liqueur (such as	1/4 cup	60 mL
Kahlúa), 2 oz.		
Cocoa, sifted if lumpy	2 tbsp.	30 mL
Ground cinnamon	1/2 tsp.	2 mL

Orange Dream Topping: Beat first 3 ingredients in small bowl until soft peaks form. Makes about 1 cup (250 mL) topping. Chill.

Measure next 5 ingredients into heatproof pitcher. Stir well. Makes about 5 cups (1.25 L). Pour into 4 large mugs. Spoon 1/4 cup (60 mL) topping onto each. Serves 4.

1 serving: 319 Calories; 21.2 g Total Fat (6.2 g Mono, 0.7 g Poly, 13.2 g Sat); 75 mg Cholesterol; 22 g Carbohydrate; 1 g Fibre; 3 g Protein; 43 mg Sodium

Note: For extra-strong flavour, use espresso.

Serving Suggestion: Sprinkle finely grated orange zest over topping for added zip!

Paré Pointer
Say cheers in Finnish: "Kippis!" (KIP-his)

Café Vienna

This delicious brew will warm you up on a chilly evening.

Milk	1 cup	250 mL
Instant coffee granules	1 1/2 tsp.	7 mL
Ground cinnamon, just a pinch		
Chocolate-flavoured liqueur (such as Crème de cacao), 1 oz.	2 tbsp.	30 mL

Heat and stir milk, coffee granules and cinnamon in small heavy saucepan on medium until bubbles form around edge. Remove from heat.

Add liqueur. Stir. Makes about 1 cup (250 mL). Pour into small mug. Serves 1.

1 serving: 216 Calories; 7.7 g Total Fat (2.2 g Mono, 0.3 g Poly, 4.8 g Sat); 15 mg Cholesterol; 20 g Carbohydrate; 0 g Fibre; 10 g Protein; 159 mg Sodium

Serving Suggestion: For added flair, dip rim of mug into liqueur in saucer. Press rim into granulated sugar in separate saucer until coated.

Canadian Coffee

Appealing maple flavour. Not just for pancakes anymore!

Hot prepared coffee	3/4 cup	175 mL
Maple-flavoured liqueur (such as Wild Maple Cream), 1/2 oz.	1 tbsp.	15 mL
Canadian whisky (rye), 1/2 oz.	1 tbsp.	15 mL
Whipped cream (or frozen whipped topping, thawed)	2 tbsp.	30 mL

Measure hot coffee, liqueur and whisky into small mug. Stir. Makes about 1 cup (250 mL).

Top with whipped cream. Serves 1.

1 serving: 134 Calories; 7.3 g Total Fat (2.1 g Mono, 0.3 g Poly, 4.6 g Sat); 20 mg Cholesterol; 5 g Carbohydrate; 0 g Fibre; 1 g Protein; 24 mg Sodium

Cinnamon Iced Coffee

Distinct cinnamon flavour in a cold coffee float. A summer's day drink.

Hot strong prepared coffee (see Note)	2 cups	500 mL
Granulated sugar	3 tbsp.	50 mL
Milk	3 cups	750 mL
Cinnamon sticks (4 inches, 10 cm, each)	3	3
Vanilla ice cream	2 cups	500 mL
White sanding (decorating) sugar, for garnish (see Note)	2 tsp.	10 mL
Ground cinnamon, for garnish	1/8 tsp.	0.5 mL

Measure hot coffee and granulated sugar into heatproof pitcher. Stir until sugar is dissolved. Let stand for 5 minutes.

Add milk to coffee mixture. Stir. Add cinnamon sticks. Cover. Chill for at least 4 hours until cold. Remove and discard cinnamon sticks. Makes about 5 cups (1.25 L) iced coffee.

Put 1/2 cup (125 mL) ice cream (about 2 scoops) into each of 4 chilled large glasses. Divide and pour coffee mixture over ice cream.

Combine sanding sugar and cinnamon in small cup. Sprinkle over each. Serves 4.

1 serving: 263 Calories; 9.7 g Total Fat (2.8 g Mono, 0.4 g Poly, 6 g Sat); 38 mg Cholesterol; 36 g Carbohydrate; 0 g Fibre; 9 g Protein; 158 mg Sodium

Pictured on page 35.

Note: For extra-strong flavour, use espresso.

Note: Sanding sugar is a coarse decorating sugar that comes in white and various colours and is available at specialty kitchen stores.

Licorice Cream Coffee

Creamy coffee with a touch of licorice. Mmm....

Hot prepared coffee	3/4 cup	175 mL
Irish cream liqueur (such as Baileys), 1 oz.	2 tbsp.	30 mL
Licorice-flavoured liqueur (such as Sambuca), 1/4 oz.	1/2 tbsp.	7 mL
Whipped cream (or frozen whipped topping, thawed), optional	2 tbsp.	30 mL

Measure hot coffee and both liqueurs into small mug. Stir. Makes about 1 cup (250 mL).

Top with whipped cream. Serves 1.

1 serving: 139 Calories; 5 g Total Fat (1.4 g Mono, 0.2 g Poly, 3.1 g Sat); 5 mg Cholesterol; 11 g Carbohydrate; 0 g Fibre; 1 g Protein; 33 mg Sodium

Maple Iced Coffee

Thick and creamy, maple-flavoured dessert coffee. Serve with a spoon or straw.

Cold strong prepared coffee (see Note)	1 1/2 cups	375 mL
Maple (or vanilla) ice cream, softened	1 cup	250 mL
Maple (or maple-flavoured) syrup	2 tbsp.	30 mL
Ice cubes	6	6

Process all 4 ingredients in blender until smooth. Makes about 2 cups (500 mL). Pour into 2 chilled medium glasses. Serves 2.

1 serving: 200 Calories; 7.7 g Total Fat (2.2 g Mono, 0.3 g Poly, 4.7 g Sat); 31 mg Cholesterol; 31 g Carbohydrate; 0 g Fibre; 3 g Protein; 65 mg Sodium

Pictured on page 35.

Note: For extra-strong flavour, use espresso.

Coffee Granita

Strong, icy and sweet with a cinnamon kick. Exhilarating!

Hot strong prepared coffee (see Note)	2 cups	500 mL
Brown sugar, packed	3 tbsp.	50 mL
Ground cinnamon	1/4 tsp.	1 mL
Coffee-flavoured liqueur (such as Kahlúa), 2 oz.	1/4 cup	60 mL

Measure hot coffee, brown sugar and cinnamon into medium bowl. Stir until sugar is dissolved. Pour into 1 quart (1 L) shallow baking dish. Cover. Freeze for about 3 hours until almost firm. Makes about 2 cups (500 mL) slush.

Scrape coffee mixture, using fork, into 2 chilled medium glasses. Drizzle 2 tbsp. (30 mL) liqueur over each. Serves 2.

1 serving: 214 Calories; 0.1 g Total Fat (0 g Mono, 0 g Poly, 0 g Sat); 0 mg Cholesterol; 40 g Carbohydrate; 0 g Fibre; 1 g Protein; 21 mg Sodium

Pictured on page 35.

Note: For extra-strong flavour, use espresso.

Serving Suggestion: Serve this coffee in a martini glass (see page 8) for a classy touch.

Eggnog Cappuccino

Deliciously strong coffee with creamy eggnog and cinnamon. Impressive presentation—festive and flavourful!

Hot strong prepared coffee (see Note)	1/2 cup	125 mL
Eggnog, warmed	2/3 cup	150 mL
Ground cinnamon, sprinkle (optional)		

Pour hot coffee into 2 small mugs.

Beat eggnog with whisk until frothy, or use milk frother. Spoon over top of coffee. Sprinkle each with cinnamon. Serves 2.

1 serving: 123 Calories; 6.7 g Total Fat (2 g Mono, 0.3 g Poly, 4 g Sat); 53 mg Cholesterol; 13 g Carbohydrate; 0 g Fibre; 4 g Protein; 51 mg Sodium

Pictured on page 18.

Note: For extra-strong flavour, use espresso.

Spiced Honey Coffee

Honey and spice make coffee so nice!

Milk	1/2 cup	125 mL
Liquid honey	2 tbsp.	30 mL
Vanilla	1/4 tsp.	1 mL
Ground cinnamon	1/8 tsp.	0.5 mL
Ground nutmeg, just a pinch		
Hot strong prepared coffee (see Note)	1 1/4 cups	300 mL
Whipped cream (or frozen whipped topping, thawed), for garnish	1/3 cup	75 mL

Heat and stir first 5 ingredients in small heavy saucepan on medium for about 5 minutes until bubbles form around edge and milk just starts to boil.

Pour milk mixture into 2 small mugs. Add hot coffee to each. Makes about 2 cups (500 mL).

Top each with whipped cream. Serves 2.

1 serving: 100 Calories; 0.7 g Total Fat (0.2 g Mono, 0 g Poly, 0.4 g Sat); 3 mg Cholesterol; 22 g Carbohydrate; 0 g Fibre; 3 g Protein; 39 mg Sodium

Note: For extra-strong flavour, use espresso.

Serving Suggestion: Add a cinnamon stick—makes a pretty garnish and a great stir stick as well!

Paré Pointer

Say cheers in Chinese: "Ganbei!" (GAHN-bay)

Orange Liqueur Coffee

Barely sweet, dark coffee with creamy orange topping.

ORANGE CREAM TOPPING

Whipping cream	1/2 cup	125 mL
Orange-flavoured liqueur (such as Grand Marnier), 1/2 oz.	1 tbsp.	15 mL
Granulated sugar	1 tbsp.	15 mL
Hot strong prepared coffee (see Note)	3 cups	750 mL
Orange-flavoured liqueur (such as Grand Marnier), 1 oz.	2 tbsp.	30 mL
Coffee-flavoured liqueur (such as Kahlúa), 1 oz.	2 tbsp.	30 mL

Cocoa, sifted if lumpy (sprinkle)

Orange Cream Topping: Beat whipping cream, first amount of liqueur and sugar in small bowl until soft peaks form. Makes about 1 cup (250 mL) topping.

Combine next 3 ingredients in 4 cup (1 L) liquid measure or small heatproof pitcher. Makes about 3 cups (750 mL). Pour into 4 small mugs. Spoon 1/4 cup (60 mL) topping onto each.

Sprinkle each with cocoa. Serves 4.

1 serving: 169 Calories; 10.1 g Total Fat (3 g Mono, 0.3 g Poly, 6.3 g Sat); 37 mg Cholesterol; 10 g Carbohydrate; 0 g Fibre; 1 g Protein; 20 mg Sodium

Note: For extra-strong flavour, use espresso.

Irish Coffee

Toast the Irish with this traditional drink.

Irish whiskey (1 1/2 oz.)	3 tbsp.	50 mL
Granulated sugar	1/2 tsp.	2 mL
Hot strong prepared coffee (see Note)	3/4 cup	175 mL
Whipped cream (or frozen whipped topping, thawed)	2 tbsp.	30 mL

Measure whiskey and sugar into small mug. Add hot coffee. Stir. Makes about 1 cup (250 mL).

Top with whipped cream. Serves 1.

1 serving: 159 Calories; 4.9 g Total Fat (1.4 g Mono, 0.2 g Poly, 3 g Sat); 18 mg Cholesterol; 4 g Carbohydrate; 0 g Fibre; 1 g Protein; 13 mg Sodium

Note: For extra-strong flavour, use espresso.

Irish Cream Floats

Ice cream and liqueur make this coffee a rich, creamy dessert to eat with a spoon!

Hot strong prepared coffee (see Note)	1 1/2 cups	375 mL
Brown sugar, packed	1 tbsp.	15 mL
Irish cream liqueur (such as Baileys), 2 1/2 oz.	1/3 cup	75 mL
Chocolate ice cream	1 cup	250 mL

Measure hot coffee and brown sugar into 2 cup (500 mL) liquid measure. Stir until sugar is dissolved. Add liqueur. Stir. Makes about 2 cups (500 mL). Pour into 2 chilled large glasses or mugs.

Add 1/2 cup (125 mL) ice cream (about 2 scoops) to each. Serves 2.

1 serving: 353 Calories; 14.5 g Total Fat (4.2 g Mono, 0.6 g Poly, 9 g Sat); 30 mg Cholesterol; 44 g Carbohydrate; 0 g Fibre; 4 g Protein; 106 mg Sodium

Note: For extra-strong flavour, use espresso.

Variation (without alcohol): Omit liqueur. Use same amount of Irish cream-flavoured syrup (such as Torani's).

Caramel Chocolate

Dessert in a mug! Sweet, smooth, caramel-flavoured coffee.
Caramelizing the milk takes time, but it's definitely worth it.

Can of sweetened condensed milk	11 oz.	300 mL
Hot strong prepared coffee (see Note)	4 cups	1 L
Chocolate syrup	1/4 cup	60 mL

Pour condensed milk into 9 inch (22 cm) glass pie plate. Cover tightly with foil. Placed in medium roasting pan. Pour hot water into roasting pan until 1 inch (2.5 cm) deep. Bake in 425°F (220°C) oven for about 80 minutes until milk is thickened and caramel-coloured. Remove pie plate from roasting pan. Transfer caramelized milk to large bowl.

Add hot coffee and chocolate syrup. Stir well. Makes about 5 cups (1.25 L). Spoon into 6 small mugs. Serves 6.

1 serving: 243 Calories; 5.8 g Total Fat (1.6 g Mono, 0.2 g Poly, 3.6 g Sat); 22 mg Cholesterol; 44 g Carbohydrate; 0 g Fibre; 6 g Protein; 102 mg Sodium

Note: For extra-strong flavour, use espresso.

To Make Ahead: Prepare caramelized milk. Cover. Chill until ready to use. Place caramelized milk in medium saucepan. Add hot coffee and chocolate syrup. Heat on medium-low, stirring occasionally, until hot. Do not boil. Serve immediately.

Cocoa-Nut Coffee

You'll enjoy the hazelnut aroma of this coffee topped
with a rich chocolate cream. So tempting.

COCOA CREAM TOPPING

Whipping cream	1/2 cup	125 mL
Granulated sugar	1 tbsp.	15 mL
Cocoa, sifted if lumpy	1 tsp.	5 mL
Hot prepared coffee	4 cups	1 L
Hazelnut-flavoured liqueur (such as Frangelico), 4 oz.	1/2 cup	125 mL

(continued on next page)

32 Coffee Drinks

Cocoa Cream Topping: Beat whipping cream, sugar and cocoa in small bowl until stiff peaks form. Makes about 1 cup (250 mL) topping.

Pour hot coffee into 4 large mugs. Add 2 tbsp. (30 mL) liqueur to each. Stir. Spoon 1/4 cup (60 mL) topping onto each. Serves 4.

1 serving: 226 Calories; 10.3 g Total Fat (3 g Mono, 0.4 g Poly, 6.4 g Sat); 37 mg Cholesterol; 17 g Carbohydrate; trace Fibre; 1 g Protein; 19 mg Sodium

Variation (without alcohol): Omit liqueur. Use same amount of hazelnut-flavoured syrup (such as Torani's).

Serving Suggestion: Garnish with chocolate curls or sprinkle with cocoa for added appeal and taste.

Chocolate Coffee

Chocolate in creamy, hot coffee. A luscious treat.
Use homogenized milk for a richer flavour.

Milk	1 cup	250 mL
Chopped dark chocolate (about 1 3/4 oz., 50 g)	1/4 cup	60 mL
Granulated sugar	3 tbsp.	50 mL
Milk	4 cups	1 L
Hot strong prepared coffee (see Note)	3 cups	750 mL
Vanilla	1 tsp.	5 mL
Large marshmallows	12	12

Heat and stir first 3 ingredients in large heavy saucepan on medium-low for 8 to 10 minutes until chocolate is melted.

Slowly add second amount of milk, stirring constantly. Increase heat to medium. Heat and stir until mixture is hot.

Add hot coffee and vanilla. Stir well. Makes about 8 cups (2 L). Pour into 6 large mugs.

Top each with 2 marshmallows. Serves 6.

1 serving: 203 Calories; 4.5 g Total Fat (1.4 g Mono, 0.2 g Poly, 2.7 g Sat); 9 mg Cholesterol; 34 g Carbohydrate; trace Fibre; 8 g Protein; 120 mg Sodium

Note: For extra-strong flavour, use espresso.

Apple Iced Tea

Fruity amber tea sweetened with honey. Perfect for a cold winter evening.

Boiling water	3 cups	750 mL
Orange pekoe tea bags	4	4
Apple juice	3 cups	750 mL
Liquid honey	1/3 cup	75 mL
Lemon juice	2 tbsp.	30 mL
Ice		

Pour boiling water into teapot. Add tea bags. Cover. Let steep for 5 minutes. Squeeze and discard tea bags.

Combine apple juice, honey and lemon juice in pitcher. Add tea. Stir. Cover. Chill for 4 to 6 hours until cold. Makes about 6 cups (1.5 L). Pour over ice in 4 large glasses. Serves 4.

1 serving: 203 Calories; 0.2 g Total Fat (0 g Mono, 0.1 g Poly, 0 g Sat); 0 mg Cholesterol; 53 g Carbohydrate; trace Fibre; 0 g Protein; 13 mg Sodium

Serving Suggestion: Garnish with slices of lemon or apple.

1. Maple Iced Coffee, page 27
2. Coffee Granita, page 28
3. Cinnamon Iced Coffee, page 26

Props Courtesy Of: Stokes
The Bay

Earl Grey Iced Tea

*Crisp, natural iced tea flavour with just
a hint of mint. A refreshing summer drink.*

Boiling water	8 cups	2 L
Granulated sugar	1/3 cup	75 mL
Lemon juice	1/4 cup	60 mL
Chopped fresh mint leaves	1/4 cup	60 mL
Earl Grey tea bags	4	4
Cinnamon sticks (4 inches, 10 cm, each)	2	2
Thin lemon slices	6	6
Ice		

Measure first 6 ingredients into large heatproof bowl. Stir until sugar is dissolved. Cover. Chill for at least 8 hours or overnight to blend flavours.

Strain tea mixture through sieve into pitcher. Discard solids. Add lemon slices. Stir. Makes about 7 cups (1.75 L). Pour over ice in 6 large glasses. Serves 6.

*1 serving: 51 Calories; 0 g Total Fat (0 g Mono, 0 g Poly, 0 g Sat); 0 mg Cholesterol;
14 g Carbohydrate; 0 g Fibre; 0 g Protein; 10 mg Sodium*

Pictured on page 54.

1. Honey Ginger Iced Tea, page 41
2. Queen Bee Sparkle, page 38
3. Spiced Chai Tea, page 39

Props Courtesy Of: Dansk Gifts
Pier 1 Imports
Stokes
The Bay

Queen Bee Sparkle

Golden yellow with a splash of licorice flavour.
It'll be the buzz of the party!

Boiling water	3 cups	750 mL
Green tea bags	3	3
Yellow-coloured, licorice-flavoured liqueur (such as Galliano), 4 oz. (see Note)	1/2 cup	125 mL
Lemon juice	1/4 cup	60 mL
Liquid honey	2 tbsp.	30 mL
Ginger ale	2 cups	500 mL
Lemon slices		
Ice		

Pour boiling water into teapot. Add tea bags. Cover. Let steep for 5 minutes. Squeeze and discard tea bags.

Combine liqueur, lemon juice and honey in pitcher. Add tea. Stir. Cover. Chill for 4 to 6 hours until cold.

Add ginger ale and lemon slices. Stir gently. Makes about 7 cups (1.75 L). Pour over ice in 6 large glasses. Serves 6.

1 serving: 143 Calories; 0.1 g Total Fat (0 g Mono, 0 g Poly, 0 g Sat); 0 mg Cholesterol; 24 g Carbohydrate; 0 g Fibre; 0 g Protein; 11 mg Sodium

Pictured on page 36.

Note: If you cannot find Galliano, add several drops of yellow liquid food colouring to same amount of clear licorice-flavoured liqueur (such as Sambuca) until desired shade is reached.

Serving Suggestion: Garnish with lemon wedge on glass.

Spiced Chai Tea

Caramel-coloured, mildly spiced East Indian tea. Delicious hot or cold.

Water	2 1/2 cups	625 mL
Thinly sliced, peeled gingerroot	2 tbsp.	30 mL
Fennel seed	1/2 tsp.	2 mL
Whole cloves	5	5
Whole black peppercorns	5	5
Whole green cardamom, bruised (see Tip, below)	5	5
Whole allspice	5	5
Orange pekoe tea bags	3	3
Vanilla bean, split (or 1 tsp., 5 mL, vanilla)	1	1
Milk	2 1/2 cups	625 mL
Liquid honey	3 tbsp.	50 mL

Combine first 9 ingredients in large saucepan. Bring to a boil on medium. Reduce heat to medium-low. Simmer, uncovered, for about 20 minutes until fragrant. Remove from heat. Strain through sieve into large bowl. Discard solids. Return tea mixture to same saucepan.

Add milk and honey. Stir well. Heat on medium until bubbles form around edge. Remove from heat. Makes about 4 cups (1 L). Pour into 4 small mugs. Serves 4.

1 serving: 121 Calories; 1.7 g Total Fat (0.5 g Mono, 0.1 g Poly, 1.1 g Sat); 6 mg Cholesterol; 21 g Carbohydrate; 0 g Fibre; 5 g Protein; 86 mg Sodium

Pictured on page 36.

CHOCOLATE CHAI: Omit milk. Use same amount of chocolate milk.

ICED SPICED CHAI: Chill Spiced Chai Tea. Pour over ice in large glasses or process with ice cubes in blender, using 3 to 4 ice cubes per serving.

 *To bruise cardamom, hit cardamom pods with mallet or flat side of wide knife to "bruise" or crack them open slightly.*

Brandy Tea Slush

Sure to become a favourite. Apricot-coloured slush with a mild, refreshing flavour.

Boiling water	2 cups	500 mL
Orange pekoe tea bags	4	4
Water	7 cups	1.75 L
Granulated sugar	1 cup	250 mL
Apricot (or peach) brandy (16 oz.)	2 cups	500 mL
Can of frozen concentrated lemonade, thawed	12 1/2 oz.	355 mL
Can of frozen concentrated orange juice, thawed	12 1/2 oz.	355 mL
Ginger ale	12 cups	3 L

Pour boiling water into extra-large heatproof bowl. Add tea bags. Let steep for 10 minutes. Squeeze and discard tea bags.

Combine water and sugar in large saucepan. Bring to a boil on medium. Boil for about 1 minute, stirring occasionally, until sugar is dissolved. Remove from heat. Add to tea.

Add brandy and concentrated lemonade and orange juice. Stir well. Pour into large plastic container with tight-fitting lid (one 16 cup, 4 L, ice cream pail works well). Cover. Freeze until firm. Makes about 14 cups (3.5 L) slush.

Scoop slush into chilled large glasses until 2/3 full. Fill each with about 2/3 cup (150 mL) ginger ale. Serve with a straw and spoon. Serves 20.

1 serving: 222 Calories; 0.1 g Total Fat (0 g Mono, 0 g Poly, 0 g Sat); 0 mg Cholesterol; 43 g Carbohydrate; trace Fibre; 1 g Protein; 13 mg Sodium

Tea Drinks

Honey Ginger Iced Tea

Semi-sweet iced tea with a lemon and ginger snap!

Water	4 cups	1 L
Thinly sliced, peeled gingerroot	2 tbsp.	30 mL
Orange pekoe tea bags	3	3
Liquid honey	1/3 cup	75 mL
Lemon juice	2 tbsp.	30 mL
Ice		
Fresh mint sprigs, for garnish		

Combine water and ginger in medium saucepan. Bring to a boil on medium-high. Remove from heat.

Add tea bags. Let steep for 5 minutes. Strain through sieve into heatproof pitcher. Discard solids.

Add honey and lemon juice. Stir. Cover. Chill for 4 to 6 hours until cold. Makes about 4 cups (1 L).

Pour over ice in 4 large glasses. Garnish with mint sprigs. Serves 4.

1 serving: 111 Calories; 0 g Total Fat (0 g Mono, 0 g Poly, 0 g Sat); 0 mg Cholesterol; 30 g Carbohydrate; 0 g Fibre; 0 g Protein; 9 mg Sodium

Pictured on page 36.

Serving Suggestion: Serve over crushed ice for a sparkling presentation on a hot summer day.

Paré Pointer
Say cheers in French: "Santé!" (SAHN-tay)

Iced Pineapple Tea

Pleasantly sweet pineapple with a gentle ginger mist.

Can of frozen concentrated pineapple juice	12 1/2 oz.	355 mL
Cold strong prepared tea	3 cups	750 mL
Lemon juice	3 tbsp.	50 mL
Ginger ale	3 cups	750 mL
Ice		

Combine concentrated pineapple juice, tea and lemon juice in pitcher. Add ginger ale. Stir gently. Makes about 7 1/2 cups (1.9 L).

Pour over ice in 6 large glasses. Serves 6.

1 serving: 177 Calories; 0.1 g Total Fat (0 g Mono, 0 g Poly, 0 g Sat); 0 mg Cholesterol; 45 g Carbohydrate; 0 g Fibre; 1 g Protein; 19 mg Sodium

Serving Suggestion: Place wedge of fresh pineapple (with peel) on edge of glass or thread canned pineapple tidbits alternating with maraschino cherries onto cocktail pick for garnish.

Orange Ginger Infusion

A tasty beverage any time, but especially calming when you have a head cold. It will have you feeling better in no time!

Water	3 1/2 cups	875 mL
Thinly sliced, peeled gingerroot	1/4 cup	60 mL
Frozen concentrated orange juice	1/4 cup	60 mL
Sweetened powdered orange-flavoured drink crystals	2 tbsp.	30 mL
Liquid honey (optional)	2 tsp.	10 mL

Combine first 4 ingredients in medium saucepan. Bring to a boil on medium. Reduce heat to medium-low. Simmer, uncovered, for about 5 minutes until fragrant. Remove from heat. Remove and discard ginger.

Add honey. Stir. Makes about 4 cups (1 L). Pour into 4 small mugs. Serves 4.

1 serving: 53 Calories; 0 g Total Fat (0 g Mono, 0 g Poly, 0 g Sat); 0 mg Cholesterol; 13 g Carbohydrate; trace Fibre; 0 g Protein; 2 mg Sodium

Chamomile Refresher

Mild flavours of chamomile, pineapple and mint
in a refreshing, pale yellow tea.

Boiling water	2 cups	500 mL
Chamomile tea bags	3	3
Fresh mint sprigs	2	2
Sparkling bottled water (such as Perrier)	1 1/2 cups	375 mL
Pineapple juice	1 cup	250 mL
White grape juice	1 cup	250 mL
Orange juice	1/2 cup	125 mL
Sweetened powdered lemon-flavoured drink crystals	2 – 3 tbsp.	30 – 50 mL
Ice		

Pour boiling water into heatproof medium bowl. Add tea bags and mint. Let steep for 10 minutes. Strain through sieve into pitcher. Discard solids.

Add next 5 ingredients. Stir until drink crystals are dissolved. Makes about 6 cups (1.5 L). Pour over ice in 4 large glasses. Serves 4.

1 serving: 122 Calories; 0.2 g Total Fat (0 g Mono, 0.1 g Poly, 0 g Sat); 0 mg Cholesterol; 30 g Carbohydrate; trace Fibre; 1 g Protein; 8 mg Sodium

Paré Pointer
Say cheers in German: "Proest!" (PROHST)

Cranberry Iced Tea

Cold cranberry and orange tea. Satisfying, thirst-quenching beverage.

Boiling water	3 cups	750 mL
Orange pekoe tea bags	5	5
Can of frozen concentrated cranberry cocktail	9 1/2 oz.	275 mL
Orange juice	1 cup	250 mL
Fresh (or frozen, thawed) cranberries	3 tbsp.	50 mL
Thin orange slices, halved	4	4
Ice		

Pour boiling water into teapot. Add tea bags. Cover. Let steep for 5 minutes. Squeeze and discard tea bags.

Combine concentrated cranberry cocktail and orange juice in pitcher. Add tea. Stir. Cover. Chill for 4 to 6 hours until cold. Makes 5 cups (1.25 L).

Add cranberries and orange slice halves. Stir.

Pour over ice in 4 large glasses. Serves 4.

1 serving: 191 Calories; 0.1 g Total Fat (0 g Mono, 0 g Poly, 0 g Sat); 0 mg Cholesterol; 48 g Carbohydrate; trace Fibre; 1 g Protein; 9 mg Sodium

CRANBERRY TEA SPRITZER: Pour Cranberry Iced Tea into large glasses until 1/2 to 2/3 full. Fill with ginger ale, club soda or sparkling bottled water (such as Perrier).

Mango Tea

Enjoy this fruity, hot drink. A refreshing break in your day.

Water	3 1/2 cups	875 mL
Can of frozen concentrated mango punch	12 1/2 oz.	355 mL
Almond-flavoured syrup (such as Torani's)	1 tbsp.	15 mL
Ground cinnamon	1/4 tsp.	1 mL
Orange pekoe tea bags	3 – 4	3 – 4

(continued on next page)

Combine first 4 ingredients in medium saucepan. Bring to a boil on medium. Remove from heat.

Add tea bags. Cover. Let steep for 5 minutes. Squeeze and discard tea bags. Makes about 5 cups (1.25 L). Pour into 4 large mugs. Serves 4.

1 serving: 203 Calories; 0.8 g Total Fat (0.1 g Mono, 0.2 g Poly, 0.1 g Sat); 0 mg Cholesterol; 50 g Carbohydrate; 0 g Fibre; 0 g Protein; 20 mg Sodium

Variation (with alcohol): Omit almond-flavoured syrup. Use same amount of almond-flavoured liqueur (such as Amaretto).

Serving Suggestion: Garnish with cinnamon sticks.

Sweet Spiced Tea

Mildly spiced, sweet and satisfying. Good hot or cold.

Water	6 cups	1.5 L
Granulated sugar	1/4 – 1/3 cup	60 – 75 mL
Whole green cardamom, bruised (see Tip, page 39)	4	4
Whole cloves	4	4
Cinnamon stick (4 inches, 10 cm)	1	1
Orange pekoe tea bags	3	3

Heat and stir first 5 ingredients in medium saucepan on medium-high until sugar is dissolved. Bring to a boil. Remove from heat. Let stand for 15 minutes.

Add tea bags. Bring to a boil on medium-high. Reduce heat to medium-low. Simmer, uncovered, for 3 minutes. Remove from heat. Strain through sieve into teapot. Discard solids. Makes about 5 cups (1.25 L). Pour into 4 large mugs. Serves 4.

1 serving: 53 Calories; 0 g Total Fat (0 g Mono, 0 g Poly, 0 g Sat); 0 mg Cholesterol; 14 g Carbohydrate; 0 g Fibre; 0 g Protein; 6 mg Sodium

Serving Suggestion: Add a fresh cinnamon stick to your cup of tea for extra spice.

Banana Egg Flip

Creamy white and frothy. A nourishing combination in a delicious milkshake!

Milk	2 cups	500 mL
Vanilla ice cream	1 cup	250 mL
Plain yogurt	3 tbsp.	50 mL
Liquid honey	2 tbsp.	30 mL
Ripe medium banana, cut up	1	1
Large egg (see Note)	1	1
Ice cubes	3	3

Process all 7 ingredients in blender until smooth. Makes about 4 1/2 cups (1.1 L). Pour into 4 chilled medium glasses. Serves 4.

1 serving: 209 Calories; 6.8 g Total Fat (2 g Mono, 0.4 g Poly, 3.8 g Sat); 75 mg Cholesterol; 31 g Carbohydrate; trace Fibre; 8 g Protein; 117 mg Sodium

Note: Eggs used in beverages should be cold. Remove egg from refrigerator just before adding. Beverages containing uncooked egg should be served immediately.

Peanut Butter Blast

Familiar flavour combination—peanut butter, chocolate and banana—in a breakfast or snack beverage.

Milk	1 1/2 cups	375 mL
Chocolate ice cream	1 cup	250 mL
Frozen ripe medium banana (see Tip, page 21)	1	1
Smooth (or crunchy) peanut butter	1 tbsp.	15 mL

Process all 4 ingredients in blender until smooth. Makes about 3 1/2 cups (875 mL). Pour into 4 chilled small glasses. Serves 4.

1 serving: 167 Calories; 7.1 g Total Fat (2.4 g Mono, 0.8 g Poly, 3.5 g Sat); 16 mg Cholesterol; 22 g Carbohydrate; 1 g Fibre; 6 g Protein; 94 mg Sodium

Pictured on page 53.

Kids' Drinks

Apple Ginger Mocktail

Light, carbonated drink with a crisp, clean taste. Sweet and tangy.

Apple juice	1 cup	250 mL
Lemon juice	1 tbsp.	15 mL
Grenadine syrup	1 tsp.	5 mL
Crushed ice		
Ginger ale	1 1/2 cups	375 mL

Combine apple juice, lemon juice and grenadine in 2 cup (500 mL) liquid measure. Pour over crushed ice in 2 medium glasses.

Slowly add ginger ale until full. Stir gently. Makes about 2 1/2 cups (625 mL). Serves 2.

1 serving: 140 Calories; 0.1 g Total Fat (0 g Mono, 0 g Poly, 0 g Sat); 0 mg Cholesterol; 36 g Carbohydrate; trace Fibre; 0 g Protein; 20 mg Sodium

Serving Suggestion: Garnish with thin apple slices.

Rainbow Floats

Sweet and fruity with a fun, foamy rainbow top. Kids will love it!

Lemon lime soft drink	1 cup	250 mL
Cranberry cocktail	1/2 cup	125 mL
Rainbow sherbet	1 cup	250 mL

Pour lemon lime soft drink and cranberry cocktail into 2 chilled large glasses. Stir gently.

Carefully add 1/2 cup (125 mL) sherbet (about 2 scoops) to each glass. Mixture will foam. Makes about 3 cups (750 mL). Serves 2.

1 serving: 230 Calories; 2.1 g Total Fat (0.5 g Mono, 0.1 g Poly, 1.2 g Sat); 5 mg Cholesterol; 54 g Carbohydrate; 0 g Fibre; 1 g Protein; 62 mg Sodium

Pictured on page 53.

Serving Suggestion: Add a straw and spoon so kids of all ages will be able to enjoy this drink to the last drop!

Kids' Drinks

Grape Lemonade

This pink punch gets more purple as the grape-flavoured ice cubes melt. Cold, sweet and tart.

Can of frozen concentrated grape juice, thawed	12 oz.	341 mL
Water	1 1/2 cups	375 mL
Can of frozen concentrated pineapple juice, partially thawed	12 1/2 oz.	355 mL
Frozen concentrated lemonade, partially thawed	1/2 cup	125 mL
Grenadine syrup	1 tbsp.	15 mL
Water	5 cups	1.25 L

Lemon slices, for garnish

Combine concentrated grape juice and water in 4 cup (1 L) liquid measure. Pour into ice cube trays. Freeze until firm. Makes about 24 cubes.

Combine next 4 ingredients in small punch bowl. Add frozen grape juice cubes. Makes about 9 1/2 cups (2.4 L).

Garnish with lemon slices. Serves 10.

1 serving: 189 Calories; 0.2 g Total Fat (0 g Mono, 0.1 g Poly, 0.1 g Sat); 0 mg Cholesterol; 47 g Carbohydrate; trace Fibre; 1 g Protein; 6 mg Sodium

Pictured on page 53.

 *At the peak of melon season, chop watermelon into bite-size pieces. Freeze in single layer on ungreased baking sheet. Store in resealable freezer bags for up to 12 months. Use in a variety of beverages. Enjoy a taste of summer in the middle of winter!*

Watermelon Slush

Kids and adults will love this on a hot day.
Yummy and fun—the ginger ale tickles the tongue.

Chopped seedless watermelon (see Tip, page 48)	3 cups	750 mL
Can of frozen concentrated white grape cocktail, partially thawed	12 oz.	341 mL
Ginger ale	6 cups	1.5 L

Process watermelon and concentrated grape cocktail in blender until smooth. Pour into 2 quart (2 L) shallow baking dish. Cover. Freeze for about 2 hours until almost firm. Makes about 3 3/4 cups (925 mL) slush.

Scrape about 2/3 cup (150 mL) slush, using fork, into each of 6 chilled large glasses. Slowly add ginger ale until full. Stir gently. Serves 6.

1 serving: 239 Calories; 0.6 g Total Fat (0 g Mono, 0.1 g Poly, 0.1 g Sat); 0 mg Cholesterol; 59 g Carbohydrate; 1 g Fibre; 1 g Protein; 25 mg Sodium

Serving Suggestion: Garnish each glass with small slice of watermelon and fresh strawberry.

Peach Dream

Lightly flavoured peach drink with a subtle hint of orange.

Milk	2 1/2 cups	625 mL
Can of sliced peaches (with juice)	14 oz.	398 mL
Vanilla ice cream	1 cup	250 mL
Orange juice	1/3 cup	75 mL
Vanilla	1/4 tsp.	1 mL
Ice cubes		

Process first 5 ingredients in blender until smooth. Makes about 6 2/3 cups (1.65 L). Pour over ice cubes in 6 chilled medium glasses. Serves 6.

1 serving: 129 Calories; 3.8 g Total Fat (1.1 g Mono, 0.2 g Poly, 2.3 g Sat); 15 mg Cholesterol; 20 g Carbohydrate; 1 g Fibre; 5 g Protein; 75 mg Sodium

Apple "Moose"

A "moose" you can drink!
This frothy mousse tastes like apple pie and ice cream.

Vanilla ice cream	1 cup	250 mL
Milk	1 cup	250 mL
Unsweetened applesauce	1/4 cup	60 mL
Lemon juice	1 tsp.	5 mL

Process all 4 ingredients in blender until smooth. Makes about 2 1/3 cups (575 mL). Pour into 2 chilled medium glasses. Serves 2.

1 serving: 209 Calories; 9.1 g Total Fat (2.6 g Mono, 0.3 g Poly, 5.6 g Sat); 36 mg Cholesterol; 27 g Carbohydrate; 1 g Fibre; 7 g Protein; 121 mg Sodium

Serving Suggestion: Serve with a straw. Top with candy sprinkles just for fun!

Just Peachy

Refreshing peach flavour.

Peach nectar	1/2 cup	125 mL
Orange juice	1/3 cup	75 mL
Lemon juice	2 tsp.	10 mL
Crushed ice	1/4 cup	60 mL
Lemon lime soft drink (or ginger ale)	1/2 cup	125 mL

Combine first 3 ingredients in 1 cup (250 mL) liquid measure.

Measure crushed ice into chilled large glass. Pour peach mixture over top. Slowly add lemon lime soft drink until full. Stir gently. Makes about 1 2/3 cups (400 mL). Serves 1.

1 serving: 165 Calories; 0.2 g Total Fat (0 g Mono, 0.1 g Poly, 0 g Sat); 0 mg Cholesterol; 42 g Carbohydrate; 1 g Fibre; 1 g Protein; 24 mg Sodium

Serving Suggestion: Garnish with thin slice of fresh peach. Use club soda in place of soft drink for a less sweet alternative.

Frosty Mandarin

Rich, cold orange cream.

Can of mandarin orange segments (with juice)	10 oz.	284 mL
Vanilla ice cream (or frozen yogurt)	1 cup	250 mL
Orange sherbet	1/2 cup	125 mL

Process all 3 ingredients in blender until smooth. Makes about 2 1/2 cups (625 mL). Pour into 2 chilled medium glasses. Serves 2.

1 serving: 265 Calories; 8.7 g Total Fat (2.5 g Mono, 0.3 g Poly, 5.3 g Sat); 33 mg Cholesterol; 46 g Carbohydrate; 1 g Fibre; 4 g Protein; 87 mg Sodium

Pictured on page 53.

Midnight Punch

Sweet purple punch kids will love. Great to serve at a party.

Club soda	8 cups	2 L
Granulated sugar	1 cup	250 mL
Envelope of unsweetened powdered grape-flavoured drink crystals	1/4 oz.	6 g
Envelope of unsweetened powdered orange-flavoured drink crystals	1/4 oz.	6 g
Ginger ale	8 cups	2 L

Combine first 4 ingredients in small punch bowl. Stir gently until sugar is dissolved.

Add ginger ale. Stir gently. Makes about 16 cups (4 L). Serves 16.

1 serving: 95 Calories; 0 g Total Fat (0 g Mono, 0 g Poly, 0 g Sat); 0 mg Cholesterol; 24 g Carbohydrate; 0 g Fibre; 0 g Protein; 36 mg Sodium

Serving Suggestion: For a spooky effect at Halloween, fill 2 plastic gloves with water, secure tightly and freeze until firm. Carefully peel or cut away gloves and place frozen "hands" in punch bowl.

Pink Moo Juice

Strawberry flavour in a satisfying, creamy beverage.
Add more ice cream topping or yogurt if you prefer a sweeter taste.

Milk	2 cups	500 mL
Frozen whole strawberries, chopped	1 cup	250 mL
Strawberry ice cream topping (or jam)	1/4 cup	60 mL
Fresh strawberries, for garnish	4	4

Process first 3 ingredients in blender until smooth. Makes about 3 3/4 cups (925 mL). Pour into 4 chilled small glasses.

Garnish each with fresh strawberry. Serves 4.

1 serving: 132 Calories; 1.5 g Total Fat (0.4 g Mono, 0.1 g Poly, 0.9 g Sat); 5 mg Cholesterol; 27 g Carbohydrate; 1 g Fibre; 5 g Protein; 70 mg Sodium

Variation: Omit milk. Use same amount of plain or flavoured yogurt for a thicker drink.

1. Rainbow Floats, page 47
2. Frosty Mandarin, page 51
3. Grape Lemonade, page 48
4. Peanut Butter Blast, page 46

Props Courtesy Of: Cherison Enterprises Inc.
Wal-Mart Canada Inc.
Zellers

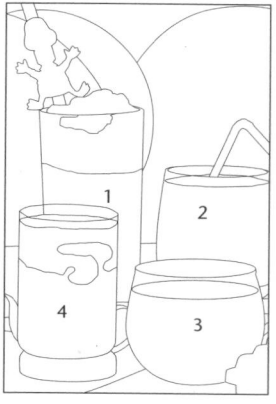

Kids' Drinks

Hot Chocolate For Two

*A great winter warm-up for the kids after school
or at the end of a day playing in the snow.*

Cocoa, sifted if lumpy	1 tbsp.	15 mL
Granulated sugar	1 tbsp.	15 mL
Water	3/4 cup	175 mL
Skim evaporated milk	3/4 cup	175 mL
Vanilla	3/4 tsp.	4 mL

Miniature marshmallows, for garnish

Combine cocoa and sugar in small cup. Divide and spoon into 2 small mugs.

Combine water, evaporated milk and vanilla in 2 cup (500 mL) liquid measure. Microwave on high (100%) for about 2 minutes until boiling. Pour into mugs. Stir until smooth. Makes about 1 1/2 cups (375 mL).

Garnish with marshmallows. Serves 2.

1 serving: 106 Calories; 0.5 g Total Fat (0.2 g Mono, 0 g Poly, 0.3 g Sat); 3 mg Cholesterol; 18 g Carbohydrate; 1 g Fibre; 7 g Protein; 107 mg Sodium

1. Pink Summer Slush, page 58
2. Earl Grey Iced Tea, page 37
3. Citrus Sunburst, page 68

Props Courtesy Of: Danesco Inc.
                              Dansk Gifts
                              Pier 1 Imports

Fruit Salad Chiller

This cold, fruity drink will give you the chills! Sweet, creamy cantaloupe flavour.

Vanilla ice cream	1 cup	250 mL
Sliced fresh strawberries	1/2 cup	125 mL
Sliced ripe banana	1/2 cup	125 mL
Chopped cantaloupe	1/2 cup	125 mL
Liquid honey	2 – 3 tbsp.	30 – 50 mL
Ice cubes	3	3

Process all 6 ingredients in blender until smooth. Makes about 2 cups (500 mL). Pour into 2 chilled medium glasses. Serves 2.

1 serving: 259 Calories; 8.1 g Total Fat (2.3 g Mono, 0.4 g Poly, 4.8 g Sat); 31 mg Cholesterol; 47 g Carbohydrate; 2 g Fibre; 3 g Protein; 61 mg Sodium

Serving Suggestion: Garnish each glass with a fresh strawberry.

Malted Milkshake

This is so frothy, it will make a great moustache!

Chocolate ice cream	2 cups	500 mL
Milk	1 cup	250 mL
Chocolate syrup	2 tbsp.	30 mL
Malt drink mix (such as Ovaltine)	2 tbsp.	30 mL

Process all 4 ingredients in blender until smooth. Makes about 3 cups (750 mL). Pour into 3 chilled medium glasses. Serves 3.

1 serving: 290 Calories; 11.5 g Total Fat (3.4 g Mono, 0.4 g Poly, 7.1 g Sat); 35 mg Cholesterol; 44 g Carbohydrate; 0 g Fibre; 7 g Protein; 167 mg Sodium

MALTED BANANA SHAKE: Add 1 ripe medium banana, cut up, to other ingredients. Process until smooth.

Kids' Drinks

Berry Shake Up

Pleasant purple pick-me-up! Adults will like this one too.

Strawberry ice cream	2 cups	500 mL
Milk	2 cups	500 mL
Frozen blueberries	3/4 cup	175 mL
Vanilla	1/2 tsp.	2 mL

Process all 4 ingredients in blender until smooth. Makes about 4 2/3 cups (1.15 L). Pour into 4 chilled medium glasses. Serves 4.

1 serving: 205 Calories; 7.4 g Total Fat (0.4 g Mono, 0.1 g Poly, 0.9 g Sat); 25 mg Cholesterol; 29 g Carbohydrate; 1 g Fibre; 7 g Protein; 107 mg Sodium

Serving Suggestion: Garnish with fresh blueberries threaded onto cocktail picks.

Purple Cow

A creamy banana and blueberry drink that's not overly sweet.

Milk	1 cup	250 mL
Frozen ripe medium banana (see Tip, page 21)	1	1
Frozen blueberries	1/3 cup	75 mL
Berry (or plain) yogurt	3 tbsp.	50 mL
Liquid honey	1 – 2 tbsp.	15 – 30 mL

Process all 5 ingredients in blender until smooth. Makes about 2 cups (500 mL). Pour into 2 chilled medium glasses. Serves 2.

1 serving: 177 Calories; 2.2 g Total Fat (0.5 g Mono, 0.1 g Poly, 1.2 g Sat); 7 mg Cholesterol; 36 g Carbohydrate; 2 g Fibre; 6 g Protein; 77 mg Sodium

Summer Slush

Slushy drink perfect for that summer barbecue or backyard party.

Pineapple juice	6 cups	1.5 L
Orange juice	6 cups	1.5 L
Water	6 cups	1.5 L
Can of frozen concentrated orange juice, thawed	12 1/2 oz.	355 mL
Can of frozen concentrated lemonade, thawed	12 1/2 oz.	355 mL
Ripe medium bananas, cut up	4	4
Container of frozen strawberries in syrup, thawed	15 oz.	425 g
Vodka (or gin), 26 oz.	3 cups	750 mL
Lemon lime soft drink	24 cups	6 L

Divide and measure first 5 ingredients into 2 large plastic containers with tight-fitting lids (two 16 cup, 4 L, ice cream pails work well). Stir.

Process bananas and strawberries with syrup in blender until smooth. Divide and add to juice mixture in each plastic container.

Add 1 1/2 cups (375 mL) vodka to each. Stir well. Cover. Freeze until firm. Makes about 27 cups (6.75 L) slush.

Scoop slush into chilled large glasses until 3/4 full. Slowly add lemon lime soft drink until full. Serves about 36.

1 serving: 221 Calories; 0.3 g Total Fat (0 g Mono, 0.1 g Poly, 0 g Sat); 0 mg Cholesterol; 44 g Carbohydrate; 1 g Fibre; 1 g Protein; 21 mg Sodium

KIDS' SLUSH: Omit alcohol. Slush will freeze more firmly, but can still be scooped into glasses. Fill with soft drink.

PINK SUMMER SLUSH: Omit lemon lime soft drink. Use same amount of cream soda for a sweeter, pink slush.

Pictured on page 54.

Serving Suggestion: Great to have on hand for summer company. Slush can be frozen for up to 1 month. Just scoop into glasses and add soft drink, a straw and a spoon.

Pink Margarita Slush

Cool, tangy and deliciously refreshing.

Can of frozen concentrated cranberry lemonade	12 1/2 oz.	355 mL
Tequila (6 oz.)	3/4 cup	175 mL
Orange-flavoured liqueur (such as Grand Marnier), 6 oz.	3/4 cup	175 mL
Ice cubes	20 – 24	20 – 24

Measure concentrated lemonade, tequila and liqueur into blender. Cover. Process, adding ice cubes 2 or 3 at a time through hole in blender lid, scraping down sides if necessary, until thick and slushy. Makes about 5 cups (1.25 L). Pour into 6 chilled small glasses. Serves 6.

1 serving: 261 Calories; 0.1 g Total Fat (0 g Mono, 0 g Poly, 0 g Sat); 0 mg Cholesterol; 35 g Carbohydrate; 0 g Fibre; 0 g Protein; 3 mg Sodium

Serving Suggestion: Dampen rims of margarita glasses (see page 8) with lemon wedge, or dip into lemon juice in saucer. Press rims into granulated sugar in separate saucer until coated. Fill glasses with slush. Garnish each with lemon wedge.

Fruity Yogurt Freeze

A drink that is thick enough to eat with a spoon until it starts to melt. Perfect on a hot summer day when you need to cool down!

Frozen whole strawberries, chopped	1 cup	250 mL
Pineapple tidbits (with juice), about 1/2 of 14 oz. (398 mL) can	3/4 cup	175 mL
Frozen ripe medium banana (see Tip, page 21)	1	1
Vanilla frozen yogurt	1/2 cup	125 mL
Vanilla	1/2 tsp.	2 mL

Process all 5 ingredients in blender until smooth. Makes about 3 cups (750 mL). Pour into 2 chilled large glasses. Serves 2.

1 serving: 217 Calories; 2.6 g Total Fat (0.7 g Mono, 0.2 g Poly, 1.4 g Sat); 1 mg Cholesterol; 49 g Carbohydrate; 4 g Fibre; 3 g Protein; 37 mg Sodium

Berry Citrus Freeze

Strawberry and orange-flavoured margarita with a lime tang. Not overly sweet.

Frozen whole strawberries, chopped	2 cups	500 mL
Orange juice	1 1/2 cups	375 mL
Strawberry ice cream topping	1/4 cup	60 mL
Lime juice	3 tbsp.	50 mL
Tequila (3 oz.)	6 tbsp.	100 mL
Orange-flavoured liqueur (such as Grand Marnier), 1 1/2 oz.	3 tbsp.	50 mL

Process first 4 ingredients in blender until smooth. Pour into 2 quart (2 L) shallow baking dish. Cover. Freeze for about 2 hours until almost firm.

Scrape strawberry mixture, using fork, into blender. Add tequila and liqueur. Process until smooth. Makes about 3 1/2 cups (875 mL). Pour into 4 chilled small glasses. Serves 4.

1 serving: 219 Calories; 0.4 g Total Fat (0.1 g Mono, 0.1 g Poly, 0 g Sat); 0 mg Cholesterol; 37 g Carbohydrate; 2 g Fibre; 1 g Protein; 9 mg Sodium

Pictured on page 108.

Serving Suggestion: To dress up this drink, dampen rims of glasses with lime wedge, or dip into lime juice in saucer. Press rims into coloured sugar in separate saucer until coated. Garnish each with half of a fresh strawberry.

Lemonade Shake

Refreshing lemonade in a shake—sure to be a favourite. Delicious!

Vanilla ice cream	2 cups	500 mL
Sparkling lemonade soft drink	1 cup	250 mL
Frozen concentrated pink lemonade (or lemonade), partially thawed	1/4 cup	60 mL

Process all 3 ingredients in blender until smooth. Makes about 2 2/3 cups (650 mL). Pour into 2 chilled medium glasses. Serves 2.

1 serving: 403 Calories; 15.4 g Total Fat (4.4 g Mono, 0.6 g Poly, 9.5 g Sat); 61 mg Cholesterol; 65 g Carbohydrate; 0 g Fibre; 5 g Protein; 117 mg Sodium

Banana Colada Cooler

Creamy, cold tropical drink with rich banana and coconut flavours.

Pineapple juice	2 cups	500 mL
Frozen ripe medium bananas (see Tip, page 21)	3	3
Can of coconut milk	14 oz.	398 mL
White (light) rum (5 oz.)	2/3 cup	150 mL

Pour pineapple juice into ice cube trays. Freeze for about 4 hours until firm.

Put 1/2 of frozen pineapple juice cubes into blender. Add 1 1/2 bananas, 1/2 can of coconut milk and 1/3 cup (75 mL) rum. Process until smooth. Transfer to large pitcher. Repeat with remaining juice cubes, bananas, coconut milk and rum. Makes about 7 cups (1.75 mL). Pour into 6 chilled medium glasses. Serves 6.

1 serving: 287 Calories; 13.9 g Total Fat (0.6 g Mono, 0.2 g Poly, 12.1 g Sat); 0 mg Cholesterol; 27 g Carbohydrate; 1 g Fibre; 2 g Protein; 10 mg Sodium

Peach Melba

Creamy milkshake fashioned after the classic dessert. Sweet peach with tangy raspberry.

Can of sliced peaches (with juice)	14 oz.	398 mL
Vanilla ice cream	1 cup	250 mL
Milk	1/2 cup	125 mL
Raspberry jam	2 tbsp.	30 mL

Process all 4 ingredients in blender until smooth. Makes about 3 cups (750 mL). Pour into 2 chilled large glasses. Serves 2.

1 serving: 308 Calories; 8.5 g Total Fat (2.5 g Mono, 0.4 g Poly, 5.2 g Sat); 33 mg Cholesterol; 57 g Carbohydrate; 2 g Fibre; 6 g Protein; 104 mg Sodium

Serving Suggestion: Garnish with whipped topping mixed with almond flavouring. Top with a fresh raspberry for a splash of colour.

Raspberry Margarita

Brilliant raspberry-red refreshment. Yum!

Container of frozen raspberries in syrup, thawed	15 oz.	425 g
Lemon juice	1/4 cup	60 mL
Raspberry jam	3 tbsp.	50 mL
Tequila (2 oz.)	1/4 cup	60 mL
Orange-flavoured liqueur (such as Grand Marnier), 2 oz.	1/4 cup	60 mL
Crushed ice	1 cup	250 mL

Combine first 3 ingredients in medium bowl. Strain raspberry mixture through sieve into 1 quart (1 L) shallow baking dish. Discard seeds. Spread raspberry mixture evenly in baking dish. Cover. Freeze for about 3 hours until almost firm.

Scrape raspberry mixture, using fork, into blender. Add tequila, liqueur and crushed ice. Process until smooth. Makes about 3 3/4 cups (925 mL). Pour into 4 small chilled glasses. Serves 4.

1 serving: 218 Calories; 0.2 g Total Fat (0 g Mono, 0.1 g Poly, 0 g Sat); 0 mg Cholesterol; 39 g Carbohydrate; 5 g Fibre; 1 g Protein; 8 mg Sodium

Pictured on page 71.

Serving Suggestion: Dampen rims of margarita glasses (see page 8) with lemon wedge, or dip into lemon juice in saucer. Press rims into coloured sugar in separate saucer until coated.

Frozen Drinks

Orange Frostbite

Smooth and frothy—just right for the summer! Placing glasses in freezer before serving will make this yummy drink even frostier!

Medium oranges, peeled, seeds and white pith removed	4	4
Vanilla ice cream	1 3/4 cups	425 mL
Orange Dream Liqueur, page 139 (or vodka), 4 oz. (optional)	1/2 cup	125 mL

Cut oranges into quarters. Place in blender.

Add ice cream and liqueur. Process until smooth. Makes about 4 cups (1 L). Pour into 4 chilled medium glasses. Serves 4.

1 serving (with alcohol): 266 Calories; 7.9 g Total Fat (2.3 g Mono, 0.3 g Poly, 4.8 g Sat); 31 mg Cholesterol; 41 g Carbohydrate; 2 g Fibre; 4 g Protein; 65 mg Sodium

Pictured on page 71.

Serving Suggestion: Use "glasses" made from whole oranges. Cut tops off large oranges about 1/4 of the way from stem end. Carefully cut around inside edge of orange to loosen. Remove fruit and juice to blender, using spoon, to use in recipe. Freeze shells for at least 2 hours until firm. Fill with drink. Add a short straw.

Paré Pointer

Say cheers in Greek: "Eis Igian!" (is-i EE-an)

Caesar Granita

Mildly spiced, icy Caesar. Stays cold until the last sip.

Clam tomato beverage (such as Clamato juice)	2 cups	500 mL
Vodka (2 oz.), optional	1/4 cup	60 mL
Lemon juice	1 tbsp.	15 mL
Worcestershire sauce	1/4 tsp.	1 mL
Celery salt	1/4 tsp.	1 mL
Hot pepper sauce	1/4 tsp.	1 mL
Pickled pepper rings, for garnish	2	2

Combine first 6 ingredients in medium bowl. Pour into 1 quart (1 L) shallow baking dish. Cover. Freeze for about 3 hours until almost firm. Makes about 2 2/3 cups (650 mL).

Scrape tomato mixture, using fork, into 2 chilled medium glasses. Garnish each with pepper ring. Serves 2.

1 serving (with alcohol): 189 Calories; 0.3 g Total Fat (0 g Mono, 0.1 g Poly, 0 g Sat); 0 mg Cholesterol; 29 g Carbohydrate; 0 g Fibre; 2 g Protein; 1200 mg Sodium

Bananarama

Velvety smooth, thick and creamy.

Vanilla ice cream	2 cups	500 mL
Brandy (1/2 oz.)	1 tbsp.	15 mL
Banana-flavoured liqueur (such as Crème de banane), 1/2 oz.	1 tbsp.	15 mL
Orange-flavoured liqueur (such as Grand Marnier), 1/4 oz.	1/2 tbsp.	7 mL
Grated chocolate (or chocolate curls), for garnish		

Process first 4 ingredients in blender until smooth. Makes about 1 1/3 cups (325 mL). Pour into 2 chilled small glasses.

Sprinkle each with grated chocolate. Serves 2.

1 serving: 336 Calories; 15.4 g Total Fat (4.4 g Mono, 0.6 g Poly, 9.5 g Sat); 61 mg Cholesterol; 36 g Carbohydrate; 0 g Fibre; 5 g Protein; 112 mg Sodium

Tropical Daiquiri

Refreshing pineapple and coconut combination.
Half-and-half makes it creamier.

Fresh pineapple, cut into 1 inch (2.5 cm) cubes (or canned pineapple chunks, drained)	3 cups	750 mL
Milk (or half-and-half cream)	1 cup	250 mL
Crushed ice	1 cup	250 mL
Cream of coconut syrup	1/3 cup	75 mL
White (light) rum (2 1/2 oz.)	1/3 cup	75 mL
Maraschino cherries (with stems), for garnish	4	4

Spread pineapple cubes in single layer in 2 quart (2 L) shallow baking dish. Cover. Freeze for 2 to 3 hours until firm.

Measure next 4 ingredients into blender. Add 1/2 of frozen pineapple. Process until smooth. Add remaining pineapple. Process until smooth. Makes about 4 cups (1 L). Pour into 4 chilled medium glasses.

Garnish each with maraschino cherry. Serves 4.

1 serving: 182 Calories; 5.8 g Total Fat (0.5 g Mono, 0.3 g Poly, 4.5 g Sat); 3 mg Cholesterol; 20 g Carbohydrate; 2 g Fibre; 3 g Protein; 47 mg Sodium

Pictured on page 71.

Serving Suggestion: For a festive presentation, dampen rims of glasses with lemon wedge, or dip into lemon juice in small saucer. Press rims into coloured sugar in separate saucer until coated.

Paré Pointer

Say cheers in Hebrew: "L'chaim!" (le-HI-m)

Mocha Frappuccino

Slushy chocolate coffee—sweet and creamy.

Hot strong prepared coffee (see Note)	2 cups	500 mL
Brown sugar, packed	2 tbsp.	30 mL
Vanilla (or chocolate) ice cream, softened	1 cup	250 mL
Chocolate ice cream topping	1/4 cup	60 mL
Finely grated chocolate, for garnish	2 tbsp.	30 mL

Measure hot coffee and brown sugar into small bowl. Stir until sugar is dissolved. Pour into 1 quart (1 L) shallow baking dish. Cover. Freeze for about 3 hours until almost firm.

Scrape coffee mixture, using fork, into blender. Add ice cream and chocolate topping. Process until smooth. Makes about 2 2/3 cups (650 mL). Pour into 2 chilled medium glasses.

Sprinkle each with grated chocolate. Serves 2.

1 serving: 359 Calories; 13.7 g Total Fat (3.9 g Mono, 1.7 g Poly, 7.3 g Sat); 36 mg Cholesterol; 59 g Carbohydrate; 0 g Fibre; 5 g Protein; 130 mg Sodium

Note: For extra-strong flavour, use espresso.

Serving Suggestion: Add a straw to each glass for sipping.

Honeydew Granita

Processing it twice gives this granita a smooth texture. Superb!

Water	1 1/2 cups	375 mL
Granulated sugar	2/3 cup	150 mL
Chopped honeydew	3 cups	750 mL
Lemon juice	1 tbsp.	15 mL

Heat and stir water and sugar in medium saucepan on medium until sugar is dissolved. Increase heat to high. Bring to a boil. Boil, uncovered, for 3 minutes. Remove from heat. Cool.

Process sugar mixture, honeydew and lemon juice in blender until smooth. Pour into 2 quart (2 L) shallow baking dish. Cover. Freeze for about 4 hours until almost firm. Scrape mixture, using fork, into blender. Process until smooth. Makes about 5 cups (1.25 L). Pour into 4 chilled medium glasses. Serves 4.

1 serving: 185 Calories; 0.1 g Total Fat (0 g Mono, 0 g Poly, 0 g Sat); 0 mg Cholesterol; 48 g Carbohydrate; 1 g Fibre; 1 g Protein; 14 mg Sodium

Variation (with alcohol): Drizzle each with 2 to 3 tsp. (10 to 15 mL) melon-flavoured liqueur (such as Bols).

 *To reduce the heat in chili peppers and jalapeño peppers, remove the seeds and ribs. Wear rubber gloves and avoid touching your eyes when handling hot peppers. Wash your hands well afterwards.*

Citrus Sunburst

A refreshing, eye-catching drink, bursting with orange flavour.

CITRUS CREAM

Orange sherbet	2 cups	500 mL
Pink grapefruit juice	2/3 cup	150 mL
Can of mandarin orange segments (with juice)	10 oz.	284 mL
Ice cubes	6	6
Gin (3 oz.), optional	6 tbsp.	100 mL
Grenadine syrup	1/2 tsp.	2 mL
Lime slices, for garnish	4	4

Citrus Cream: Process first 4 ingredients in blender until smooth. Makes 3 1/2 cups (875 mL) cream.

Divide and measure gin and grenadine into 4 chilled small glasses. Pour Citrus Cream over top of each.

Garnish each with lime slice. Serves 4.

1 serving (with alcohol): 239 Calories; 2.1 g Total Fat (0.6 g Mono, 0.1 g Poly, 1.2 g Sat); 5 mg Cholesterol; 44 g Carbohydrate; trace Fibre; 2 g Protein; 52 mg Sodium

Pictured on page 54.

Paré Pointer
Say cheers in Icelandic: "Skal!" (SKOHL)

Frozen Drinks

Watermelon Daiquiri

Thick and slushy watermelon with a splash of orange and lime.

Chopped seedless watermelon (see Tip, page 48)	4 cups	1 L
Lemon lime soft drink	3/4 cup	175 mL
White (light) rum (2 oz.)	1/4 cup	60 mL
Orange-flavoured liqueur (such as Grand Marnier), 2 oz.	1/4 cup	60 mL
Lime juice	3 tbsp.	50 mL

Spread watermelon in single layer in 2 quart (2 L) shallow baking dish. Cover. Freeze for about 3 hours until firm.

Place 1/2 of frozen watermelon in blender. Add next 4 ingredients. Process until smooth. Add remaining watermelon. Process until smooth. Makes about 4 cups (1 L). Pour into 4 chilled medium glasses. Serves 4.

1 serving: 145 Calories; 0.7 g Total Fat (0 g Mono, 0 g Poly, 0 g Sat); 0 mg Cholesterol; 18 g Carbohydrate; 1 g Fibre; 1 g Protein; 9 mg Sodium

Vanilla Malted

Tastes like chocolate malt balls, with a vanilla finish. This one's sure to make you feel like a kid in a soda shop!

Vanilla ice cream	2 cups	500 mL
Sparkling bottled water (such as Perrier)	1/2 cup	125 mL
Malt drink mix (such as Ovaltine)	6 tbsp.	100 mL
Vanilla	1 1/2 tsp.	7 mL

Process all 4 ingredients in blender until just smooth. Do not over-process, as mixture thins quickly. Makes about 2 cups (500 mL). Pour into 2 chilled medium glasses. Serves 2.

1 serving: 346 Calories; 15.9 g Total Fat (4.6 g Mono, 0.6 g Poly, 9.8 g Sat); 62 mg Cholesterol; 47 g Carbohydrate; 0 g Fibre; 6 g Protein; 206 mg Sodium

CHOCOLATE MALTED: Omit vanilla ice cream. Use same amount of chocolate ice cream.

Serving Suggestion: Add a straw and sip to your heart's content.

Spiced Frozen Nog

Just when you thought eggnog couldn't get any better!
A cool holiday treat.

Vanilla ice cream	2 cups	500 mL
Eggnog	3/4 cup	175 mL
Ground cinnamon	1/8 tsp.	0.5 mL
Ground nutmeg	1/16 tsp.	0.5 mL
Ground ginger	1/16 tsp.	0.5 mL

Ground cinnamon (or nutmeg), sprinkle

Process first 5 ingredients in blender until smooth. Makes about 2 cups (500 mL). Pour into 2 chilled medium glasses.

Sprinkle each with cinnamon. Serves 2.

1 serving: 417 Calories; 22.9 g Total Fat (6.7 g Mono, 0.9 g Poly, 14 g Sat); 121 mg Cholesterol; 47 g Carbohydrate; trace Fibre; 9 g Protein; 167 mg Sodium

1. Raspberry Margarita, page 62
2. Tropical Daiquiri, page 65
3. Orange Frostbite, page 63

Props Courtesy Of: Pier 1 Imports

Frozen Drinks

Straw-Barb Juice

Strawberries and rhubarb were surely made for each other!

Fresh strawberries	1 1/2 cups	375 mL
Fresh rhubarb stalks, cut up	2	2
Liquid honey	2 tbsp.	30 mL
Ginger ale	1 cup	250 mL

Push strawberries and rhubarb through juicer feed chute. Discard pulp. Transfer juice to pitcher.

Add honey. Stir. Add ginger ale. Stir gently. Makes about 2 cups (500 mL). Pour into 2 medium glasses. Serves 2.

1 serving: 160 Calories; 0.5 g Total Fat (0 g Mono, 0.2 g Poly, 0 g Sat); 0 mg Cholesterol; 41 g Carbohydrate; 1 g Fibre; 1 g Protein; 13 mg Sodium

Pictured on page 72.

Serving Suggestion: Use other soft drink flavours, such as cream soda, lemon lime or club soda, for a new twist on this delicious combination.

1. Straw-Barb Juice, above
2. Fizzy Ale, page 74
3. Green Zinger, page 75
4. Orange Vegetable Brew, page 77

Props Courtesy Of: Pier 1 Imports
The Bay

Fizzy Ale

Good for what ails you! Delicious any time.

Large lemon wedge	1	1
Seedless green grapes	1 1/2 lbs.	680 g
Piece of peeled gingerroot (about 1/4 inch, 6 mm)	1	1
Sparkling bottled water (such as Perrier)	2 cups	500 mL
Ice		

Remove and discard thin layer of peel from lemon, leaving white pith on fruit. Push through juicer feed chute.

Push grapes and gingerroot through chute. Discard pulp. Transfer juice to pitcher.

Add sparkling water. Stir gently. Makes about 3 3/4 cups (925 mL).

Pour over ice in 4 medium glasses. Serves 4.

1 serving: 109 Calories; 0.6 g Total Fat (0 g Mono, 0.2 g Poly, 0.2 g Sat); 0 mg Cholesterol; 30 g Carbohydrate; trace Fibre; 1 g Protein; 5 mg Sodium

Pictured on page 72.

Serving Suggestion: Thread 2 grapes onto cocktail pick and place on side of each glass for garnish.

Winter Veggies Drink

Not getting enough veggies? Here's an answer.

Small yellow turnip, cut up	1	1
Small parsnips	6	6
Medium carrots	4	4

Push all 3 vegetables through juicer feed chute. Discard pulp. Makes about 1 2/3 cups (400 mL). Pour into 2 small glasses. Serves 2.

1 serving: 257 Calories; 1.1 g Total Fat (0.3 g Mono, 0.3 g Poly, 0.2 g Sat); 0 mg Cholesterol; 61 g Carbohydrate; 3 g Fibre; 5 g Protein; 121 mg Sodium

Green Zinger

Bright green, with fresh-from-the-garden flavour.

Medium zucchini (with peel), cut up	1	1
English cucumber (with peel), cut up	1	1
Small apple (with peel), core removed, cut up	1	1
Fresh whole green beans	1 cup	250 mL
Fresh pea pods	1 cup	250 mL
Fresh parsley sprigs	3	3
Fresh spinach leaves	15	15
Large dark green lettuce leaves	4	4

Push first 5 ingredients through juicer feed chute.

Roll parsley tightly in spinach and lettuce leaves. Push through chute. Discard pulp. Makes about 1 2/3 cups (400 mL). Pour into 2 small glasses. Serves 2.

1 serving: 126 Calories; 0.9 g Total Fat (0.1 g Mono, 0.4 g Poly, 0.2 g Sat); 0 mg Cholesterol; 27 g Carbohydrate; 1 g Fibre; 7 g Protein; 45 mg Sodium

Pictured on page 72.

Tropical Breeze

Delicious tropical flavour. Sunshine in a glass!

Medium mango, peeled and pitted, cut up	1	1
Medium papaya, peeled and seeds removed, cut up	1/2	1/2
Fresh pineapple slices (1/2 inch, 12 mm, thick), core removed	2	2

Push all 3 fruits through juicer feed chute. Discard pulp. Makes about 2 1/3 cups (575 mL). Pour into 2 medium glasses. Serves 2.

1 serving: 142 Calories; 0.8 g Total Fat (0.2 g Mono, 0.2 g Poly, 0.1 g Sat); 0 mg Cholesterol; 36 g Carbohydrate; 1 g Fibre; 1 g Protein; 5 mg Sodium

Pictured on page 90.

Serving Suggestion: Serve over ice, with a splash of club soda for sparkle.

Fruit Punch

Pretty pink, frothy refreshment.

Cantaloupe, seeds removed, cut up	1/2	1/2
Small apple (with peel), core removed, cut up	1	1
Fresh strawberries, cut up	6	6
Seedless red (or green) grapes	1/2 cup	125 mL
Fresh cranberries	1/2 cup	125 mL

Push all 5 fruits through juicer feed chute. Discard pulp (see Serving Suggestion). Makes about 1 1/2 cups (375 mL). Pour into 2 small glasses. Serves 2.

1 serving: 117 Calories; 0.8 g Total Fat (0 g Mono, 0.2 g Poly, 0.1 g Sat); 0 mg Cholesterol; 29 g Carbohydrate; 1 g Fibre; 2 g Protein; 13 mg Sodium

Serving Suggestion: To make a thicker drink, add small amount of pulp to juice. Stir.

Spicy Veggie Brew

You can substitute a few drops of hot pepper sauce for the chili pepper to spice up this juice to your taste.

Medium roma (plum) tomatoes, cut up	4	4
Small head of broccoli, cut up	1	1
Large orange (or red) pepper, cut up	1	1
English cucumber (with peel), cut up	1/2	1/2
Medium carrots, cut up	2	2
Celery ribs, cut up	2	2
Small fresh chili pepper, seeds and ribs removed (see Tip, page 67)	1	1

Push all 7 vegetables through juicer feed chute. Discard pulp. Makes about 2 cups (500 mL). Pour into 2 medium glasses. Serves 2.

1 serving: 167 Calories; 1.7 g Total Fat (0.2 g Mono, 0.8 g Poly, 0.3 g Sat); 0 mg Cholesterol; 37 g Carbohydrate; 2 g Fibre; 8 g Protein; 120 mg Sodium

Orange Vegetable Brew

Subtle and sweet flavours blend well in this brightly coloured brew.

Medium carrots, cut up	8	8
Celery ribs, cut up	3	3
Medium sweet potato (or yam), about 12 oz. (340 g), peeled and cut up	1	1
Acorn (or banana) squash, peeled and seeds removed, cut up	1	1

Push all 4 vegetables through juicer feed chute. Discard pulp. Makes about 2 1/4 cups (550 mL). Pour into 2 medium glasses. Serves 2.

1 serving: 251 Calories; 0.9 g Total Fat (0.1 g Mono, 0.4 g Poly, 0.2 g Sat); 0 mg Cholesterol; 61 g Carbohydrate; 2 g Fibre; 5 g Protein; 138 mg Sodium

Pictured on page 72.

Serving Suggestion: Add celery rib to each glass for the perfect stir stick!

Orchard Juice

Good rich flavour. Add enough honey to make as sweet as you like.

Medium apples (with peel), core removed, cut up	3	3
Fresh black (or red) plums, pitted	4	4
Fresh pears (with peel), core removed, cut up	3	3
Fresh apricots, pitted, cut up	3	3
Nectarines (or fresh peaches), pitted, cut up	2	2
Liquid honey (optional)	1 – 2 tbsp.	15 – 30 mL

Push all 5 fruits through juicer feed chute, alternating apple pieces with softer fruits. Discard pulp. Makes about 3 1/2 cups (875 mL). Transfer juice to pitcher. Juice will be foamy and will settle into layers.

Add honey. Stir well. Pour into 4 small glasses. Serve immediately. Serves 4.

1 serving: 169 Calories; 1.1 g Total Fat (0.3 g Mono, 0.2 g Poly, 0.1 g Sat); 0 mg Cholesterol; 43 g Carbohydrate; 1 g Fibre; 2 g Protein; 4 mg Sodium

Almond Soda

Lightly sweet almond flavour with a delicate lime zing.
A great choice for a hot summer's day.

Ice cubes	3	3
Almond-flavoured syrup (such as Torani's)	2 tbsp.	30 mL
Lime juice	2 tsp.	10 mL
Club soda	1 cup	250 mL
Lime slice, for garnish	1	1

Put ice cubes into medium glass. Add almond syrup, lime juice and club soda. Stir gently. Makes about 1 cup (250 mL).

Garnish with lime slice. Serves 1.

1 serving: 131 Calories; 0 g Total Fat (0 g Mono, 0 g Poly, 0 g Sat); 0 mg Cholesterol; 35 g Carbohydrate; trace Fibre; 0 g Protein; 83 mg Sodium

ALMOND SPRITZER: Omit almond-flavoured syrup. Use same amount (30 mL, 1 oz.) of almond-flavoured liqueur (such as Amaretto).

Cran-Almond Delight

Crisp cranberry with a delicate almond accent.

Crushed ice	1/4 cup	60 mL
Cranberry cocktail	3/4 cup	175 mL
Almond-flavoured liqueur (such as Amaretto), 1 oz.	2 tbsp.	30 mL
Club soda	1/4 cup	60 mL

Measure crushed ice into large glass. Add cranberry cocktail, liqueur and club soda. Stir gently. Makes about 1 1/4 cups (300 mL). Serves 1.

1 serving: 241 Calories; 0.3 g Total Fat (0 g Mono, 0.1 g Poly, 0.1 g Sat); 0 mg Cholesterol; 43 g Carbohydrate; 0 g Fibre; 0 g Protein; 19 mg Sodium

Pictured on page 108.

Variation (without alcohol): Omit liqueur. Use same amount of almond-flavoured syrup (such as Torani's).

Cocktails

Spicy Caesar

*A popular drink. Spices can be increased
or decreased according to personal taste.*

Clam tomato beverage (such as Clamato juice)	3 cups	750 mL
Vodka (4 oz.)	1/2 cup	125 mL
Prepared horseradish	1/2 – 1 tsp.	2 – 5 mL
Hot pepper sauce	1/2 tsp.	2 mL
Worcestershire Sauce	1/2 tsp.	2 mL
Ice		
Pickled asparagus spears, for garnish	4	4
Small lemon (or lime) wedges, for garnish	4	4

Measure first 5 ingredients into 4 cup (1 L) liquid measure. Stir. Makes about 3 1/2 cups (875 mL). Pour over ice in 4 medium glasses.

Garnish each with asparagus spear. Place lemon wedge on rim of each glass. Serves 4.

1 serving: 157 Calories; 0.2 g Total Fat (0 g Mono, 0 g Poly, 0 g Sat); 0 mg Cholesterol; 21 g Carbohydrate; trace Fibre; 1 g Protein; 775 mg Sodium

VIRGIN SPICY CAESAR: Omit vodka.

SPICY BLOODY MARY: Omit clam tomato beverage. Use same amount of tomato juice.

SALT AND PEPPER CAESAR: Omit vodka. Use same amount of Peppercorn Vodka, page 149.

Serving Suggestion: Dampen rims of glasses with lemon (or lime) wedge, or dip into lemon (or lime) juice in saucer. Press rims into celery salt in separate saucer until coated.

Banana Froster

*The classic Bananas Foster dessert is banana sautéed in rum
and brown sugar, served over vanilla ice cream. In this "Froster,"
these flavours are now in a glass. Yum!*

Half-and-half cream (or milk)	1/4 cup	60 mL
Banana-flavoured liqueur (such as Crème de banane), 1 oz.	2 tbsp.	30 mL
Dark (navy) rum (1/4 oz.)	1/2 tbsp.	7 mL
Brown sugar, packed	1 tsp.	5 mL
Crushed ice	1/4 cup	60 mL

Measure first 4 ingredients into cocktail shaker. Add crushed ice. Replace lid. Hold firmly and shake vigorously until cold and sugar is dissolved. Strain through sieve into small glass. Makes about 1/2 cup (125 mL). Serves 1.

1 serving: 236 Calories; 6.6 g Total Fat (1.9 g Mono, 0.3 g Poly, 4 g Sat); 20 mg Cholesterol; 22 g Carbohydrate; 0 g Fibre; 2 g Protein; 30 mg Sodium

Serving Suggestion: For a delectable difference, dampen rim of glass with lemon wedge, or dip into lemon juice in saucer. Press into brown sugar in separate saucer until coated.

Granny Smith

Slightly tart apple flavour with a citrus finish. Pucker up!

Ice cubes	3	3
Apple juice	1/4 cup	60 mL
Sour apple-flavoured liqueur (such as Sour Puss), 3/4 oz.	1 1/2 tbsp.	25 mL
Vodka (1/4 oz.)	1/2 tbsp.	7 mL
Sparkling lemonade (or lemonade)	1/2 cup	125 mL

Put ice cubes into medium glass. Add remaining 4 ingredients. Stir gently. Makes about 1 cup (250 mL). Serves 1.

1 serving: 149 Calories; 0.1 g Total Fat (0 g Mono, 0 g Poly, 0 g Sat); 0 mg Cholesterol; 21 g Carbohydrate; trace Fibre; 0 g Protein; 6 mg Sodium

Pictured on page 108.

Brandy Alexandra

A sister to "Brandy Alexander." Made with milk for a light, creamy cocktail.

Milk	3/4 cup	175 mL
Brandy (1 oz.)	2 tbsp.	30 mL
Chocolate-flavoured liqueur (such as Crème de cacao), 1/2 oz.	1 tbsp.	15 mL
Ice cubes	2 – 4	2 – 4

Ground nutmeg, sprinkle

Measure first 3 ingredients into cocktail shaker. Add ice cubes. Replace lid. Hold firmly and shake vigorously until cold. Strain through sieve into small glass. Makes about 1 cup (250 mL).

Sprinkle with nutmeg. Serves 1.

1 serving: 198 Calories; 4.5 g Total Fat (1.3 g Mono, 0.2 g Poly, 2.8 g Sat); 10 mg Cholesterol; 13 g Carbohydrate; 0 g Fibre; 7 g Protein; 112 mg Sodium

Serving Suggestion: To make this drink extra-special, dip rim of martini glass (see page 8) into melted chocolate in saucepan. Let stand until set.

Cold Buttered Rum

Indulge yourself with this creamy butterscotch treat.

Milk	2/3 cup	150 mL
Vanilla ice cream	1/2 cup	125 mL
Butterscotch ice cream topping	3 tbsp.	50 mL
Spiced rum (1 oz.)	2 tbsp.	30 mL
Ice		

Process first 4 ingredients in blender until smooth. Makes about 1 1/2 cups (375 mL). Pour over ice in 2 small glasses. Serves 2.

1 serving: 217 Calories; 4.8 g Total Fat (1.4 g Mono, 0.2 g Poly, 3 g Sat); 19 mg Cholesterol; 33 g Carbohydrate; 0 g Fibre; 5 g Protein; 180 mg Sodium

Variation (without alcohol): Omit spiced rum. Use 1/2 tsp. (2 mL) rum flavouring.

Cran-Razz Soda

Tangy, berry-flavoured soda, just sweet enough to satisfy. Exhilarating!

Cranberry cocktail	1/2 cup	125 mL
Raspberry-flavoured syrup (such as Torani's)	1/4 cup	60 mL
Can of club soda	12 1/2 oz.	355 mL
Ice		

Combine cranberry cocktail and raspberry syrup in 4 cup (1 L) liquid measure. Add club soda. Stir gently. Makes about 3 cups (750 mL). Pour over ice in 2 large glasses. Serves 2.

1 serving: 172 Calories; 0.1 g Total Fat (0 g Mono, 0 g Poly, 0 g Sat); 0 mg Cholesterol; 45 g Carbohydrate; 0 g Fibre; 0 g Protein; 70 mg Sodium

Pictured on page 89.

CRAN-RAZZ COCKTAIL: Add 1/4 cup (60 mL, 2 oz.) vodka to first 3 ingredients. Stir gently. Makes about 3 1/4 cups (800 mL). Serves 2.

Ginger "Ale"

Strong ginger and mild apple flavours come together in this sparkling, lime-coloured drink.

Crushed ice	1/4 cup	60 mL
Apple juice	1/2 cup	125 mL
Sour apple-flavoured liqueur (such as Sour Puss), 1 oz.	2 tbsp.	30 mL
Irish whiskey (1/4 oz.)	1/2 tbsp.	7 mL
Ginger beer	1/2 cup	125 mL

Measure crushed ice into large glass. Add remaining 4 ingredients. Stir gently. Makes about 1 1/2 cups (375 mL). Serves 1.

1 serving: 187 Calories; 0.1 g Total Fat (0 g Mono, 0 g Poly, 0 g Sat); 0 mg Cholesterol; 27 g Carbohydrate; trace Fibre; 0 g Protein; 13 mg Sodium

Variation: For a milder ginger flavour, omit ginger beer. Use same amount of ginger ale.

Ginger Orange Dream

A smooth blend of orange and ginger to warm the insides.

Ginger Orange Liqueur, page 138 (1 1/4 oz.)	2 1/2 tbsp.	37 mL
Orange Dream Liqueur, page 139 (3/4 oz.)	1 1/2 tbsp.	25 mL
Ice cubes	2 – 4	2 – 4
Orange slice, for garnish	1	1

Measure both liqueurs into cocktail shaker. Add ice cubes. Replace lid. Hold firmly and shake vigorously until cold. Strain through sieve into small glass. Makes about 1/3 cup (75 mL).

Garnish with orange slice. Serves 1.

1 serving: 140 Calories; 0.8 g Total Fat (0.2 g Mono, 0 g Poly, 0.5 g Sat); 3 mg Cholesterol; 13 g Carbohydrate; trace Fibre; 1 g Protein; 12 mg Sodium

Cranberry Charm

Sweet and fruity, with a licorice finish.

Cranberry cocktail	1 cup	250 mL
Frozen concentrated orange juice	1/4 cup	60 mL
Yellow-coloured, licorice-flavoured liqueur (such as Galliano), 1 oz. (see Note)	2 tbsp.	30 mL
Melon-flavoured liqueur (such as Bols), 1 oz.	2 tbsp.	30 mL
Ice cubes	4	4

Measure first 4 ingredients into cocktail shaker. Add ice cubes. Replace lid. Hold firmly and shake vigorously until cold. Strain through sieve into 2 small glasses. Makes about 1 1/2 cups (375 mL). Serves 2.

1 serving: 259 Calories; 0.3 g Total Fat (0 g Mono, 0.1 g Poly, 0.1 g Sat); 0 mg Cholesterol; 49 g Carbohydrate; trace Fibre; 1 g Protein; 6 mg Sodium

Note: If you cannot find Galliano, add several drops of yellow liquid food colouring to same amount of clear licorice-flavoured liqueur (such as Sambuca) until desired shade is reached.

Jelly Bean

Looks like grape, but tastes like licorice. A pleasant surprise!

Ice cubes	3	3
Licorice-flavoured liqueur (such as Sambuca), 3/4 oz.	1 1/2 tbsp.	25 mL
Blue-coloured, orange-flavoured liqueur (such as Blue Curaçao), 1/2 oz. (see Note)	1 tbsp.	15 mL
Grenadine syrup	1 tbsp.	15 mL
Lemon lime soft drink	3/4 cup	175 mL

Put ice cubes into medium glass. Add remaining 4 ingredients. Stir gently. Makes about 1 cup (250 mL). Serves 1.

1 serving: 250 Calories; 0.1 g Total Fat (0 g Mono, 0 g Poly, 0 g Sat); 0 mg Cholesterol; 45 g Carbohydrate; 0 g Fibre; 0 g Protein; 37 mg Sodium

Pictured on page 89.

Note: If you cannot find Blue Curaçao, add several drops of blue liquid food colouring to same amount of clear Curaçao until desired shade is reached.

Pepper Martini

A twist on the traditional martini. Warms you from the inside out.

Peppercorn Vodka, page 149 (2 oz.)	1/4 cup	60 mL
Dry vermouth (1/8 oz.)	3/4 tsp.	4 mL
Ice cubes	2 – 4	2 – 4

Lemon twist (or olive), for garnish

Measure vodka and dry vermouth into cocktail shaker. Add ice cubes. Replace lid. Hold firmly and shake vigorously until cold. Strain through sieve into martini glass (see page 8). Makes about 1/3 cup (75 mL).

Garnish with lemon twist. Serves 1.

1 serving: 140 Calories; 0 g Total Fat (0 g Mono, 0 g Poly, 0 g Sat); 0 mg Cholesterol; 0 g Carbohydrate; 0 g Fibre; 0 g Protein; 1 mg Sodium

Cocktails

Limey Coconut

Remember the old Harry Nilsson song "You put the lime in the coconut...?"
You may feel like singing it as you make this frothy, creamy drink.

Half-and-half cream (or milk)	2 tbsp.	30 mL
Coconut-flavoured rum (such as Malibu), 1/2 oz.	1 tbsp.	15 mL
White (light) rum (1/2 oz.)	1 tbsp.	15 mL
Cream of coconut	1 tbsp.	15 mL
Lime juice	1 tbsp.	15 mL
Crushed ice	1/2 cup	125 mL
Lime twist, for garnish	1	1

Measure first 5 ingredients into cocktail shaker. Add crushed ice. Replace lid. Hold firmly and shake vigorously until cold. Strain through sieve into small glass. Makes about 2/3 cup (150 mL).

Garnish with lime twist. Serves 1.

1 serving: 156 Calories; 8.4 g Total Fat (1.1 g Mono, 0.2 g Poly, 6.6 g Sat); 10 mg Cholesterol; 4 g Carbohydrate; trace Fibre; 2 g Protein; 14 mg Sodium

Ginger Fizz

Bright orange drink infused with intense ginger flavour.
Sure to add zip to your day!

Ice cubes	4	4
Pineapple juice	1/2 cup	125 mL
Apricot nectar	1/4 cup	60 mL
Ginger beer	1/4 cup	60 mL
Ginger Orange Liqueur, page 138 (1 oz.)	2 tbsp.	30 mL

Put ice cubes into large glass. Add remaining 4 ingredients. Stir gently. Makes about 1 3/4 cups (425 mL). Serves 1.

1 serving: 198 Calories; 0.2 g Total Fat (0 g Mono, 0.1 g Poly, 0 g Sat); 0 mg Cholesterol; 38 g Carbohydrate; 1 g Fibre; 1 g Protein; 8 mg Sodium

Variation: For a milder ginger flavour, omit ginger beer. Use same amount of ginger ale.

Classic Martini

Whether shaken or stirred, the proportions in these recipes can be varied to suit your personal taste: the less vermouth, the drier the drink. Crisp, cold, dry—the ultimate martini. Simple to prepare, elegant to serve.

Gin (1 1/2 oz.)	3 tbsp.	50 mL
Dry vermouth (3/4 oz.)	1 1/2 tbsp.	25 mL
Ice cubes	2 – 4	2 – 4
Pimiento-stuffed olives	2	2

Stirred Method: Measure gin and dry vermouth into 1 cup (250 mL) liquid measure. Add ice cubes. Stir until cold. Strain through sieve into martini glass (see page 8). Makes about 1/3 cup (75 mL).

Thread olives onto cocktail pick. Place in glass. Serves 1.

Shaken Method: Measure gin and dry vermouth into cocktail shaker. Add ice cubes. Replace lid. Hold firmly and shake vigorously until cold. Strain through sieve into martini glass (see page 8). Makes about 1/3 cup (75 mL).

Thread olives onto cocktail pick. Place in glass. Serves 1.

1 serving: 131 Calories; 2 g Total Fat (1.4 g Mono, 0.2 g Poly, 0.3 g Sat); 0 mg Cholesterol; 0 g Carbohydrate; 1 g Fibre; 0 g Protein; 376 mg Sodium

VODKA MARTINI: Omit gin. Use same amount of vodka.

DRY MARTINI: Measure 1/4 cup (60 mL, 2 oz.) gin and 1/2 tbsp. (7 mL, 1/4 oz.) dry vermouth into liquid measure or cocktail shaker. Add ice cubes. Stir or shake until cold. Strain through sieve into martini glass (see page 8). Garnish with olives.

Serving Suggestion: Lemon twists are an attractive alternative to the traditional olive-embellished martini. Choose a pickled onion instead and you've just made a "Gibson!"

Cocktails

Oogy Wawa

A booze-y, fruity drink for those hot summer days
after the yard work is done.

Pineapple juice	2 tbsp.	30 mL
Orange juice	2 tbsp.	30 mL
Apricot nectar	2 tbsp.	30 mL
Dark (navy) rum (1 oz.)	2 tbsp.	30 mL
White (light) rum (1/2 oz.)	1 tbsp.	15 mL
Lime juice	1 tbsp.	15 mL
Grenadine syrup	1/8 tsp.	0.5 mL
Bitters (such as Angostura)	3 drops	3 drops
Club soda	1/4 cup	60 mL
Crushed ice	1/4 cup	60 mL

Measure first 9 ingredients into cocktail shaker. Add crushed ice. Replace lid. Hold firmly and shake vigorously until cold. Strain through sieve into medium glass. Makes about 1 cup (250 mL). Serves 1.

1 serving: 155 Calories; 0.1 g Total Fat (0 g Mono, 0 g Poly, 0 g Sat); 0 mg Cholesterol; 14 g Carbohydrate; trace Fibre; 1 g Protein; 16 mg Sodium

Pictured on page 90.

Serving Suggestion: Dampen rim of glass with lime wedge, or dip into lime juice in saucer. Press rim into medium sweetened coconut, toasted (see Tip, page 23), in separate saucer until coated.

Paré Pointer
Say cheers in Zulu: "Oogy Wawa!" (OO-gee WAH-wah)

Morning Glory

Tart lemon and licorice are a delightful mix.

Half-and-half cream (or milk)	2 tbsp.	30 mL
Lemon juice	1 1/2 tbsp.	25 mL
Licorice-flavoured liqueur (such as Sambuca), 1/2 oz.	1 tbsp.	15 mL
Egg white (large), see Note	1	1
Ice cubes	2 – 4	2 – 4
Lemon peel spiral, for garnish	1	1

Measure first 4 ingredients into cocktail shaker. Add ice cubes. Replace lid. Hold firmly and shake vigorously until cold. Strain through sieve into small glass. Makes about 1/2 cup (125 mL).

Garnish with lemon peel spiral. Serves 1.

1 serving: 122 Calories; 3.1 g Total Fat (0.9 g Mono, 0.1 g Poly, 1.9 g Sat); 10 mg Cholesterol; 11 g Carbohydrate; trace Fibre; 4 g Protein; 68 mg Sodium

Note: Eggs used in beverages should be cold. Remove egg from refrigerator just before adding. Beverages containing uncooked egg should be served immediately.

1. Cran-Razz Soda, page 82
2. Robin's Egg, page 96
3. Jelly Bean, page 84
4. Melon Cooler, page 96

Props Courtesy Of: Mikasa Home Store

Blue Dazzler

Looks like a calm, clear blue ocean on a sunny day.
Light, refreshing and smooth.

Sparkling lemonade	1/2 cup	125 mL
Blue-coloured, orange-flavoured liqueur	1 tbsp.	15 mL
(such as Blue Curaçao), 1/2 oz. (see Note)		
Tequila (1/2 oz.)	1 tbsp.	15 mL
Scotch-based liqueur (such as Drambuie),	1 tbsp.	15 mL
1/2 oz.		
Crushed ice	1/2 cup	125 mL
Lemon twist, for garnish	1	1

Measure first 4 ingredients into cocktail shaker. Add crushed ice. Replace lid. Hold firmly and shake vigorously until cold. Strain through sieve into small glass. Makes about 1 cup (250 mL).

Garnish with lemon twist. Serves 1.

1 serving: 177 Calories; 0.1 g Total Fat (0 g Mono, 0 g Poly, 0 g Sat); 0 mg Cholesterol; 22 g Carbohydrate; 0 g Fibre; 0 g Protein; 6 mg Sodium

Pictured on page 90.

Note: If you cannot find Blue Curaçao, add several drops of blue liquid food colouring to same amount of clear Curaçao until desired shade is reached.

1. Tropical Breeze, page 75
2. Sunburn, page 95
3. Blue Dazzler, above
4. Oogy Wawa, page 87

Props Courtesy Of: Pier 1 Imports
The Bay

Orange Almond Cocktail

Red grenadine settles to the bottom of the glass for
an attractive, vibrant presentation. It's delicious, too.

Orange juice	1 cup	250 mL
Vodka (2 oz.)	1/4 cup	60 mL
Almond-flavoured liqueur (such as Amaretto), 1 oz.	2 tbsp.	30 mL
Ice cubes	4	4
Crushed ice	1/4 cup	60 mL
Grenadine syrup	1/4 tsp.	1 mL

Measure orange juice, vodka and liqueur into cocktail shaker. Add ice cubes. Replace lid. Hold firmly and shake vigorously until cold. Strain through sieve into 2 cup (500 mL) liquid measure. Makes about 1 1/3 cups (325 mL).

Spoon crushed ice into 2 small glasses. Pour orange juice mixture over top. Drizzle each with grenadine. Do not stir. Serves 2.

1 serving: 193 Calories; 0.3 g Total Fat (0.1 g Mono, 0.1 g Poly, 0 g Sat); 0 mg Cholesterol; 21 g Carbohydrate; trace Fibre; 1 g Protein; 3 mg Sodium

Pictured on front cover.

Serving Suggestion: Serve this drink in martini glasses (see page 8) to show off its colour.

Paré Pointer
Say cheers in Italian: "Alla salute!" (AH-lah sal-OO-tay)

Pearl Drop

Creamy white chocolate flavour with a surprise at the bottom of the glass!

Milk chocolate kiss	1	1
Half-and-half cream (or milk)	2 tbsp.	30 mL
Vodka (1 oz.)	2 tbsp.	30 mL
Chocolate-flavoured liqueur (such as Crème de cacao), 1/4 oz.	1/2 tbsp.	7 mL
Irish cream liqueur (such as Baileys), 1/4 oz.	1/2 tbsp.	7 mL
Ice cubes	2 – 4	2 – 4

Place chocolate kiss in bottom of small glass.

Measure next 4 ingredients into cocktail shaker. Add ice cubes. Replace lid. Hold firmly and shake vigorously until cold. Strain through sieve into prepared glass. Makes about 1/3 cup (75 mL). Serves 1.

1 serving: 173 Calories; 6.8 g Total Fat (2 g Mono, 0.3 g Poly, 4.2 g Sat); 13 mg Cholesterol; 7 g Carbohydrate; trace Fibre; 2 g Protein; 31 mg Sodium

Serving Suggestion: This is a fun drink to serve in a martini glass (see page 8).

Curried Tomato Juice

A good aperitif for a summer barbecue. Mild curry flavour in a creamy, tangy tomato drink.

Tomato juice	1 cup	250 mL
Buttermilk	1/4 cup	60 mL
Gin (1 oz.), optional	2 tbsp.	30 mL
Plain yogurt	1 tbsp.	15 mL
Curry paste	1/4 tsp.	1 mL
Ice cubes	4	4

Measure first 5 ingredients into cocktail shaker. Add ice cubes. Replace lid. Hold firmly and shake vigorously until creamy and cold. Strain through sieve into 2 small glasses. Makes about 1 1/2 cups (375 mL). Serves 2.

1 serving (with alcohol): 73 Calories; 0.5 g Total Fat (0.1 g Mono, 0.1 g Poly, 0.3 g Sat); 2 mg Cholesterol; 8 g Carbohydrate; 1 g Fibre; 3 g Protein; 509 mg Sodium

Spiced Berry

Ruby red with subtle spice and full berry flavours.

Cranberry cocktail	3/4 cup	175 mL
Spiced rum (1 1/2 oz.)	3 tbsp.	50 mL
Raspberry-flavoured liqueur (such as Chambord), 3/4 oz.	1 1/2 tbsp.	25 mL
Ice cubes	4	4

Measure first 3 ingredients into cocktail shaker. Add ice cubes. Replace lid. Hold firmly and shake vigorously until cold. Strain through sieve into 2 small glasses. Makes about 1 1/4 cups (300 mL). Serves 2.

1 serving: 114 Calories; 0.1 g Total Fat (0 g Mono, 0 g Poly, 0 g Sat); 0 mg Cholesterol; 14 g Carbohydrate; 0 g Fibre; 0 g Protein; 2 mg Sodium

Serving Suggestion: Combine 3 tbsp. (50 mL) granulated sugar and 1 tsp. (5 mL) ground cinnamon in saucer. Dip rims of 2 martini glasses (see page 8) into cranberry cocktail in separate saucer. Press into sugar mixture until coated. Pour cocktail mixture into glasses.

Sham Champagne

This recipe can be easily increased to make a large quantity. The sugar cube produces a steady supply of small bubbles—just like the real thing.

White grape juice	1/2 cup	125 mL
Club soda	1/2 cup	125 mL
Sugar cube (optional)	1	1

Measure grape juice and club soda into champagne flute (see page 8). Stir gently.

Drop sugar cube into grape juice mixture. Makes 1 cup (250 mL). Serve immediately. Serves 1.

1 serving: 82 Calories; 0.1 g Total Fat (0 g Mono, 0 g Poly, 0 g Sat); 0 mg Cholesterol; 20 g Carbohydrate; trace Fibre; 1 g Protein; 31 mg Sodium

Cocktails

Sunburn

Attractive tangerine-red colour with a pleasing fruity flavour.

Ice cubes	4	4
Mango tangerine cocktail (such as Sunrype)	2/3 cup	150 mL
Pineapple juice	1/3 cup	75 mL
Dark (navy) rum (3/4 oz.)	1 1/2 tbsp.	25 mL
Grenadine syrup	1 tbsp.	15 mL
Almond-flavoured liqueur (such as Amaretto), 1/4 oz.	1/2 tbsp.	7 mL
Peach-flavoured liqueur (such as Southern Comfort), 1/4 oz.	1/2 tbsp.	7 mL

Put ice cubes into large glass. Add remaining 6 ingredients. Stir. Makes about 1 1/4 cups (300 mL). Serves 1.

1 serving: 297 Calories; 0.5 g Total Fat (0.1 g Mono, 0.1 g Poly, 0.1 g Sat); 0 mg Cholesterol; 54 g Carbohydrate; trace Fibre; 0 g Protein; 25 mg Sodium

Pictured on page 90.

Tropical Sunrise

Luscious, citrus-filled beverage. Pure ambrosia!

Pineapple juice	1 cup	250 mL
Frozen concentrated orange juice	1/4 cup	60 mL
Coconut milk	1/4 cup	60 mL
Crushed ice	3 tbsp.	50 mL
Lime juice	1 tbsp.	15 mL

Process all 5 ingredients in blender until smooth. Makes about 1 3/4 cups (425 mL). Pour into 2 medium glasses. Serves 2.

1 serving: 195 Calories; 6.6 g Total Fat (0.3 g Mono, 0.1 g Poly, 5.7 g Sat); 0 mg Cholesterol; 34 g Carbohydrate; trace Fibre; 2 g Protein; 6 mg Sodium

VODKA SUNRISE: Add 1/4 cup (60 mL, 2 oz.) vodka or white (light) rum to blender with all 5 ingredients. Process until smooth. Makes about 2 cups (500 mL).

Cocktails

Robin's Egg

The robin's egg blue colour catches your eye. The combination of orange and chocolate satisfies your taste buds.

Ice cubes	4	4
Blue-coloured, orange-flavoured liqueur (such as Blue Curaçao), 3/4 oz. (see Note)	1 1/2 tbsp.	25 mL
White chocolate-flavoured liqueur (such as Godet), 1/2 oz.	1 tbsp.	15 mL
Milk	1/2 cup	125 mL

Put ice cubes into medium glass. Add both liqueurs and milk. Stir. Makes about 2/3 cup (150 mL). Serves 1.

1 serving: 195 Calories; 3.9 g Total Fat (1.1 g Mono, 0.2 g Poly, 2.4 g Sat); 8 mg Cholesterol; 22 g Carbohydrate; 0 g Fibre; 5 g Protein; 81 mg Sodium

Pictured on page 89.

Note: If you cannot find Blue Curaçao, add several drops of blue liquid food colouring to same amount of clear Curaçao until desired shade is reached.

Melon Cooler

Sweet, sparkling cooler for a hot summer's day.

Melon-flavoured liqueur (such as Bols), 1/2 oz.	1 tbsp.	15 mL
Sparkling sweet wine (such as Asti Spumante), 4 oz.	1/2 cup	125 mL

Measure liqueur into small glass. Add sparkling wine. Stir gently. Makes about 1/2 cup (125 mL). Serves 1.

1 serving: 117 Calories; 0 g Total Fat (0 g Mono, 0 g Poly, 0 g Sat); 0 mg Cholesterol; 1 g Carbohydrate; 0 g Fibre; 0 g Protein; 6 mg Sodium

Pictured on page 89.

Serving Suggestion: Serve this cooler in a cocktail glass or champagne flute (see page 8) for an attractive presentation.

Raspberry Spritzer

Sweet ginger ale releases the fresh raspberry flavour
in this brilliant red drink. Pretty and festive.

Package of frozen raspberries in syrup, thawed	15 oz.	425 g
Ginger ale	3 cups	750 mL

Press raspberries through sieve into small bowl or 2 cup (500 mL) liquid measure. Discard seeds. Makes about 1 1/4 cups (300 mL) juice. Measure 3 tbsp. (50 mL) juice into each of 6 small glasses.

Add 1/2 cup (125 mL) ginger ale to each. Stir gently. Serves 6.

1 serving: 117 Calories; 0.1 g Total Fat (0 g Mono, 0.1 g Poly, 0 g Sat); 0 mg Cholesterol; 30 g Carbohydrate; 3 g Fibre; 1 g Protein; 10 mg Sodium

Pineapple Alaska

Light yellow foam tops this fluffy pineapple treat.

Crushed ice	2 cups	500 mL
Can of crushed pineapple (with juice)	14 oz.	398 mL
Pineapple juice	1/2 cup	125 mL
Brown sugar, packed	1 1/2 tbsp.	25 mL
Egg white (large), see Note	1	1

Process all 5 ingredients in blender until cream-coloured and foamy. Makes about 6 2/3 cups (1.65 L). Pour into 6 medium glasses. Let stand for 1 minute. Foam will rise to top. Serves 6.

1 serving: 70 Calories; 0.1 g Total Fat (0 g Mono, 0 g Poly, 0 g Sat); 0 mg Cholesterol; 18 g Carbohydrate; 1 g Fibre; 1 g Protein; 11 mg Sodium

Note: Eggs used in beverages should be cold. Remove egg from refrigerator just before adding. Beverages containing uncooked egg should be served immediately.

PINEAPPLE RUM ALASKA: Add 6 tbsp. (100 mL, 3 oz.) white (light) rum to ingredients in blender before processing.

Orange Apricot Delight

Subtle hint of licorice makes this smooth,
fruity beverage delightfully different.

Orange juice	1/2 cup	125 mL
Apricot brandy (1 1/2 oz.)	3 tbsp.	50 mL
Vodka (1 oz.)	2 tbsp.	30 mL
Yellow-coloured, licorice-flavoured liqueur	1 tbsp.	15 mL
(such as Galliano), 1/2 oz. (see Note)		
Ginger ale	1/2 cup	125 mL
Ice		

Combine first 4 ingredients in 2 cup (500 mL) liquid measure. Add ginger ale. Stir gently. Makes about 1 1/2 cups (375 mL). Pour over ice in 2 small glasses. Serves 2.

1 serving: 164 Calories; 0.2 g Total Fat (0 g Mono, 0 g Poly, 0 g Sat); 0 mg Cholesterol; 16 g Carbohydrate; trace Fibre; 0 g Protein; 6 mg Sodium

Note: If you cannot find Galliano, add several drops of yellow liquid food colouring to same amount of clear licorice-flavoured liqueur (such as Sambuca) until desired shade is reached.

Strawberry Blonde

Sparkling apple cider is a perfect partner to Madeira—a sweet,
fortified wine that gives this drink its unusual colour and taste.

Ice cubes	4 – 5	4 – 5
Sparkling apple cider	3/4 cup	175 mL
Madeira wine (1 1/2 oz.)	3 tbsp.	50 mL
Grenadine syrup	1/8 tsp.	0.5 mL
Fresh strawberry, for garnish	1	1

Put ice cubes into medium glass. Add apple cider, wine and grenadine. Stir gently. Makes about 1 cup (250 mL).

Garnish with strawberry. Serves 1.

1 serving: 128 Calories; 0.2 g Total Fat (0 g Mono, 0.1 g Poly, 0 g Sat); 0 mg Cholesterol; 25 g Carbohydrate; trace Fibre; 0 g Protein; 9 mg Sodium

Cocktails

Misty Evening

Soothing beverage with a lemon mist.

Whole cloves	3	3
Lemon slice (1/2 inch, 12 mm, thick)	1	1
Cinnamon stick (4 inches, 10 cm)	1	1
Boiling water	2/3 cup	150 mL
Canadian whisky (rye), 1 oz.	2 tbsp.	30 mL
Liquid honey	1 tsp.	5 mL

Place first 3 ingredients in small mug.

Add boiling water, whisky and honey. Stir, using cinnamon stick. Let stand for 2 to 3 minutes. Remove and discard cloves, lemon slice and cinnamon stick. Makes about 1 cup (250 mL). Serves 1.

1 serving: 87 Calories; 0 g Total Fat (0 g Mono, 0 g Poly, 0 g Sat); 0 mg Cholesterol; 6 g Carbohydrate; 0 g Fibre; 0 g Protein; 1 mg Sodium

Pictured on page 107.

Serving Suggestion: Add a fresh cinnamon stick wrapped with a spiral of lemon zest to mug for garnish.

Nutty Irish

Nutty flavour with a creamy texture. A comforting late-night drink.

Milk	1 cup	250 mL
Hazelnut-flavoured liqueur (such as Frangelico), 1/2 oz.	1 tbsp.	15 mL
Irish cream liqueur (such as Baileys), 1/2 oz.	1 tbsp.	15 mL

Heat and stir milk in small heavy saucepan on medium until bubbles form around edge. Remove from heat.

Add both liqueurs. Stir. Makes about 1 cup (250 mL). Pour into small mug. Serves 1.

1 serving: 214 Calories; 5.3 g Total Fat (1.5 g Mono, 0.2 g Poly, 3.2 g Sat); 13 mg Cholesterol; 21 g Carbohydrate; 0 g Fibre; 9 g Protein; 145 mg Sodium

Dutch Eggnog

Creamy yellow with a sprinkle of spice.

Milk	3/4 cup	175 mL
Apricot brandy (1/2 oz.)	1 tbsp.	15 mL
Apricot nectar	1 tbsp.	15 mL
Eggnog-flavoured liqueur (such as Advocaat), 1 oz.	2 tbsp.	30 mL
Ground nutmeg, sprinkle		

Heat and stir milk, brandy and apricot nectar in small heavy saucepan on medium until bubbles form around edge. Remove from heat.

Add liqueur. Stir. Makes about 1 cup (250 mL). Pour into small mug. Sprinkle with nutmeg. Serves 1.

1 serving: 188 Calories; 2.1 g Total Fat (0.6 g Mono, 0.1 g Poly, 1.3 g Sat); 8 mg Cholesterol; 12 g Carbohydrate; trace Fibre; 6 g Protein; 98 mg Sodium

Serving Suggestion: Add extra nutmeg for a more traditional eggnog.

Snow-Capped Mountain

This drink will remind you of a purple mountain with a snow-covered peak.

Milk	3/4 cup	175 mL
Raspberry-flavoured liqueur (such as Chambord), 3/4 oz.	1 1/2 tbsp.	25 mL
Vodka (1/2 oz.)	1 tbsp.	15 mL
Whipped cream (or frozen whipped topping, thawed)	2 tbsp.	30 mL

Heat and stir milk in small heavy saucepan on medium until bubbles form around edge. Remove from heat.

Add liqueur and vodka. Stir. Makes about 1 cup (250 mL). Pour into small glass mug.

Top with whipped cream. Serves 1.

1 serving: 209 Calories; 6.9 g Total Fat (2 g Mono, 0.2 g Poly, 4.3 g Sat); 25 mg Cholesterol; 10 g Carbohydrate; 0 g Fibre; 7 g Protein; 103 mg Sodium

Toasted Almond

Fragrant almond and coffee aromas emanate from this soothing, warm milk.

Milk	1 1/2 cups	375 mL
Almond-flavoured liqueur (such as Amaretto), 1 oz.	2 tbsp.	30 mL
Coffee-flavoured liqueur (such as Kahlúa), 1 oz.	2 tbsp.	30 mL
Whipped cream (or frozen whipped topping, thawed), for garnish	2 tbsp.	30 mL
Finely chopped almonds, toasted (see Tip, page 23), for garnish	1 tbsp.	15 mL

Heat and stir milk in small heavy saucepan on medium until bubbles form around edge. Remove from heat.

Add both liqueurs. Stir. Makes about 1 1/2 cups (375 mL). Pour into 2 small mugs.

Top each with whipped cream and almonds. Serves 2.

1 serving: 199 Calories; 2.2 g Total Fat (0.6 g Mono, 0.1 g Poly, 1.3 g Sat); 8 mg Cholesterol; 22 g Carbohydrate; 0 g Fibre; 6 g Protein; 99 mg Sodium

Applecot Cider

Sweet apple cider mingled with tangy apricot and ginger.

Package of apple cider mix (such as Lynch)	3/4 oz.	23 g
Apricot brandy (1/2 oz.)	1 tbsp.	15 mL
Ginger Orange Liqueur, page 138 (or peach-flavoured liqueur, such as peach schnapps), 1/2 oz.	1 tbsp.	15 mL

Prepare apple cider mix in small mug according to package directions.

Add brandy and liqueur. Stir. Makes about 1 cup (250 mL). Serves 1.

1 serving: 188 Calories; 0.3 g Total Fat (0 g Mono, 0.1 g Poly, 0.1 g Sat); 0 mg Cholesterol; 33 g Carbohydrate; trace Fibre; 0 g Protein; 8 mg Sodium

Maple Toddy

Apple and vanilla flavours with the sweetness of maple syrup.

Apple cider (or apple juice)	4 cups	1 L
Maple (or maple-flavoured) syrup	3 tbsp.	50 mL
Vanilla bean, split	1	1
Cinnamon stick (4 inches, 10 cm)	1	1
Whole allspice	10	10
Brandy (2 1/2 oz.), optional	1/3 cup	75 mL

Combine first 5 ingredients in medium saucepan. Bring to a boil on medium. Reduce heat to medium-low. Simmer, uncovered, for about 25 minutes until fragrant. Remove from heat. Strain through sieve into 4 cup (1 L) liquid measure. Discard solids.

Add brandy. Stir. Makes about 3 1/3 cups (825 mL). Pour into 4 small mugs. Serves 4.

1 serving: 162 Calories; 0.3 g Total Fat (0 g Mono, 0.1 g Poly, 0.1 g Sat); 0 mg Cholesterol; 41 g Carbohydrate; trace Fibre; 0 g Protein; 9 mg Sodium

Pictured on page 107.

Serving Suggestion: Add a fresh cinnamon stick for garnish, or serve with maple-flavoured chocolates.

Last Call

Sweet apple cider with a black raspberry finish. Delicious!

Package of apple cider mix (such as Lynch)	3/4 oz.	23 g
Boiling water	1 cup	250 mL
Raspberry-flavoured liqueur (such as Chambord), 1 oz.	2 tbsp.	30 mL
Cinnamon stick (4 inches, 10 cm)	1	1

Combine apple cider mix and boiling water in large mug.

Add liqueur. Stir. Makes about 1 cup (250 mL). Add cinnamon stick. Serves 1.

1 serving: 242 Calories; 0.4 g Total Fat (0 g Mono, 0.1 g Poly, 0.1 g Sat); 0 mg Cholesterol; 47 g Carbohydrate; trace Fibre; 0 g Protein; 11 mg Sodium

Sweet Dreams

Two-layered dessert in a glass. Well worth the extra effort.
The foamy egg layer makes this drink a decadent dream.

Chocolate milk	2 1/2 cups	625 mL
Almond-flavoured liqueur (such as Amaretto), 4 oz.	1/2 cup	125 mL
ORANGE SABAYON		
Egg yolks (large)	2	2
Granulated sugar	2 1/2 tbsp.	37 mL
Orange juice	2 tbsp.	30 mL

Heat and stir chocolate milk in heavy medium saucepan on medium until bubbles form around edge. Remove from heat.

Add liqueur. Stir. Cover to keep warm. Makes about 3 cups (750 mL).

Orange Sabayon: Beat egg yolks and sugar on medium in small bowl over saucepan of simmering water for about 1 minute until combined. Add orange juice. Beat for about 5 minutes until foamy and thickened. Makes about 1 1/4 cups (300 mL) sabayon.

Pour about 3/4 cup (175 mL) chocolate milk mixture into each of 4 large mugs. Top each with about 1/3 cup (75 mL) sabayon. Serves 4.

1 serving: 314 Calories; 6 g Total Fat (2 g Mono, 0.5 g Poly, 2.9 g Sat); 119 mg Cholesterol; 41 g Carbohydrate; 1 g Fibre; 7 g Protein; 105 mg Sodium

Pictured on page 18 and on back cover.

Variation (without alcohol): Omit liqueur. Use same amount of almond-flavoured syrup (such as Torani's).

Serving Suggestion: Garnish with chocolate curls. To make curls, peel room temperature chocolate with vegetable peeler.

Sunset Tea

A mellow blend of orange and almond flavours in a dusk-red tea.
Fill your cup and enjoy the evening twilight.

Boiling water	2 cups	500 mL
Orange and peach-flavoured tea bags (such as Tetley)	2	2
Cognac (or brandy), 1/2 oz.	1 tbsp.	15 mL
Almond-flavoured liqueur (such as Amaretto), 1/2 oz.	1 tbsp.	15 mL
Orange-flavoured liqueur (such as Grand Marnier), 1 oz.	2 tbsp.	30 mL
Lemon juice	2 tsp.	10 mL

Pour boiling water into teapot. Add tea bags. Cover. Let steep for 5 minutes. Squeeze and discard tea bags.

Add remaining 4 ingredients. Stir. Makes about 2 1/2 cups (625 mL). Pour into 2 large mugs. Serves 2.

1 serving: 84 Calories; 0 g Total Fat (0 g Mono, 0 g Poly, 0 g Sat); 0 mg Cholesterol; 4 g Carbohydrate; 0 g Fibre; 0 g Protein; 3 mg Sodium

Serving Suggestion: Add a citrus knot to each cup of tea for extra zest. To make knots, choose firm, smooth-skinned orange, lemon or lime. Wash and dry fruit. Remove 4 inch (10 cm) thin strip of peel from fruit, using citrus stripper. Tie peel in a knot and drop into tea.

Minty Thaw

Tastes like a peppermint patty!

Chocolate milk	2 cups	500 mL
Mint-flavoured liqueur (such as peppermint schnapps), 2 oz.	1/4 cup	60 mL
Whipped cream (or frozen whipped topping, thawed), optional	2 tbsp.	30 mL

(continued on next page)

Nightcaps

Heat and stir chocolate milk in small heavy saucepan on medium until bubbles form around edge. Remove from heat.

Add liqueur. Stir. Makes about 2 1/2 cups (625 mL). Pour into 2 large mugs.

Top each with whipped cream. Serves 2.

1 serving: 322 Calories; 5.4 g Total Fat (1.6 g Mono, 0.3 g Poly, 3.3 g Sat); 18 mg Cholesterol; 42 g Carbohydrate; 2 g Fibre; 8 g Protein; 161 mg Sodium

Pictured on page 107.

Serving Suggestion: Sprinkle crushed mint candies over whipped cream for colour, and add a candy cane or peppermint stick for stirring.

White Hot Chocolate

Oh, so sweet and chocolaty! A dessert you can drink.

Milk	1 cup	250 mL
White chocolate bar, chopped (about 1/2 cup, 125 mL)	3 1/2 oz.	100 g
Vanilla	1/4 tsp.	1 mL
Whipped cream (or frozen whipped topping, thawed)	1/4 cup	60 mL

Heat and stir milk in small heavy saucepan on medium until bubbles form around edge. Remove from heat.

Add chocolate bar pieces and vanilla. Stir until chocolate is melted and mixture is smooth. Makes about 1 1/3 cups (325 mL). Pour into 2 small mugs.

Top each with whipped cream. Serves 2.

1 serving: 370 Calories; 21.7 g Total Fat (6.7 g Mono, 0.6 g Poly, 12.9 g Sat); 35 mg Cholesterol; 37 g Carbohydrate; 0 g Fibre; 8 g Protein; 115 mg Sodium

Serving Suggestion: Use espresso cups for this decadent dessert beverage—a little goes a long way! Serves 4.

After-Dinner Mint

Minted chocolate with an eggnog flavour and a chocolate stir stick.

Chocolate milk	3/4 cup	175 mL
Mint-flavoured liqueur (such as Crème de menthe), 1/4 oz.	1/2 tbsp.	7 mL
Chocolate-flavoured liqueur (such as Crème de cacao), 1/2 oz.	1 tbsp.	15 mL
Eggnog-flavoured liqueur (such as Advocaat), 1/2 oz. (optional)	1 tbsp.	15 mL
Chocolate stick with mint filling (such as Ovation), for garnish	1	1

Heat and stir chocolate milk in small heavy saucepan on medium until bubbles form around edge. Remove from heat.

Add all 3 liqueurs. Stir. Makes about 1 cup (250 mL). Pour into large mug.

Garnish with chocolate stick. Serves 1.

1 serving: 225 Calories; 6.5 g Total Fat (1.9 g Mono, 0.3 g Poly, 4 g Sat); 16 mg Cholesterol; 28 g Carbohydrate; 1 g Fibre; 7 g Protein; 135 mg Sodium

1. Minty Thaw, page 104
2. Misty Evening, page 99
3. Maple Toddy, page 102

Props Courtesy Of: Wal-Mart Canada Inc.

Nightcaps

Vanilla Milk

Can't sleep? This beats counting sheep to help you relax.

Milk	2 cups	500 mL
White corn syrup	3 tbsp.	50 mL
Clear vanilla	2 tsp.	10 mL

Heat and stir all 3 ingredients in small heavy saucepan on medium until bubbles form around edge. Makes about 2 cups (500 mL). Pour into 2 small mugs. Serves 2.

1 serving: 217 Calories; 2.7 g Total Fat (0.8 g Mono, 0.1 g Poly, 1.7 g Sat); 10 mg Cholesterol; 38 g Carbohydrate; 0 g Fibre; 8 g Protein; 151 mg Sodium

Variation: Omit corn syrup and vanilla. Use 3 tbsp. (50 mL) vanilla-flavoured syrup (such as Torani's).

VANILLA MALTED MILK: Add 3 tbsp. (50 mL) malt drink mix (such as Ovaltine) to milk mixture before heating.

VANILLA HAZELNUT MILK: Add 2 tbsp. (30 mL, 1 oz.) hazelnut-flavoured liqueur (such as Frangelico) to each mug.

1. Cran-Almond Delight, page 78
2. South Seas Sangria, page 113
3. Granny Smith, page 80
4. Berry Citrus Freeze, page 60

Props Courtesy Of: Canhome Global
Pier 1 Imports
Winners Stores

Apple Ginger Punch

Sparkling, tart apple flavour goes well with ginger. So delicious!

Tart medium cooking apples (such as Granny Smith), peeled and core removed, diced	4	4
Water	1 cup	250 mL
Brown sugar, packed	1/4 cup	60 mL
Finely grated, peeled gingerroot	2 tsp.	10 mL
Bottles of sparkling apple cider (with alcohol), 12 oz. (341 mL) each	4	4
Ginger ale	3 cups	750 mL
Ice cubes	12	12
Thin slices of apple (with peel), core removed, for garnish	12 – 16	12 – 16

Heat and stir first 4 ingredients in large saucepan on medium until mixture just starts to boil. Reduce heat to medium-low. Cover. Simmer for 10 to 15 minutes, stirring occasionally, until apple is softened. Remove from heat. Cool. Transfer to blender. Process until smooth. Transfer to small punch bowl. Cover. Chill for at least 4 hours until cold.

Just before serving, add apple cider and ginger ale. Stir gently. Add ice cubes and apple slices. Makes about 16 cups (4 L). Serves 14.

1 serving: 104 Calories; 0.1 g Total Fat (0 g Mono, 0 g Poly, 0 g Sat); 0 mg Cholesterol; 20 g Carbohydrate; 1 g Fibre; 0 g Protein; 14 mg Sodium

Variation (without alcohol): Omit sparkling apple cider (with alcohol). Use same amount of alcohol-free sparkling apple cider.

Fizzy Lemon Refresher

Tart, but not sour, with a sweet, fizzy finish. You'll want to pour this refreshing drink over plenty of ice.

Boiling water	3 cups	750 mL
Medium lemons, sliced	3	3
Diced, peeled gingerroot	1 tbsp.	15 mL
Granulated sugar	1 cup	250 mL
Lemon juice	1/2 cup	125 mL
Club soda	4 cups	1 L
Ice cubes		

Pour boiling water into large heatproof bowl. Add lemon slices and ginger. Cover. Let stand at room temperature for at least 12 hours. Strain lemon mixture through sieve into medium saucepan. Discard solids.

Add sugar. Heat and stir on medium-high until boiling. Reduce heat to medium. Boil, uncovered, for 15 to 20 minutes, stirring occasionally, until reduced by half and slightly thickened. Remove from heat. Let stand until cooled completely.

Add lemon juice. Stir. Pour into pitcher. Cover. Chill for at least 4 hours until cold.

Just before serving, add club soda. Stir gently. Makes about 5 1/2 cups (1.4 L).

Pour over ice cubes in 6 medium glasses. Serves 6.

1 serving: 143 Calories; 0 g Total Fat (0 g Mono, 0 g Poly, 0 g Sat); 0 mg Cholesterol; 37 g Carbohydrate; trace Fibre; 0 g Protein; 37 mg Sodium

Paré Pointer
Say cheers in Maori: "Kia Ora!" (KEE-ah Or-AH)

Sangria

Full-bodied flavour, lightened with soda.
Fruit slices add a pretty contrast to the wine's deep red colour.

Brandy (8 oz.)	1 cup	250 mL
Granulated sugar	2/3 cup	150 mL
Medium oranges, sliced	2	2
Medium lemons, sliced	2	2
Medium limes, sliced	2	2
Bottles of dry red (or alcohol-free) wine (26 oz., 750 mL, each)	2	2
Club soda	4 cups	1 L
Ice cubes	24	24

Measure brandy and sugar into small punch bowl. Stir until sugar is dissolved. Add orange, lemon and lime slices. Stir. Cover. Let stand for 1 1/2 hours.

Add wine. Stir. Chill for at least 4 hours until cold.

Just before serving, remove citrus slices using slotted spoon, leaving 6 to 8 slices in bowl for garnish. Add club soda. Stir gently. Add ice cubes. Makes 14 cups (3.5 L). Serves 25.

1 serving: 95 Calories; 0 g Total Fat (0 g Mono, 0 g Poly, 0 g Sat); 0 mg Cholesterol; 9 g Carbohydrate; trace Fibre; 0 g Protein; 12 mg Sodium

Pictured on page 125.

South Seas Sangria

*This cool wine and fruit punch has a tropical flair
and is not too sweet. Good for sipping.*

Can of sliced peaches in pear juice	14 oz.	398 mL
Dry white (or alcohol-free) wine (26 oz.)	3 cups	750 mL
Pear juice (such as Ceres)	1/2 cup	125 mL
Blue-coloured, orange-flavoured liqueur	1/4 cup	60 mL
(such as Blue Curaçao), 2 oz. (see Note)		
Can of club soda	12 1/2 oz.	355 mL

Drain peaches, reserving juice. Chop peaches. Transfer peaches and reserved juice to pitcher.

Add wine, pear juice and liqueur. Cover. Chill for at least 4 hours until cold.

Just before serving, add club soda. Stir gently. Makes about 7 1/2 cups (1.9 L). Pour into 12 chilled small glasses. Serves 12.

*1 serving: 84 Calories; 0 g Total Fat (0 g Mono, 0 g Poly, 0 g Sat); 0 mg Cholesterol;
9 g Carbohydrate; trace Fibre; 0 g Protein; 12 mg Sodium*

Pictured on page 108.

Note: If you cannot find Blue Curaçao, add several drops of blue liquid food colouring to same amount of clear Curaçao until desired shade is reached.

Paré Pointer
Say cheers in Polish: "Na Zdrowoie!" (NAH zdrav-EE)

Pineapple Citrus Punch

Tangy fruit blend in a beautiful amber-coloured punch. Refreshing, flavourful and without alcohol. Add an ice ring for a decorative flair.

Pineapple juice	4 cups	1 L
Orange juice	2 cups	500 mL
Ruby red grapefruit juice	2 cups	500 mL
Lemon juice	1/4 cup	60 mL
Large oranges, peeled and sectioned, membranes and seeds discarded, cut bite size	2	2
Large pink grapefruit, peeled and sectioned, membranes and seeds discarded, cut bite size	1	1
Lemon lime soft drink	4 cups	1 L

Combine first 6 ingredients in small punch bowl. Chill for at least 4 hours until cold.

Just before serving, add lemon lime soft drink. Stir gently. Makes about 14 1/2 cups (3.6 L). Serves 25.

1 serving: 69 Calories; 0.1 g Total Fat (0 g Mono, 0 g Poly, 0 g Sat); 0 mg Cholesterol; 17 g Carbohydrate; trace Fibre; 1 g Protein; 6 mg Sodium

ICE RING: Put crushed ice into bottom of 12 cup (3 L) bundt pan. Arrange various fruit pieces in and on top of ice. Freeze for 1 hour. Pour 2 cups (500 mL) punch or fruit juice over top of fruit. (Do not use alcohol in ice ring because alcohol will not freeze.) Freeze for 8 hours or overnight. Run warm water over underside of bundt pan. Carefully remove ice ring. Gently place in punch.

Variation: To keep ice ring from thawing too quickly, omit punch or fruit juice. Use clear sugar-free soft drink, such as lemon lime or ginger ale, to pour over top of fruit.

Rhubarb Punch

*Tangy and sweet—very refreshing. Make the juice
the day before for easy assembly just before guests arrive.*

RHUBARB JUICE

Package of frozen (or fresh, chopped) rhubarb, thawed	2 1/4 lbs.	1 kg
Whole cloves	4	4
Water	1 cup	250 mL
Granulated sugar	1/4 cup	60 mL
Ginger ale	3 cups	750 mL
Sliced fresh strawberries	1 cup	250 mL
Ice cubes	12	12

Rhubarb Juice: Combine rhubarb, cloves and water in large saucepan. Bring to a boil on high. Reduce heat to medium-low. Cover. Simmer for about 25 minutes, stirring occasionally, until rhubarb is softened. Remove from heat. Strain through sieve into medium bowl. Press gently with back of spoon to extract juice. Discard solids.

Add sugar. Stir until sugar is dissolved. Let stand for 5 minutes. Cover. Chill for at least 4 hours until cold. Makes about 3 cups (750 mL) juice.

Pour juice into small punch bowl. Add ginger ale. Stir gently. Add strawberries and ice cubes. Makes about 8 cups (2 L). Serves 14.

1 serving: 52 Calories; 0.1 g Total Fat (0 g Mono, 0 g Poly, 0 g Sat); 0 mg Cholesterol; 13 g Carbohydrate; 1 g Fibre; 0 g Protein; 5 mg Sodium

Pictured on page 125.

Paré Pointer

Say cheers in Portuguese: Saude! (sah-OOD)

Soda-licious Punch

Peachy-pink with pretty strawberry ice cubes. Subtly sweet.

Apple juice	2 cups	500 mL
Fresh (or frozen) whole strawberries, sliced	1 cup	250 mL
Blush wine (such as Zinfandel), 26 oz.	3 cups	750 mL
Apple juice	1/2 cup	125 mL
Brandy (4 oz.)	1/2 cup	125 mL
Ginger ale	2 cups	500 mL
Club soda	2 cups	500 mL

Pour first amount of apple juice into ice cube trays for a total of about 20 cubes. Add 2 strawberry slices to each cube. Freeze for at least 4 hours until firm.

Combine wine, second amount of apple juice and brandy in small punch bowl. Add ginger ale and club soda. Stir gently. Add strawberry ice cubes. Makes about 11 cups (2.75 L). Serves 20.

1 serving: 66 Calories; 0.1 g Total Fat (0 g Mono, 0 g Poly, 0 g Sat); 0 mg Cholesterol; 7 g Carbohydrate; trace Fibre; 0 g Protein; 10 mg Sodium

Apricot Orange Punch

Easy to make, this brightly coloured punch is perfect for a party.

Cans of mandarin orange segments (with juice), 10 oz. (284 mL) each	3	3
Apricot nectar	2 cups	500 mL
Orange juice	2 cups	500 mL
Yellow-coloured lemon lime soft drink (such as Mountain Dew)	2 1/2 cups	625 mL
Ice cubes (or Ice Ring, page 114)	12	12

Combine first 3 ingredients in small punch bowl. Add lemon lime soft drink. Stir gently. Add ice cubes. Makes about 11 cups (2.75 L). Serves 20.

1 serving: 56 Calories; 0.1 g Total Fat (0 g Mono, 0 g Poly, 0 g Sat); 0 mg Cholesterol; 14 g Carbohydrate; trace Fibre; 1 g Protein; 7 mg Sodium

Cherry Lemon Sipper

Pretty, light, purple sparkling punch with a delicate dash of lemon.

Can of frozen concentrated lemonade, partially thawed	12 1/2 oz.	355 mL
Club soda	4 cups	1 L
Ginger ale	4 cups	1 L
Cherry brandy (3 oz.)	6 tbsp.	100 mL
Can of pitted Bing cherries, drained	14 oz.	398 mL

Measure first 3 ingredients into small punch bowl. Stir gently until concentrated lemonade is dissolved.

Add brandy and cherries. Stir. Makes about 11 cups (2.75 L). Serves 20.

1 serving: 77 Calories; 0.1 g Total Fat (0 g Mono, 0 g Poly, 0 g Sat); 0 mg Cholesterol; 17 g Carbohydrate; trace Fibre; 0 g Protein; 16 mg Sodium

Variation (without alcohol): Omit cherry brandy. Reserve syrup from canned cherries. Add 1/2 cup (125 mL) reserved syrup to punch.

Sparkling Strawberry Bubbly

Sweet and fruity coral-coloured drink that's light and refreshing.

Sliced fresh strawberries	3 cups	750 mL
Icing (confectioner's) sugar	3/4 cup	175 mL
Orange-flavoured liqueur (such as Grand Marnier), 2 1/2 oz.	1/3 cup	75 mL
Bottles of sparkling dry white (or alcohol-free) wine (26 oz., 750 mL, each)	2	2
Sliced fresh strawberries (optional)	1 1/2 cups	375 mL

Process first 3 ingredients in blender until smooth. Transfer to small punch bowl.

Add wine and second amount of strawberries. Stir gently. Makes about 10 cups (2.5 L). Serves 18.

1 serving: 95 Calories; 0.1 g Total Fat (0 g Mono, 0.1 g Poly, 0 g Sat); 0 mg Cholesterol; 8 g Carbohydrate; 1 g Fibre; 0 g Protein; 5 mg Sodium

Serving Suggestion: This pretty punch looks best served in champagne flutes (see page 8).

Cold And Winey

*Have this ready for the group after a day of outdoor winter activities.
The strong flavours will warm them from the inside out.*

Orange juice	2 cups	500 mL
Lemon juice	1/2 cup	125 mL
Grenadine syrup	1/4 cup	60 mL
Frozen whole blackberries (or raspberries)	24	24
Bottles of dry red (or alcohol-free) wine (26 oz., 750 mL, each)	2	2
Blackberry brandy (4 oz.)	1/2 cup	125 mL
Orange-flavoured liqueur (such as Grand Marnier), 4 oz.	1/2 cup	125 mL
Granulated sugar	1/4 cup	60 mL

Combine orange juice, lemon juice and grenadine in 4 cup (1 L) liquid measure. Pour into ice cube trays for a total of 24 cubes. Add 1 blackberry to each cube. Freeze for at least 4 hours until firm.

Measure remaining 4 ingredients into small punch bowl. Stir until sugar is dissolved. Add frozen orange juice cubes. Makes about 8 1/2 cups (2.1 L). Serves 14.

1 serving: 176 Calories; 0.1 g Total Fat (0 g Mono, 0 g Poly, 0 g Sat); 0 mg Cholesterol; 17 g Carbohydrate; 1 g Fibre; 1 g Protein; 10 mg Sodium

Serving Suggestion: Serve in small wine glasses (see page 8) so your guests can appreciate its deep, rich colour.

Minted Citrus Punch

Sweet and refreshing citrus tang with a hint of mint.

Can of mandarin orange segments (with juice)	10 oz.	284 mL
Boiling water	4 cups	1 L
Fresh mint leaves	1 cup	250 mL
Peel of medium orange, white pith removed, cut into strips	1	1
Peel of medium lemon, white pith removed, cut into strips	1	1
Can of frozen concentrated lemonade, partially thawed	12 1/2 oz.	355 mL
Can of frozen concentrated orange juice, partially thawed	12 1/2 oz.	355 mL
Grapefruit soft drink	4 cups	1 L

Spoon mandarin orange segments and juice into ice cube tray for a total of about 12 cubes (see Note). Freeze for at least 4 hours until firm.

Pour boiling water into large heatproof bowl. Add mint and both peels. Stir. Cover. Let stand for 1 hour.

Strain mint mixture through sieve into small punch bowl. Discard solids. Add remaining 3 ingredients. Stir gently. Add frozen mandarin orange cubes. Makes about 10 1/2 cups (2.6 L). Serves 18.

1 serving: 111 Calories; 0.1 g Total Fat (0 g Mono, 0 g Poly, 0 g Sat); 0 mg Cholesterol; 28 g Carbohydrate; trace Fibre; 1 g Protein; 9 mg Sodium

Pictured on page 125.

Note: Add fresh mint leaves to mandarin orange segments in ice cube tray before freezing for extra colour and flavour.

Party Eggnog

Spicy, foamy eggnog your guests will love.

Large eggs (see Note)	12	12
Icing (confectioner's) sugar	2 cups	500 mL
Vanilla	3 tbsp.	50 mL
Salt	1/2 tsp.	2 mL
Homogenized milk	8 cups	2 L
Spiced rum (or brandy), 4 – 8 oz.	1/2 – 1 cup	125 – 250 mL
Ground nutmeg	1 tsp.	5 mL
Ground cinnamon	1/2 tsp.	2 mL

Beat eggs in large bowl until frothy.

Add icing sugar, 1/4 cup (60 mL) at a time while beating, until combined. Add vanilla and salt. Stir. Pour into small punch bowl.

Add remaining 4 ingredients. Stir well. Makes about 14 cups (3.5 L). Serve immediately. Serves 25.

1 serving: 142 Calories; 5.2 g Total Fat (1.7 g Mono, 0.4 g Poly, 2.5 g Sat); 115 mg Cholesterol; 15 g Carbohydrate; 0 g Fibre; 6 g Protein; 118 mg Sodium

Note: Eggs used in beverages should be cold. Remove eggs from refrigerator just before adding. Beverages containing uncooked egg should be served immediately.

Paré Pointer

Say cheers in Romanian: "Noroc!" (nor-OOK)

Ginger Lemonade

Pleasantly sweet and refreshing lemon ginger flavour.

Boiling water	3 cups	750 mL
Granulated sugar	1 1/2 cups	375 mL
Chopped, peeled gingerroot	1 cup	250 mL
Water	3 cups	750 mL
Lemon juice	1/2 cup	125 mL
Whole cloves	8	8
Ice		

Pour boiling water into large heatproof bowl. Add sugar and ginger. Stir until sugar is dissolved. Cover. Let stand for 2 hours. Strain through cheesecloth into separate large bowl. Squeeze cheesecloth to extract liquid. Discard ginger. Pour liquid into pitcher.

Add water, lemon juice and cloves. Stir. Cover. Chill for at least 4 hours until cold. Remove and discard cloves. Makes about 7 cups (1.75 L). Pour over ice in 8 chilled medium glasses. Serves 8.

1 serving: 157 Calories; 0 g Total Fat (0 g Mono, 0 g Poly, 0 g Sat); 0 mg Cholesterol; 41 g Carbohydrate; trace Fibre; 0 g Protein; 1 mg Sodium

Pineapple Delight

A thirst-quenching punch. The pineapple ice mold gives it extra flavour.

Pineapple juice	2 cups	500 mL
Ginger ale	8 cups	2 L
Pineapple juice	2 cups	500 mL
Can of pineapple tidbits (with juice)	14 oz.	398 mL
Apricot brandy (6 oz.)	3/4 cup	175 mL

Pour first amount of pineapple juice into 2 cup (500 mL) shallow jelly mold. Freeze for at least 4 hours until firm.

Measure remaining 4 ingredients into small punch bowl. Stir gently. Add frozen pineapple juice mold. Makes about 10 cups (2.5 L). Serves 22.

1 serving: 89 Calories; 0.1 g Total Fat (0 g Mono, 0 g Poly, 0 g Sat); 0 mg Cholesterol; 18 g Carbohydrate; trace Fibre; 0 g Protein; 7 mg Sodium

Orange Mango Punch

A thick, tropical-flavoured punch. You may need a whisk to mix in the coconut milk.

Granulated sugar	1/4 cup	60 mL
Water	3 tbsp.	50 mL
Cans of sliced mango (with syrup), 14 oz. (398 mL) each	2	2
Orange juice	3 cups	750 mL
Can of coconut milk	14 oz.	398 mL
Orange-flavoured liqueur (such as Grand Marnier), 2 1/2 oz.	1/3 cup	75 mL
Yellow-coloured, licorice-flavoured liqueur (such as Galliano), 1 1/2 oz. (see Note)	3 tbsp.	50 mL
Ice cubes	12	12

Combine sugar and water in small saucepan. Bring to a boil on medium-high. Boil, uncovered, for about 1 minute until slightly thickened and sugar is dissolved. Remove from heat. Cool.

Chop portion of mango into 1/4 inch (6 mm) pieces to fill 1 cup (250 mL) measure. Set aside. Process remaining mango with syrup in blender until smooth.

Measure next 4 ingredients into small punch bowl. Add processed mango, chopped mango and sugar mixture. Stir. Add ice cubes. Makes about 9 cups (2.25 L). Serves 16.

1 serving: 127 Calories; 5.3 g Total Fat (0.3 g Mono, 0.1 g Poly, 4.5 g Sat); 0 mg Cholesterol; 16 g Carbohydrate; 1 g Fibre; 1 g Protein; 5 mg Sodium

Note: If you cannot find Galliano, add several drops of yellow food colouring to same amount of clear licorice-flavoured liqueur (such as Sambuca) until desired shade is reached.

Variation (without alcohol): Omit liqueurs. Use same amount of orange juice.

Serving Suggestion: Use mandarin-mint ice cubes (Minted Citrus Punch, page 119) for a special touch. If you prefer a less thick punch, add lemon lime soft drink or club soda until desired consistency.

Mocha Punch

*Chocolate syrup in the bottom of the glass gives
this creamy treat a layered look. Whipped cream and
grated chocolate add a special touch your guests will love.*

Hot strong prepared coffee (see Note)	4 cups	1 L
Granulated sugar	1/2 cup	125 mL
Salt	1/4 tsp.	1 mL
Cold strong prepared coffee (see Note)	4 cups	1 L
Chocolate ice cream	4 cups	1 L
Vanilla ice cream	4 cups	1 L
Almond flavouring	1/4 tsp.	1 mL
Chocolate syrup	3/4 cup	175 mL
Ice cubes	36	36
Whipped cream, for garnish		
Grated chocolate, for garnish		

Measure hot coffee, sugar and salt into large bowl. Stir until sugar is dissolved.

Add next 4 ingredients. Stir until ice cream is melted. Makes about 11 cups (2.75 L). Transfer to large pitcher.

Measure about 1 tbsp. (15 mL) chocolate syrup into each of 12 medium glasses. Add 3 ice cubes to each. Fill with ice cream mixture.

Garnish with whipped cream and grated chocolate. Serves 12.

1 serving: 278 Calories; 10.4 g Total Fat (3 g Mono, 0.4 g Poly, 6.4 g Sat); 36 mg Cholesterol; 46 g Carbohydrate; 0 g Fibre; 4 g Protein; 148 mg Sodium

Note: For extra-strong flavour, use espresso.

Serving Suggestion: Place small pitcher of chocolate syrup and a bucket of ice on buffet table. Write directions for making 1 glass of punch on pretty recipe card and set it beside pitcher of punch. Guests will have fun mixing their own drink! Be sure to have plenty of whipped cream and grated chocolate available.

Melon Lemonade

A delightful combination of fresh flavours.

Can of frozen concentrated lemonade, partially thawed	12 1/2 oz.	355 mL
White (light) rum (6 oz.)	3/4 cup	175 mL
Melon-flavoured liqueur (such as Bols), 4 oz.	1/2 cup	125 mL
Lemon lime soft drink	5 cups	1.25 L

Ice
Small honeydew slices, for garnish

Combine concentrated lemonade, rum and liqueur in pitcher. Add lemon lime soft drink. Stir gently. Makes about 8 cups (2 L).

Pour over ice in 8 large glasses. Garnish each with honeydew slice. Serves 8.

1 serving: 249 Calories; 0.1 g Total Fat (0 g Mono, 0 g Poly, 0 g Sat); 0 mg Cholesterol; 43 g Carbohydrate; 0 g Fibre; 0 g Protein; 20 mg Sodium

Serving Suggestion: Add small slices of honeydew and watermelon to water in ice cube trays. Freeze until firm. Makes pretty ice cubes for this, or any other, fruity beverage.

1. Minted Citrus Punch, page 119
2. Sangria, page 112
3. Rhubarb Punch, page 115

Props Courtesy Of: Dansk Gifts
Sears Canada
The Bay

Winter Season's Brew

A delectable hot drink full of spice.

Cranberry cocktail	4 cups	1 L
Pineapple juice	4 cups	1 L
Granulated sugar	1/3 cup	75 mL
Whole cloves	1 tbsp.	15 mL
Whole allspice	2 tsp.	10 mL
Cinnamon sticks (4 inches, 10 cm, each), broken up	4	4
Salt	1/4 tsp.	1 mL

Measure cranberry cocktail and pineapple juice into percolator (see Note). Insert stem and basket.

Place remaining 5 ingredients in basket. Perk as usual. Makes about 8 cups (2 L). Pour into 6 large mugs. Serves 6.

1 serving: 245 Calories; 0.3 g Total Fat (0 g Mono, 0.1 g Poly, 0.1 g Sat); 0 mg Cholesterol; 62 g Carbohydrate; trace Fibre; 1 g Protein; 104 mg Sodium

Note: Don't have a percolator? Measure cocktail and juice, sugar and salt into large saucepan. Stir. Tie spices in cheesecloth. Add to saucepan. Bring to a boil on medium. Reduce heat to medium-low. Simmer, uncovered, for about 20 minutes, stirring occasionally, until fragrant. Remove and discard cheesecloth with spices.

1. Peppercorn Vodka, page 149
2. Ginger Orange Liqueur, page 138
3. Hot Tequila Cider, page 132

Props Courtesy Of: Pier 1 Imports

Percolator Punch

This mellow, spiced fruit drink is perfect
for a relaxing evening shared with friends.

Apple cider (or juice)	4 cups	1 L
Orange juice	4 cups	1 L
Cranberry cocktail	4 cups	1 L
Lemon juice	2 tbsp.	30 mL
Salt	1/8 tsp.	0.5 mL
Brown sugar, packed	3/4 cup	175 mL
Cinnamon stick (4 inches, 10 cm), broken up	1	1
Whole cloves	1 1/2 tsp.	7 mL
Whole allspice	1 1/2 tsp.	7 mL

Measure first 5 ingredients into percolator (see Note). Insert stem and basket.

Place remaining 4 ingredients in basket. Perk as usual. Makes about 12 cups (3 L). Pour into 12 small mugs. Serves 12.

1 serving: 187 Calories; 0.4 g Total Fat (0 g Mono, 0.1 g Poly, 0.1 g Sat); 0 mg Cholesterol; 47 g Carbohydrate; trace Fibre; 1 g Protein; 37 mg Sodium

Note: Don't have a percolator? Measure first 5 ingredients and brown sugar into large saucepan. Stir. Tie spices in cheesecloth. Add to saucepan. Bring to a boil on medium. Reduce heat to medium-low. Simmer, uncovered, for about 20 minutes, stirring occasionally, until fragrant. Remove and discard cheesecloth with spices.

Paré Pointer

Say cheers in Russian: "Na Zdrovia!" (NAH zdor-OH-vEEa)

Warm Spiced Rum

Clear, golden colour with lightly spiced apple flavour. Soothing and warming.

Apple cider	6 cups	1.5 L
Apple juice	1 cup	250 mL
Whole allspice	8	8
Cinnamon sticks (4 inches, 10 cm, each)	2	2
Spiced rum (4 oz.)	1/2 cup	125 mL
Brandy (1 1/2 oz.)	3 tbsp.	50 mL

Measure first 4 ingredients into large saucepan. Stir. Heat on medium for 20 to 30 minutes, stirring occasionally, until fragrant.

Add rum and brandy. Stir. Remove from heat. Strain through sieve into heatproof pitcher. Discard solids. Makes about 7 cups (1.75 L). Pour into 8 small mugs. Serves 8.

1 serving: 154 Calories; 0.3 g Total Fat (0 g Mono, 0.1 g Poly, 0 g Sat); 0 mg Cholesterol; 27 g Carbohydrate; trace Fibre; 0 g Protein; 7 mg Sodium

Warm Apricot Honey Punch

A sweet, delicious way to warm up after skiing or skating.

Apricot nectar	6 cups	1.5 L
Liquid honey	3 tbsp.	50 mL
Lemon juice	2 tbsp.	30 mL
Medium orange, sliced thinly	1	1

Heat and stir apricot nectar, honey and lemon juice in large saucepan on medium until just boiling. Remove from heat. Makes about 6 cups (1.5 L).

Pour into 6 large mugs. Garnish each with orange slice. Serves 6.

1 serving: 192 Calories; 0.3 g Total Fat (0.1 g Mono, 0.1 g Poly, 0 g Sat); 0 mg Cholesterol; 50 g Carbohydrate; 2 g Fibre; 1 g Protein; 8 mg Sodium

Golden Wedding Punch

Pleasantly sweet citrus and apple combination bubbling with flavour.

Apple juice	4 cups	1 L
Can of frozen concentrated lemonade, partially thawed	12 1/2 oz.	355 mL
Can of frozen concentrated orange juice, partially thawed	12 1/2 oz.	355 mL
Ginger ale	8 cups	2 L

Combine first 3 ingredients in small punch bowl. Add ginger ale. Stir gently. Makes about 15 1/2 cups (3.75 L). Serves 28.

1 serving: 95 Calories; 0.1 g Total Fat (0 g Mono, 0 g Poly, 0 g Sat); 0 mg Cholesterol; 24 g Carbohydrate; trace Fibre; 0 g Protein; 7 mg Sodium

Variation (with alcohol): Add 1 1/2 cups (375 mL, 13 oz.) gin (or vodka) to punch.

Serving Suggestion: Make Ice Ring, page 114, using orange and lemon slices. Add to punch in large punch bowl. Arrange small glasses around punch bowl for an attractive presentation.

Cranberry Lime Sparkle

A refreshing balance of tart and sweet in a drink.
Cranberry Lime Punch (below) is a simple yet elegant way
to dress up your holiday party, with or without alcohol.

Cranberry cocktail	1/3 cup	75 mL
Lime cordial (alcohol-free)	1 tbsp.	15 mL
Sparkling dry white (or alcohol-free) wine	2/3 cup	150 mL

Measure cranberry cocktail and lime cordial into small glass.

Top with sparkling wine. Stir gently. Makes about 1 cup (250 mL).
Serves 1.

1 serving: 168 Calories; 0 g Total Fat (0 g Mono, 0 g Poly, 0 g Sat); 0 mg Cholesterol;
16 g Carbohydrate; trace Fibre; 0 g Protein; 10 mg Sodium

CRANBERRY GINGER SPARKLE: Omit sparkling wine. Use same amount of ginger ale.

CRANBERRY LEMON SPARKLE: Omit sparkling wine. Use same amount of lemon lime soft drink.

CRANBERRY LIME PUNCH: Measure 1/2 cup (125 mL) lime cordial, 3 cups (750 mL) cranberry cocktail and 6 cups (1.5 L) sparkling dry white (or alcohol-free) wine into small punch bowl. Stir gently. Makes about 9 1/2 cups (2.4 L). Serves 10.

Paré Pointer
Say cheers in Gaelic: "Schlante!" (sh-LAHN-tee)

Cranberry Champagne

Something a little different, but a lovely combination of flavours.

Bottles of sparkling dry white (or alcohol-free) wine (26 oz., 750 mL, each)	2	2
Cranberry cocktail	1 1/2 cups	375 mL
Orange-flavoured liqueur (such as Grand Marnier), 2 oz.	1/4 cup	60 mL

Measure all 3 ingredients into small punch bowl or large pitcher. Stir gently. Makes about 8 1/2 cups (2.1 L). Serves 12.

1 serving: 115 Calories; 0 g Total Fat (0 g Mono, 0 g Poly, 0 g Sat); 0 mg Cholesterol; 6 g Carbohydrate; 0 g Fibre; 0 g Protein; 7 mg Sodium

Serving Suggestion: Show off this pretty mixture by serving it in champagne flutes (see page 8).

Hot Tequila Cider

Seamless blend of tequila, apple and cinnamon in a pale red cider.

Sparkling apple cider (with alcohol)	4 cups	1 L
Cranberry cocktail	1 1/2 cups	375 mL
Tequila (2 oz.)	1/4 cup	60 mL
Orange-flavoured liqueur (such as Grand Marnier), 2 oz.	1/4 cup	60 mL
Cinnamon sticks (4 inches, 10 cm, each)	2	2

Heat and stir all 5 ingredients in large saucepan on medium-low for about 20 minutes until hot. Do not boil. Remove and discard cinnamon sticks. Makes about 6 cups (1.5 L). Pour into 6 small mugs. Serves 6.

1 serving: 166 Calories; 0.1 g Total Fat (0 g Mono, 0 g Poly, 0 g Sat); 0 mg Cholesterol; 20 g Carbohydrate; 0 g Fibre; 0 g Protein; 16 mg Sodium

Pictured on page 126.

Strawberry Cupid

A pretty pink drink for Valentine's Day with a creamy strawberry taste.
Adults will love it as much as the kids will!

Boiling water	1/2 cup	125 mL
Package of strawberry-flavoured jelly powder (gelatin)	3 oz.	85 g
Strawberry ice cream	2 cups	500 mL
Milk	1 cup	250 mL
Crushed ice	1/2 cup	125 mL

Pour boiling water into 2 cup (500 mL) liquid measure. Add jelly powder. Stir until dissolved. Let stand for 5 minutes. Transfer to blender. Process on medium for 1 minute.

Add ice cream, 1/4 cup (60 mL) at a time (about 1 scoop), processing after each addition until smooth.

Add milk and crushed ice. Process for 30 seconds. Makes about 4 cups (1 L). Pour into 4 chilled medium glasses. Serves 4.

1 serving: 242 Calories; 6.5 g Total Fat (0.2 g Mono, 0 g Poly, 0.4 g Sat); 23 mg Cholesterol; 42 g Carbohydrate; 0 g Fibre; 6 g Protein; 128 mg Sodium

Pictured on page 144.

Variation: Try other flavours of jelly powder with vanilla ice cream for a new taste experience.

Paré Pointer
Say cheers in Spanish: "Salud!" (SAH-lood)

Malted Easter Egg

Creamy chocolate with subtle malt flavour.
Kids will love the marshmallow flavour and crunchy sprinkles.

Chocolate ice cream	2 cups	500 mL
Milk	1 cup	250 mL
Miniature marshmallows	1/4 cup	60 mL
Malt drink mix (such as Ovaltine)	2 tbsp.	30 mL
Coloured candy sprinkles, for garnish	1 tbsp.	15 mL

Process first 4 ingredients in blender for about 1 minute until frothy. Makes about 2 3/4 cups (675 mL). Pour into 2 chilled medium glasses.

Garnish each with candy sprinkles. Serves 2.

1 serving: 412 Calories; 17.1 g Total Fat (5 g Mono, 0.7 g Poly, 10.5 g Sat); 53 mg Cholesterol; 59 g Carbohydrate; 0 g Fibre; 10 g Protein; 236 mg Sodium

Pictured on page 144.

Paré Pointer
Say cheers in Swedish: "Skal!" (SKOHL)

Witch's Brew

A deep red, cherry-flavoured beverage—just right for your Halloween party.

Cranberry-apple juice	4 cups	1 L
Orange juice	1 cup	250 mL
Maraschino cherry juice	1/4 cup	60 mL
Cinnamon stick (4 inches, 10 cm)	1	1
Whole cloves	3	3
Whole allspice	3	3
Medium orange, sliced thinly (optional)	1	1
Maraschino cherries (optional)	4	4

Measure first 6 ingredients into large saucepan. Bring to a boil on medium-high. Reduce heat to medium-low. Simmer, uncovered, for 15 minutes, stirring occasionally. Remove from heat. Strain through sieve into 4 cup (1 L) liquid measure. Discard solids. Makes about 4 cups (1 L).

Place 1 or 2 orange slices and 1 maraschino cherry in each of 4 small mugs. Pour cranberry mixture over top of each. Serves 4.

1 serving: 208 Calories; 0.1 g Total Fat (0 g Mono, 0 g Poly, 0 g Sat); 0 mg Cholesterol; 52 g Carbohydrate; trace Fibre; 1 g Protein; 6 mg Sodium

Pictured on page 143.

Serving Suggestion: Cool this brew slightly when serving to children. To make a special brew for adults, omit maraschino cherry juice. Add 1/4 cup (60 mL) cherry brandy to strained, hot cranberry mixture. Stir. Pour into small mugs. Garnish with orange slices.

Nuclear Waste

Bright neon green with a slightly cloudy appearance. Looks radioactive!
Alcohol taste is masked by citrus flavours, so be warned!

Orange juice	4 cups	1 L
Blue-coloured, orange-flavoured liqueur (such as Blue Curaçao), 4 oz. (see Note)	1/2 cup	125 mL
Vodka (2 1/2 oz.)	1/3 cup	75 mL
Ginger ale	3 cups	750 mL
Ice		

Combine orange juice, liqueur and vodka in small punch bowl or large pitcher. Chill for about 3 hours until cold.

Just before serving, add ginger ale. Stir gently. Makes about 8 cups (2 L). Pour over ice in 8 medium glasses. Serves 8.

1 serving: 176 Calories; 0.3 g Total Fat (0.1 g Mono, 0.1 g Poly, 0.1 g Sat); 0 mg Cholesterol; 31 g Carbohydrate; trace Fibre; 1 g Protein; 10 mg Sodium

Pictured on page 143.

Note: If you cannot find Blue Curaçao, add several drops of blue liquid food colouring to same amount of clear Curaçao until desired shade is reached.

Swamp Water

Visually fascinating—purple and orange jelly pieces suspended in a fizzy drink. Great for Halloween or a child's birthday party.

Package of grape-flavoured jelly powder (gelatin)	3 oz.	85 g
Package of orange-flavoured jelly powder (gelatin)	3 oz.	85 g
Prepared grape-flavoured drink	4 cups	1 L
Lemon lime soft drink	4 cups	1 L

Prepare jelly powders in two 8 × 8 inch (20 × 20 cm) pans, according to package directions. Chill for about 4 hours until firm. Flake with fork or cut into small shapes using cookie cutter. Transfer to small punch bowl.

Add grape drink and lemon lime soft drink. Stir gently. Makes about 12 3/4 cups (3.2 L). Serves 16.

1 serving: 96 Calories; 0 g Total Fat (0 g Mono, 0 g Poly, 0 g Sat); 0 mg Cholesterol; 24 g Carbohydrate; 0 g Fibre; 1 g Protein; 38 mg Sodium

Pictured on page 143.

Variation: Experiment with colours and flavours by changing jelly powders and prepared drink.

Paré Pointer

Say cheers in Thai: "Sawasdi!" (SAH-wahs-DEE)

Ginger Orange Liqueur

A little patience brings great reward—a mildly spiced, orange-flavoured liqueur. Straining mixture through cheesecloth will result in a bright, clear appearance.

Vodka (26 oz.)	3 cups	750 mL
Grated orange zest	1/2 cup	125 mL
Piece of peeled gingerroot (3 inches, 7.5 cm), sliced	1	1
Granulated sugar	2/3 cup	150 mL
Water	1/3 cup	75 mL

Combine vodka, orange zest and ginger in sterile glass jar with tight-fitting lid. Let stand for 1 week at room temperature. Strain through sieve into 4 cup (1 L) liquid measure. Discard solids. Return liquid to same jar.

Combine sugar and water in small saucepan. Bring to a boil on medium. Heat and stir until sugar is dissolved. Remove from heat. Cool. Add to vodka mixture in jar. Makes about 3 1/2 cups (875 mL). Let stand for 1 week at room temperature. Strain through cheesecloth into 4 cup (1 L) liquid measure. Discard solids. Transfer to storage jar or fancy bottle with tight-fitting lid. Store for up to 1 month at room temperature or in refrigerator. Serves 30.

1 serving: 73 Calories; 0 g Total Fat (0 g Mono, 0 g Poly, 0 g Sat); 0 mg Cholesterol; 5 g Carbohydrate; 0 g Fibre; 0 g Protein; 0 mg Sodium

Pictured on page 126.

Serving Suggestion: Equally good served at room temperature or over ice. Use as substitute for orange-flavoured liqueurs in mixed drinks.

Orange Dream Liqueur

Creamy, thick orange liqueur—reminiscent of an orange ice cream bar.
Flavours will mellow with time. Makes a nice gift.

Water	1 cup	250 mL
Granulated sugar	1/2 cup	125 mL
Vodka (13 oz.)	1 1/2 cups	375 mL
Can of sweetened condensed milk	11 oz.	300 mL
Frozen concentrated orange juice	1/3 cup	75 mL
Vanilla	2 tsp.	10 mL

Measure water and sugar into small saucepan. Bring to a boil on medium. Heat and stir until sugar is dissolved. Remove from heat. Let stand until cooled completely.

Measure next 4 ingredients into blender. Add sugar mixture. Process for about 1 minute until smooth. Makes about 4 cups (1 L). Pour into sterile glass jar with tight-fitting lid. Store for up to 1 month in refrigerator. Serves 32.

1 serving: 83 Calories; 1.1 g Total Fat (0.3 g Mono, 0 g Poly, 0.7 g Sat); 4 mg Cholesterol; 11 g Carbohydrate; 0 g Fibre; 1 g Protein; 16 mg Sodium

Serving Suggestion: Serve over ice or in your favourite coffee.

ORANGE DREAM CLOUD: Pour equal amounts of Orange Dream Liqueur and club soda over ice in medium glass. Stir gently. Serves 1.

Paré Pointer
Say cheers in Turkish: "Serefe!" (sher-FAY)

Christmas Spirit

A robust, spiced berry liqueur to serve as an aperitif or after-dinner drink. Can be used as a base for your Christmas punch, too.

Granulated sugar	2 cups	500 mL
Fresh (or frozen, thawed) raspberries	1 1/2 cups	375 mL
Fresh (or frozen, thawed) cranberries	1 1/3 cups	325 mL
Water	1 cup	250 mL
Medium orange, zest and juice only	1	1
Whole cloves	6	6
Whole allspice	4	4
Cinnamon sticks (4 inches, 10 cm, each)	2	2
Gin (or vodka), 26 oz.	3 cups	750 mL

Combine first 8 ingredients in large pot or Dutch oven. Bring to a boil on medium. Reduce heat to medium-low. Simmer, uncovered, for about 20 minutes until fragrant. Remove from heat. Cool.

Add gin. Stir well. Pour into 2 sterile 4 cup (1 L) glass jars with tight-fitting lids. Let stand at room temperature for 2 weeks. Shake gently once every 2 days. Strain through sieve into 8 cup (2 L) liquid measure. Do not push through. Gently lift berry mixture in sieve, using spoon, allowing liquid to flow through. Discard solids. Return liquid to same jars with tight-fitting lids. Let stand at room temperature for 2 weeks. Strain through double layer of cheesecloth into 2 cup (500 mL) liquid measure. Discard solids. Makes about 2 cups (500 mL). Transfer to storage jar or fancy bottle with tight-fitting lid. Store for up to 1 month at room temperature or in refrigerator. Serves 16.

1 serving: 211 Calories; 0.1 g Total Fat (0 g Mono, 0 g Poly, 0 g Sat); 0 mg Cholesterol; 28 g Carbohydrate; trace Fibre; 0 g Protein; 1 mg Sodium

Licorice Twist Nog

Here are just a few ways to add a twist to your favourite eggnog.
A nice change from the ordinary.

Ice cubes	3	3
Eggnog	3/4 cup	175 mL
Licorice-flavoured liqueur (such as Sambuca), 1/2 – 1 oz.	1 – 2 tbsp.	15 – 30 mL

Put ice cubes into medium glass. Add eggnog and liqueur. Stir. Makes about 1 cup (250 mL). Serves 1.

1 serving: 335 Calories; 15.2 g Total Fat (4.5 g Mono, 0.7 g Poly, 9 g Sat); 118 mg Cholesterol; 34 g Carbohydrate; 0 g Fibre; 8 g Protein; 111 mg Sodium

TROPICAL TWIST NOG: Measure 1 tbsp. (15 mL, 1/2 oz.) each, banana-flavoured liqueur (such as Crème de banane) and coconut-flavoured rum (such as Malibu), over ice in medium glass. Add 1 cup (250 mL) eggnog. Stir. Sprinkle with toasted coconut (see Tip, page 23). Serves 1.

ORANGE TWIST NOG: Measure 1 tbsp. (15 mL, 1/2 oz.) Orange Dream Liqueur, page 139, 1 tbsp. (15 mL) frozen concentrated orange juice and 2/3 cup (150 mL) eggnog into cocktail shaker. Add ice cubes. Replace lid. Hold firmly and shake vigorously until cold. Strain through sieve into small glass. Sprinkle with ground ginger. Serves 1.

Pictured on page 144.

Paré Pointer

Say cheers in Yugoslavian: "Zivio!" (ziv-EE-oh)

Hot Buttered Cranberry

Rich, buttery cranberry and spice. Tastes great!

Cans of jellied cranberry sauce (14 oz., 398 mL, each)	2	2
Pineapple juice	4 cups	1 L
Water	3 cups	750 mL
Brown sugar, packed	1/2 cup	125 mL
Ground cinnamon	1/2 tsp.	2 mL
Ground cloves	1/2 tsp.	2 mL
Ground nutmeg	1/4 tsp.	1 mL
Ground allspice	1/4 tsp.	1 mL
Salt	1/8 tsp.	0.5 mL
Butter (not margarine)	1/4 cup	60 mL
Navy (dark) rum (8 oz.), optional	1 cup	250 mL

Measure first 9 ingredients into 3 1/2 quart (3 1/2 L) slow cooker. Stir well. Cover. Cook on Low for 4 hours.

Add butter and rum. Stir until butter is melted. Makes about 12 cups (3 L). Serves 12.

1 serving: 240 Calories; 4.3 g Total Fat (1.2 g Mono, 0.2 g Poly, 2.6 g Sat); 11 mg Cholesterol; 52 g Carbohydrate; 1 g Fibre; 0 g Protein; 95 mg Sodium

HOT SPICED CRANBERRY: Omit butter.

1. Nuclear Waste, page 136
2. Witch's Brew, page 135
3. Swamp Water, page 137

Props Courtesy Of: Casa Bugatti
Dansk Gifts

Melted Snowball

Sweet butterscotch and spiced rum will warm and relax you.
Great after a day of outdoor winter activities.

Butter (not margarine), softened	2/3 cup	150 mL
Brown sugar, packed	1 1/2 cups	375 mL
Icing (confectioner's) sugar	1 cup	250 mL
Vanilla ice cream, softened	2 cups	500 mL
Spiced rum (8 oz.)	1 cup	250 mL
Boiling water	6 cups	1.5 L

Beat butter in large bowl until smooth. Add brown sugar and icing sugar. Beat until thick and creamy.

Add ice cream. Stir until well combined. Makes about 4 cups (1 L) ice cream mixture. Transfer to plastic container with tight-fitting lid. Freeze for at least 6 hours until firm.

Scoop about 1/2 cup (125 mL) ice cream mixture (about 2 scoops) into each of 8 large mugs. Add 2 tbsp. (30 mL, 1 oz.) rum and 3/4 cup (175 mL) boiling water to each. Stir. Serves 8.

1 serving: 507 Calories; 20.1 g Total Fat (5.8 g Mono, 0.8 g Poly, 12.5 g Sat); 59 mg Cholesterol; 66 g Carbohydrate; 0 g Fibre; 1 g Protein; 211 mg Sodium

1. Malted Easter Egg, page 134
2. Orange Twist Nog, page 141
3. Strawberry Cupid, page 133

Props Courtesy Of: Dansk Gifts
                     Pier 1 Imports

Slow Cooker Wassail

Pronounced WAH-sul or WAH-sayl.
A warming winter beverage any way you say it!

Cinnamon sticks (4 inches, 10 cm, each)	2	2
Whole allspice	12	12
Peel of small orange, white pith removed, chopped	1	1
Piece of peeled gingerroot (about 1 inch, 2.5 cm), chopped	1	1
Apple cider	12 cups	3 L
Liquid honey (optional)	1/3 cup	75 mL

Place cinnamon sticks and allspice in small plastic bag. Pound with hammer or meat mallet until crushed. Transfer to 6 inch (15 cm) square double layer of cheesecloth.

Add orange peel and ginger. Tie cheesecloth with string to enclose spices.

Pour apple cider into 4 quart (4 L) slow cooker. Add honey. Stir. Add spice bag. Cook on Low for about 6 hours or on High for about 3 hours until fragrant. Remove and discard spice bag. Makes about 12 1/2 cups (3.1 L). Serves 12.

1 serving: 123 Calories; 0.3 g Total Fat (0 g Mono, 0.1 g Poly, 0.1 g Sat); 0 mg Cholesterol; 31 g Carbohydrate; trace Fibre; 0 g Protein; 8 mg Sodium

Variation (with alcohol): Add 1 cup (250 mL, 8 oz.) brandy or apple brandy near end of cooking time.

Paré Pointer
Say cheers in Norwegian: "Skal!" (SKAHL)

Spiced Peach Eggnog

Peach-flavoured eggnog with potent spiced rum. A little goes a long way.

Egg yolks (large), see Note	3	3
Icing (confectioner's) sugar	1/4 cup	60 mL
Sweetened powdered peach-flavoured drink crystals	1/4 cup	60 mL
Spiced rum (4 – 8 oz.)	1/2 – 1 cup	125 – 250 mL
Half-and-half cream (or milk)	2 cups	500 mL
Peach schnapps (2 oz.)	1/4 cup	60 mL
Egg whites (large), see Note	3	3
Ground nutmeg, sprinkle		

Beat egg yolks in medium bowl for about 5 minutes until pale.

Slowly add icing sugar and drink crystals while beating until well combined.

Slowly add rum while beating until drink crystals are dissolved. Cover. Chill for at least 1 hour until cold.

Add half-and-half cream and peach schnapps. Stir.

Beat egg whites in separate medium bowl with clean beaters until soft peaks form. Fold rum mixture into egg whites until no white streaks remain. Makes about 5 1/2 cups (1.4 L). Pour into 10 chilled small glasses.

Sprinkle each with nutmeg. Serves 10.

1 serving: 155 Calories; 6.6 g Total Fat (2.1 g Mono, 0.4 g Poly, 3.7 g Sat); 81 mg Cholesterol; 11 g Carbohydrate; 0 g Fibre; 3 g Protein; 46 mg Sodium

Note: Eggs used in beverages should be cold. Remove eggs from refrigerator just before adding. Beverages containing uncooked egg should be served immediately.

Brandy Mint Cream

Make ahead and refrigerate—stays thick for at least one hour.
Great as an after-dinner drink or dessert.

Vanilla ice cream, softened	4 cups	1 L
Brandy (4 oz.)	1/2 cup	125 mL
Mint-flavoured liqueur (such as Crème de menthe), 2 oz.	1/4 cup	60 mL

Process all 3 ingredients in blender until smooth. Makes about 5 cups (1.25 L). Pour into 6 chilled small glasses. Serves 6.

1 serving: 276 Calories; 10.3 g Total Fat (3 g Mono, 0.4 g Poly, 6.3 g Sat); 41 mg Cholesterol; 27 g Carbohydrate; 0 g Fibre; 3 g Protein; 75 mg Sodium

Serving Suggestion: Use green Crème de menthe instead of clear for a festive Christmas treat. Serve in parfait glasses or champagne flutes (see page 8)—just add a straw and enjoy!

Mulled Wine

Rich, red wine colour and flavour with citrus and spice tones.
Use a full-bodied red wine for best results.

Water	2 cups	500 mL
Granulated sugar	1/2 cup	125 mL
Whole cloves	8	8
Cinnamon stick (4 inches, 10 cm)	1	1
Dry red (or alcohol-free) wine (26 oz.)	3 cups	750 mL
Medium orange, sliced thinly	1	1

Measure first 4 ingredients into large saucepan. Bring to a boil on medium. Reduce heat to medium-low. Simmer, uncovered, for 10 to 15 minutes, stirring occasionally, until sugar is dissolved and mixture is fragrant. Remove and discard cloves and cinnamon stick.

Add wine and orange slices. Heat and stir until just hot. Do not boil. Makes about 6 cups (1.5 L). Pour into 6 small mugs. Place 1 orange slice in each. Serves 6.

1 serving: 168 Calories; 0 g Total Fat (0 g Mono, 0 g Poly, 0 g Sat); 0 mg Cholesterol; 22 g Carbohydrate; trace Fibre; 0 g Protein; 6 mg Sodium

Peppercorn Vodka

Spicy and warming. Use instead of regular vodka when you want to kick things up a notch. Will keep for up to one year, tightly sealed. Makes a great spicy Caesar.

Vodka (13 oz.)	1 1/2 cups	375 mL
Whole black peppercorns	2 tbsp.	30 mL

Combine vodka and peppercorns in sterile glass jar with tight-fitting lid. Let stand at room temperature for 1 week. Shake gently once a day. Strain through sieve into storage jar or fancy bottle with tight-fitting lid. Discard solids. Makes about 1 1/2 cups (375 mL). Serves 12.

1 serving: 68 Calories; 0 g Total Fat (0 g Mono, 0 g Poly, 0 g Sat); 0 mg Cholesterol; 0 g Carbohydrate; 0 g Fibre; 0 g Protein; 0 mg Sodium

Pictured on page 126.

SPICY CAESAR: Dampen rim of cocktail glass with lime wedge, or dip into lime juice in saucer. Press into salt in separate saucer until coated. Pour 2 tbsp. (30 mL, 1 oz.) Peppercorn Vodka over ice in glass. Add clam tomato beverage to fill.

Paré Pointer

Say cheers in Latin: Propino Tibi Salutem!
(proh-PEEN-oh tib-EE sa-LOO-tem)

Measurement Tables

Throughout this book measurements are given in Conventional and Metric measure. To compensate for differences between the two measurements due to rounding, a full metric measure is not always used. The cup used is the standard 8 fluid ounces. Temperature is given in degrees Fahrenheit and Celsius. Baking pan measurements are in inches and centimetres as well as quarts and litres. An exact metric conversion is given below as well as the working equivalent (Metric Standard Measure).

Oven Temperatures

Fahrenheit (°F)	Celsius (°C)
175°	80°
200°	95°
225°	110°
250°	120°
275°	140°
300°	150°
325°	160°
350°	175°
375°	190°
400°	205°
425°	220°
450°	230°
475°	240°
500°	260°

Pans

Conventional Inches	Metric Centimetres
8x8 inch	20x20 cm
9x9 inch	22x22 cm
9x13 inch	22x33 cm
10x15 inch	25x38 cm
11x17 inch	28x43 cm
8x2 inch round	20x5 cm
9x2 inch round	22x5 cm
10x4 1/2 inch tube	25x11 cm
8x4x3 inch loaf	20x10x7.5 cm
9x5x3 inch loaf	22x12.5x7.5 cm

Spoons

Conventional Measure	Metric Exact Conversion Millilitre (mL)	Metric Standard Measure Millilitre (mL)
1/8 teaspoon (tsp.)	0.6 mL	0.5 mL
1/4 teaspoon (tsp.)	1.2 mL	1 mL
1/2 teaspoon (tsp.)	2.4 mL	2 mL
1 teaspoon (tsp.)	4.7 mL	5 mL
2 teaspoons (tsp.)	9.4 mL	10 mL
1 tablespoon (tbsp.)	14.2 mL	15 mL

Cups

Conventional Measure	Metric Exact Conversion Millilitre (mL)	Metric Standard Measure Millilitre (mL)
1/4 cup (4 tbsp.)	56.8 mL	60 mL
1/3 cup (5 1/3 tbsp.)	75.6 mL	75 mL
1/2 cup (8 tbsp.)	113.7 mL	125 mL
2/3 cup (10 2/3 tbsp.)	151.2 mL	150 mL
3/4 cup (12 tbsp.)	170.5 mL	175 mL
1 cup (16 tbsp.)	227.3 mL	250 mL
4 1/2 cups	1022.9 mL	1000 mL (1 L)

Dry Measurements

Conventional Measure Ounces (oz.)	Metric Exact Conversion Grams (g)	Metric Standard Measure Grams (g)
1 oz.	28.3 g	28 g
2 oz.	56.7 g	57 g
3 oz.	85.0 g	85 g
4 oz.	113.4 g	125 g
5 oz.	141.7 g	140 g
6 oz.	170.1 g	170 g
7 oz.	198.4 g	200 g
8 oz.	226.8 g	250 g
16 oz.	453.6 g	500 g
32 oz.	907.2 g	1000 g (1 kg)

Casseroles

CANADA & BRITAIN		UNITED STATES	
Standard Size Casserole	Exact Metric Measure	Standard Size Casserole	Exact Metric Measure
1 qt. (5 cups)	1.13 L	1 qt. (4 cups)	900 mL
1 1/2 qts. (7 1/2 cups)	1.69 L	1 1/2 qts. (6 cups)	1.35 L
2 qts. (10 cups)	2.25 L	2 qts. (8 cups)	1.8 L
2 1/2 qts. (12 1/2 cups)	2.81 L	2 1/2 qts. (10 cups)	2.25 L
3 qts. (15 cups)	3.38 L	3 qts. (12 cups)	2.7 L
4 qts. (20 cups)	4.5 L	4 qts. (16 cups)	3.6 L
5 qts. (25 cups)	5.63 L	5 qts. (20 cups)	4.5 L

Recipe Index

151

G

I

J

H

153

154

155

156

Recipe Notes

Recipe Notes

Starters

Jean Paré

companyscoming.com
visit our ↟ website

Divider Photo

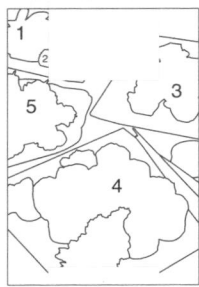

1. Salami Rolls, page 100
2. Shrimp Tomatoes, page 57
3. Phyllo Nests, page 85, with
   Ham Filling, page 92
   Mango Chutney Dip, page 39
   Piquant Beef Filling, page 85
4. Sushi, page 102
5. Yakitori, page 68

Props Courtesy Of:
Scona Clayworks
The Bay

We gratefully acknowledge the following suppliers for their generous support of our Test Kitchen and Photo Studio:

Broil King Barbecues
Corelle®
HamiltonBeach ® Canada
Lagostina®
Proctor Silex® Canada
Tupperware®

Need more recipes?

Six *"sneak preview"* recipes are featured online with every new book released.

Visit us at ↴
www.companyscoming.com

Table of Contents

Snacks

Spreads

Salads

Soups

5

Foreword

Starters are those morsels that we serve at the beginning of an evening of entertaining. They can be bite-size appetizers and finger foods, or a served soup or salad. They make a great start to any gathering and often help to get conversation going.

Appetizers and finger foods became fashionable in the early twentieth century. Since then, they have evolved into a multitude of morsels. With the explosion over the past one hundred years of canned and packaged ingredients, there is no end to what can be tucked inside phyllo pastry or stuffed into a mushroom cap.

Today's appetizers are fresh and varied, bright in colors, and even exotic in appearance. But they are all easy and most can be made ahead and frozen. What a welcome surprise for unexpected company to be served warm-from-the-oven Mushroom Pastries or Green Chili Bites—both from your freezer not 12 minutes earlier! Try to keep your serving sizes to one or two bites, and always serve with small plates or cocktail napkins. You may want to invest in decorative cocktail picks and small fancy spreaders.

Choose starters that have a variety of textures, colors and tastes. The ratio of hot to cold will depend on the time of year, the time of day and whether additional food will be offered. You don't want your appetizers to spoil dinner, but if you aren't serving a larger meal, you won't want your guests to go hungry.

Consider passing around only a few appetizers; then begin your meal with a starter soup or salad. The purpose of the starter is to stimulate the appetite for the meal to follow—not to compete with it. Starter soups and salads in this book are light and mellow in flavor and are meant to be served in smaller portions.

Cocktail parties, bridal showers, office gatherings, aprés-ski groups and even your volunteer-windup, are perfect opportunities for appetizers. Pass around a plate of hot Shrimp Kabobs, or have a platter of Beefy Roll-Ups and Chili Rolls handy for guests to serve themselves. Even Sushi and Dolmades can be assembled with relative ease for a trendy treat.

For a great beginning — choose Starters!

Jean Paré

Each recipe has been analyzed using the most updated version of the Canadian Nutrient File from Health and Welfare Canada which is based upon the United States Department of Agriculture (USDA) Nutrient Data Base.

Margaret Ng, B.Sc. (Hon), M.A.
Registered Dietitian

PARMESAN TOAST

It doesn't get much easier than this.

Hard margarine (or butter), softened	½ cup	125 mL
Grated Parmesan cheese	¼ cup	60 mL
Baguette, cut into ½ inch (12 mm) slices	½	½

Mash margarine and cheese with fork on plate.

Arrange baguette slices on ungreased broiler tray. Broil to toast 1 side. Turn slices over. Spread 1 tbsp. (15 mL) cheese mixture on each slice. Broil until golden. Makes 12.

1 slice: 137 Calories; 9.4 g Total Fat; 245 mg Sodium; 3 g Protein; 11 g Carbohydrate; trace Dietary Fiber

CHEESY PARTY BREAD

This canapé has a good flavor served cold but it's even better when served warm.

Pork sausage meat	½ lb.	225 g
Lean ground beef	½ lb.	225 g
Process cheese loaf (such as Velveeta), cut up	½ lb.	225 g
Salt	¼ tsp.	1 mL
Pepper	⅛ tsp.	0.5 mL
Garlic powder	¼ tsp.	1 mL
Dried whole oregano	½ tsp.	2 mL
Cayenne pepper	⅛ tsp.	0.5 mL
Cocktail-size rye bread slices	32	32

Scramble-fry sausage meat and ground beef in frying pan until no longer pink. Drain.

Add next 6 ingredients. Stir until cheese is melted. Cool slightly. Makes 2 cups (500 mL) filling.

Arrange bread slices on ungreased baking sheet. Spread 1 tbsp. (15 mL) filling on each slice. (May be frozen at this point.) Bake in 350°F (175°C) oven for about 10 minutes. Makes 32.

1 canapé: 63 Calories; 3.4 g Total Fat; 218 mg Sodium; 4 g Protein; 4 g Carbohydrate; trace Dietary Fiber

MOZZA PEPPER TOAST

Roasted pepper with cheese is a delight to eat.

Medium red pepper	1	1
Water	½ cup	125 mL
Cornstarch	1 tsp.	5 mL
Balsamic vinegar	¼ cup	60 mL
White vinegar	2 tbsp.	30 mL
Prepared mustard	1½ tbsp.	25 mL
Prepared horseradish	1 tsp.	5 mL
Cooking oil	1 tsp.	5 mL
Worcestershire sauce	¼ tsp.	1 mL
Cayenne pepper	⅛ tsp.	0.5 mL
Garlic powder (or 1 clove, minced)	¼ tsp.	1 mL
Part-skim mozzarella cheese, cut into ¼ inch (6 mm) cubes	8 oz.	250 g
Chopped pitted ripe olives	¼ cup	60 mL
Baguette, cut into ½ inch (12 mm) slices	1	1

Set red pepper on ungreased pie plate. Bake in 350°F (175°C) oven for 15 minutes. Turn pepper. Bake for 15 to 20 minutes. Cool enough to handle. Peel, seed and dice. Turn into medium bowl.

Stir water and cornstarch together in small saucepan. Heat and stir until boiling and thickened. Remove from heat. Set aside.

Stir in next 8 ingredients. Add to red pepper. Cool.

Add cheese cubes and olives. Stir well. Cover. Marinate in refrigerator for several hours or overnight, stirring occasionally. Drain well. Makes 1⅔ cups (400 mL) topping.

Arrange baguette slices on ungreased broiler tray. Broil to toast top sides. Turn slices over. Using a slotted spoon, place 1 tbsp. (15 mL) cheese mixture on each slice. Broil until golden. Makes about 24.

1 slice: 86 Calories; 2.5 g Total Fat; 175 mg Sodium; 4 g Protein; 11 g Carbohydrate; trace Dietary Fiber

Pictured on page 89.

SHRIMP CURRY ON TOAST

Delicate curry flavor. Toast points always go quickly.

Cooking oil	2 tsp.	10 mL
Chopped onion	1/2 cup	125 mL
Chopped fresh mushrooms	1/2 cup	125 mL
Grated carrot	1/3 cup	75 mL
Garlic clove, minced (or 1/4 tsp., 1 mL, garlic powder)	1	1
Reserved liquid from shrimp		
Vegetable (or seafood) bouillon powder	1 tsp.	5 mL
Curry powder	1/2 tsp.	2 mL
Canned cocktail (or broken) shrimp, drained and rinsed, liquid reserved	4 oz.	113 g
Light cream cheese, softened	4 oz.	125 g
White (or whole wheat) sandwich bread slices, crusts removed	10	10
Medium coconut, sprinkle (optional)		

Heat cooking oil in frying pan. Add onion, mushrooms, carrot and garlic. Sauté until onion is soft.

Stir in reserved shrimp liquid, bouillon powder and curry powder. Cook until most of liquid is evaporated. Remove from heat.

Add shrimp and cream cheese. Mash together to make spreadable mixture. Makes 1 1/4 cups (300 mL) shrimp spread.

Toast 1 side of bread. Spread 2 tbsp. (30 mL) shrimp spread on untoasted side of each bread slice. Cut into Toast Points, page 14. Sprinkle with coconut. Arrange on ungreased baking sheet. Broil about 6 inches (15 cm) from heat until hot and coconut is toasted. Makes about 40.

1 toast point: 30 Calories; 1 g Total Fat; 81 mg Sodium; 2 g Protein; 4 g Carbohydrate; trace Dietary Fiber

Variation: Omit coconut. Broil then garnish with a bit of seafood sauce or mango chutney.

Breads

BACON CHEESE FILLING

Fill Toast Cups, page 14, or mini puff pastry patty shells, with about ¹/₂ tbsp. (7 mL) filling. Works great as a spread too. Lots of bacon flavor. Chives add a zestiness.

Bacon slices	4	4
Light cream cheese, softened	4 oz.	125 g
Milk	1¹/₂ tbsp.	25 mL
Dried chopped chives (or green onion)	1 tbsp.	15 mL

Cook bacon in frying pan until crisp. Drain. Cool. Crumble or chop.

Mash cream cheese and milk together well in small bowl. Mix in bacon and chives. Makes ²/₃ cup (150 mL).

¹/₂ tbsp. (7 mL): 17 Calories; 1.4 g Total Fat; 68 mg Sodium; 1 g Protein; trace Carbohydrate; 0 g Dietary Fiber

HAM PINWHEELS

Make one day ahead or make and freeze ahead.

Canned ham flakes	6¹/₂ oz.	184 g
Salad dressing (or mayonnaise)	3 tbsp.	50 mL
Worcestershire sauce	1 tbsp.	15 mL
Prepared mustard	1 tsp.	5 mL
Onion powder	¹/₄ tsp.	1 mL
Day-old unsliced white (or whole wheat) bread loaf, sliced lengthwise (at bakery)	1	1
Hard margarine (or butter), softened	¹/₄ cup	60 mL
Gherkins, approximately	9	9

Mash first 5 ingredients together with fork in small bowl.

Remove crusts from 3 long slices of bread. Roll each slice with rolling pin to flatten slightly. Thinly spread each slice with margarine to edge. Spread with ham mixture to edge. Place gherkins, end to end, along short edge of each slice. Roll up. Place seam side down in container. Cover with damp tea towel. Chill. Slice thinly to serve. Cuts into 12 pinwheel slices per roll, for a total of 36.

1 pinwheel: 65 Calories; 3.3 g Total Fat; 185 mg Sodium; 2 g Protein; 7 g Carbohydrate; trace Dietary Fiber

CRAB PUFFS

Tasty and colorful. Freezing is not recommended.

Salad dressing (or mayonnaise)	2 tbsp.	30 mL
Milk	3 tbsp.	50 mL
Prepared mustard	1 tsp.	5 mL
Hot pepper sauce	$1/8$ tsp.	0.5 mL
Lemon juice	1 tsp.	5 mL
Parsley flakes	$1/2$ tsp.	2 mL
Onion powder	$1/4$ tsp.	1 mL
Salt	$1/4$ tsp.	1 mL
Chopped pimiento	1 tbsp.	15 mL
Canned crabmeat, drained and cartilage removed	$4^{1/4}$ oz.	120 g
All-purpose flour	1 tsp.	5 mL
Egg whites (large), room temperature	3	3
White (or whole wheat) sandwich bread slices, crusts removed	12	12
Grated part-skim mozzarella cheese	$3/4$ cup	175 mL
Pimiento strips (or pimiento-stuffed green olive slices)	48	48

Stir first 11 ingredients in medium bowl in order given.

Beat egg whites in small bowl until stiff. Fold into crab mixture.

Arrange bread slices on ungreased baking sheet. Spread about 2 tbsp. (30 mL) crab mixture over each slice. Sprinkle with cheese. Top with pimiento strip placed down center of each side of crab mixture. Bake in 350°F (175°C) oven for 15 to 20 minutes until puffed and golden. Cut each slice into Toast Triangles, page 14. Makes 48.

1 toast triangle: 37 Calories; 1.3 g Total Fat; 95 mg Sodium; 2 g Protein; 5 g Carbohydrate; trace Dietary Fiber

ONION TOAST POINTS

Broils to an orange shade. Tangy.

Salad dressing (or mayonnaise)	$1/2$ cup	125 mL
Finely chopped red onion	$1/2$ cup	125 mL
Paprika	1 tsp.	5 mL
Cayenne pepper	$1/8$ tsp.	0.5 mL
Salt	$1/8$ tsp.	0.5 mL
Pepper, just a pinch		

(continued on next page)

Breads

| White (or whole wheat) sandwich | 6 | 6 |
| bread slices, crusts removed | | |

Stir first 6 ingredients in small bowl. Makes 1 cup (250 mL).

Arrange bread slices on ungreased broiler tray. Broil to toast on 1 side only. Turn over. Spread untoasted sides of slices with about 2½ tbsp. (37 mL) onion mixture. Broil about 6 inches (15 cm) from heat for about 4 minutes until bubbly hot. Watch closely. Cut into Toast Points, page 14. Makes 24.

1 toast point: 44 Calories; 2.7 g Total Fat; 79 mg Sodium; 1 g Protein; 4 g Carbohydrate; trace Dietary Fiber

TENDERLOIN ON TOAST

A make-ahead sure-to-be-a-hit canapé.

Soy sauce	3 tbsp.	50 mL
Ketchup	3 tbsp.	50 mL
Brown sugar, packed	3 tbsp.	50 mL
Sherry (or alcohol-free sherry)	3 tbsp.	50 mL
Red food coloring	1 tsp.	5 mL
Pork tenderloin	1 lb.	454 g
Toast Rounds, page 14	24	24
Hard margarine (or butter), softened	2 tbsp.	30 mL

Mix first 5 ingredients in small bowl. Pour into sealable plastic bag.

Place tenderloin in bag. Seal. Marinate in refrigerator all day or overnight, turning bag occasionally. Remove pork from marinade. Place in ungreased 8 or 9 inch (20 or 22 cm) square pan. Cook, uncovered, in 375°F (190°C) oven for 20 minutes. Brush with marinade. Cook for 10 to 20 minutes until cooked. Chill. Slice into ⅛ inch (3 mm) slices.

Spread margarine on 1 side of each Toast Round. Serve slice of tenderloin on buttered side. Makes 96.

1 canapé: 23 Calories; 0.5 g Total Fat; 71 mg Sodium; 1 g Protein; 3 g Carbohydrate; trace Dietary Fiber

TOAST CUPS

Quick-and-easy containers for spreads or a mousse.

White (or whole wheat) sandwich bread 9   9
slices, crusts removed

Cut each bread slice into 4 squares. Press into ungreased muffin cups. Bake on bottom rack in 350°F (175°C) oven for about 15 minutes until browned. Cool. Store in plastic bag or other container. Fill before serving, or let guests help themselves. Makes 36.

1 toast cup: 17 Calories; 0.2 g Total Fat; 32 mg Sodium; 1 g Protein; 3 g Carbohydrate; trace Dietary Fiber

Variation: Lightly butter both sides of bread before pressing into muffin cups. Bread may also be cut into $2\frac{1}{2}$ inch (6.4 cm) circles, both sides buttered, and pressed into cups. Bake as above.

TOAST POINTS: Arrange uncut bread slices on ungreased broiler tray. Broil 1 side only until lightly browned. ❶ Cut each slice down the center to make 2 rectangles. Cut each rectangle cornerwise to make 4 elongated triangles.

TOAST SQUARES: Arrange uncut bread slices on ungreased broiler tray. Broil 1 side only until lightly browned. ❷ Cut each slice into 4 squares rather than elongated triangles.

TOAST TRIANGLES: Arrange uncut bread slices on ungreased broiler tray. Broil 1 side only until lightly browned. ❸ Cut each slice into 4 even triangles, cutting diagonally from corner to corner.

TOAST ROUNDS: Slice small loaf, such as submarine bun or baguette, into round slices. Broil 1 side, or leave plain.

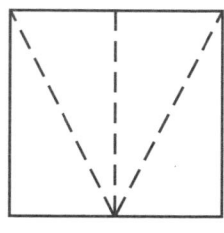 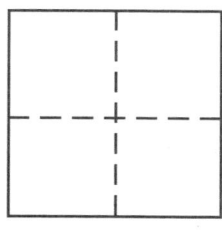 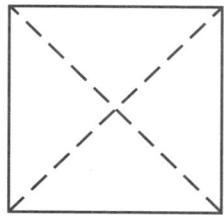

❶ Toast Points   ❷ Toast Squares   ❸ Toast Triangles

These can be made ahead. Cover to reheat.

Biscuit mix	**2 cups**	**500 mL**
Milk	**½ cup**	**125 mL**
Onion powder	**¼ tsp.**	**1 mL**
Grated medium or sharp Cheddar cheese	**1 cup**	**250 mL**
Grated Monterey Jack cheese	**1 cup**	**250 mL**
Canned broken shrimp, drained and rinsed	**2 × 4 oz.**	**2 × 113 g**
Canned crabmeat, drained and cartilage removed	**5 oz.**	**142 g**
Large eggs	**6**	**6**
Light cream (half-and-half)	**2 cups**	**500 mL**
Salt	**½ tsp.**	**2 mL**
Pepper	**¼ tsp.**	**1 mL**

Stir biscuit mix, milk and onion powder together in medium bowl to form a soft ball. Press in bottom of ungreased 9 x 13 inch (22 x 33 cm) pan. Bake in 375°F (190°C) oven for 15 minutes to partially cook.

Sprinkle crust with both cheeses, shrimp and crabmeat.

Beat eggs in medium bowl until frothy. Add cream, salt and pepper. Mix. Pour over top of seafood. Bake for about 35 minutes until knife inserted in center comes out clean. Let stand for 5 to 10 minutes. Cut into squares. Makes 54.

1 square: 65 Calories; 3.7 g Total Fat; 151 mg Sodium; 4 g Protein; 4 g Carbohydrate; trace Dietary Fiber

All leaping lettuce is found in a tossed salad.

SHRIMP SQUARES

Serve as a finger food or as a first course starter.

White (or whole wheat) sandwich bread slices, crusts removed	6	6
Hard margarine (or butter), softened	2 tbsp.	30 mL
Canned small shrimp, drained and rinsed	4 oz.	113 g
Grated medium Cheddar cheese	1/2 cup	125 mL
Mayonnaise (not salad dressing)	2 tbsp.	30 mL
Parsley flakes	1 tsp.	5 mL
Worcestershire sauce	1/4 tsp.	1 mL
Onion salt	1/4 tsp.	1 mL
Paprika, sprinkle		

Arrange bread slices on ungreased broiler tray. Lightly butter 1 side of each slice. Cut each slice into 4 smaller squares. Broil buttered sides until lightly browned. Turn over. Set aside.

Mash shrimp, cheese and mayonnaise together in medium bowl, adding more mayonnaise if too dry. Mix in parsley, Worcestershire sauce and onion salt. Spread unbuttered side of each toast square with 1 1/2 tsp. (7 mL) shrimp mixture.

Sprinkle with paprika. Broil until sizzling hot. Serve. Makes 24 small squares, or serves 6 as a first course appetizer.

1 square: 49 Calories; 3 g Total Fat; 87 mg Sodium; 2 g Protein; 3 g Carbohydrate; trace Dietary Fiber

CRAB SQUARES: Use crabmeat instead of shrimp.

1. Wiener Wisps, page 73
2. Spinach Dip 'N' Bowl, page 31
3. Snackin' Potato Skins (Variations), page 79
4. Toads, page 23
5. Stuffed Mushrooms, page 78
6. Southern Pizza, page 22
7. Chicken Pizza, page 20
8. Beefy Roll-Ups, page 94

The Company's Coming Story

Jean Paré (pronounced "Perry") grew up understanding that the combination of family, friends and home cooking is the best recipe for a good life. From her mother, she learned to appreciate good cooking, while her father praised even her earliest attempts in the kitchen. When Jean left home, she took with her many acquired family recipes, a love of cooking and an intriguing desire to read recipe books like novels!

"never share a recipe you wouldn't use yourself"

In 1963, when her four children had all reached school age, Jean volunteered to cater the 50th Anniversary of the Vermilion School of Agriculture, now Lakeland College, in Alberta, Canada. Working out of her home, Jean prepared a dinner for over 1,000 people which launched a flourishing catering operation that continued for over eighteen years. During that time, she was provided with countless opportunities to test new ideas with immediate feedback—resulting in empty plates and contented customers! Whether preparing cocktail sandwiches for a house party or serving a hot meal for 1,500 people, Jean Paré earned a reputation for good food, courteous service and reasonable prices.

As requests for her recipes mounted, Jean was often asked the question, "Why don't you write a cookbook?" Jean responded by teaming up with her son, Grant Lovig, in the fall of 1980 to form Company's Coming Publishing Limited. The publication of the first Company's Coming cookbook on April 14, 1981 marked the debut of what would soon become one of the world's most popular cookbook series.

The company has grown since those early days when Jean worked from a spare bedroom in her home. Today she leads a team of writers and testers in the development of new recipes. Under the guidance of Jean's daughter, Gail Lovig, Company's Coming cookbooks are now distributed throughout Canada, in addition to the United States and numerous overseas markets. Rounding off three generations is Jean's granddaughter (Grant's daughter), Amanda Jean Lovig, who looks after publicity and arranges personal appearances for her grandmother.

Bestsellers many times over in English, Company's Coming cookbooks have also been published in French and Spanish. Familiar and trusted in home kitchens around the world, Company's Coming cookbooks are offered in a variety of formats. Highly regarded as kitchen workbooks, the softcover Original Series, with its lay-flat plastic comb binding, is still the favourite with readers.

Jean Paré's approach to cooking has always called for *quick and easy recipes* using *everyday ingredients*. Even when travelling, she is constantly on the lookout for new ideas to share with her readers. At home, she can usually be found researching and writing recipes, or helping in the company's test kitchen. Jean continues to gain new supporters by adhering to what she calls The Golden Rule of Cooking: *"Never share a recipe you wouldn't use yourself."* It's an approach that has worked—*millions of times over!*

Recipe Notes

Recipe Notes

156

Make ahead...

When making up your appetizer menu, look for recipes that can be made ahead of time. Many hot appetizers can be prepared and frozen several weeks in advance, then reheated just before serving. Dips and spreads can be made the day before and stored in the refrigerator. Fresh vegetables for your crudités platter are best prepared on the same day.

BRUSCHETTA PIZZA

An attractive twist to the usual bruschetta. Colorful with flavor to match.

BASIC PIZZA CRUST		
All-purpose flour	1½ cups	375 mL
Instant yeast	1¼ tsp.	6 mL
Salt	¼ tsp.	1 mL
Cooking oil	2 tbsp.	30 mL
Very warm water	½ cup	125 mL
TOPPING		
Salad dressing (or mayonnaise)	½ cup	125 mL
Grated Parmesan cheese	¼ cup	60 mL
Dried whole oregano	1 tsp.	5 mL
Dried sweet basil	½ tsp.	2 mL
Pepper	½ tsp.	2 mL
Garlic cloves, minced (or ½ tsp., 2 mL, garlic powder), optional	2	2
Chopped pitted ripe olives	⅓ cup	75 mL
Plum tomatoes, seeded and diced	3	3
Grated part-skim mozzarella cheese	1½ cups	375 mL

Basic Pizza Crust: Put flour, yeast and salt into food processor fitted with dough blade.

With machine running, pour cooking oil and warm water through feed tube. Process for about 30 seconds. Let dough rest, covered, for 15 minutes. Roll out on lightly floured surface. Press in greased 12 inch (30 cm) pizza pan or 9 x 13 inch (22 x 33 cm) pan. Poke holes all over crust, except edge, with fork. Bake on bottom rack in 425°F (220°C) oven for 8 minutes. Press down any bulges. Cool slightly.

Topping: Mix first 6 ingredients well in medium bowl. Spread over crust.

Sprinkle with olives, tomato and mozzarella cheese. Bake for about 8 minutes. Cuts into 16 long thin appetizer wedges or 24 squares.

1 wedge: 144 Calories; 8.3 g Total Fat; 193 mg Sodium; 5 g Protein; 12 g Carbohydrate; 1 g Dietary Fiber

Pictured on page 89.

CHICKEN PIZZA

Guests will love to fill their plates with these small wedges.

SWEET BISCUIT PIZZA CRUST

All-purpose flour	2 cups	500 mL
Baking powder	1 tbsp.	15 mL
Granulated sugar	1 tsp.	5 mL
Salt	1/4 tsp.	1 mL
Milk	2/3 cup	150 mL
Cooking oil	1 tbsp.	15 mL

TOPPING

Cooking oil	2 tsp.	10 mL
Boneless, skinless chicken breast halves (about 1/2 lb., 225 g), cut into very small dice	2	2
Chopped onion	3/4 cup	175 mL
Chopped green pepper	1/3 cup	75 mL
Garlic powder	1/8 tsp.	0.5 mL
Chili powder	1/8 tsp.	0.5 mL
Ground thyme	1/8 tsp.	0.5 mL
Cayenne pepper	1/8 tsp.	0.5 mL
Salt	1 tsp.	5 mL
Pepper	1/8 tsp.	0.5 mL
Picante salsa	6 tbsp.	100 mL
Grated part-skim mozzarella cheese	1 1/2 cups	375 mL

Sweet Biscuit Pizza Crust: Combine first 4 ingredients in medium bowl.

Add milk and cooking oil. Stir to form a soft ball. Turn out onto lightly floured surface. Knead 8 times. Divide into 4 equal portions. Roll out each portion into 7 inch (18 cm) diameter circle. Place on large greased baking sheet. Bake in 425°F (220°C) oven for 8 minutes to partially cook.

Topping: Heat cooking oil in frying pan. Add chicken, onion and green pepper. Scramble-fry until chicken is no longer pink and onion is golden.

Stir in next 6 ingredients.

(continued on next page)

Breads

Spread ¼ of salsa over each crust. Scatter ¼ of chicken mixture over salsa. Sprinkle each with ¼ of cheese. Bake for 6 minutes until hot and cheese is melted. Cut each pizza into 8 wedges. Makes 32 wedges.

1 wedge: 66 Calories; 1.9 g Total Fat; 186 mg Sodium; 4 g Protein; 8 g Carbohydrate; trace Dietary Fiber

Pictured on page 17.

Note: To make without partially baking crust, put topping onto unbaked crust. Bake on bottom rack in 450°F (230°C) oven for 10 minutes.

CHEESE TOASTIES

Be prepared to make lots. A popular flavor.

Grated sharp Cheddar cheese	1 cup	250 mL
Grated onion	2 tsp.	10 mL
Worcestershire sauce	¼ tsp.	1 mL
Lemon juice	1½ tsp.	7 mL
Cayenne pepper	¹⁄₁₆ tsp.	0.5 mL
Salt	¼ tsp.	1 mL
White (or whole wheat) sandwich bread slices, with crusts	8	8
Hard margarine (or butter), softened	3 tbsp.	50 mL

Mix first 6 ingredients well in small bowl.

Lay 4 bread slices on working surface. Divide cheese mixture among slices. Spread. Cover with remaining 4 slices. Spread tops with margarine. Turn over. Spread again with margarine. Cut off crusts. Cut each sandwich into 4 squares. Place all 16 squares in hot frying pan. Brown each side. Serve. Makes 16.

1 toastie: 84 Calories; 5.1 g Total Fat; 179 mg Sodium; 3 g Protein; 7 g Carbohydrate; trace Dietary Fiber

When tires get old there is nothing left to do but retire them.

SOUTHERN PIZZA

Little bit of corn and chili powder on a biscuit crust. A bit of the South.

BISCUIT PIZZA CRUST

All-purpose flour	2 cups	500 mL
Baking powder	1 tbsp.	15 mL
Salt	1/4 tsp.	1 mL
Water	2/3 cup	150 mL
Cooking oil	1 tbsp.	15 mL

TOPPING

Cooking oil	2 tsp.	10 mL
Lean ground beef	1/2 lb.	225 g
Chopped onion	1/2 cup	125 mL
Chopped green pepper	1/4 cup	60 mL
Canned tomatoes, drained, chopped and drained again	14 oz.	398 mL
Frozen kernel corn	1/2 cup	125 mL
Chili powder	1 tsp.	5 mL
Dried whole oregano	1/2 tsp.	2 mL
Garlic powder	1/4 tsp.	1 mL
Dried sweet basil	1/4 tsp.	1 mL
Salt	1/2 tsp.	2 mL
Pepper	1/8 tsp.	0.5 mL
Grated part-skim mozzarella cheese	1 1/3 cups	325 mL

Biscuit Pizza Crust: Measure flour, baking powder and salt into medium bowl. Stir.

Add water and cooking oil. Mix into soft ball. Turn out onto lightly floured surface. Knead 8 times. Divide and roll into 4 circles, 7 inches (18 cm) in diameter. Place on greased baking sheets.

Topping: Heat cooking oil in frying pan. Add ground beef, onion and green pepper. Scramble-fry until beef is no longer pink and onion and pepper are soft and golden. Drain.

Stir next 8 ingredients together in medium bowl. Spread 1/4 of corn mixture over each crust. Spoon 1/4 of meat mixture over corn mixture.

(continued on next page)

Breads

Sprinkle each pizza with ¼ of cheese. Bake on bottom rack in 425°F (220°C) oven for about 15 minutes. Cut each pizza into 8 wedges, for a total of 32.

1 wedge: 64 Calories; 2 g Total Fat; 113 mg Sodium; 4 g Protein; 8 g Carbohydrate; 1 g Dietary Fiber

Pictured on page 17.

TOADS

Serve hot from the oven or reheat later.

Cooking oil	**1 tsp.**	**5 mL**
Cocktail-size sausages (or small sausages, halved)	**12**	**12**
All-purpose flour	**1 cup**	**250 mL**
Salt	**¼ tsp.**	**1 mL**
Large egg	**1**	**1**
Milk	**1¼ cups**	**300 mL**
Cooking oil	**2 tbsp.**	**30 mL**

Heat first amount of cooking oil in frying pan. Add sausages. Brown.

Place flour, salt, egg and milk in small bowl. Beat until smooth.

Put ½ tsp. (2 mL) second amount of cooking oil and 1 small browned sausage into each muffin cup. Heat in 425°F (220°C) oven for 5 minutes. Pour milk mixture quickly over each sausage. Bake for 20 minutes until risen and golden brown. Makes 12.

1 toad: 126 Calories; 7.5 g Total Fat; 227 mg Sodium; 4 g Protein; 10 g Carbohydrate; trace Dietary Fiber

Pictured on page 17.

Paré Pointer

She was enjoying the spring flowers until she heard the cro-cuss.

Breads

SHRIMP CANAPÉS

Looks pretty on the darkest bread you can find.

SHRIMP FILLING

Canned shrimp, drained and rinsed	4 oz.	113 g
Salad dressing (or mayonnaise)	3 tbsp.	50 mL
Ketchup	1½ tbsp.	25 mL
Prepared horseradish	¼ tsp.	1 mL
Cocktail-size dark (such as pumpernickel) bread slices	20	20
Pimiento strips, for garnish		

Shrimp Filling: Mash first 4 ingredients together in small bowl. Makes ⅞ cup (200 mL) filling.

Cut bread slices into rounds with 1¾ inch (4.5 cm) cookie cutter. Spoon or pipe shrimp mixture over top of each slice. Garnish with pimiento. Makes 20.

1 canapé: 34 Calories; 1.3 g Total Fat; 75 mg Sodium; 2 g Protein; 4 g Carbohydrate; trace Dietary Fiber

HAMWICHES

A very moist filling that can be used in Mini Cream Puff Shells, page 88.

HAM FILLING

Canned ham flakes, with liquid	6½ oz.	184 g
Salad dressing (or mayonnaise)	1½ tbsp.	25 mL
Sweet pickle relish	1 tbsp.	15 mL
Dried chives	2 tsp.	10 mL
Pumpernickel bread slices	6	6
Hard margarine (or butter), softened	2 tbsp.	30 mL

Ham Filling: Break up ham with liquid in small bowl. Add salad dressing, relish and chives. Mash together well. Makes ¾ cup (175 mL) filling.

Make sandwiches with 3 pieces of bread and 2 layers of filling, buttering bread on both sides of filling. Cut off crusts. Cut into four 1 inch (2.5 cm) slices. Lay slices flat. Cut into thirds. Serve sandwiches on their sides. Makes 24.

1 hamwich: 48 Calories; 3 g Total Fat; 160 mg Sodium; 2 g Protein; 4 g Carbohydrate; trace Dietary Fiber

EGG RIBBONS

These eye-appealing little sandwiches are enjoyed by all.

Large hard-boiled eggs, chopped	6	6
Finely diced celery	1/4 cup	60 mL
Salad dressing (or mayonnaise)	1/4 cup	60 mL
Sweet pickle relish	2 tbsp.	30 mL
Onion powder	1/4 tsp.	1 mL
Salt	1/2 tsp.	2 mL
Day-old dark bread slices	8	8
Day-old white bread slices	4	4
Hard margarine (or butter), softened	1/4 cup	60 mL

Mix first 6 ingredients in small bowl.

Use 2 dark bread slices and 1 white bread slice per stack. Lightly butter 1 side of each dark slice. Spread with 1/8 of egg mixture. Lightly butter both sides of white slice. Place on top of egg mixture. Spread top side with 1/8 of egg mixture. Place remaining dark slice, buttered side down, on top of egg mixture. Repeat with remaining 6 dark slices and 3 white slices, to make a total of 4 stacks. Cut off crusts. Wrap each stack. Chill. To serve, cut into 1/2 inch (12 mm) layered slices. Cut each slice into 3 or 4 finger sandwiches. Makes about 48.

1 sandwich: 42 Calories; 2.5 g Total Fat; 92 mg Sodium; 1 g Protein; 4 g Carbohydrate; trace Dietary Fiber

SESAME ROUNDS

Serve these hot or cold.

White (or whole wheat or pumpernickel) bread slices	12	12
Hard margarine (or butter), softened	1/2 cup	125 mL
Toasted sesame seeds	1/3 cup	75 mL

Cut 4 rounds per slice of bread, using 1 3/4 inch (4.5 cm) cookie cutter. Generously butter 1 side of each round to edge. Press buttered side into sesame seeds to coat. Arrange, seed side up, on greased baking sheet. Bake in 350°F (175°C) oven for about 15 minutes until browned. Makes 48.

1 round: 41 Calories; 2.8 g Total Fat; 56 mg Sodium; 1 g Protein; 3 g Carbohydrate; trace Dietary Fiber

Pictured on page 107.

HOT BREAD PUFFS

Cheese-coated cubes are bites of bliss. Recipe may easily be halved.

Day-old unsliced white (or whole wheat) bread loaf, crust removed	1	1
Hard margarine (or butter)	1 cup	250 mL
Cream cheese	8 oz.	250 g
Grated sharp Cheddar cheese	3 cups	750 mL
Worcestershire sauce	2 tsp.	10 mL
Egg whites (large), room temperature	4	4

Cut bread loaf into 1 inch (2.5 cm) cubes. Place in freezer for about 30 minutes until partially frozen.

Combine next 4 ingredients in top of double boiler over simmering water. Stir often as mixture melts. Remove from heat.

Beat egg whites in small bowl until stiff. Fold into hot mixture until no streaks appear. Pierce partially frozen bread cubes with fork. Dip into hot mixture to coat. Transfer to ungreased baking sheet. Chill all day or overnight. Just before serving, bake in 400°F (205°C) oven for about 10 minutes until lightly browned. To keep on hand, freeze on tray. Store in plastic container or bag. Thaw before baking. Makes about 120.

1 bread puff: 43 Calories; 3.4 g Total Fat; 64 mg Sodium; 1 g Protein; 2 g Carbohydrate; trace Dietary Fiber

SAUSAGE BREAD ROLLS

A very different sausage roll. Encased in bread and cheese. Quick to prepare.

Link sausages (about ½ lb., 225 g)	8	8
Hard margarine (or butter), softened	¼ cup	60 mL
Grated medium Cheddar cheese	1 cup	250 mL
White (or whole wheat) sandwich bread slices, crusts removed	8	8

Poke holes in sausages with tip of paring knife so fat can drain out. Cook sausages in frying pan. Drain. Cool.

Cream margarine and cheese together in small bowl.

(continued on next page)

Roll each bread slice flat with rolling pin. Spread both sides of each slice with cheese mixture using about 1 tbsp. (15 mL) per side. Place sausage on 1 edge. Roll up snugly like jelly roll. Repeat. Arrange on greased baking sheet. Bake in 375°F (190°C) oven for about 12 minutes until very hot. Cut each sausage roll into 3 pieces to serve. Makes 24.

1 piece: *78 Calories; 5.6 g Total Fat; 133 mg Sodium; 3 g Protein; 4 g Carbohydrate; trace Dietary Fiber*

GRILLED CHEESE BITES

Guests will love these tiny sandwiches.

White (or whole wheat) sandwich bread slices, crusts removed	3	3
Pepper Monterey Jack cheese, sliced	3 oz.	85 g
White (or whole wheat) sandwich bread slices, crusts removed	3	3
Jalapeño pepper jelly	3 tbsp.	50 mL
Medium Cheddar cheese, thinly sliced	3 oz.	85 g
White (or whole wheat) sandwich bread slices, crusts removed	3	3
Large eggs, fork-beaten	2	2
Water	¼ cup	60 mL

Lay 3 bread slices on working surface. Divide Monterey Jack cheese slices on top of each slice. Set second bread slice over each. Spread each with 1 tbsp. (15 mL) jalapeño jelly. Layer Cheddar cheese slices over jelly followed by third bread slice. Cut each stack into 4 squares.

Mix egg and water in small bowl. Dip top and bottom of each small sandwich into egg mixture. Grill in hot well-greased frying pan, browning both sides. These can be made ahead, frozen in single layer on tray and stored in container in freezer. They are good thawed and eaten cold, or thaw and heat in 350°F (175°C) oven for about 5 minutes. Makes 12.

1 bite: *127 Calories; 5.9 g Total Fat; 197 mg Sodium; 6 g Protein; 12 g Carbohydrate; trace Dietary Fiber*

BEEF BUNS

You can choose either small appetizer-size or larger lunch-size buns.

Beef stew meat, cut into ¾ inch (2 cm) cubes	1½ lbs.	680 g
Water, to cover		
Salt	1 tsp.	5 mL
Pepper	½ tsp.	2 mL
Cooking oil	2 tsp.	10 mL
Medium onion, chopped	1	1
Shredded cabbage, packed	⅔ cup	150 mL
Grated gingerroot	1-2 tbsp.	15-30 mL
Soy sauce	¼ cup	60 mL
Finely chopped green onion	¼ cup	60 mL
Brown sugar, packed	2 tbsp.	30 mL
Salt	½ tsp.	2 mL
Dried crushed chilies	½ tsp.	2 mL
Garlic powder	¼ tsp.	1 mL
Cornstarch	2 tsp.	10 mL
Liquid gravy browner	2 tsp.	10 mL
Frozen dinner roll dough, thawed (see Note)	30	30
Large egg, fork-beaten	1	1
Sesame seeds (not toasted)	1 tbsp.	15 mL

Boil stew meat, water, first amount of salt and pepper gently in large saucepan for at least 1½ hours until very tender. Strain and reserve ⅔ cup (150 mL) liquid. Cool meat. Process in food processor until shredded.

Heat cooking oil in large frying pan. Add onion. Sauté until soft.

Add cabbage and gingerroot. Sauté until cabbage is soft.

Stir in next 6 ingredients.

Mix reserved liquid, cornstarch and gravy browner in small cup. Stir into cabbage mixture until boiling and thickened. Add shredded meat. Stir. Cool. Makes about 3½ cups (875 mL) filling.

(continued on next page)

Breads

Divide buns in half. Roll each half into 2½ inch (6.4 cm) circle. Place 1 scant tbsp. (15 mL) beef filling in center. Moisten edge with water. Gather edge up to top, pinching to seal. Place seam side down, 1 inch (2.5 cm) apart, on 2 greased 11 x 17 inch (28 x 43 cm) baking sheets. Cover each with damp tea towel. Let stand in oven with light on and door closed for about 40 minutes until buns are doubled in size.

Brush buns with egg. Sprinkle with sesame seeds. Bake in 375°F (190°C) oven for about 15 minutes until lightly browned. Makes 60.

1 small bun: 102 Calories; 2.7 g Total Fat; 290 mg Sodium; 5 g Protein; 14 g Carbohydrate; 1 g Dietary Fiber

Pictured on page 125.

Note: For larger buns, roll whole bun into 4 inch (10 cm) circle. Spoon about 1½ tbsp. (25 mL) beef filling in center. Bake for about 20 minutes. Makes 30.

TUNA TOWERS

The unusual addition of grated apple gives this its good flavor. Contrasting colors of bread and filling make this very attractive.

TUNA FILLING

Canned flaked tuna, drained	6½ oz.	184 g
Grated peeled apple	⅓ cup	75 mL
Finely chopped celery	¼ cup	60 mL
Sweet pickle relish	1 tsp.	5 mL
Onion powder	¼ tsp.	1 mL
Salad dressing (or mayonnaise)	¼ cup	60 mL
Salt	⅛ tsp.	0.5 mL
Cocktail-size dark (such as pumpernickel) bread slices	60	60
Hard margarine (or butter), softened	3 tbsp.	50 mL
Pimiento-stuffed green olive slices, for garnish		

Tuna Filling: Combine first 7 ingredients in medium bowl. Stir together. Makes 1⅓ cups (325 mL) filling.

Cut out 1½ inch (3.8 cm) circles from each bread slice. Spread margarine and 1½ tsp. (7 mL) filling on each of 2 slices. Top with third slice. Repeat with remaining filling and bread slices. Garnish with olive slices. Makes 20.

1 tiered sandwich: 91 Calories; 3.7 g Total Fat; 200 mg Sodium; 4 g Protein; 11 g Carbohydrate; 1 g Dietary Fiber

STUFFING BALLS

What an aroma and with flavor to match!

Chopped onion	¼ cup	60 mL
Chopped celery	¼ cup	60 mL
Hard margarine (or butter)	2 tbsp.	30 mL
Canned cream-style corn	¾ cup	175 mL
Water	¼ cup	60 mL
Parsley flakes	1 tsp.	5 mL
Poultry seasoning	1 tsp.	5 mL
Salt	½ tsp.	2 mL
Pepper	⅛ tsp.	0.5 mL
Large eggs, fork-beaten	2	2
Fine dry bread crumbs	2 cups	500 mL
Thin bacon slices (about 1½ lbs., 680 g)	20	20

Sauté onion and celery in margarine in small frying pan until soft.

Combine corn, water, parsley flakes, poultry seasoning, salt, and pepper in large bowl. Stir in eggs. Add onion and celery mixture.

Add bread crumbs. Mix well. Chill for 30 minutes. Shape into 1 inch (2.5 cm) balls.

Cut bacon slices in half. Wrap each ball with bacon. Secure with wooden pick. To serve, place on ungreased baking sheet. Bake in 400°F (205°C) oven for 10 minutes. Drain. Turn. Bake for 10 minutes until bacon is cooked and browned. Drain on paper towel. Makes about 40.

4 stuffing balls: 54 Calories; 2.7 g Total Fat; 152 mg Sodium; 2 g Protein; 5 g Carbohydrate; trace Dietary Fiber

Better quit preening or you'll end up like a duck—down in the mouth.

SAVORY CURRY DIP

Curry flavor is middle of the road. Add as much as you like. Serve with fresh vegetables.

Salad dressing (or mayonnaise)	1 cup	250 mL
Onion flakes	1 tbsp.	15 mL
Prepared horseradish	2 tsp.	10 mL
Curry powder	1 tsp.	5 mL
Salt	1 tsp.	5 mL
Milk	$\frac{1}{2}$ cup	125 mL

Mix all 6 ingredients in small bowl. Makes 1⅓ cups (325 mL).

1 tbsp. (15 mL): 59 Calories; 5.6 g Total Fat; 196 mg Sodium; trace Protein; 2 g Carbohydrate; trace Dietary Fiber

SPINACH DIP 'N' BOWL

This makes a large amount, but don't be concerned, you make the dish to serve it in too! Serve surrounded with vegetables, bread chunks and crackers.

Frozen chopped spinach, thawed and squeezed dry	10 oz.	300 g
Salad dressing (or mayonnaise)	1 cup	250 mL
Sour cream	1 cup	250 mL
Chopped onion	$\frac{1}{2}$ cup	125 mL
Envelope dry vegetable soup mix	1 × 1½ oz.	1 × 45 g
Canned chopped water chestnuts, drained	10 oz.	284 mL
Round bread loaf, hollowed out	1	1

Place first 4 ingredients in blender. Process until smooth. Turn into medium bowl.

Stir in vegetable soup mix and water chestnuts. Cover. Chill for at least 2 hours. Makes 3¾ cups (925 mL).

Fill bread loaf with dip. Serve at room temperature or wrap in foil and heat in 300°F (150°C) oven for 2 to 3 hours.

2 tbsp. (30 mL) dip only: 63 Calories; 5.4 g Total Fat; 132 mg Sodium; 1 g Protein; 3 g Carbohydrate; trace Dietary Fiber

Pictured on page 17.

Dips

GUACAMOLE

Spiced just right. Green in color with tomato showing through. Serve with corn chips, tortilla chips or raw vegetables.

Medium avocados, peeled and mashed	2	2
Lime (or lemon) juice	3 tbsp.	50 mL
Finely chopped white (or red) onion	2 tbsp.	30 mL
Medium tomato, seeded and diced	1	1
Chili powder	1 tsp.	5 mL
Garlic powder	1/4 tsp.	1 mL
Cayenne pepper	1/4 tsp.	1 mL
Salt	1 tsp.	5 mL
Pepper	1/4 tsp.	1 mL

Mix all 9 ingredients in medium bowl. Makes 1¾ cups (425 mL).

1 tbsp. (15 mL): 24 Calories; 2.1 g Total Fat; 96 mg Sodium; trace Protein; 2 g Carbohydrate; trace Dietary Fiber

Pictured on page 35.

CHILI CON QUESO

Looks so inviting. For even more zip use Pepper Jack cheese in place of Monterey Jack. Keep hot in chafing dish or fondue pot. A must for tortilla chips.

Skim evaporated milk	13½ oz.	385 mL
All-purpose flour	3 tbsp.	50 mL
Canned stewed tomatoes, drained, chopped and drained again	14 oz.	398 mL
Canned diced green chilies, drained	4 oz.	114 mL
Chili powder	1/2 tsp.	2 mL
Garlic powder	1/8 tsp.	0.5 mL
Cayenne pepper	1/4 tsp.	1 mL
Salt	1/2 tsp.	2 mL
Grated Monterey Jack cheese	3 cups	750 mL

(continued on next page)

Whisk evaporated milk into flour in large saucepan until no lumps remain. Heat and stir until boiling and thickened.

Add remaining 7 ingredients, stirring often until cheese is melted. Serve hot. Makes 4 cups (1 L).

1 tbsp. (15 mL): 28 Calories; 1.7 g Total Fat; 82 mg Sodium; 2 g Protein; 2 g Carbohydrate; trace Dietary Fiber

Pictured on page 35.

HOT BROCCOLI DIP

Chunky and cheesy. A different dip than the usual. Serve in chafing dish to keep hot. Have melba toast, crackers, corn chips, and toast rounds on the side.

Frozen chopped broccoli	10 oz.	300 g
Water	1 cup	250 mL
Hard margarine (or butter)	½ cup	125 mL
Chopped onion	½ cup	125 mL
Condensed cream of mushroom soup	10 oz.	284 mL
Grated medium Cheddar cheese	2 cups	500 mL
Garlic powder	¼ tsp.	1 mL
Canned mushroom pieces, drained and chopped	10 oz.	284 mL

Cook broccoli in water in small saucepan until barely tender. Drain. Chop larger pieces.

Melt margarine in large saucepan. Add onion. Sauté until soft and clear.

Add remaining 4 ingredients. Stir. Add broccoli mixture. Heat and stir until cheese is melted. Serve hot. Makes 4 cups (1 L).

2 tbsp. (30 mL): 69 Calories; 6 g Total Fat; 172 mg Sodium; 2 g Protein; 2 g Carbohydrate; trace Dietary Fiber

Business is when you don't have any of, you go out of.

GARBANZO DIP

Serve with crackers, or Tortilla Crisps, page 115.

Cooking oil	2 tbsp.	30 mL
Chopped onion	1 cup	250 mL
Small green pepper, chopped	1	1
Chopped celery	1/3 cup	75 mL
Canned garbanzo beans (chick peas), drained	14 oz.	398 mL
Lemon juice	4 tsp.	20 mL
Dried whole oregano	1 tsp.	5 mL
Garlic powder	1/4 tsp.	1 mL
Salt	1/2 tsp.	2 mL
Pepper	1/8 tsp.	0.5 mL
Sliced ripe olives, for garnish		

Heat cooking oil in non-stick frying pan. Add onion, green pepper and celery. Sauté for 10 to 15 minutes until soft.

Combine next 6 ingredients in food processor or blender. Add onion mixture. Process until smooth.

Just before serving, garnish with olive slices. Makes 1$\frac{3}{4}$ cups (425 mL).

1 tbsp. (15 mL): 24 Calories; 1.2 g Total Fat; 65 mg Sodium; 1 g Protein; 3 g Carbohydrate; trace Dietary Fiber

Pictured on page 35.

1. Chili Con Queso, page 32
2. Tortilla Crisps, page 115
3. Tortilla Chips, page 113
4. Kidney Bean Dip, page 37
5. Guacamole, page 32
6. Green Chili Bites, page 52
7. Garbanzo Dip, page 34
8. Cheesy Roll-Ups, page 97
9. Chili Rolls, page 101
10. Tortilla Roll-Ups, page 95

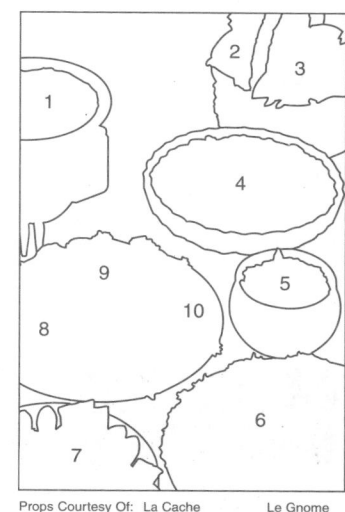

How much to serve...

How much to serve depends on the time of day and whether additional food will be offered. Allow four to five appetizers per person if your guests have already eaten, or if a meal is part of the event. If you're making an entire meal of hors d'oeuvres, use 10 to 12 pieces per guest as your guide. Keep a variety of cheeses and crackers on hand, as well as some ready-to-heat appetizers in your freezer, just in case people are hungrier than expected.

If you're into "hot" you can add more cayenne pepper to this. It has a good flavor and an attractive browned top. Serve with tortilla chips, raw vegetables or corn chips.

BOTTOM LAYER

Canned kidney beans, drained	**2 × 14 oz.**	**2 × 398 mL**
Salsa (mild or medium)	**6 tbsp.**	**100 mL**
Sliced green onion	**½ cup**	**125 mL**
Chili powder	**1 tsp.**	**5 mL**
Onion powder	**½ tsp.**	**2 mL**
Garlic powder	**¼ tsp.**	**1 mL**
White vinegar	**1 tsp.**	**5 mL**
Parsley flakes	**2 tsp.**	**10 mL**
Cayenne pepper	**¼ tsp.**	**1 mL**
Salt	**½ tsp.**	**2 mL**

TOP LAYER

Grated medium Cheddar cheese	**1 cup**	**250 mL**
Grated Monterey Jack cheese	**1 cup**	**250 mL**
Chili powder	**1 tsp.**	**5 mL**

Bottom Layer: Mash kidney beans with fork in medium bowl.

Add next 9 ingredients. Mix well. Spread in ungreased 9 inch (22 cm) pie plate or shallow casserole.

Top Layer: Sprinkle with layer of Cheddar cheese, followed by layer of Monterey Jack cheese. Sprinkle with chili powder. Bake, uncovered, in 350°F (175°C) oven for about 30 minutes. Makes about 4 cups (1 L).

1 tbsp. (15 mL): 24 Calories; 1.2 g Total Fat; 79 mg Sodium; 2 g Protein; 2 g Carbohydrate; 1 g Dietary Fiber

Pictured on page 35.

When the little worm grows up he wants to join the apple core.

BLUE CHEESE DIP

A robust flavor yet not overbearing. Serve with chips or vegetables. Great with Buffalo Wings, page 69.

Sour cream	1 cup	250 mL
Cream cheese, softened	4 oz.	125 g
Blue cheese, crumbled	1/2 cup	125 mL
Prepared horseradish	1 tsp.	5 mL
Lemon juice	1 tsp.	5 mL
Parsley flakes	1 tsp.	5 mL
Minced onion flakes	1 1/2 tsp.	7 mL
Salt	1/2 tsp.	2 mL

Mash all 8 ingredients in small bowl with fork or spoon. Beat with electric beater until fluffy. Makes 2 1/8 cups (530 mL).

1 tbsp. (15 mL): 30 Calories; 2.8 g Total Fat; 80 mg Sodium; 1 g Protein; 1 g Carbohydrate; trace Dietary Fiber

Pictured on page 107.

STRAWBERRY DIP

A pretty pink coating for fruit and cake.

Cut up fresh strawberries	1 cup	250 mL
Granulated sugar	1/4 cup	60 mL
Creamed cottage cheese, drained	1/3 cup	75 mL
Sour cream	1/3 cup	75 mL

Combine strawberries and sugar in small bowl. Stir. Let stand for 10 minutes, stirring twice. Drain in sieve. Place berries in blender.

Add cottage cheese and sour cream. Process until smooth. Turn into small bowl. Garnish as desired. Chill. Makes 1 1/2 cups (375 mL).

1 tbsp. (15 mL): 17 Calories; 0.5 g Total Fat; 15 mg Sodium; 1 g Protein; 3 g Carbohydrate; trace Dietary Fiber

Paré Pointer

When the prisoners put on a play, it was a cell out.

Dips

MANGO CHUTNEY DIP

This is also a good filling for Phyllo Nests, page 85. Fill each with 1½ tsp. (7 mL) filling. Serve with assorted crackers and chips.

Spreadable cream cheese	8 oz.	250 g
Mango chutney, chopped	⅓ cup	75 mL
Ground walnuts (or pecans)	½ cup	125 mL

Mix all 3 ingredients well in small bowl. Makes 1½ cups (375 mL).

1 tbsp. (15 mL): 51 Calories; 4.7 g Total Fat; 30 mg Sodium; 1 g Protein; 2 g Carbohydrate; trace Dietary Fiber

Pictured on front cover.

CRANBERRY DIP

So pretty for dunking fruit. But also a nice change with meat appetizers such as Party Meatballs, page 65, or Chicken Nuggets, page 62.

Canned cranberry jelly	14 oz.	398 mL
Lemon juice	2 tsp.	10 mL
Prepared mustard	½ tsp.	2 mL
Granulated sugar	2 tbsp.	30 mL

Mix all 4 ingredients in small bowl. Stir well. Makes 1½ cups (375 mL).

1 tbsp. (15 mL): 32 Calories; trace Total Fat; 7 mg Sodium; trace Protein; 8 g Carbohydrate; trace Dietary Fiber

Pictured on page 71.

FRUIT FROSTING

A dream dip that makes up quickly. Serve with fresh fruit.

Cream cheese, softened	8 oz.	250 g
Jar marshmallow cream	7 oz.	200 g
Milk	2 tbsp.	30 mL
Lemon juice	⅛ tsp.	0.5 mL

Beat all 4 ingredients together. Makes about 2 cups (500 mL).

1 tbsp. (15 mL): 45 Calories; 2.6 g Total Fat; 25 mg Sodium; 1 g Protein; 5 g Carbohydrate; 0 g Dietary Fiber

SPICY DIP

This cinnamon-flavored dip is just right for apples and other fruit. Place in a small dish in the center of a large plate or platter. Surround with cut fruit.

Sour cream	1 cup	250 mL
Brown sugar, packed	2 tbsp.	30 mL
Ground cinnamon	$1/8$ tsp.	0.5 mL
Brandy flavoring	1 tsp.	5 mL

Stir all 4 ingredients together in small bowl. Makes 1 cup (250 mL).

1 tbsp. (15 mL): 29 Calories; 2 g Total Fat; 7 mg Sodium; trace Protein; 2 g Carbohydrate; trace Dietary Fiber

MUSHROOM DIP

A chunky dip. Serve with potato chips or assorted crackers.

Hard margarine (or butter)	2 tbsp.	30 mL
Coarsely chopped fresh mushrooms (or sliced button mushrooms)	4 cups	1 L
Finely chopped onion	$1/2$ cup	125 mL
Worcestershire sauce	1 tbsp.	15 mL
Garlic powder	$1/2$ tsp.	2 mL
Light sour cream (see Note)	$1 1/2$ cups	375 mL
Dill weed	1 tsp.	5 mL

Melt margarine in large frying pan. Add mushrooms, onion, Worcestershire sauce and garlic powder. Sauté for 20 to 25 minutes, stirring often, until onion is soft and all liquid is evaporated.

Stir in sour cream and dill weed. Heat through. Turn into chafing dish. Makes $2 1/2$ cups (625 mL).

2 tbsp. (30 mL): 32 Calories; 2.4 g Total Fat; 30 mg Sodium; 1 g Protein; 2 g Carbohydrate; trace Dietary Fiber

Note: Add up to $1/2$ cup (125 mL) more sour cream if dip thickens while heating in chafing dish.

SIMPLE SWEET AND SOUR SAUCE

Perfect to dunk meatballs in this.

Brown sugar, packed	1 cup	250 mL
Cornstarch	2 tbsp.	30 mL
White vinegar	1/2 cup	125 mL
Pineapple juice (or water)	1/2 cup	125 mL

Stir brown sugar and cornstarch together in small saucepan.

Add vinegar and pineapple juice. Bring to a boil over medium stirring constantly until mixture is thickened. Makes 1 1/3 cups (325 mL).

1 tbsp. (15 mL): 46 Calories; trace Total Fat; 3 mg Sodium; trace Protein; 12 g Carbohydrate; trace Dietary Fiber

Pictured on page 125 and on back cover.

MUSHROOM DILL DIP

Very tasty. Dill adds a nice touch. Serve with assorted crackers, chips or raw vegetables.

Hard margarine (or butter)	1 tsp.	5 mL
Finely chopped fresh mushrooms	1 cup	250 mL
Chopped green onion	1/2 cup	125 mL
Light cream cheese, softened	4 oz.	125 g
Light sour cream	1/3 cup	75 mL
Light salad dressing (or mayonnaise)	3 tbsp.	50 mL
Dill weed	1 tsp.	5 mL
Garlic powder	1/8 tsp.	0.5 mL
Salt	1/8 tsp.	0.5 mL

Heat margarine in frying pan. Add mushrooms and green onion. Sauté until golden. Cool.

Beat remaining 6 ingredients together well in medium bowl until creamy. Fold in mushroom mixture. Makes 1 1/2 cups (375 mL).

1 tbsp. (15 mL): 15 Calories; 0.9 g Total Fat; 32 mg Sodium; 1 g Protein; 1 g Carbohydrate; trace Dietary Fiber

MEATBALL SAUCE

Double duty sauce. Drizzle over Party Meatballs, page 65, or other meatballs, or use as a dip.

Light sour cream	1 cup	250 mL
Prepared horseradish (not hot)	$\frac{1}{4}$ cup	60 mL
Onion salt	$\frac{1}{4}$ tsp.	1 mL
Seasoned salt	$\frac{1}{4}$ tsp.	1 mL

Mix all 4 ingredients in small bowl. Cover. Refrigerate until ready to serve. Makes about 1$\frac{1}{4}$ cups (300 mL).

1 tbsp. (15 mL): 12 Calories; 0.8 g Total Fat; 41 mg Sodium; trace Protein; 1 g Carbohydrate; trace Dietary Fiber

Pictured on page 71.

ORANGE COCONUT FRUIT DIP

Pale yellow in color. Serve with fruit pieces.

Creamed cottage cheese	2 cups	500 mL
Sour cream	$\frac{1}{4}$ cup	60 mL
Frozen concentrated orange juice	2 tbsp.	30 mL
Granulated sugar	2 tbsp.	30 mL
Fine (or medium) coconut	$\frac{1}{4}$ cup	60 mL
Finely grated orange peel, for garnish		

Measure first 4 ingredients into blender. Process until smooth. Turn into medium bowl.

Stir in coconut. Garnish with orange peel. Makes 1$\frac{1}{2}$ cups (375 mL).

1 tbsp. (15 mL): 30 Calories; 1.2 g Total Fat; 81 mg Sodium; 3 g Protein; 2 g Carbohydrate; trace Dietary Fiber

Paré Pointer

When the tailor couldn't find his scissors his pet frog said, "Rippit, rippit."

Dips

DOUBLE DILL DIP

Double the pleasure. A treat with fresh veggies.

Cream cheese, softened	4 oz.	125 g
Sour cream	2 cups	500 mL
Lemon juice	1 tsp.	5 mL
Parsley flakes	2 tsp.	10 mL
Onion flakes	2 tsp.	10 mL
Dill weed	2 tsp.	10 mL
Onion salt	1 tsp.	5 mL
Garlic powder	1/2 tsp.	2 mL
Jar of tangy dill bits, drained	13½ oz.	375 mL

Combine first 8 ingredients in blender. Process until smooth. Turn into medium bowl.

Stir in dill bits. Makes 4½ cups (1.1 L).

1 tbsp. (15 mL): 17 Calories; 1.5 g Total Fat; 68 mg Sodium; trace Protein; 1 g Carbohydrate; trace Dietary Fiber

ARTICHOKE DIP

Exceptionally good. Serve with chips or bread chunks.

Canned artichoke hearts, drained and finely chopped	14 oz.	398 mL
Salad dressing (or mayonnaise)	3/4 cup	175 mL
Sour cream	1/4 cup	60 mL
Grated Parmesan cheese	1/2 cup	125 mL
Onion salt	1/16 tsp.	0.5 mL
Garlic powder	1/16 tsp.	0.5 mL
Hot pepper sauce	1/16 tsp.	0.5 mL
Sliced (or slivered) almonds, toasted in 350°F (175°C) oven for about 5 minutes	1/2 cup	125 mL
Paprika	1/2 tsp.	2 mL

Mix first 7 ingredients well in medium bowl. Turn into ungreased 9 inch (22 cm) pie plate. Bake, uncovered, in 350°F (175°C) oven for 15 to 20 minutes until hot.

Sprinkle dip with almonds and paprika. Makes 2 cups (500 mL).

1 tbsp. (15 mL): 48 Calories; 4.1 g Total Fat; 87 mg Sodium; 1 g Protein; 2 g Carbohydrate; 1 g Dietary Fiber

HERB DIP

Vegetables and chips go well with this dip.

Cream cheese, softened	8 oz.	250 g
Plain yogurt	1 cup	250 mL
Salad dressing (or mayonnaise)	¼ cup	60 mL
Dried chopped chives	1 tbsp.	15 mL
Parsley flakes	1 tsp.	5 mL
Celery salt	½ tsp.	2 mL
Salt	¼ tsp.	1 mL
Dried thyme	¼ tsp.	1 mL
Garlic powder	¼ tsp.	1 mL
Dried sweet basil	¼ tsp.	1 mL
Onion powder	¼ tsp.	1 mL
Paprika, for garnish		

Beat first 11 ingredients together in small bowl until smooth. Chill for at least 2 hours before serving.

Garnish with paprika. Makes generous 2 cups (500 mL).

1 tbsp. (15 mL): 41 Calories; 3.7 g Total Fat; 80 mg Sodium; 1 g Protein; 1 g Carbohydrate; trace Dietary Fiber

SWEET CURRY DIP

Serve with assorted crackers, chips, raw vegetables or fresh fruit. Curry flavor is middle of the road.

Low-fat sweetened condensed milk	11 oz.	300 mL
White vinegar	⅓ cup	75 mL
Dry mustard	¾ tsp.	4 mL
Curry powder, more or less	¾ tsp.	4 mL
Garlic powder	⅛ tsp.	0.5 mL

Stir all 5 ingredients together well in small bowl. Makes 1⅓ cups (325 mL).

1 tbsp. (15 mL): 60 Calories; 0.7 g Total Fat; 23 mg Sodium; 1 g Protein; 10 g Carbohydrate; trace Dietary Fiber

Pictured on page 53.

APPLE AND DIP

A merry-go-round of red-edged apple slices makes for a very showy appetizer. Invite guests to help themselves. This is good enough to be dessert.

Light cream cheese, softened	8 oz.	250 g
Brown sugar, packed	3/4 cup	175 mL
Vanilla	1 tbsp.	15 mL
Red-skinned apples, cut into thin wedges (about 32 in total)	2	2
Lemon juice	1/4 cup	60 mL

Beat cream cheese, brown sugar and vanilla in medium bowl until smooth. Turn into small serving dish on plate.

Dip apple wedges into lemon juice to prevent browning. Arrange on plate, surrounding dip. Makes 1 cup (250 mL).

1 tbsp. (15 mL) plus 2 apple wedges: 67 Calories; 1.3 g Total Fat; 75 mg Sodium; 1 g Protein; 13 g Carbohydrate; trace Dietary Fiber

SPRING DIP

The color of daffodils with orange and green flecks. Exceptionally good. Serve with assorted raw vegetables, cut bite size.

Chopped onion	1 tbsp.	15 mL
Grated carrot, packed	1/3 cup	75 mL
Medium green pepper, cut up	1/2	1/2
White vinegar	1 tbsp.	15 mL
Salad dressing (or mayonnaise)	1/2 cup	125 mL
Process yellow cheese spread	1/2 cup	125 mL

Place first 4 ingredients in blender. Process until crumbly smooth, not puréed.

Add salad dressing and cheese. Stir well. Best served same day. Makes generous 1 1/3 cups (325 mL).

1 tbsp. (15 mL): 47 Calories; 4 g Total Fat; 133 mg Sodium; 1 g Protein; 2 g Carbohydrate; trace Dietary Fiber

HOT CRAB DIP

Just the right amount of zip to this good dip. Serve hot with assorted crackers.

Cream cheese, softened	8 oz.	250 g
White (or alcohol-free white) wine	1 tbsp.	15 mL
Salad dressing (or mayonnaise)	2 tbsp.	30 mL
Prepared mustard	1/2 tsp.	2 mL
Onion flakes	2 tsp.	10 mL
Seasoned salt	1/2 tsp.	2 mL
Canned crabmeat, drained and cartilage removed	5 oz.	142 g

Place first 6 ingredients in small bowl. Beat until smooth. Turn into double boiler.

Fold crabmeat into cream cheese mixture using a spatula. Heat over simmering water. Makes 1²/₃ cups (400 mL).

1 tbsp. (15 mL): 41 Calories; 3.7 g Total Fat; 93 mg Sodium; 1 g Protein; 1 g Carbohydrate; trace Dietary Fiber

BACON DIP

Smoky, creamy taste. Quite thick. Creamy white with green and brown bits. Serve with fresh assorted vegetables and potato chips. Also good spread on crackers.

Bacon slices, diced, cooked and drained (1/2 lb., 225 g)	8	8
Sour cream	2/3 cup	150 mL
Parsley flakes	1 tsp.	5 mL
Onion powder	1/8 tsp.	0.5 mL
Garlic salt	1/8 tsp.	0.5 mL
Cayenne pepper	1/16 tsp.	0.5 mL

Stir all 6 ingredients together in small bowl. Cover. Store in refrigerator overnight to blend flavors. Makes 1 cup (250 mL).

1 tbsp. (15 mL): 33 Calories; 2.9 g Total Fat; 63 mg Sodium; 1 g Protein; trace Carbohydrate; trace Dietary Fiber

An elegant first course, especially the mini cheeses.

PASTRY

All-purpose flour	¾ cup	175 mL
Brown sugar, packed	1 tsp.	5 mL
Baking powder	¼ tsp.	1 mL
Salt	¼ tsp.	1 mL
Hard margarine (or butter)	6 tbsp.	100 mL
Cold water	2 tbsp.	30 mL
Gouda cheese rounds, red wax removed	2 × 7 oz.	2 × 200 g
Ground walnuts (or pecans)	½ cup	125 mL

Pastry: Stir flour, brown sugar, baking powder and salt in medium bowl. Cut in margarine with pastry blender until mixture is crumbly.

Add cold water. Mix dough into a ball, adding a bit more water if needed. Divide into 4 equal portions. Roll out each portion on lightly floured surface into 6 inch (15 cm) circles.

Set cheese rounds on 2 pastry circles. Cover tops of cheese with walnuts. Set remaining 2 pastry circles in place over walnuts. Moisten edges with water. Crimp together to seal. Bake in 425°F (220°C) oven for 20 to 25 minutes until lightly browned. Each round cuts into 10 wedges, for a total of 20.

1 wedge: 139 Calories; 10.7 g Total Fat; 243 mg Sodium; 6 g Protein; 5 g Carbohydrate; trace Dietary Fiber

BABY GOUDAS EN CROÛTE:
Pastry, see above

Baby Gouda cheese rounds, red wax removed	6 × ¾ oz.	6 × 21 g
Ground walnuts (or pecans)	2 tbsp.	30 mL

Divide pastry into 12 portions. Roll out each portion on lightly floured surface into 3 inch (7.5 cm) circles.

Place 1 baby Gouda on each of 6 pastry circles. Sprinkle with 1 tsp. (5 mL) walnuts. Cover with remaining 6 pastry circles. Moisten edges with water. Crimp together to seal. Bake in 425°F (220°C) oven for 12 to 15 minutes. Makes 6.

BRIE EN CROÛTE: Omit Gouda cheese and use Brie instead.

CRAB-STUFFED EGGS

Always a winner on an appetizer tray. Also used as an extra for a cold salad plate. Cut eggs lengthwise, or crosswise—either way works just fine.

Large hard-boiled eggs, peeled	12	12
Mayonnaise (not salad dressing)	$1/3$ cup	75 mL
Prepared mustard	$1/2$ tsp.	2 mL
Lemon juice	$1/2$ tsp.	2 mL
Dill weed	$1/8$ tsp.	0.5 mL
Seasoned salt	$1/4$ tsp.	1 mL
Chopped chives	2 tsp.	10 mL
Dried whole oregano	$1/8$ tsp.	0.5 mL
Canned crabmeat, drained and cartilage removed	1 cup	250 mL
Paprika, sprinkle		

Cut eggs in half crosswise. Carefully remove yolks to small bowl. Place egg white halves on flat surface. Set aside. Mash yolks with fork.

Add next 8 ingredients. Mix well. If too dry, add a bit of milk. Makes 2 cups (500 mL) filling. Fill egg white halves. A pastry tube makes an attractive design.

Sprinkle with paprika. Makes 24.

1 stuffed egg half: 67 Calories; 5.3 g Total Fat; 106 mg Sodium; 4 g Protein; trace Carbohydrate; trace Dietary Fiber

Pictured on page 53.

SHRIMP-STUFFED EGGS: Use chopped cooked fresh (or frozen, thawed) shrimp instead of crabmeat.

FROZEN CHEESE PUFFS

Rich-tasting pastry encloses green olives. These look great.

Hard margarine (or butter), softened	$1/2$ cup	125 mL
All-purpose flour	1 cup	250 mL
Grated sharp Cheddar cheese, room temperature	2 cups	500 mL
Small pimiento-stuffed green olives	30	30

(continued on next page)

Work margarine and flour together well in large bowl.

Add cheese. Mix well, warming with your hands to work mixture together. Divide and roll into 1 inch (2.5 cm) balls.

Flatten each ball and shape around olive, sealing dough together. Freeze in single layer on baking sheet. Store in plastic bag or container in freezer. Bake from frozen state on ungreased baking sheet in 375°F (190°C) oven for 10 to 15 minutes until puffy and lightly browned. Makes 2½ dozen.

1 cheese puff: 117 Calories; 10.3 g Total Fat; 904 mg Sodium; 3 g Protein; 4 g Carbohydrate; 2 g Dietary Fiber

CHEESE THINS

Large thin wafers that are crispy good. Makes a showy basketful. Serve with Double Dill Dip, page 43.

All-purpose flour	2 cups	500 mL
Grated sharp Cheddar cheese	1 cup	250 mL
Granulated sugar	1 tbsp.	15 mL
Baking soda	½ tsp.	2 mL
Salt	½ tsp.	2 mL
Onion powder	¼ tsp.	1 mL
Cayenne pepper	¹⁄₁₆ tsp.	0.5 mL
Cooking oil	¼ cup	60 mL
Water	½ cup	125 mL

Measure first 7 ingredients into medium bowl. Stir well.

Add cooking oil and water. Mix until dough forms a ball. Cover. Let stand for 20 minutes. Divide into 4 portions. Roll out 1 portion paper thin on lightly floured surface. Cut into 8 wedges. Arrange wedges on ungreased baking sheet. Bake in 375°F (190°C) oven for about 10 minutes until crisp and browned. Repeat for remaining dough. Makes 32 wedges.

1 wedge: 63 Calories; 3.1 g Total Fat; 87 mg Sodium; 2 g Protein; 7 g Carbohydrate; trace Dietary Fiber

Paré Pointer

Woman complaining to marriage counselor about her husband: "When he won a trip for two to Hawaii, he went twice!"

MINI CHEESE BALLS

Offer a variety of tastes and colors with these tiny individual balls.

Grated sharp Cheddar cheese	2 cups	500 mL
Cream cheese, softened	4 oz.	125 g
Worcestershire sauce	½ tsp.	2 mL
Lemon juice	1 tsp.	5 mL
Seasoned salt	½ tsp.	2 mL
COATINGS		
Toasted sesame seeds	2 tbsp.	30 mL
Chili powder	2 tsp.	10 mL
Dill weed	2 tsp.	10 mL

Combine first 5 ingredients in medium bowl. Mix. Shape into 24 walnut-size balls.

Coatings: Roll ⅓ of balls in sesame seeds. Roll ⅓ of balls in chili powder until dark. Roll remaining ⅓ of balls in dill weed. If you prefer, all balls can be rolled to look the same. Makes 24.

1 cheese ball: 64 Calories; 5.5 g Total Fat; 110 mg Sodium; 3 g Protein; 1 g Carbohydrate; trace Dietary Fiber

Pictured on page 53.

SPINACH SQUARES

Cheese and spinach are a natural combination.

Hard margarine (or butter)	¼ cup	60 mL
Large eggs	3	3
All-purpose flour	1 cup	250 mL
Milk	1 cup	250 mL
Salt	1 tsp.	5 mL
Baking powder	1 tsp.	5 mL
Grated Havarti cheese	4 cups	1 L
Frozen chopped spinach, thawed and squeezed dry	2 × 10 oz.	2 × 300 g

Melt margarine in large saucepan.

Add next 5 ingredients. Mix.

(continued on next page)

Add cheese and spinach. Stir together. Turn into greased 9 x 13 inch (22 x 33 cm) pan. Bake in 350°F (175°C) oven for about 35 minutes until set and browned. Cool. Cuts into 54 squares.

1 square: 56 Calories; 3.6 g Total Fat; 142 mg Sodium; 3 g Protein; 3 g Carbohydrate; trace Dietary Fiber

CRISPY CHEESE WAFERS

These deliver crunch and heat. A winner.

Hard margarine (or butter), softened	1 cup	250 mL
Grated medium Cheddar cheese, room temperature	2 cups	500 mL
Cayenne pepper	½ tsp.	2 mL
Salt	½ tsp.	2 mL
All-purpose flour	2 cups	500 mL
Crisp rice cereal	2 cups	500 mL

Cream margarine and cheese in large bowl. Mix in cayenne pepper and salt.

Add flour. Work in until dough is soft.

Add cereal. Mix. Shape into 2 rolls about 2 inches (5 cm) in diameter. Roll up in waxed paper. Chill for 2 hours. Slice 1/4 inch (6 mm) thick. Arrange on well-greased baking sheet. Bake in 350°F (175°C) oven for 15 to 16 minutes until browned. Makes about 60.

1 wafer: 65 Calories; 4.6 g Total Fat; 96 mg Sodium; 2 g Protein; 4 g Carbohydrate; trace Dietary Fiber

Yeast is one of the major causes of inflation.

GREEN CHILI BITES

This really is yummy. Both spicy-hot and oven-hot.

Large eggs	5	5
All-purpose flour	1/4 cup	60 mL
Baking powder	1/2 tsp.	2 mL
Salt	1/4 tsp.	1 mL
Pepper	1/8 tsp.	0.5 mL
Hard margarine (or butter), melted	1/4 cup	60 mL
Canned diced green chilies, drained	4 oz.	114 mL
Grated Monterey Jack cheese	2 cups	500 mL
Creamed cottage cheese, mashed with fork	1 cup	250 mL
Hot pepper sauce	1/4 tsp.	1 mL

Beat eggs in medium bowl until frothy. Add flour, baking powder, salt, pepper, and margarine. Beat well.

Stir in green chilies, Monterey Jack cheese, cottage cheese and hot pepper sauce. Pour into greased 9 x 9 inch (22 x 22 cm) square pan. Bake in 350°F (175°C) oven for 35 to 45 minutes until lightly browned and set. Serve hot. Cuts into 36 appetizer squares, or serves 9 as a main course starter.

1 appetizer square: *56 Calories; 4.2 g Total Fat; 126 mg Sodium; 3 g Protein; 1 g Carbohydrate; trace Dietary Fiber*

Pictured on page 35.

1. Ham Turnovers, page 91
2. Cheese Triangles, page 93
3. Sweet Curry Dip, page 44
4. Gougère, page 55
5. Apricot Cheese Spread, page 122
6. Party Crackers, page 117
7. Salad Horns, page 138
8. Crab-Stuffed Eggs, page 48
9. Bruschetta Brie, page 124
10. Mini Cheese Balls, page 50
11. Dolmades, page 104

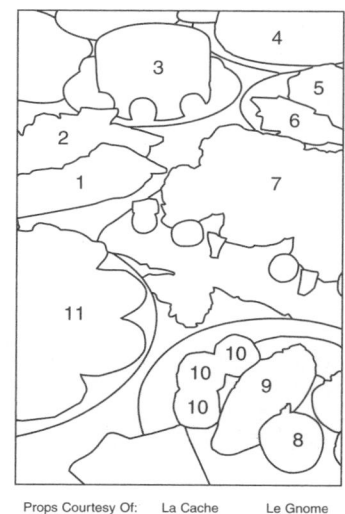

Props Courtesy Of: La Cache   Le Gnome
Stokes   The Bay

Hors d'Oeuvres

Getting ready...

For early evening nibbling, set out snacks, nuts, marinated olives and, just before guests are to arrive, cold dips and dippers. Divide cold selections into two serving vessels to make replenishment easy. With hot hors d'oeuvres, prepare as much as you can in advance. Before the party, arrange them on baking trays for reheating or quick baking in the oven at serving time.

This is a sort of cheese cake from the Burgundy region in France. Goo-ZHAIR resembles cream puffs or Yorkshire Pudding. Can be served hot or cold, but should be cut first as it is a bit greasy in the hands because of the cheese.

Water	1 cup	250 mL
Hard margarine (or butter)	½ cup	125 mL
Salt	1 tsp.	5 mL
All-purpose flour	1 cup	250 mL
Large eggs	4	4
Grated Gruyère cheese	1 cup	250 mL
Large egg, fork-beaten, for topping	1	1
Grated Gruyère cheese, for topping	¼ cup	60 mL

Bring water, margarine and salt to a boil in medium saucepan.

Add flour all at once. Stir briskly until mixture is smooth and thickened and pulls away from sides of pan. Remove from heat.

Add eggs, 1 at a time, beating thoroughly with a spoon after each addition.

Add first amount of cheese. Work into mixture. Using greased 9 or 10 inch (22 or 25 cm) pie plate, pipe or pile dough into puffs around edge. Fill in center and pile on top as necessary. Brush top with egg.

Sprinkle with second amount of Gruyère cheese. Bake in 400°F (205°C) oven for 30 to 35 minutes until puffed and browned. Serve hot or cold. Cuts into 16 wedges.

1 wedge: 145 Calories; 10.6 g Total Fat; 291 mg Sodium; 6 g Protein; 7 g Carbohydrate; trace Dietary Fiber

Pictured on page 53.

You better keep going even if you are on the right track. You could get run over.

MARINATED SHRIMP

Takes extra time to get this into the refrigerator but it's ready to serve with barely any effort. Serve with wooden picks.

Water	2½ qts.	2.5 L
Salt	4 tsp.	20 mL
Mustard seed	1 tsp.	5 mL
Bay leaves	3	3
Whole allspice	1 tsp.	5 mL
Whole cloves	1 tsp.	5 mL
Dried crushed chilies	2 tsp.	10 mL
Whole peppercorns	1 tsp.	5 mL
Fresh medium shrimp in shells (70-80 shrimp)	2 lbs.	900 g
MARINADE		
Cooking oil	¼ cup	60 mL
White vinegar	⅓ cup	75 mL
Water	½ cup	125 mL
Celery seed	1 tsp.	5 mL
Celery salt	½ tsp.	2 mL
Cayenne pepper	⅛ tsp.	0.5 mL
Salt	½ tsp.	2 mL
Worcestershire sauce	2 tbsp.	30 mL
Prepared mustard	1 tsp.	5 mL
Large onion, thinly sliced	1	1

Heat water and salt in large pot or Dutch oven until boiling.

Tie next 6 ingredients in double layer of cheesecloth. Add to boiling water.

Add shrimp. Return to a boil. Boil, uncovered, for 2 to 3 minutes until shrimp are curled and pinkish. Drain. Cool and shell. Discard cheesecloth bag and contents.

Marinade: Mix first 9 ingredients in small bowl. Layer ½ of shrimp in large bowl.

Add ½ of onion over top. Cover with second ½ of shrimp and remaining ½ of onion. Pour marinade over all. Cover. Let stand in refrigerator for at least 24 hours. Turn out into dish or onto large platter. Makes about 75.

1 shrimp (with marinade): 20 Calories; 0.9 g Total Fat; 56 mg Sodium; 3 g Protein; trace Carbohydrate; trace Dietary Fiber

Pictured on page 89.

Hors d'Oeuvres

This makes a large quantity. Filling freezes well, allowing you to prepare as much as you like.

Boiling water	1 tbsp.	15 mL
Seafood bouillon powder	1 tsp.	5 mL
Cream cheese, softened	8 oz.	250 g
Pepper	1/16 tsp.	0.5 mL
Worcestershire sauce	1/8 tsp.	0.5 mL
Onion powder	1/4 tsp.	1 mL
Parsley flakes	1 tsp.	5 mL
Prepared horseradish	1/2 tsp.	2 mL
Balsamic vinegar (or lemon juice)	1 tsp.	5 mL
Cooked fresh (or frozen cooked, thawed) shrimp, chopped	6 oz.	170 g
Cherry tomatoes	36	36

Stir boiling water into bouillon powder in small bowl. Add next 7 ingredients. Mash together well with fork.

Add shrimp. Mix well. Makes 1½ cups (375 mL) filling.

Cut tomatoes in half crosswise. Scoop out seeds. Stuff with cream cheese filling by piping or spooning 1 tsp. (5 mL) into each half. Makes 72.

*1 **stuffed tomato half:** 16 Calories; 1.3 g Total Fat; 25 mg Sodium; 1 g Protein; trace Carbohydrate; trace Dietary Fiber*

Pictured on front cover.

You can eat beef all your life and be as strong as an ox, but you can eat fish all your life and not swim a stroke.

SHRIMP KABOBS

Succulent. Fancy to look at, but easy to make ahead of time.

Cooking oil	1 tbsp.	15 mL
Hard margarine (or butter), melted	3 tbsp.	50 mL
Lemon juice	1 tbsp.	15 mL
Soy sauce	1 tbsp.	15 mL
Parsley flakes	1 tbsp.	15 mL
Garlic salt	1/8 tsp.	0.5 mL
Fresh medium shrimp, peeled and deveined	24	24

Combine first 6 ingredients in medium bowl. Stir.

Add shrimp. Place in plastic bag. Close tightly. Marinate in refrigerator for 20 minutes, turning bag often. Empty contents into medium-hot frying pan. Stir-fry for about 5 minutes until shrimp are curled and pinkish. Cool shrimp and marinade. Soak twelve 4 inch (10 cm) wooden skewers in water for 10 minutes. Place 2 shrimp on each skewer. Chill skewers and marinade until just before serving. When ready to serve, heat marinade. Place skewers on ungreased baking sheet. Brush shrimp with marinade. Discard any remaining marinade. Heat kabobs in 400°F (205°C) oven for 3 to 5 minutes until hot. Makes 12.

1 kabob: *43 Calories; 3.9 g Total Fat; 148 mg Sodium; 2 g Protein; trace Carbohydrate; trace Dietary Fiber*

Pictured on page 71.

CRAB RANGOON

Serve these wontons hot from the fresh or frozen state. Try dipping in Simple Sweet And Sour Sauce, page 41.

Cream cheese, softened	4 oz.	125 g
Garlic cloves, minced (or 1/4-1/2 tsp., 1-2 mL, garlic powder)	1-2	1-2
Salt	1/4 tsp.	1 mL
Hot pepper sauce	1/8 tsp.	0.5 mL
Green onions, thinly sliced	2	2
Canned crabmeat, drained and cartilage removed	1 cup	250 mL
Square wonton wrappers	48	48
Cooking oil, for deep-frying		

(continued on next page)

Mash cream cheese, garlic, salt and hot pepper sauce well in small bowl. Mix in green onion and crabmeat.

❶ Place about 1 tsp. (5 mL) filling in center of each wrapper. Moisten 2 adjoining edges. ❷ Fold center moistened point over filling, tucking point under filling. ❸ Bring remaining 2 moistened corners to center just above tucked edge, overlapping slightly. Press down on points to seal.

Deep-fry a few at a time in hot 375°F (190°C) cooking oil for about 1 minute until golden brown. Serve immediately, or cool and freeze at this point. Reheat on greased baking sheet in 400°F (205°C) oven for about 5 minutes until hot. Makes 48.

1 appetizer: *23 Calories; 1.6 g Total Fat; 54 mg Sodium; 1 g Protein; 1 g Carbohydrate; trace Dietary Fiber*

Pictured on page 125 and on back cover.

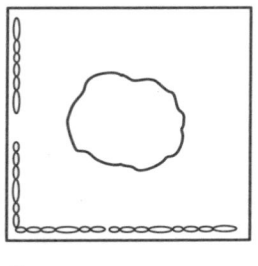

❶

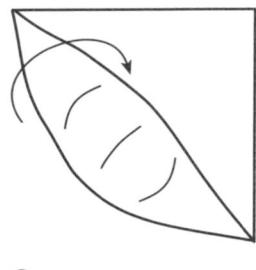

❷

❸

TRIPLE SATAY

Wonderful flavor. Melt-in-your-mouth tender.

Boneless, skinless chicken breast halves (about 2), cut into ¾ inch (2 cm) cubes	½ lb.	225 g
Beef tenderloin, cut into ¾ inch (2 cm) cubes	½ lb.	225 g
Pork tenderloin, cut into ¾ inch (2 cm) cubes	½ lb.	225 g
Soy sauce	½ cup	125 mL
Cooking oil	2 tbsp.	30 mL
White vinegar	¼ cup	60 mL
Granulated sugar	¼ cup	60 mL
Ground ginger	½ tsp.	2 mL
Garlic powder	¼ tsp.	1 mL
Chili powder	½ tsp.	2 mL
SATAY SAUCE		
Smooth peanut butter	½ cup	125 mL
Soy sauce	1 tbsp.	15 mL
Chili sauce	2 tbsp.	30 mL
Dried crushed chilies	¼ tsp.	1 mL
Fine coconut	1 tbsp.	15 mL
Brown sugar, packed	2 tbsp.	30 mL
Onion powder	¼ tsp.	1 mL
Skim evaporated milk	½ cup	125 mL

Put chicken, beef and pork cubes into medium bowl with tight fitting lid, or into 3 separate bowls if desired.

Mix remaining 7 ingredients in small bowl. Pour over cubes. Cover. Shake or turn to coat. Chill for several hours or overnight. Soak eighteen 4 inch (10 cm) wooden skewers in water for 10 minutes. Thread 1 cube of each meat onto each skewer. Lay on ungreased broiler tray. Broil about 4 inches (10 cm) from heat for about 5 minutes, turning at half-time, until cooked.

Satay Sauce: Mix all 8 ingredients in medium saucepan. Heat and stir until boiling. Simmer for 5 minutes, stirring constantly. Makes 1 cup (250 mL) sauce. Serve in small bowl with kabobs. Makes 18.

1 kabob (with sauce): 134 Calories; 6.7 g Total Fat; 608 mg Sodium; 11 g Protein; 8 g Carbohydrate; 1 g Dietary Fiber

Pictured on page 71.

And a snap to make. Good taste. Sweet and dark soy flavor.

Whole chicken wings (or drumettes)	3 lbs.	1.4 kg
Apple juice	½ cup	125 mL
Soy sauce	½ cup	125 mL
Brown sugar, packed	½ cup	125 mL
Garlic powder (optional)	⅛ tsp.	0.5 mL

Remove wing tips and discard. Cut wings apart at joint. Arrange in single layer on greased baking sheet with sides or pan lined with greased foil.

Stir remaining 4 ingredients together well in medium bowl. Pour over chicken. Bake, uncovered, in 400°F (205°C) oven for about 1 hour, basting frequently, until sticky and glazed. Makes about 36 wing pieces or 24 drumettes.

1 piece (with sauce): 100 Calories; 6.1 g Total Fat; 270 mg Sodium; 7 g Protein; 4 g Carbohydrate; trace Dietary Fiber

Pictured on page 71.

Caramel-colored sauce sticks well to each sausage. Very quick and easy.

Brown sugar, packed	½ cup	125 mL
All-purpose flour	2 tbsp.	30 mL
White vinegar	⅓ cup	75 mL
Pineapple juice	½ cup	125 mL
Soy sauce	2 tsp.	10 mL
Ketchup	1 tsp.	5 mL
Smoked cocktail sausages	1½ lbs.	680 g

Stir brown sugar and flour in small saucepan until well mixed.

Add vinegar, pineapple juice, soy sauce, and ketchup. Heat and stir until sauce is boiling and thickened.

Add sausages. Cover. Simmer to heat through. Serve in chafing dish. Makes about 48.

1 sausage (with sauce): 52 Calories; 3.6 g Total Fat; 152 mg Sodium; 2 g Protein; 3 g Carbohydrate; trace Dietary Fiber

Pictured on page 89.

CHICKEN NUGGETS

Ground turkey may also be used for this. Bite-size balls are very tasty.

Ground raw chicken	1 lb.	454 g
Onion flakes	2 tsp.	10 mL
Large egg	1	1
Fine dry bread crumbs	1/2 cup	125 mL
Milk	1/3 cup	75 mL
Dried thyme	1/2 tsp.	2 mL
Salt	3/4 tsp.	4 mL
Salad dressing (or mayonnaise)	1/4 cup	60 mL
Milk	2 tbsp.	30 mL
Fine dry bread crumbs	2/3 cup	150 mL
Paprika	1 tsp.	5 mL

Combine first 7 ingredients in medium bowl. Mix well. Let chill in refrigerator for about 1 hour to firm for easier rolling. Shape into 1 inch (2.5 cm) balls.

Mix salad dressing and second amount of milk in small bowl.

Stir second amount of bread crumbs and paprika together. Dip chicken balls into salad dressing mixture then coat with crumb mixture. Arrange in single layer on greased baking sheet or pan lined with greased foil. Bake in 425°F (220°C) oven for 15 to 20 minutes until cooked. Makes about 36.

1 nugget: 41 Calories; 1.4 g Total Fat; 106 mg Sodium; 4 g Protein; 3 g Carbohydrate; trace Dietary Fiber

Pictured on page 71.

CRUSTY PARMESAN WINGS

Flavorful Parmesan gives wings a real lift. Great for munching.

Grated Parmesan cheese	1 cup	250 mL
Fine dry bread crumbs	1/2 cup	125 mL
Paprika	1 1/2 tsp.	7 mL
Golden Italian dressing	3/4 cup	175 mL
Whole chicken wings (or drumettes)	3 lbs.	1.4 kg

(continued on next page)

Hors d'Oeuvres

Combine cheese, bread crumbs and paprika in small bowl. Stir well.

Pour dressing into separate small bowl.

Remove wing tips and discard. Cut wings apart at joint. Dip each piece into dressing then coat with cheese mixture. Arrange in single layer on greased baking sheet with sides or pan lined with greased foil. Bake in 350°F (175°C) oven for about 45 minutes until tender. Serve warm. These may be prepared ahead. Reheat in 350°F (175°C) oven for about 10 minutes until hot. Makes about 36 wing pieces or 24 drumettes.

1 coated piece: 136 Calories; 10.6 g Total Fat; 176 mg Sodium; 8 g Protein; 2 g Carbohydrate; trace Dietary Fiber

Pictured on page 71.

CHICKEN WINGS SESAME

The sesame flavor comes through well in these delicious morsels. Nice in appearance too.

Large eggs	2	2
Prepared mustard	2 tbsp.	30 mL
Cooking oil	2 tbsp.	30 mL
Brown sugar, packed	2 tbsp.	30 mL
Salt	1 tsp.	5 mL
Fine dry bread crumbs	1¼ cups	300 mL
Sesame seeds	⅓ cup	75 mL
Whole chicken wings (or drumettes)	3 lbs.	1.4 kg

Beat eggs with whisk or fork in small bowl. Add next 4 ingredients. Mix well.

Mix bread crumbs and sesame seeds in separate small bowl.

Remove wing tips and discard. Cut wings apart at joint. Dip pieces into egg mixture then into bread crumb mixture. Arrange in single layer on greased baking sheet with sides or pan lined with greased foil. Bake in 425°F (220°C) oven for 25 to 30 minutes, turning at halftime. Makes about 36 wing pieces or 24 drumettes.

1 coated piece: 123 Calories; 8.1 g Total Fat; 148 mg Sodium; 8 g Protein; 4 g Carbohydrate; trace Dietary Fiber

Pictured on page 71.

SWEET AND SOUR SAUSAGE BALLS

Sauce is more sweet than sour.

Sausage meat	2 lbs.	900 g
Fine dry bread crumbs	⅔ cup	150 mL
Large egg, fork-beaten	1	1
SWEET AND SOUR SAUCE		
Canned pineapple tidbits, drained	14 oz.	398 mL
Ketchup	¾ cup	175 mL
Chili sauce	½ cup	125 mL
Brown sugar, packed	⅓ cup	75 mL
Soy sauce	1 tbsp.	15 mL
Lemon juice	1 tbsp.	15 mL
Garlic powder	⅛ tsp.	0.5 mL
Ground ginger	⅛ tsp.	0.5 mL

Shape sausage meat into 1 inch (2.5 cm) balls. Arrange in single layer on ungreased baking sheet. Bake in 350°F (175°C) oven for 15 to 20 minutes. Drain well.

Sweet And Sour Sauce: Combine all 8 ingredients in large frying pan. Add cooked sausage balls. Bring sauce to a boil. When hot, turn into chafing dish. Makes about 40.

1 ball (with sauce): 72 Calories; 4.1 g Total Fat; 240 mg Sodium; 2 g Protein; 7 g Carbohydrate; trace Dietary Fiber

Pictured on page 107.

SZECHUAN SATAY

So rich looking. Delicious ginger and garlic flavors.

Beef sirloin steak	1 lb.	454 g
Soy sauce	3 tbsp.	50 mL
Granulated sugar	2 tsp.	10 mL
Minced gingerroot	1 tbsp.	15 mL
Garlic powder (or 2 cloves, minced)	½ tsp.	2 mL
Dried crushed chilies	½ tsp.	2 mL

Cut steak into ⅛ inch (3 mm) thick slices. Cut long slices in half. This is easier to do if steak is partially frozen.

Stir remaining 5 ingredients in medium bowl. Add meat strips. Stir to coat. Let stand for 30 minutes, stirring often.

(continued on next page)

Hors d'Oeuvres

Soak twenty-six 4 inch (10 cm) wooden skewers in water for 10 minutes. Thread skewers with meat strips. Place on wire rack over baking sheet with sides. Broil about 5 inches (12.5 cm) from heat for 6 to 8 minutes, turning once, until medium doneness. When ready to serve, set on greased baking sheet. Bake in 400°F (205°C) oven for 5 minutes until hot. Makes about 26.

1 kabob: 24 Calories; 0.7 g Total Fat; 129 mg Sodium; 4 g Protein; 1 g Carbohydrate; trace Dietary Fiber

Pictured on page 71.

PARTY MEATBALLS

Contains beef and turkey. Gently spiced. Serve with cocktail picks.

Fine dry bread crumbs	²/₃ **cup**	**150 mL**
Salt	1¹/₂ **tsp.**	**7 mL**
Pepper	¹/₄ **tsp.**	**1 mL**
Garlic powder	¹/₂ **tsp.**	**2 mL**
Onion powder	¹/₂ **tsp.**	**2 mL**
Ground nutmeg, large measure	¹/₄ **tsp.**	**1 mL**
Large egg, fork-beaten	**1**	**1**
Water	¹/₄ **cup**	**60 mL**
Lean ground beef	**1 lb.**	**454 g**
Lean ground raw turkey	**1 lb.**	**454 g**

Combine first 6 ingredients in large bowl.

Stir in egg and water.

Add ground beef and ground turkey. Mix well. Shape into 1 inch (2.5 cm) balls. Arrange in single layer on greased baking sheets with sides. Bake in 350°F (175°C) oven for 15 to 18 minutes. May be cooled, then frozen in single layer and placed in plastic bags or containers. Reheat from frozen state in 400°F (205°C) oven for 5 to 10 minutes until hot. Makes about 80.

1 coated meatball: 23 Calories; 1.1 g Total Fat; 64 mg Sodium; 2 g Protein; 1 g Carbohydrate; trace Dietary Fiber

Pictured on front cover and on page 71.

PACIFIC RIBS

The thick brown sauce clings to the ribs. This one doesn't take much attention while cooking.

Pork spareribs, cut into short lengths (sweet and sour cut)	2 lbs.	900 g
Strained plums (baby food)	4½ oz.	128 mL
Apple cider vinegar	3 tbsp.	50 mL
Brown sugar, packed	½ cup	125 mL
Ketchup	3 tbsp.	50 mL
Ground ginger	1 tsp.	5 mL
Garlic powder	½ tsp.	2 mL
Salt	½ tsp.	2 mL
Pepper	⅛ tsp.	0.5 mL

Cut ribs apart into individual bones. Place in small roaster lined with greased foil.

Stir remaining 8 ingredients together in small bowl. Pour over ribs. Stir to coat. Cover. Bake in 350°F (175°C) oven for 2 hours, stirring every 20 to 30 minutes. Remove cover. Bake for 10 to 15 minutes. Drain. Makes about 40.

1 rib (with sauce): 42 Calories; 2 g Total Fat; 58 mg Sodium; 2 g Protein; 4 g Carbohydrate; trace Dietary Fiber

Pictured on page 71.

SWEET BACON DOGS

So easy and so good.

Wieners (1 lb., 454 g)	12	12
Thin bacon slices, each cut into 3 pieces	16	16
Brown sugar, packed	¼ cup	60 mL

Cut each wiener into 4 pieces. Wrap each piece with bacon, securing with wooden pick. Roll in brown sugar. Arrange in single layer on greased baking sheet or pan lined with greased foil. Sprinkle any remaining brown sugar over top. Bake in 250°F (120°C) oven for about 1½ hours. Serve warm. May be cooled and frozen. Reheat in 350°F (175°C) oven until bacon just begins to sizzle. Makes 48.

1 bacon dog: 47 Calories; 3.8 g Total Fat; 139 mg Sodium; 2 g Protein; 1 g Carbohydrate; trace Dietary Fiber

Pictured on page 107.

A different and satisfying way to serve ribs without the usual sweet, sticky sauce.

Pork spareribs	2¹⁄₄ lbs.	1 kg
Water	1 cup	250 mL
White vinegar	3 tbsp.	50 mL
Soy sauce	2 tbsp.	30 mL
Salt	1 tsp.	5 mL
Pepper	¹⁄₂ tsp.	2 mL
Garlic powder	¹⁄₂ tsp.	2 mL
Bay leaves	2	2
Oyster sauce (optional)	1 tbsp.	15 mL

Cut meat between ribs to separate. Place in large saucepan.

Stir remaining 8 ingredients together in small bowl. Pour over ribs. Marinate for 1 hour in refrigerator, stirring often so top ribs are coated. Cover. Bring to a boil. Simmer for about 1 hour until tender. Discard bay leaves. Drain and reserve liquid. To serve, brush ribs with liquid. Arrange in single layer in baking pan lined with greased foil. Bake in 400°F (205°C) oven for 5 to 10 minutes until hot. Makes about 36.

1 rib (with sauce): 34 Calories; 2.5 g Total Fat; 142 mg Sodium; 3 g Protein; trace Carbohydrate; trace Dietary Fiber

Pictured on page 71.

You could quit your job due to illness and fatigue. You might be sick and tired of it.

YAKITORI

Little picks or skewers hold this delicious chicken. An attractive finger food.

Light-colored soy sauce	¾ cup	175 mL
Granulated sugar	¼ cup	60 mL
Sherry (or alcohol-free sherry)	¼ cup	60 mL
Garlic powder	¼ tsp.	1 mL
Pepper	⅛ tsp.	0.5 mL
Boneless, skinless chicken breast halves (about 1¾ lbs., 790 g), cut into 1 inch (2.5 cm) cubes	7	7
Medium green, red or yellow peppers, cut into 1 inch (2.5 cm) pieces to make about 30	2	2
Medium onions, cut into 1 inch (2.5 cm) pieces to make about 30	1-2	1-2

Combine first 5 ingredients in small saucepan. Stir. Bring to a boil over medium. Remove from heat.

Soak thirty 4 inch (10 cm) wooden skewers in water for 10 minutes. Thread each skewer with chicken, green pepper and onion. Place in hot sauce for 20 minutes. Spoon sauce over top several times during marinating. Remove from sauce. Arrange in single layer on greased broiler tray. Broil about 5 inches (12.5 cm) from heat for 2 minutes. Brush with sauce. Turn skewers over. Brush with sauce. Broil for 2 minutes. Repeat until chicken is cooked. Makes about 30.

1 kabob: 45 Calories; 0.4 g Total Fat; 454 mg Sodium; 7 g Protein; 3 g Carbohydrate; trace Dietary Fiber

PARTY WINGS

These have a sweet and sour taste with a rich brown glaze.

Apricot jam	½ cup	125 mL
Ketchup	⅓ cup	75 mL
Soy sauce	3 tbsp.	50 mL
Garlic powder	½ tsp.	2 mL
Whole chicken wings (or drumettes)	3 lbs.	1.4 kg

(continued on next page)

Mix first 4 ingredients in small bowl.

Remove wing tips and discard. Cut wings apart at joint. Arrange in single layer on greased baking sheet or pan lined with greased foil. Brush enough jam mixture over chicken to coat. Bake in 350°F (175°C) oven for 30 minutes. Brush with jam mixture. Bake for 10 minutes. Brush with remaining jam mixture. Bake for 10 minutes until tender. Makes about 36 wing pieces or 24 drumettes.

1 coated piece: 101 Calories; 6.1 g Total Fat; 147 mg Sodium; 7 g Protein; 4 g Carbohydrate; trace Dietary Fiber

Pictured on page 71.

BUFFALO WINGS

Another choice to make. Decide if you want hot wings or "suicide hot" wings.

Large eggs, fork-beaten	**2**	**2**
Milk	**¼ cup**	**60 mL**
Hot pepper sauce	**1 tbsp.**	**15 mL**
All-purpose flour	**⅔ cup**	**150 mL**
Seasoned salt	**2 tsp.**	**10 mL**
Pepper	**½ tsp.**	**2 mL**
Whole chicken wings (or drumettes)	**3 lbs.**	**1.4 kg**
Cooking oil, for deep-frying		
Commercial Louisiana Hot Sauce	**1-4 tbsp.**	**15-60 mL**

Combine eggs, milk and hot pepper sauce in small bowl.

Combine flour, seasoned salt and pepper in separate small bowl.

Remove wing tips and discard. Cut wings apart at joint. Dip a few pieces into egg mixture then into flour mixture to coat. Deep-fry in hot 375°F (190°C) cooking oil for 8 to 10 minutes until browned and crisp. Drain on paper towels. Put cooked chicken into large pail or bowl with cover.

Drizzle cooked chicken with hot sauce. Cover. Shake and toss for 1 to 2 minutes to distribute sauce evenly. Serve with Blue Cheese Dip, page 38. Makes about 36 wing pieces or 24 drumettes.

1 coated piece (with sauce): 108 Calories; 7.5 g Total Fat; 108 mg Sodium; 8 g Protein; 2 g Carbohydrate; trace Dietary Fiber

Pictured on page 107.

GLAZED MEATBALLS

So easy to cook these by simmering in a sauce. Dark brown glaze.

Lean ground beef	1½ lbs.	680 g
Envelope dry onion soup mix	1 × 1.4 oz.	1 × 38 g
Large egg	1	1
Ketchup	¼ cup	60 mL
Fine dry bread crumbs	⅓ cup	75 mL
Poultry seasoning, just a pinch		
Parsley flakes	¼ tsp.	1 mL
GLAZE		
Grape jelly	1½ cups	375 mL
Ketchup	¾ cup	175 mL
Lemon juice (or white vinegar), to taste (optional)		

Mix all 7 ingredients in medium bowl. Shape into 1 inch (2.5 cm) balls.

Glaze: Heat jelly and ketchup in frying pan until hot. Stir in lemon juice. Add meatballs. Stir gently to coat. Simmer, covered, for 20 to 25 minutes. Turn into chafing dish. Serve with wooden picks. Makes 60.

*1 **meatball** **(with glaze):** 58 Calories; 1.9 g Total Fat; 134 mg Sodium; 3 g Protein; 8 g Carbohydrate; trace Dietary Fiber*

Pictured on page 71.

1. Ribs Adobo, page 67
2. Pacific Ribs, page 66
3. Triple Satay, page 60
4. Shrimp Kabobs, page 58
5. Szechuan Satay, page 64
6. Party Wings, page 68
7. Chicken Nuggets, page 62
8. Snap Wings, page 61
9. Chicken Wings Sesame, page 63
10. Crusty Parmesan Wings, page 62
11. Cranberry Dip, page 39
12. Party Meatballs, page 65, with Meatball Sauce, page 42
13. Glazed Meatballs, page 70

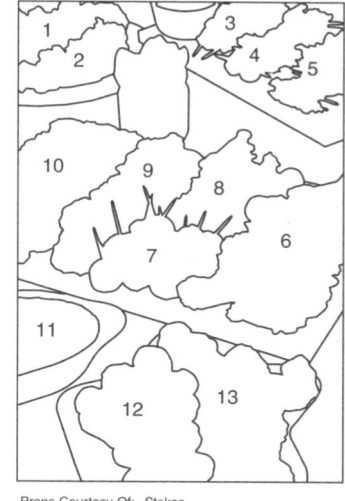

Props Courtesy Of: Stokes
The Bay

Hosting with ease...

Make a greater quantity of fewer items—
two or three kinds of appetizers with different
garnishes offer variety and simplify preparation.
Keep finger foods fairly small so they're easy
for guests to manage, and set out small plates
and cocktail napkins so your guests can help
themselves.

WIENER WISPS

Serve these wonderful morsels with picks. Sauce is thick and delectable.

Ketchup	½ cup	125 mL
Brown sugar, packed	½ cup	125 mL
Prepared mustard	1 tsp.	5 mL
Onion powder	¼ tsp.	1 mL
Rum flavoring	½ tsp.	2 mL
Water	½ cup	125 mL
Wieners (about 1 lb., 454 g), each cut into 6 pieces	12	12

Measure first 6 ingredients into medium saucepan. Stir.

Add wiener pieces. Bring to a boil. Cover. Simmer for about 15 minutes. Serve hot in chafing dish. Makes 72.

1 piece (with sauce): 28 Calories; 1.8 g Total Fat; 95 mg Sodium; 1 g Protein; 2 g Carbohydrate; trace Dietary Fiber

Pictured on page 17.

SAUCY GARLIC SAUSAGE: Rather than wieners, slice garlic sausage into sauce. Excellent.

POLYNESIAN SAUSAGES

These are outstanding. Coated with a sweet and tangy sauce.

Apricot jam	1 cup	250 mL
Apple cider vinegar	3 tbsp.	50 mL
Paprika	¼ tsp.	1 mL
Onion powder	¼ tsp.	1 mL
Parsley flakes	¼ tsp.	1 mL
Garlic powder	¼ tsp.	1 mL
Salami cocktail sausages, cooked	1 lb.	454 g

Measure first 6 ingredients into 3½ quart (3.5 L) slow cooker. Stir well.

Add sausages. Stir. Cover. Cook on Low for 2 to 4 hours or on High for 1 to 2 hours until heated through. Serve with wooden picks. Makes about 22.

1 sausage (with sauce): 100 Calories; 5.2 g Total Fat; 199 mg Sodium; 2 g Protein; 11 g Carbohydrate; trace Dietary Fiber

SIMPLE MEATBALLS

These are extra good on their own, or serve with Simple Sweet And Sour Sauce, page 41. The sauce can be served as a dip beside the meatballs or can be poured over them.

Fine dry bread crumbs	½ cup	125 mL
Finely minced onion	¼ cup	60 mL
Water	⅓ cup	75 mL
Prepared horseradish	1 tsp.	5 mL
Salt	1 tsp.	5 mL
Pepper	¼ tsp.	1 mL
Lean ground beef	1 lb.	454 g

Stir first 6 ingredients together well in medium bowl.

Add ground beef. Mix well. Shape into 1 inch (2.5 cm) balls. Arrange in single layer on greased baking sheet or pan. Bake in 375°F (190°C) oven for about 15 minutes until no longer pink. Drain. Makes 40.

1 meatball (with sauce): 23 Calories; 1 g Total Fat; 83 mg Sodium; 2 g Protein; 1 g Carbohydrate; trace Dietary Fiber

TORTILLA STACKS

Easy to serve on small plates in the living room before the call to the table. Delicious.

Lean ground beef	½ lb.	225 g
Finely chopped onion	½ cup	125 mL
Picante salsa	3 tbsp.	50 mL
Flour tortillas (10 inch, 25 cm, size)	3	3
Canned diced green chilies, drained	4 oz.	114 mL
Medium tomato, seeded and diced	1	1
Grated Monterey Jack cheese	⅓ cup	75 mL
Grated medium Cheddar cheese	⅓ cup	75 mL

(continued on next page)

Hors d'Oeuvres

Scramble-fry ground beef and onion in non-stick frying pan until beef is no longer pink and onion is soft. Drain well.

Stir in salsa. Cool.

Lay 1 tortilla on greased baking sheet. Spread meat sauce over top to edge. Cover with second tortilla. Sprinkle with green chilies. Top with third tortilla. Scatter tomato over tortilla.

Toss both cheeses together. Sprinkle over top. Bake in 425°F (220°C) oven for about 15 minutes. Cuts into 8 wedges.

1 wedge: 155 Calories; 5.8 g Total Fat; 318 mg Sodium; 10 g Protein; 15 g Carbohydrate; 1 g Dietary Fiber

GLAZED HAM CANAPÉS

An appetizer with sustenance. Especially good when serving an appetizer meal.

Canned cola-flavored beverage	1 × 12½ oz.	1 × 355 mL
Apricot (or peach) jam	¼ cup	60 mL
Ground cloves	¼ tsp.	1 mL
Cooked smoked ham	1½ lbs.	680 g
Small butter crackers (such as Ritz)	48	48
Prepared mustard	3 tbsp.	50 mL

Stir first 3 ingredients in ungreased 2 quart (2 L) casserole.

Set ham in cola mixture. Cover. Bake in 325°F (160°) oven for 2 hours, turning ham several times. Cool. Chill until needed.

Serve thin slices, cut to fit, over crackers that have been spread with a little prepared mustard. Makes 48.

1 canapé: 46 Calories; 1.8 g Total Fat; 427 mg Sodium; 4 g Protein; 3 g Carbohydrate; trace Dietary Fiber

Paré Pointer

You get a hangover by eating too much.

WIENER BITES

Tart, sweet sauce that complements the wiener pieces. Serve hot with picks.

Black currant (or blackberry) jelly	1¼ cups	300 mL
Prepared mustard	½ cup	125 mL
Wieners (1 lb., 454 g), each cut into 6 pieces	12	12

Heat jelly and mustard in large saucepan.

Add wiener pieces. Cover. Simmer, stirring often, until wiener pieces are puffed. Serve with wooden picks. Makes about 72.

1 piece (with sauce): 37 Calories; 1.9 g Total Fat; 94 mg Sodium; 1 g Protein; 4 g Carbohydrate; trace Dietary Fiber

COCKTAIL SAUSAGES

A bit sweet and a bit tangy.

Grape jelly	1 cup	250 mL
Chili sauce	1 cup	250 mL
Lemon juice	1 tsp.	5 mL
Frozen concentrated orange juice	3 tbsp.	50 mL
Salami cocktail sausages, cooked	2 lbs.	900 g

Combine first 4 ingredients in 3½ quart (3.5 L) slow cooker. Stir well.

Add sausages. Stir gently. Cover. Cook on Low for 4 to 5 hours or on High for 2 to 2½ hours until hot. Makes 44.

1 sausage (with sauce): 107 Calories; 5.8 g Total Fat; 346 mg Sodium; 3 g Protein; 11 g Carbohydrate; 1 g Dietary Fiber

Paré Pointer

You know a mummy has a cold when it starts coffin.

BEEF SKEWERS

Once these marinated and broiled appetizers show up, they are gone in a flash. Can be prepared on skewers, chilled and broiled at the last minute.

Light soy sauce	²⁄₃ cup	150 mL
Lemon juice	1 tbsp.	15 mL
White vinegar	1 tbsp.	15 mL
Brown sugar, packed	¼ cup	60 mL
Ground ginger	1 tsp.	5 mL
Garlic powder	¼ tsp.	1 mL
Onion powder	¼ tsp.	1 mL
Pepper	¼ tsp.	1 mL
Beef sirloin steak, cut into ¾ inch (2 cm) cubes	1½ lbs.	680 g

Mix first 8 ingredients in medium bowl with tight fitting cover.

Add steak cubes. Stir. Cover tightly. Marinate in refrigerator for 6 to 8 hours or overnight. Flip bowl or stir cubes occasionally. Soak thirty 4 inch (10 cm) wooden skewers in water for 10 minutes. Remove meat from marinade with slotted spoon. Discard marinade. Thread 3 cubes on each skewer. Place on greased broiling tray. Broil 4 inches (10 cm) from heat for 4 to 8 minutes, turning as needed, until desired doneness. Makes about 30.

1 kabob: 24 Calories; 0.8 g Total Fat; 56 mg Sodium; 4 g Protein; trace Carbohydrate; 0 g Dietary Fiber

He just swallowed a bone. He's not choking—he's serious.

STUFFED MUSHROOMS

A bit gooey and a real hit.

Fresh medium mushrooms	36	36
Pork sausage meat	1/2 lb.	225 g
All-purpose flour	1 tbsp.	15 mL
Fine dry bread crumbs	1/4 cup	60 mL
Picante salsa	1/4 cup	60 mL
Process mozzarella cheese slices, each cut into 12 smaller squares	3	3

Carefully twist stems from mushrooms. Chop stems.

Scramble-fry sausage meat and mushroom stems until no pink remains in sausage. Drain.

Sprinkle flour over sausage meat mixture. Mix. Add bread crumbs. Stir. Stir in salsa until mixture comes to a boil. Remove from heat. Stuff mushroom caps. Arrange in single layer on ungreased baking sheet.

Place cheese square over top of each. Bake in 400°F (205°C) oven for about 12 minutes. Serve warm. Makes 36.

1 stuffed mushroom: 27 Calories; 1.6 g Total Fat; 85 mg Sodium; 1 g Protein; 2 g Carbohydrate; trace Dietary Fiber

Pictured on page 17.

STUFFED PEA PODS

Cute and colorful. Different from the usual stuffed pea pods.

Fresh pea pods	24	24
Boiling water, to cover		
Canned ham flakes, drained	6 1/2 oz.	184 g
Salad dressing (or mayonnaise)	1 tbsp.	15 mL
Sweet pickle relish	1 1/2 tsp.	7 mL
Prepared mustard	1/4 tsp.	1 mL
Chopped chives	2 tsp.	10 mL

(continued on next page)

Put pea pods into medium bowl. Pour boiling water over to cover well. Let stand for 1 minute. Drain. Rinse in cold water until cooled. Drain. Slit top sides (least curved sides) open.

Mash remaining 5 ingredients with fork in small bowl. Makes 1 cup (250 mL) filling. Stuff each pea pod with about 2 tsp. (10 mL) filling. Makes 24.

1 stuffed pea pod: 24 Calories; 1.8 g Total Fat; 111 mg Sodium; 1 g Protein; 1 g Carbohydrate; trace Dietary Fiber

Pictured on page 89.

SNACKIN' POTATO SKINS

Always a favorite. Seasoned and crisp. Serve with sour cream and chopped green onion on the side.

Medium baking potatoes, baked and cooled	5	5
Hard margarine (or butter), melted	¼ **cup**	**60 mL**
Seasoned salt, sprinkle		

Cut potatoes in half lengthwise. Cut each half lengthwise. Now cut all 20 strips in half crosswise making 40 pieces. Scoop away most of the potato leaving a thin layer on each skin.

Brush both sides with margarine. Sprinkle with seasoned salt. Place, skin side up, on ungreased baking sheet. Bake in 400°F (205°C) oven for 10 to 15 minutes until crisp. Makes 40 pieces.

1 coated potato skin: 24 Calories; 1.1 g Total Fat; 15 mg Sodium; trace Protein; 3 g Carbohydrate; trace Dietary Fiber

Variation #1: Omit seasoned salt. Sprinkle with ½ envelope of taco seasoning. Bake as above. Serve with Guacamole, page 32.

Pictured on page 17.

Variation #2: Omit margarine and seasoned salt. Place potato wedges, skin side down, on ungreased baking sheet. Sprinkle with 1 cup (250 mL) grated Cheddar cheese. Add either ⅓ cup (75 mL) cooked and crumbled bacon or ⅓ cup (75 mL) chopped green onion, or a combination of both. Bake as above.

Pictured on page 17.

PRIZE MUSHROOMS

Attractive and so different.

Large fresh portobello mushrooms, 5-6 inches (12.5-15 cm) in diameter	6	6
Cooking oil	2 tsp.	10 mL
Hard margarine (or butter)	1 tsp.	5 mL
Garlic clove, minced (or ¼ tsp., 1 mL, garlic powder)	1	1
Chopped onion	1 cup	250 mL
Finely chopped red pepper	2 tbsp.	30 mL
Salt	¼ tsp.	1 mL
Pepper, sprinkle		
Grated part-skim mozzarella cheese	1 cup	250 mL
Chopped chives	1 tbsp.	15 mL
Grated Parmesan cheese	1 tbsp.	15 mL

Remove stems from mushrooms. Brush both sides of caps with cooking oil. Arrange in single layer on ungreased baking sheet. Broil both sides, about 6 inches (15 cm) from heat for 4 to 5 minutes per side until caps begin to soften.

Heat margarine in frying pan. Add garlic, onion and red pepper. Sprinkle with salt and pepper. Sauté until golden. Divide and spoon into mushroom caps.

Divide and layer remaining 3 ingredients over onion mixture in each cap. Broil until cheese is melted and nicely browned. Makes 6 servings.

1 stuffed mushroom: 118 Calories; 7.4 g Total Fat; 255 mg Sodium; 7 g Protein; 7 g Carbohydrate; 1 g Dietary Fiber

Pictured on page 143.

CARROT CURLS

A colorful, crisp and easy addition to salads or to a raw vegetable platter with dip.

Large carrots	2	2
Cold water, to cover		

(continued on next page)

Peel carrots lengthwise into wide strips using vegetable peeler.

Curl each carrot strip around finger. Fasten with wooden pick. Place in large bowl filled with enough water to cover all curls. Chill for at least 2 hours. Drain. Set curls on paper towels. Remove wooden picks just before placing on salad or on tray. Makes about 16.

1 carrot curl: 5 Calories; trace Total Fat; 4 mg Sodium; trace Protein; 1 g Carbohydrate; trace Dietary Fiber

Pictured on page 89.

MYSTERY APPETIZER

A real conversation item. Have friends guess what it is.

Fine dry bread crumbs	²/₃ cup	150 mL
Grated Parmesan cheese	¹/₂ cup	125 mL
Parsley flakes	¹/₂ tsp.	2 mL
Poultry seasoning	¹/₄ tsp.	1 mL
Onion powder	¹/₄ tsp.	1 mL
Salt	¹/₁₆ tsp.	0.5 mL
Pepper, just a pinch		
Large eggplant, peeled and cut like french fries	1	1
Salad dressing (or mayonnaise)	²/₃ cup	150 mL

Stir first 7 ingredients together in small bowl.

Dip eggplant pieces into salad dressing to coat. Roll in crumb mixture. Arrange in single layer on greased baking sheet. Bake in 400°F (205°C) oven for about 12 minutes until browned. Serve immediately as eggplant tends to darken upon standing. Makes about 60.

1 coated "fry": 24 Calories; 1.7 g Total Fat; 46 mg Sodium; 1 g Protein; 2 g Carbohydrate; trace Dietary Fiber

Pictured on page 107.

Paré Pointer

Honey is very scarce in Thailand. Bangkok has only one "B."

MARINATED VEGETABLES

A bright and colorful addition to a tray of starters.

Cooking oil	½ cup	125 mL
Lemon juice	2 tbsp.	30 mL
White vinegar	2 tbsp.	30 mL
Granulated sugar	1½ tsp.	7 mL
Salt	½ tsp.	2 mL
Dry mustard	¼ tsp.	1 mL
Onion salt	¼ tsp.	1 mL
Paprika	¼ tsp.	1 mL
Dried whole oregano	¼ tsp.	1 mL
Garlic salt	¼ tsp.	1 mL
Ground thyme	¹⁄₁₆ tsp.	0.5 mL
Cauliflower florets	1½ cups	375 mL
Broccoli florets	1½ cups	375 mL
Small fresh mushrooms	1 cup	250 mL
Medium green pepper, cut into strips	1	1
Cherry tomatoes	1½ cups	375 mL
Diagonally sliced celery	1 cup	250 mL
Medium carrot, cut into sticks	1	1

Stir first 11 ingredients together well in large bowl with tight fitting lid. Makes ¾ cup (175 mL) marinade.

Add remaining 7 ingredients. Cover. Turn over to coat vegetables. Chill for several hours or overnight, turning or shaking bowl occasionally. Serve in marinade with slotted spoon. Makes 8 cups (2 L).

¼ cup (60 mL): 23 Calories; 1.9 g Total Fat; 39 mg Sodium; trace Protein; 2 g Carbohydrate; trace Dietary Fiber

Pictured on page 89.

When asked if he'd lived here all his life, he replied, "Not yet."

SAVORY PALMIERS

Cute little treats that will please everyone. Real showstoppers, but not hard to make at all. This version is without the sugar.

Cooking oil	2 tsp.	10 mL
Finely chopped onion	1 cup	250 mL
Finely chopped fresh mushrooms	2 cups	500 mL
Hard margarine (or butter)	1 tsp.	5 mL
All-purpose flour	4 tsp.	20 mL
Salt	$\frac{1}{4}$ tsp.	1 mL
Pepper	$\frac{1}{16}$ tsp.	0.5 mL
Garlic powder	$\frac{1}{4}$ tsp.	1 mL
Light sour cream	$\frac{1}{4}$ cup	60 mL
Frozen puff pastry, thawed according to package directions	$\frac{1}{2} \times$ 14.1 oz.	$\frac{1}{2} \times$ 397 g

Heat cooking oil in frying pan. Add onion. Sauté until soft. Blot onions on paper towel. Spoon into small bowl.

Add mushrooms and margarine to frying pan. Sauté until golden. Add onion to mushrooms.

Sprinkle with flour, salt, pepper and garlic powder. Mix well.

Stir in sour cream until mixture is boiling and thickened. Cool.

Roll out pastry on lightly floured surface to rectangle measuring 11 x 13 inches (28 x 33 cm). Cut lengthwise, down center, forming 2 long rectangles. Spread $\frac{1}{2}$ of mushroom mixture over surface, leaving $\frac{1}{2}$ inch (12 mm) space down each side. Roll each long side to meet in center just touching each other. Dampen pastry along each edge. Press together lightly. Wrap in plastic wrap. Chill for 30 to 40 minutes. Cut each chilled roll into 24 slices, each slice about $\frac{1}{2}$ inch (12 mm) wide. Arrange on greased baking sheet, cut side down. Bake in upper third of 375°F (190°C) oven for about 12 minutes until golden. Serve warm. Makes 48.

1 palmier: 26 Calories; 1.7 g Total Fat; 39 mg Sodium; trace Protein; 2 g Carbohydrate; trace Dietary Fiber

Pictured on page 89.

IMPOSSIBLE BACON QUICHE

This makes its own crust while baking. Nice flavor of bacon and onion.

Bacon slices, cooked crisp and crumbled	12-15	12-15
Shredded Swiss cheese	1 cup	250 mL
Finely chopped onion	1/4 cup	60 mL
Milk	2 cups	500 mL
Biscuit mix	1 cup	250 mL
Large eggs	4	4
Salt	1/4 tsp.	1 mL
Pepper	1/8 tsp.	0.5 mL

Grease 10 inch (25 cm) pie plate. Sprinkle bacon over bottom. Scatter cheese over bacon. Scatter onion over cheese.

Put milk, biscuit mix, eggs, salt and pepper into blender or medium bowl. Process or beat together well. Pour into pie plate. Bake in 400°F (205°C) oven for about 35 minutes until knife inserted near center comes out clean. Cuts into 10 wedges for a sit-down appetizer.

1 wedge: 197 Calories; 11.1 g Total Fat; 446 mg Sodium; 11 g Protein; 13 g Carbohydrate; trace Dietary Fiber

CHEESE TARTS

A winner every time.

Grated medium Cheddar cheese	1/2 cup	125 mL
Grated Havarti (or other white) cheese	1/2 cup	125 mL
Chopped onion	1 tbsp.	15 mL
Salt	1/4 tsp.	1 mL
Pepper, just a pinch		
Dry mustard, just a pinch		
Large egg	1	1
Milk	1/2 cup	125 mL
Unbaked mini-tart shells	24	24

Measure first 8 ingredients into blender. Process until smooth.

Pour into tart shells. Bake in 350°F (175°C) oven for 20 to 25 minutes until set. Makes 24.

1 tart: 59 Calories; 4.1 g Total Fat; 111 mg Sodium; 2 g Protein; 3 g Carbohydrate; trace Dietary Fiber

PHYLLO NESTS

Very pretty. Ready for the filling of your choice.

Frozen phyllo pastry sheets, thawed according to package directions	3	3
Hard margarine (or butter), melted	2 tbsp.	30 mL

Lay 1 pastry sheet on working surface. Working quickly, brush with melted margarine. Cover with second sheet. Brush with melted margarine. Repeat with remaining sheet. Cut layered strip into 2½ inch (6.4 cm) squares. Carefully press into greased mini-muffin pans. Bake in 375°F (190°C) oven for 5 to 6 minutes until browned. Let stand for 5 minutes before removing to rack to cool. Makes 20.

1 unfilled nest: 21 Calories; 1.2 g Total Fat; 33 mg Sodium; trace Protein; 2 g Carbohydrate; trace Dietary Fiber

Pictured on front cover.

PIQUANT BEEF FILLING

The dark meaty filling complements the light-colored pastry.

Lean ground beef	½ lb.	225 g
Finely chopped onion	¼ cup	60 mL
All-purpose flour	1 tbsp.	15 mL
Salt	¼ tsp.	1 mL
Pepper, sprinkle		
Soy sauce	1 tbsp.	15 mL
Milk	⅓ cup	75 mL

Scramble-fry ground beef and onion in non-stick frying pan until no pink remains in meat and onion is soft.

Sprinkle with flour, salt and pepper. Mix well.

Stir in soy sauce and milk until boiling. Remove from heat. Chill until needed. Reheat filling just before serving. Serve in Toast Cups, page 14, or Phyllo Nests, above. Makes 1⅓ cups (325 mL).

1 tbsp. (15 mL): 26 Calories; 1.6 g Total Fat; 86 mg Sodium; 2 g Protein; 1 g Carbohydrate; trace Dietary Fiber

Pictured on front cover.

MUSHROOM PASTRIES

Pass these lavish pastries and watch them disappear.

CREAM CHEESE PASTRY

Cream cheese, softened	4 oz.	125 g
Hard margarine (or butter), softened	1/2 cup	125 mL
All-purpose flour	1 1/2 cups	375 mL

MUSHROOM FILLING

Hard margarine (or butter)	2 tbsp.	30 mL
Chopped onion	1 cup	250 mL
Fresh mushrooms, chopped	1/2 lb.	225 g
All-purpose flour	2 tbsp.	30 mL
Salt	1 tsp.	5 mL
Pepper	1/4 tsp.	1 mL
Ground thyme	1/4 tsp.	1 mL
Salad dressing (or mayonnaise)	1/3 cup	75 mL
Worcestershire sauce	1/4 tsp.	1 mL
Large egg, fork-beaten	1	1

Cream Cheese Pastry: Beat cream cheese and margarine together well in medium bowl. Work in flour until a ball is formed. Chill for at least 1 hour.

Mushroom Filling: Melt margarine in frying pan. Add onion and mushrooms. Sauté until soft.

Add flour, salt, pepper and thyme. Stir well.

Add salad dressing and Worcestershire sauce. Stir until mixture is boiling and thickened. Remove from heat. Cool well.

Roll out pastry on lightly floured surface. Cut into thirty-six 2 inch (5 cm) circles using a scalloped edge if possible. Place 1 tsp. (5 mL) filling in center of 18 circles. Moisten edges with egg. Cover with remaining pastry circles. Seal edges with fork. Cut 2 or 3 slits in top of each. Arrange on ungreased baking sheet. Bake in 425°F (220°C) oven for about 10 minutes until browned. Makes 18.

1 pastry: 162 Calories; 11.9 g Total Fat; 284 mg Sodium; 3 g Protein; 11 g Carbohydrate; 1 g Dietary Fiber

SPICY SAUSAGE ROLLS

An all-beef make-yourself sausage. Spicy but not too hot.

Dry bread crumbs	½ cup	125 mL
Water	¼ cup	60 mL
White vinegar	2 tbsp.	30 mL
Chili powder	2 tsp.	10 mL
Salt	1 tsp.	5 mL
Pepper	¼ tsp.	1 mL
Dried whole oregano	½ tsp.	2 mL
Garlic powder	¼ tsp.	1 mL
Worcestershire sauce	½ tsp.	2 mL
Lean ground beef	1 lb.	454 g

Pastry, your own or a mix, enough for 3 crusts

Stir first 9 ingredients in medium bowl. Add ground beef. Mix well. Divide into 6 equal portions. Shape each portion into 3/4 inch (2 cm) diameter log, about 14 inches (35 cm) long.

Roll out ⅓ of pastry between 2 sheets of waxed paper to 6 x 14 inch (15 x 35 cm) rectangle. Remove top sheet of waxed paper. Cut pastry in half lengthwise. Place 1 beef log on long edge of 1 pastry half. Roll pastry over beef using waxed paper as guide. Press seam against roll to seal. Discard waxed paper. Cut into 8 equal pieces. Repeat with remaining logs and pastry, for a total of 48 pieces. Place on ungreased baking trays. Bake in 400°F (205°C) oven for 20 to 25 minutes until golden brown. Serve warm. Freezes well. Makes 48 sausage rolls.

1 sausage roll: 82 Calories; 5.3 g Total Fat; 142 mg Sodium; 3 g Protein; 6 g Carbohydrate; trace Dietary Fiber

SAUSAGE ROLLS: Precook skinless sausages in frying pan until half cooked. Cool. Roll in pastry as above.

Peanuts must be very fattening. Have you ever seen a skinny elephant?

MINI CREAM PUFF SHELLS

A versatile marvel. Fill with hot or cold fillings. You can hide a filling completely or serve these bulging.

Water	1 cup	250 mL
Hard margarine (or butter)	½ cup	125 mL
Salt	¼ tsp.	1 mL
All-purpose flour	1 cup	250 mL
Large eggs	4	4

Combine water, margarine and salt in medium saucepan. Bring to a boil over medium.

Add flour. Stir until mixture leaves sides of pan and clumps together. Remove from heat.

Beat in eggs, 1 at a time, beating well after each addition. Drop small spoonfuls onto ungreased baking sheet, leaving room for expansion. Bake in 400°F (205°C) oven for about 15 minutes until puffed and browned. They should look dry. Cool on rack. Cut tops almost, or completely, off. Fill shells. Replace tops. Makes about 72 one-bite size or 36 two-bite size.

1 one-bite size: 23 Calories; 1.7 g Total Fat; 29 mg Sodium; 1 g Protein; 1 g Carbohydrate; trace Dietary Fiber

1. Mozza Pepper Toast, page 9
2. Savory Palmiers, page 83
3. Marinated Vegetables, page 82
4. Little Smokies, page 61
5. Bruschetta Pizza, page 19
6. Veggie Chips, page 112
7. Carrot Curls, page 80
8. Stuffed Pea Pods, page 78
9. Marinated Shrimp, page 56

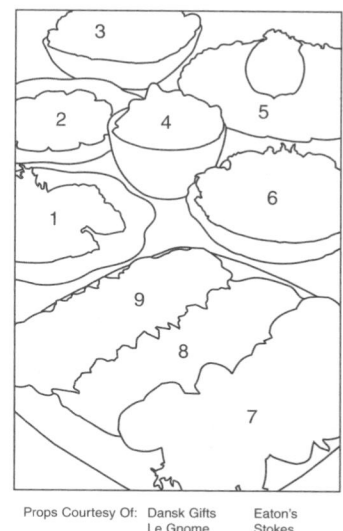

Props Courtesy Of: Dansk Gifts   Eaton's
Le Gnome   Stokes
The Bay

Pastries

Make your guests comfortable...

Arrange your party space so guests can mingle while they munch. Plan to have your buffet table and beverage area in different spots to avoid crowding. Or, set up a number of food and beverage stations throughout your home to allow movement and facilitate interaction among guests.

HAM TURNOVERS

Mild mustard and orange flavors, with a touch of sweetness.

Canned ham flakes, drained	6½ oz.	184 g
Brown sugar, packed	1 tbsp.	15 mL
Dry mustard	1 tbsp.	15 mL
Water	1½ tsp.	7 mL
Finely grated orange peel (or 1 tbsp., 15 mL, orange marmalade)	⅛ tsp.	0.5 mL
Pastry, your own or a mix, enough for 2 crusts		
Large egg, fork-beaten	1	1

Mash first 5 ingredients together well on large plate.

Roll out pastry on lightly floured surface. Cut into 3 inch (7.5 cm) squares. Place 1½ tsp. (7 mL) ham mixture in center. Moisten edges of pastry with water. Fold over, pressing with fork to seal. Cut tiny slits in tops. Arrange on ungreased baking sheet.

Brush with egg. Bake in 400°F (205°C) oven for about 15 minutes until lightly browned. Serve immediately or freeze in single layer on baking sheet then place in container. To reheat, arrange on ungreased baking sheet. Heat in 350°F (175°C) oven for 20 to 25 minutes until hot and pastry is crispy. Makes 20.

1 turnover: 121 Calories; 8.2 g Total Fat; 239 mg Sodium; 3 g Protein; 9 g Carbohydrate; trace Dietary Fiber

Pictured on page 53.

Robin Hood robbed the rich because the poor didn't have any money.

PARTY QUICHE

To make these look as good as they taste, garnish with a few shreds of cheese or a dab of sour cream. Excellent.

Grated medium Cheddar (or Swiss) cheese	1 cup	250 mL
Milk	½ cup	125 mL
Large egg	1	1
Sliced fresh mushrooms	1 cup	250 mL
Salt	¼ tsp.	1 mL
Real bacon bits (or 6 slices bacon, cooked crisp and crumbled)	½ cup	125 mL
Unbaked mini-tart shells	24	24

Place first 5 ingredients in blender. Process until smooth.

Divide bacon bits among tart shells. Spoon cheese mixture over bacon. Bake in 350°F (175°C) oven for about 25 minutes until set. Makes 24.

1 quiche: 70 Calories; 5 g Total Fat; 133 mg Sodium; 3 g Protein; 4 g Carbohydrate; trace Dietary Fiber

HAM FILLING

Makes a mellow, flavorful filling or may also be served as a dip with crackers or chips.

Canned ham flakes, drained	6½ oz.	184 g
Salad dressing (or mayonnaise)	¼ cup	60 mL
Sour cream	¼ cup	60 mL
Green onions, chopped	2	2
Prepared mustard	1 tsp.	5 mL
Prepared horseradish	1 tsp.	5 mL
Lemon juice	½ tsp.	2 mL
Pepper	1/16 tsp.	0.5 mL

Mix all 8 ingredients well in small bowl. Chill until needed. Serve in Toast Cups, page 14, or Phyllo Nests, page 85. Makes 1⅓ cups (325 mL).

1 tbsp. (15 mL): 39 Calories; 3.3 g Total Fat; 136 mg Sodium; 1 g Protein; 1 g Carbohydrate; trace Dietary Fiber

Good hot or cold. Fancy.

Large egg	1	1
Cream cheese, softened	4 oz.	125 g
Feta cheese, crumbled	8 oz.	250 g
Grated Parmesan cheese	2 tbsp.	30 mL
Parsley flakes	1 tsp.	5 mL
Frozen phyllo pastry sheets (about 1 lb., 454 g), thawed according to package directions	16	16
Hard margarine (or butter), melted	1 cup	250 mL

Beat egg in small bowl until frothy. Add all 3 cheeses and parsley. Beat until smooth.

Lay 1 pastry sheet on working surface. Cover remaining pastry with damp tea towel. Working quickly, brush sheet generously with melted margarine. ❶ Cut into four 4 inch (10 cm) wide strips, along longer edge. ❷ Fold each strip in half lengthwise to make 2 inch (5 cm) wide strips. Brush with margarine. ❸ Place 1 tsp. (5 cm) cheese mixture in center at 1 end. ❹ Fold 1 corner over to form triangle. ❺ Continue folding over in same fashion to end of strip. Brush final triangle with margarine. Place on ungreased baking sheet. Repeat with remaining cheese mixture and pastry sheets. Bake in 400°F (205°C) oven for about 15 minutes until golden. Makes 64.

1 triangle: 65 Calories; 4.5 g Total Fat; 126 mg Sodium; 1 g Protein; 5 g Carbohydrate; trace Dietary Fiber

Pictured on page 53.

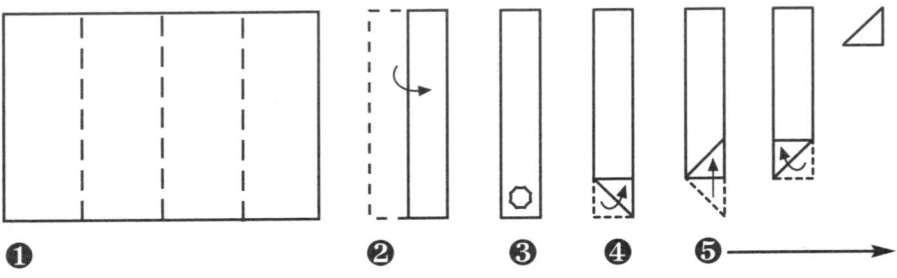

Pastries **93**

MUSHROOM TARTS

This filling can be prepared ahead along with baking the tart shells ahead too. Freezes well. Good mushroom flavor.

Hard margarine (or butter)	1 tbsp.	15 mL
Chopped fresh mushrooms	1 cup	250 mL
Chopped green onion	1 tbsp.	15 mL
All-purpose flour	2 tbsp.	30 mL
Salt	1/4 tsp.	1 mL
Skim evaporated milk (or light cream)	2/3 cup	150 mL
Unbaked mini-tart shells	18	18

Melt margarine in medium saucepan. Add mushrooms and green onion. Sauté until golden.

Mix in flour and salt.

Add evaporated milk, stirring until boiling and thickened. Cool. Makes generous 1 cup (250 mL) filling.

Bake unfilled tart shells in 400°F (205°C) oven for 10 to 13 minutes until lightly browned. Cool. Divide mushroom mixture evenly among tart shells. Bake in 400°F (205°C) oven for 5 minutes until hot. To heat from frozen state allow about 10 minutes. Makes 18.

1 tart: 53 Calories; 3 g Total Fat; 100 mg Sodium; 1 g Protein; 5 g Carbohydrate; trace Dietary Fiber

BEEFY ROLL-UPS

An attractive pinwheel effect with dark beef and orange cheese. Tasty and easy.

Light cream cheese, softened	4 oz.	125 g
Sour cream	1/4 cup	60 mL
Prepared horseradish, more or less	1 1/2 tsp.	7 mL
Prepared mustard	1 tsp.	5 mL
Chopped chives	2 tsp.	10 mL
Flour tortillas (8 inch, 20 cm, size)	4	4
Shaved deli beef	8 oz.	225 g
Grated medium Cheddar cheese	1 1/4 cups	300 mL

(continued on next page)

Mix first 5 ingredients well in small bowl.

Divide and spread over each tortilla.

Lay beef over top. Sprinkle with cheese. Roll each up as tightly as possible. Wrap in plastic wrap. Chill for at least 1 hour. Trim ends. Cut each roll into 10 slices, for a total of 40.

1 slice: 42 Calories; 2.2 g Total Fat; 163 mg Sodium; 3 g Protein; 2 g Carbohydrate; trace Dietary Fiber

Pictured on page 17.

TORTILLA ROLL-UPS

So attractive in colorful tortillas.

Cream cheese, softened	8 oz.	250 g
Salad dressing (or mayonnaise)	1/4 cup	60 mL
Envelope ranch-style salad dressing mix (stir before dividing)	1/2 x 1 oz.	1/2 x 28 g
Finely chopped green onion	1/4 cup	60 mL
Canned diced green chilies, drained and patted dry with paper towels	4 oz.	114 mL
Chopped pimiento, drained and patted dry with paper towels	2 oz.	57 mL
Plain (or dried tomato or pesto) flour tortillas (10 inch, 25 cm, size)	8	8

Beat cream cheese and salad dressing in medium bowl until smooth.

Stir in next 4 ingredients.

Spread 1/4 cup (60 mL) creamy mixture on each tortilla right to edge. Roll up snugly. Chill for at least 2 hours. Trim ends. Cut each roll into 8 slices, for a total of 64.

1 slice: 32 Calories; 1.1 g Total Fat; 63 mg Sodium; 1 g Protein; 5 g Carbohydrate; trace Dietary Fiber

Pictured on page 35.

Saleswoman at perfume counter to customer: "If this stuff really worked, would I be standing here eight hours a day?"

SALAD ROLLS

See-through rice paper wrappers. These can be picked up with fingers.

Apple cider vinegar	2 tbsp.	30 mL
Lemon juice	1 tbsp.	15 mL
Brown sugar, packed	3 tbsp.	50 mL
Plum sauce	3 tbsp.	50 mL
Soy sauce	1 tbsp.	15 mL
Hoisin sauce	1 tbsp.	15 mL
Grated gingerroot	$\frac{1}{2}$ tsp.	2 mL
Cornstarch	1 tsp.	5 mL
Dried crushed chilies	$\frac{1}{8}$-$\frac{1}{4}$ tsp.	0.5-1 mL
Shredded fresh spinach, packed	$1\frac{1}{2}$ cups	375 mL
Chopped fresh bean sprouts	$1\frac{1}{2}$ cups	375 mL
Thinly sliced fresh mushrooms	$\frac{2}{3}$ cup	150 mL
Grated carrot	$\frac{1}{2}$ cup	125 mL
Finely sliced red onion	$\frac{1}{4}$ cup	60 mL
Rice papers ($8\frac{1}{2}$ inch, 21 cm, size)	20	20
Hot water		

Chopped peanuts, for garnish (optional)

Combine first 9 ingredients in small saucepan. Heat and stir until boiling. Cool.

Combine next 5 ingredients in medium bowl. Add cooled vinegar mixture. Toss.

Soak 1 sheet of rice paper in hot water in shallow dish for about 1 minute until soft and pliable. If left too long it will become very fragile. ❶ Place about 2 tbsp. (30 mL) filling in 3 inch (7.5 cm) row off center of rice paper. ❷ Fold 1 end up and over filling, tucking under. ❸ Fold both sides over. ❹ Roll up snugly. Repeat with remaining rice papers and filling.

Garnish with peanuts. Serve immediately. Do not refrigerate. Makes 20.

1 roll: 60 Calories; 0.2 g Total Fat; 102 mg Sodium; 1 g Protein; 14 g Carbohydrate; 1 g Dietary Fiber

Pictured on page 125.

(continued on next page)

Rolls & Wraps

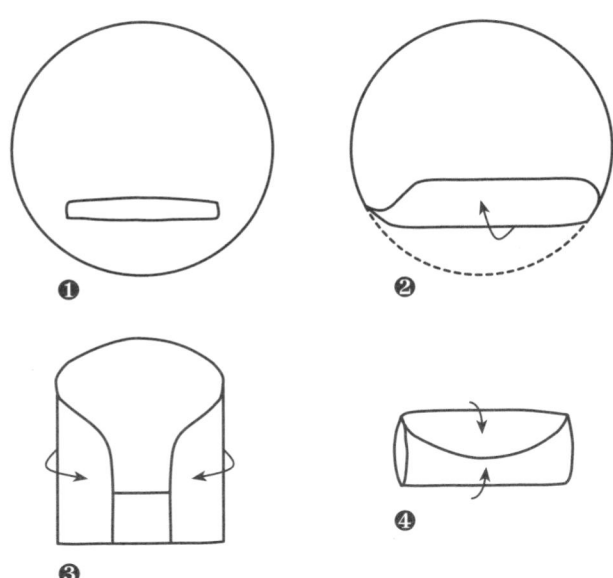

CHEESY ROLL-UPS

Basically white in color with green onion and green chilies showing in the pinwheel design.

Cream cheese, softened	**4 oz.**	**125 g**
Sour cream	**½ cup**	**125 mL**
Finely chopped green onion	**¼ cup**	**60 mL**
Canned diced green chilies, drained	**4 oz.**	**114 mL**
Seasoned salt	**¼ tsp.**	**1 mL**
Garlic powder	**⅛ tsp.**	**0.5 mL**
Flour tortillas (8 inch, 20 cm, size)	**6**	**6**

Beat cream cheese and sour cream together in small bowl until smooth.

Add next 4 ingredients. Stir. Makes 1½ cups (375 mL).

Spread each tortilla to edge with ¼ cup (60 mL) mixture. Roll up snugly, like jelly roll. Wrap in plastic wrap. Chill for at least 2 hours. Trim ends. Cut each roll into 10 slices, for a total of 60.

1 slice: 22 Calories; 1.1 g Total Fat; 38 mg Sodium; 1 g Protein; 2 g Carbohydrate; trace Dietary Fiber

Pictured on page 35.

ORIENTAL CHICKEN ROLLS

Crispy rolls. Allow a little extra time for these.

Ground raw chicken	$^1/_2$ lb.	225 g
Sliced green onion	$^1/_3$ cup	75 mL
Finely chopped celery	$^1/_3$ cup	75 mL
Grated carrot	$^1/_4$ cup	60 mL
Chopped fresh mushrooms	$^1/_2$ cup	125 mL
Garlic cloves, minced (or $^1/_2$ tsp., 2 mL, garlic powder)	2	2
Fresh bean sprouts	2 cups	500 mL
Oyster sauce	$^1/_4$ cup	60 mL
Sherry (or alcohol-free sherry)	1 tbsp.	15 mL
Granulated sugar	1 tsp.	5 mL
Cornstarch	2 tsp.	10 mL
Toasted sesame seeds	1 tbsp.	15 mL
Frozen phyllo pastry sheets (about 1 lb., 454 g), thawed according to package directions	16	16
Hard margarine (or butter), melted	6 tbsp.	100 mL
Toasted sesame seeds	1 tbsp.	15 mL

Sauté first 6 ingredients in non-stick frying pan until chicken is golden and no pink remains.

Add bean sprouts. Sauté for 2 minutes.

Mix oyster sauce, sherry, sugar and cornstarch in small cup. Stir into vegetable mixture until mixture is boiling and thickened. Cool.

Add first amount of sesame seeds. Stir. If filling becomes watery while standing, drain liquid. Makes 3 cups (750 mL) filling.

Lay 1 pastry sheet on working surface. Cover remaining sheets with damp tea towel. Working quickly, brush sheet on working surface with melted margarine. Lay a second sheet over top. Brush with margarine. ❶ Cut into 6 squares. ❷ Place about 1 tbsp. (15 mL) filling on 1 corner. ❸ Fold corner over filling, tucking in sides. ❹ Roll to opposite corner, enclosing filling in finger-size roll. Repeat with remaining 14 sheets, using 2 each time. Brush each roll with remaining margarine.

Sprinkle rolls with second amount of sesame seeds. Arrange on ungreased baking sheet. Bake in 350°F (175°C) oven for about 20 minutes until golden. Makes 48.

1 roll: 50 Calories; 1.8 g Total Fat; 187 mg Sodium; 2 g Protein; 6 g Carbohydrate; trace Dietary Fiber

Pictured on page 125 and on back cover.

(continued on next page)

Rolls & Wraps

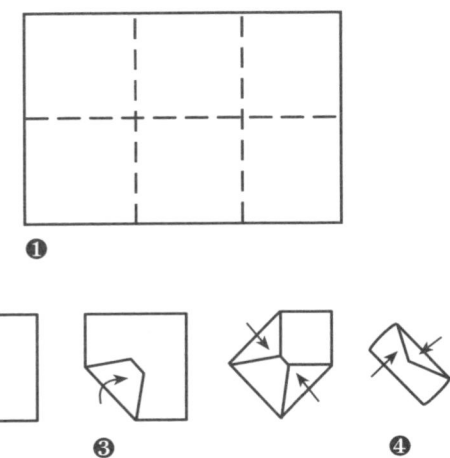

TORTILLA PINWHEELS

Nifty little rolls.

Creamed cottage cheese	2 cups	500 mL
Hard margarine (or butter)	¼ cup	60 mL
Milk	2 tbsp.	30 mL
Lemon juice	1 tbsp.	15 mL
Chopped green onion	½ cup	125 mL
Canned diced green chilies, drained	4 oz.	114 mL
Grated medium Cheddar cheese	1 cup	250 mL
Garlic salt	¼ tsp.	1 mL
Flour tortillas (8 inch, 20 cm, size)	12	12

Place first 4 ingredients in blender. Process until smooth. Turn into medium bowl.

Add green onion, green chilies, cheese and garlic salt. Stir.

Spread ¼ cup (60 mL) cheese mixture on each tortilla. Roll up like jelly roll. Wrap in plastic wrap, sealing ends. Chill for at least 2 hours. Cut each roll into 10 slices, for a total of 120.

1 slice: 22 Calories; 0.8 g Total Fat; 50 mg Sodium; 1 g Protein; 2 g Carbohydrate; trace Dietary Fiber

Rolls & Wraps

SALAMI ROLLS

Filled with a tasty, zippy spread.

Cream cheese, softened	4 oz.	125 g
Grated onion	1 tbsp.	15 mL
Prepared horseradish	2 tsp.	10 mL
Beef bouillon powder	1/4 tsp.	1 mL
Apple juice (or milk)	2 tbsp.	30 mL
Chopped chives	1 tsp.	5 mL
Very thin dry salami (or summer sausage) slices (3½ inches, 9 cm, in diameter), about ¼ lb. (113 g)	18	18

Mash first 6 ingredients well in small bowl. Add a bit more apple juice if needed to make spreadable.

Spread about 2 tsp. (10 mL) cream cheese mixture on each salami slice. Roll up. Place in covered container. Chill for 1 hour. Cut each roll into 3 slices, for a total of 54.

1 slice: 17 Calories; 1.5 g Total Fat; 48 mg Sodium; 1 g Protein; trace Carbohydrate; trace Dietary Fiber

MINI EGG ROLLS

Definitely a good choice. The shape is familiar but the size is definitely appetizer finger food.

Cooking oil	2 tbsp.	30 mL
Cooked chicken, diced and lightly packed	1/3 cup	75 mL
Fresh bean sprouts	½ lb.	225 g
Slivered onion	¼ cup	60 mL
Slivered celery	¼ cup	60 mL
Shredded cabbage	¼ cup	60 mL
Water	1 tbsp.	15 mL
Salt	½ tsp.	2 mL
Square wonton wrappers	84	84
Cooking oil, for deep-frying		

(continued on next page)

Heat first amount of cooking oil in frying pan until hot. Add next 5 ingredients. Stir-fry for 2 to 3 minutes.

Add water and salt. Cover. Steam for 1 minute. Cool.

Place ½ tsp. (2 mL) cooled filling on each wrapper, diagonally off center closer to 1 corner. Fold point over filling. Moisten open edges with water. Fold side points in over filling. Roll to opposite corner. Seal well.

When almost ready to serve, deep-fry in hot 375°F (190°C) cooking oil until golden. Makes 84.

1 roll: 18 Calories; 1.2 g Total Fat; 29 mg Sodium; trace Protein; 1 g Carbohydrate; trace Dietary Fiber

CHILI ROLLS

Pretty and bright with red and green clearly visible in the creamy filling.

Light cream cheese, softened	8 oz.	250 g
Milk	1 tbsp.	15 mL
Canned diced green chilies, drained	4 oz.	114 mL
Chopped ripe olives	2 tbsp.	30 mL
Finely chopped pecans	2 tbsp.	30 mL
Chopped chives	2 tbsp.	30 mL
Chopped pimientos	2 oz.	57 mL
Seasoned salt	⅛ tsp.	0.5 mL
Flour tortillas (8 inch, 20 cm, size)	6	6

Mash cream cheese and milk together in small bowl to make spreading consistency.

Add next 6 ingredients. Mix well.

Divide among tortillas. Spread evenly to edge. Roll up like jelly roll. Wrap each roll in plastic wrap. Refrigerate for several hours. Trim ends. Cut each roll into 10 slices, for a total of 60.

1 slice: 22 Calories; 0.9 g Total Fat; 69 mg Sodium; 1 g Protein; 3 g Carbohydrate; trace Dietary Fiber

Pictured on page 35.

Easier to make every time you try. Really good when slices are sprinkled with wasabi mixture.

Short grain white rice	1¼ cups	300 mL
Water	2½ cups	625 mL
Rice (or white) vinegar	2 tbsp.	30 mL
Granulated sugar	4 tsp.	20 mL
Salt	1 tsp.	5 mL
Sherry (or rice wine, such as sake, or alcohol-free sherry)	2 tbsp.	30 mL
Nori (roasted seaweed) sheets (available in Oriental section of grocery store)	4	4
Wasabi paste (available in Oriental section of grocery store) or 2 tbsp. (30 mL) mayonnaise	2 tsp.	10 mL

FILLING (Choose 3 or 4 for each roll)
Roasted red pepper, peeled, seeded and cut into slivers
Carrot, cut into 3 inch (7.5 cm) slivers
Green onion, cut into 3 inch (7.5 cm) slivers
English cucumber (with peel), cut into 3 inch (7.5 cm) slivers
Fresh asparagus spears, cooked and cooled
Avocado, peeled and cut into thin slices (see Note)
Fresh spinach leaves, cut into shreds
Large fried egg, with pierced yolk, cut into shreds
Canned (or imitation) crabmeat, cut into shreds

Combine first 5 ingredients in medium saucepan. Cover. Simmer for 25 to 30 minutes until rice is tender and most liquid is absorbed.

Stir in sherry. Cool.

❶ Lay 1 sheet of nori on small bamboo mat or heavy cloth napkin to assist in rolling. Spread 1 cup (250 mL) rice, using a wet fork, over nori to edge on 3 sides, leaving about 2 inches (5 cm) on long side, farthest away from you.

Spread with ¼ of wasabi paste.

(continued on next page)

Filling: ❷ Lay your choice of 3 or 4 of fillings in strip 1 inch (2.5 cm) wide, about 1 inch (2.5 cm) up from edge closest to you. Moisten nori with water on plain edge. ❸ Starting at long edge nearest you, roll up tightly using mat or cloth napkin to assist, rolling back and forth to pack tightly. Repeat with remaining 3 sheets of nori. Wrap in plastic wrap. Chill. Trim ends with wet sharp knife. Cut each roll into 5 slices, for a total of 20.

1 slice (without sauce): 93 Calories; 3.1 g Total Fat; 211 mg Sodium; 3 g Protein; 13 g Carbohydrate; 1 g Dietary Fiber

Note: Dip avocado slices into lemon juice to prevent darkening.

Variation: If you prefer not to use wasabi paste in the sushi, make a dipping sauce of ½ tsp. (2 mL) wasabi paste (or more, to taste) and ½ cup (125 mL) soy sauce.

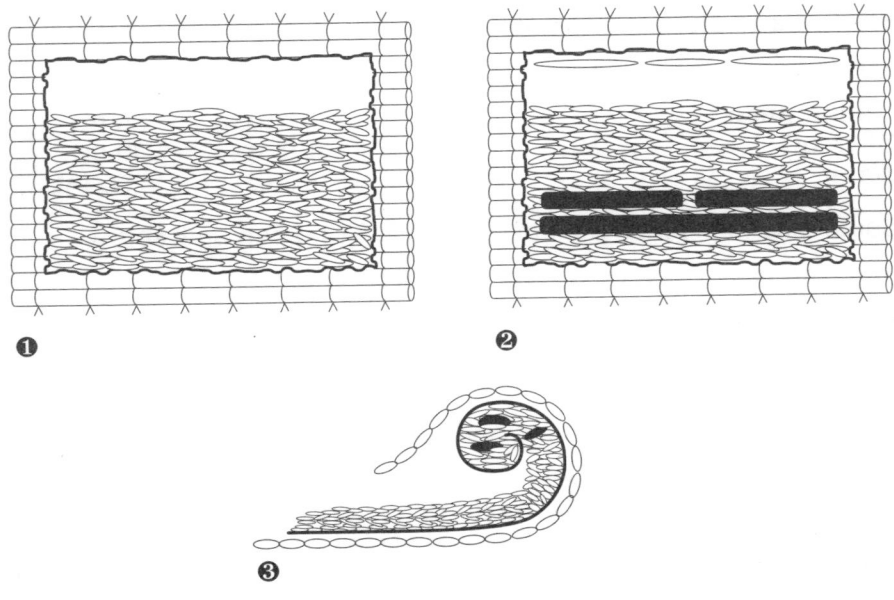

Pancakes with dents are called waffles.

DOLMADES

Pronounced dohl-MAH-dehs. A Greek favorite. These are served at room temperature or hot as a sit-down starter.

Finely chopped onion	1½ cups	375 mL
Olive oil	2 tbsp.	30 mL
Chopped pine nuts (or pecans)	½ cup	125 mL
Basmati (or long grain white) rice	1 cup	250 mL
Water	2 cups	500 mL
Raisins	⅔ cup	150 mL
Parsley flakes (or ¼ cup, 60 mL, chopped fresh)	1 tbsp.	15 mL
Salt	1 tsp.	5 mL
Pepper	⅛ tsp.	0.5 mL
Ground cinnamon	¼ tsp.	1 mL
Seeded and chopped tomato	1 cup	250 mL
Jar of grapevine leaves	17 oz.	473 mL
Lemon juice	1½ tbsp.	25 mL
Olive oil	2 tbsp.	30 mL
Water	1 cup	250 mL

Sauté onion in first amount of olive oil in frying pan until soft.

Add pine nuts. Cook for 5 minutes until browned.

Add rice, first amount of water, raisins and parsley. Stir. Bring to a gentle boil. Cover. Simmer for 15 to 20 minutes until rice is cooked and liquid is absorbed.

Stir in salt, pepper, cinnamon, and tomato. Cool enough to handle.

Rinse vine leaves under warm water. Drain. Blot dry with tea towel or paper towels. Place about 2½ tbsp. (37 mL) rice mixture on each vine leaf. Roll stem end over rice, tucking in sides as you roll to completely enclose rice. Cover bottom and sides of greased 2 quart (2 L) casserole with vine leaves. Arrange, seam side down, close together over leaves.

Sprinkle with lemon juice and second amount of olive oil. Cover surface with any remaining grape leaves. Add second amount of water. Cover. Bake in 350°F (175°C) oven for about 1 hour. Cool. Serve with a sprinkle of lemon juice. Makes 32.

1 dolmade: 66 Calories; 3.2 g Total Fat; 86 mg Sodium; 1 g Protein; 9 g Carbohydrate; 1 g Dietary Fiber

Pictured on page 53.

Good starter for a Mexican meal. Serve with sour cream. Olé.

Sausage meat	1 lb.	454 g
Chopped onion	½ cup	125 mL
Salt	¾ tsp.	4 mL
Pepper	¼ tsp.	1 mL
Commercial pizza sauce	¾ cup	175 mL
Dried whole oregano	¼ tsp.	1 mL
Flour tortillas (8 inch, 20 cm, size)	6	6
Grated part-skim mozzarella cheese	1½ cups	375 mL

Scramble-fry sausage meat and onion in frying pan until no pink remains in meat and onion is soft. Drain. Mix in salt and pepper. Cool.

Stir pizza sauce, oregano and meat mixture in small bowl. Makes 2 cups (500 mL) filling.

Spread ⅓ cup (75 mL) filling over each tortilla. Sprinkle with ¼ cup (60 mL) cheese. Roll up as tightly as possible, like jelly roll. Wrap in plastic wrap. Chill until shortly before serving. Place on greased baking sheet. Bake in 400°F (205°C) oven for 7 to 8 minutes until cheese is melted. Trim ends. ❶ Cut each roll into 4 slices, for a total of 24.

1 slice: 87 Calories; 4.6 g Total Fat; 270 mg Sodium; 4 g Protein; 7 g Carbohydrate; trace Dietary Fiber

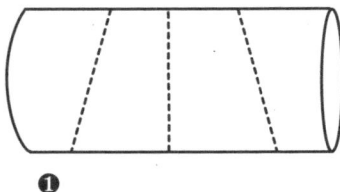

❶

ASPARAGUS ROLLS

Golden brown with asparagus, bacon and cheese showing.

White (or whole wheat) sandwich bread slices, crusts removed	16-18	16-18
Process cheese spread	¾ **cup**	**175 mL**
Bacon slices, cooked crisp and processed in blender or meat grinder	**12**	**12**
Canned (or fresh, cooked) asparagus spears	16-18	16-18
Hard margarine (or butter), melted	**3 tbsp.**	**50 mL**
Grated Parmesan cheese	1½ **tbsp.**	**25 mL**

Roll bread slices fairly flat with rolling pin.

Spread each slice with about 2 tsp. (10 mL) cheese spread. Sprinkle each with ¾ tsp. (4 mL) ground bacon. Lay asparagus spear on end of each slice, cutting off overhanging stem. Roll up snugly, like jelly roll. Secure with wooden pick if needed.

Brush each roll with melted margarine. Sprinkle with Parmesan cheese. Arrange on ungreased baking sheet. Bake in 400°F (205°C) oven for 7 to 8 minutes until golden or broil 6 inches (15 cm) from heat for 2 to 3 minutes until browned. Cut each roll in half, for a total of 32 to 36. Do not freeze.

1 half: 78 Calories; 4.1 g Total Fat; 251 mg Sodium; 3 g Protein; 7 g Carbohydrate; trace Dietary Fiber

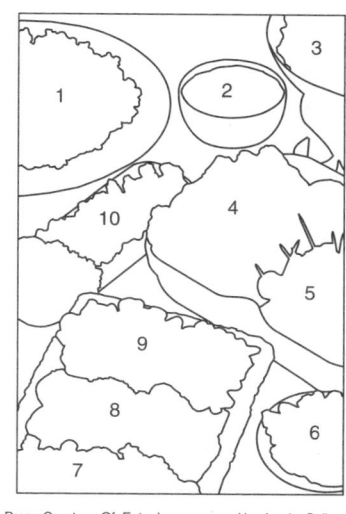

1. Cheddar Popcorn, page 112
2. Blue Cheese Dip, page 38
3. Sweet And Sour Sausage Balls, page 64
4. Buffalo Wings, page 69
5. Sweet Bacon Dogs, page 66
6. Orange Pecans, page 116
7. Deep-Fried Pasta (Variation #2), page 111
8. Sesame Rounds, page 25
9. Deep-Fried Pasta (Variation #1), page 111
10. Mystery Appetizer, page 81

Create atmosphere...

Decorating around a theme will add pizzazz to your party. Appeal to the senses: smell (scented candles, flowers), sight (colour and lighting), sound (music), and taste (food and drink). Your guests will appreciate the added touch!

A bit more time is needed to make these. They do disappear quickly.
Serve with Simple Sweet And Sour Sauce, page 41.

Ground raw chicken	½ lb.	225 g
Chopped fresh mushrooms	1½ cups	375 mL
Sesame (or cooking) oil	2 tsp.	10 mL
Salt	1 tsp.	5 mL
Granulated sugar	1 tsp.	5 mL
Ground ginger	1 tsp.	5 mL
Garlic powder	¼ tsp.	1 mL
Green onions, thinly sliced	4	4
Grated carrot	½ cup	125 mL
Chopped fresh bean sprouts	3 cups	750 mL
Oyster sauce	2 tbsp.	30 mL
Sherry (or alcohol-free sherry)	1 tbsp.	15 mL
Egg roll wrappers (about 25)	1 lb.	454 g

Cooking oil, for deep-frying

Scramble-fry ground chicken and mushrooms in sesame oil in frying pan until no pink remains in chicken and liquid is evaporated.

Sprinkle with salt, sugar, ginger and garlic. Stir. Add green onion, carrot and bean sprouts. Stir-fry over medium-high for about 5 minutes until liquid is evaporated.

Stir in oyster sauce and sherry. Stir-fry for 1 minute.

Place about 2 tbsp. (30 mL) filling on each wrapper, diagonally off center closer to 1 corner. Fold point over filling. Moisten open edges with water. Fold side points in over filling. Roll to opposite corner. Seal well.

Deep-fry in hot 375°F (190°C) cooking oil for about 5 minutes until golden. Drain on paper towel. Makes 25.

1 roll: 85 Calories; 1.9 g Total Fat; 336 mg Sodium; 4 g Protein; 12 g Carbohydrate; 1 g Dietary Fiber

Pictured on page 125 and on back cover.

Rolls & Wraps

LETTUCE WRAPS

Wrap filling in crisp lettuce leaves or leaf lettuce. An unusual treat to be sure.

Cooking oil	1 tsp.	5 mL
Boneless, skinless chicken breast half (about 4 oz., 113 g), cut into $\frac{1}{2}$ inch (12 mm) dice	1	1
Grated carrot	$\frac{1}{4}$ cup	60 mL
Sliced onion, in 1 inch (2.5 cm) long slivers	$\frac{1}{4}$ cup	60 mL
Green pepper slivers	1 tbsp.	15 mL
Red pepper slivers	1 tbsp.	15 mL
Orange pepper slivers	1 tbsp.	15 mL
Water	$\frac{1}{4}$ cup	60 mL
Package chicken-flavored Oriental soup noodles, broken into 6 pieces, seasoning packet reserved	1 x 3$\frac{1}{2}$ oz.	1 x 100 g
Reserved seasoning packet	$\frac{1}{2}$	$\frac{1}{2}$
Hoisin sauce	1 tbsp.	15 mL
Liquid honey	1 tsp.	5 mL
Pepper	$\frac{1}{8}$ tsp.	0.5 mL
Chili powder	$\frac{1}{16}$ tsp.	0.5 mL
Garlic powder	$\frac{1}{16}$ tsp.	0.5 mL
Hot pepper sauce	$\frac{1}{4}$ tsp.	1 mL
Unsalted peanuts	$\frac{1}{4}$ cup	60 mL
Lettuce leaves, from leaf or butter lettuce	8	8

Heat cooking oil in frying pan. Add chicken. Scramble-fry until no pink remains in meat.

Add carrot, onion and pepper slivers. Stir-fry until vegetables are tender crisp.

Add water. Stir in noodles. Cover. Simmer for about 2 minutes to soften.

Add next 8 ingredients. Stir well to heat through. Turn into small bowl.

(continued on next page)

Rolls & Wraps

Serve on platter with lettuce leaves. Have each person spoon about ⅛ of mixture onto leaf, roll it and eat. Makes about 8.

1 wrap: 103 Calories; 3.4 g Total Fat; 140 mg Sodium; 6 g Protein; 12 g Carbohydrate; 1 g Dietary Fiber

Pictured on page 125.

DEEP-FRIED PASTA

Tasty and crunchy. Be sure to try the variations to find your favorite.

Interesting-shaped pasta (such as rotini or tortiglioni), about	**4 cups**	**1 L**
Cooking oil, for deep-frying		
Grated Parmesan cheese	**¼ cup**	**60 mL**
Seasoned salt	**1 tsp.**	**5 mL**

Cook pasta according to package directions. Drain. Blot dry with paper towel.

Deep-fry in hot 375°F (190°C) cooking oil for 10 to 12 minutes until light golden brown, being careful not to overcook. With slotted spoon, transfer to paper towel-lined pan to drain. Do not cool. Place in large bowl.

While still hot, sprinkle with cheese and seasoned salt. Toss to coat. Makes about 4 cups (1 L).

¼ cup (60 mL): 84 Calories; 3.6 g Total Fat; 152 mg Sodium; 3 g Protein; 10 g Carbohydrate; 1 g Dietary Fiber

Variation #1: Add ½ tsp. (2 mL) cayenne pepper to seasoned salt.

Pictured on page 107.

Variation #2: Omit Parmesan cheese. Add same amount dry Cheddar cheese product.

Pictured on page 107.

TEXAS WHEELIES: Use wagon wheel pasta. Omit Parmesan cheese. Add same amount dry Cheddar cheese product and ½ tsp. (2 mL) chili powder to seasoned salt.

VEGGIE CHIPS

Make your own batch of colorful deep-fried vegetable chips.

Sweet potato, long and narrow, peeled	1	1
Medium parsnip, peeled	1	1
Medium carrot, peeled	1	1
Medium russet (or baking) potato, peeled	1	1
Ice water		
Cooking oil, for deep-frying		
Salt, sprinkle		

Using vegetable peeler, peel long thin strips from vegetables. Soak strips in large bowl in ice water for 30 minutes. Blot with paper towel or dry tea towel.

Deep-fry in batches in hot 375°F (190°C) cooking oil for about 2 minutes. Remove with slotted spoon to paper towels to drain. They should just be starting to brown. Cool. If not crisp, repeat deep-frying process, stirring continually for about 1 minute until crisp and beginning to brown. Remove with slotted spoon to paper towels to drain.

Sprinkle with salt. Cool thoroughly. Pile into large bowl. Makes about 10 cups (2.5 L).

¹/₄ cup (60 mL): 28 Calories; 2.3 g Total Fat; 2 mg Sodium; trace Protein; 2 g Carbohydrate; trace Dietary Fiber

Pictured on page 89.

CHEDDAR POPCORN

A great munchie.

Popped corn (pop about 1 cup, 250 mL)	6 qts.	6 L
Hard margarine (or butter)	¹/₂ cup	125 mL
Grated cheese product (powdered yellow Cheddar)	¹/₂ cup	125 mL
Garlic salt	¹/₄ tsp.	1 mL
Onion salt	¹/₄ tsp.	1 mL

(continued on next page)

Put popcorn into extra large container such as large roaster or preserving kettle.

Melt margarine in small saucepan.

Measure cheese into small bowl. Add garlic salt and onion salt. Stir well. Drizzle margarine over popcorn. Sprinkle with cheese mixture. Toss well. Makes 24 cups (6 L).

1 cup (250 mL): 79 Calories; 5 g Total Fat; 88 mg Sodium; 2 g Protein; 7 g Carbohydrate; 1 g Dietary Fiber

Pictured on page 107.

TORTILLA CHIPS

When making your own you have a choice of deep-frying or baking.

Corn tortillas (6 inch, 15 cm, size)	**12**	**12**
Cooking oil, for deep-frying		
Salt (or seasoned salt), sprinkle		

Cut each tortilla into 8 wedges. Deep-fry several at a time in hot 375°F (190°C) cooking oil, turning occasionally, until crisp. Transfer to paper towels to drain.

Sprinkle with salt. Makes 96.

4 chips: 72 Calories; 3.8 g Total Fat; 35 mg Sodium; 1 g Protein; 9 g Carbohydrate; 1 g Dietary Fiber

Pictured on page 35.

OVEN TORTILLA CHIPS: Arrange wedges in single layer on ungreased baking sheets. Brush lightly with water. Sprinkle with salt. Bake in 400°F (205°C) oven for about 8 minutes. Turn wedges over. Bake for about 3 minutes.

They bought a lot of ducks to try to improve their income. But they aren't picking up, they're picking down.

GOOD OL' NUTS 'N' BOLTS

Wonderful variety of shapes. A nice toasted flavor with a subtle taste of spices.

Small wheat squares cereal (such as Shreddies)	2 cups	500 mL
"O"-shaped toasted oat cereal (such as Cheerios)	1 cup	250 mL
Thin pretzels, broken in half	1 cup	250 mL
Rice and corn squares cereal (such as Crispix)	2 cups	500 mL
Mini snack crackers (such as Ritz Bits)	2 cups	500 mL
Mixed nuts	2 cups	500 mL
Hard margarine (or butter)	$\frac{1}{4}$ cup	60 mL
Cooking oil	$\frac{1}{4}$ cup	60 mL
Worcestershire sauce	2 tbsp.	30 mL
Garlic salt	1 tsp.	5 mL
Celery salt	1 tsp.	5 mL
Onion salt	1 tsp.	5 mL
Seasoned salt	1 tsp.	5 mL

Combine first 6 ingredients in large roaster. Stir.

Heat remaining 7 ingredients in small saucepan, stirring occasionally, until margarine is melted. Drizzle over dry mixture. Toss well. Bake, uncovered, in 250°F (120°C) oven for 1 hour, stirring every 20 minutes. Cool. Store in airtight containers. Makes 2 quarts (2 L).

$\frac{1}{4}$ cup (60 mL): 129 Calories; 8.8 g Total Fat; 314 mg Sodium; 3 g Protein; 11 g Carbohydrate; 1 g Dietary Fiber

Pictured on front cover.

CANDY KISS POPCORN

Good to munch on anytime.

Popped corn (pop about 1 cup, 250 mL)	6 qts.	6 L
Peanuts (optional)	1 cup	250 mL
Granulated sugar	2 cups	500 mL
Water	$\frac{1}{2}$ cup	125 mL
Fancy molasses	$\frac{1}{2}$ cup	125 mL
Salt	$\frac{1}{2}$ tsp.	2 mL
Baking soda	1 tsp.	5 mL

(continued on next page)

Snacks

Combine popcorn and peanuts in extra large container such as large roaster or preserving kettle.

Heat sugar, water, molasses and salt in heavy medium saucepan. Stir until sugar is dissolved. Boil until soft ball stage on candy thermometer and a teaspoonful forms soft ball in cold water. Remove from heat.

Sift in baking soda. Pour while foaming over popcorn mixture. Stir well until evenly coated. Turn out onto large greased baking sheets. Bake in 350°F (175°C) oven for 10 minutes to dry. Stir and break up large pieces while it cools. Makes 16 cups (4 L).

1 cup (250 mL): 192 Calories; 0.8 g Total Fat; 173 mg Sodium; 2 g Protein; 46 g Carbohydrate; 1 g Dietary Fiber

TORTILLA CRISPS

Quick to make and very tasty. Serve with Mexican-type dips or enjoy them as they are.

Hard margarine (or butter), softened	¾ cup	175 mL
Grated Parmesan cheese	½ cup	125 mL
Parsley flakes	2 tsp.	10 mL
Sesame seeds	¼ cup	60 mL
Dried whole oregano	½ tsp.	2 mL
Onion powder	¼ tsp.	1 mL
Garlic powder	¼ tsp.	1 mL
Flour tortillas (6 inch, 15 cm, size)	12	12

Combine first 7 ingredients in small bowl. Mix well.

Spread each tortilla with thick layer of cheese mixture. It will seem like too much but once cooked they will be just right. Cut each tortilla into 8 wedges. Arrange in single layer on ungreased baking sheets. Bake in 350°F (175°C) oven for 12 to 15 minutes until crisp and browned. Makes 96.

4 chips: 129 Calories; 7.8 g Total Fat; 182 mg Sodium; 3 g Protein; 12 g Carbohydrate; trace Dietary Fiber

Pictured on page 35.

SPICED NUTS

Make lots of these days before you need them.

Egg white (large), room temperature	1	1
Water	2 tsp.	10 mL
Mixed nuts (or salted peanuts)	2 cups	500 mL
Granulated sugar	1/2 cup	125 mL
Ground cinnamon	1 tsp.	5 mL
Ground nutmeg	1/2 tsp.	2 mL
Ground ginger	1/4 tsp.	1 mL
Salt	1/8 tsp.	0.5 mL

Beat egg white and water in medium bowl until smooth.

Stir in nuts.

Mix remaining 5 ingredients in small bowl. Add to nuts. Stir to coat. Spread on greased baking sheet. Bake in 250°F (120°C) oven for 1 hour, stirring every 15 minutes. Store in covered container or freeze. Makes 2 cups (500 mL).

1/4 cup (60 mL): 269 Calories; 18.7 g Total Fat; 55 mg Sodium; 7 g Protein; 23 g Carbohydrate; 2 g Dietary Fiber

ORANGE PECANS

Delicious candied nuts. Nice orange aftertaste.

Granulated sugar	1/2 cup	125 mL
Pecan halves	2 cups	500 mL
Grated orange peel	1 tbsp.	15 mL
Prepared orange juice	1/4 cup	60 mL

Combine all 4 ingredients in medium saucepan. Heat and stir until boiling. Boil, stirring constantly, until all liquid is absorbed. Turn out onto ungreased baking sheet. Separate pecans. Cool. Makes about 2 1/4 cups (550 mL).

1/4 cup (60 mL): 221 Calories; 17.4 g Total Fat; trace Sodium; 2 g Protein; 17 g Carbohydrate; 2 g Dietary Fiber

Pictured on page 107.

PARTY CRACKERS ▬

Good and crisp. Serve with a dip or spread.

Rye flour	1 cup	250 mL
All-purpose flour	1/2 cup	125 mL
Whole wheat flour	1/2 cup	125 mL
Salt	1/2 tsp.	2 mL
Baking soda	1/4 tsp.	1 mL
Celery salt	1/8 tsp.	0.5 mL
Water, approximately	1/2 cup	125 mL
Cooking oil	1/4 cup	60 mL

Measure all 3 flours, salt, baking soda and celery salt into medium bowl. Stir.

Add water and cooking oil. Mix into a ball, adding a touch more water if needed. Turn out onto lightly floured surface. Knead 20 times until smooth. Roll out 1/8 inch (3 mm) thick. Cut into 2 inch (5 cm) squares. Arrange on greased baking sheet in 275°F (140°C) oven for 30 to 40 minutes until browned. Makes about 50.

5 crackers: 136 Calories; 6.1 g Total Fat; 187 mg Sodium; 2 g Protein; 18 g Carbohydrate; 3 g Dietary Fiber

Pictured on page 53.

ROASTED NUT SNACK ▬

Dark in color. An intense flavor that keep you munching.

Soy sauce	1/2 cup	125 mL
Granulated sugar	1 tsp.	5 mL
Ground ginger	1/4 tsp.	1 mL
Garlic powder	1/4 tsp.	1 mL
Pecan halves (or peanuts)	3 cups	750 mL

Stir soy sauce, sugar, ginger and garlic in small bowl.

Add pecans. Stir well. Place pecans in greased 9 x 13 inch (22 x 33 cm) pan. Bake in 200°F (95°C) oven, stirring often, for about 1 hour until dried. Makes 3 cups (750 mL).

1/4 cup (60 mL): 203 Calories; 19.6 g Total Fat; 726 mg Sodium; 3 g Protein; 7 g Carbohydrate; 2 g Dietary Fiber

SEASONED CRACKERS

Lots of garlic flavor on these.

Water	6 tbsp.	100 mL
Cornstarch	1 tsp.	5 mL
Envelope ranch-style salad dressing mix	1 × 1 oz.	1 × 28 g
Dill weed	1 tsp.	5 mL
Garlic powder	½ tsp.	2 mL
Garlic salt	½ tsp.	2 mL
Cooking oil	2 tbsp.	30 mL
Oyster (or other small snack) crackers	5 cups	1.25 L

Stir water and cornstarch together in small saucepan. Heat and stir until boiling and thickened. Remove from heat.

Whisk in next 5 ingredients.

Measure oyster crackers into large bowl. Add dill mixture. Toss and stir well. Spread on large ungreased baking sheet. Bake in 350°F (175°C) oven for 30 minutes, stirring several times. Makes 5 cups (1.25 L).

½ cup (125 mL): 154 Calories; 7.5 g Total Fat; 557 mg Sodium; 2 g Protein; 20 g Carbohydrate; trace Dietary Fiber

BAKED MIXED NUTS

Good munchies.

Cooking oil	1 tbsp.	15 mL
Chili powder	2 tsp.	10 mL
Garlic powder	½ tsp.	2 mL
Onion powder	½ tsp.	2 mL
Hot pepper sauce	½ tsp.	2 mL
Worcestershire sauce	½ tsp.	2 mL
Unsalted mixed nuts	2 cups	500 mL

Measure first 6 ingredients into medium bowl. Mix well.

Add nuts. Stir well to coat all nuts. Spread on ungreased baking sheet. Bake in 350°F (175°C) oven for 12 to 15 minutes until browned. Makes 2 cups (500 mL).

¼ cup (60 mL): 234 Calories; 20.5 g Total Fat; 16 mg Sodium; 6 g Protein; 10 g Carbohydrate; 2 g Dietary Fiber

Snacks

ROASTED GARLIC

Makes a nice soft spread. Serve with baguette slices or crackers. Or use as a condiment with hamburgers or steak. Roast several at a time if desired.

Whole garlic bulb	1	1
Olive oil	2 tbsp.	30 mL

Turn garlic bulb on its side. Cut top just so it cuts barely through tops of garlic cloves. Set bulb, cut side up, in garlic baker or small ungreased casserole.

Drizzle olive oil over center of bulb. Cover. Bake in 350°F (175°C) oven for about 40 minutes until it looks caramelized. Squeeze softened garlic out of top of bulb. Discard skin. Combine softened garlic and olive oil in bottom of casserole. Makes 2 tbsp. (30 mL).

1 tsp. (5 mL): 52 Calories; 4.6 g Total Fat; 1 mg Sodium; trace Protein; 2 g Carbohydrate; trace Dietary Fiber

SALMON BALL

Wonderful flavor and crunch as well. Make the variation to fit a cracker.

Canned red salmon, drained, skin and round bones removed, flaked	7½ oz.	213 g
Cream cheese, softened	8 oz.	250 g
Lemon juice	1 tbsp.	15 mL
Prepared horseradish	1 tbsp.	15 mL
Salt	¼ tsp.	1 mL
Finely chopped walnuts (or pecans), toasted	½ cup	125 mL

Mix first 5 ingredients well in medium bowl. Chill for at least 3 hours until mixture can be shaped. Shape into ball.

Roll ball in walnuts to coat. Chill in covered container. Makes 1¾ cups (425 mL).

1 tbsp. (15 mL): 54 Calories; 4.9 g Total Fat; 81 mg Sodium; 2 g Protein; 1 g Carbohydrate; trace Dietary Fiber

Variation: Shape into small balls, using 1½ tsp. (7 mL) mixture, each. Roll in finely chopped walnuts or pecans. Makes 56.

TUNA PÂTÉ

Bring to room temperature before serving. Just the right spreading consistency. Serve with assorted crackers or Toast Cups, page 14.

Cream cheese, softened	8 oz.	250 g
Chili sauce	2 tbsp.	30 mL
Chopped chives	2 tsp.	10 mL
Parsley flakes	2 tsp.	10 mL
Onion powder	1/2 tsp.	2 mL
Hot pepper sauce	1 tsp.	5 mL
Chopped green onion	2 tbsp.	30 mL
Canned tuna, drained and flaked	2 × 6 1/2 oz.	2 × 184 g
Chopped fresh dill (or 1/2 tsp., 2 mL, dill weed)	2 tsp.	10 mL

CREAM CHEESE FROSTING

Cream cheese, softened	4 oz.	125 g
Skim evaporated milk (or light cream)	1 tbsp.	15 mL

Mix all 9 ingredients well in large bowl. Shape by hand into round or oblong mound on serving dish. Chill before frosting.

Cream Cheese Frosting: Beat cream cheese and evaporated milk together well. Frost top and sides of pâté mound. Chill. Makes 2 1/2 cups (625 mL).

1 tbsp. (15 mL): 42 Calories; 3.3 g Total Fat; 65 mg Sodium; 3 g Protein; 1 g Carbohydrate; trace Dietary Fiber

CRAB DELUXE

Have this in the refrigerator for a ready-to-serve tasty treat. Serve with crackers.

Cream cheese, softened	12 oz.	340 g
Salad dressing (or mayonnaise)	1/4 cup	60 mL
Worcestershire sauce	2 tbsp.	30 mL
White vinegar	1 tsp.	5 mL
Minced mild onion	1/4 cup	60 mL
Chili sauce	1/2 cup	125 mL
Canned crabmeat, drained and cartilage removed	2 × 4 1/4 oz.	2 × 120 g
Chopped green onion (or chives)	2 tbsp.	30 mL

(continued on next page)

120 Spreads

Mix first 5 ingredients in medium bowl until smooth. Spread over ungreased 12 inch (30 cm) serving plate or pizza pan.

Spread chili sauce over top, keeping in about ½ inch (12 mm) from edge. Sprinkle crabmeat over chili sauce. Sprinkle with green onion. Cover. Chill for several hours so flavors will have a chance to blend. Makes about 3½ cups (875 mL).

1 tbsp. (15 mL): 30 Calories; 2.6 g Total Fat; 77 mg Sodium; 1 g Protein; 1 g Carbohydrate; trace Dietary Fiber

LOG O' CHEESE

A very different coating for this log. Sesame seeds add a great flavor.

Grated sharp Cheddar cheese, lightly packed	2 cups	500 mL
Salad dressing (or mayonnaise)	¼ cup	60 mL
Sweet pickle relish	2 tbsp.	30 mL
Seasoned salt	½ tsp.	2 mL
Onion powder	½ tsp.	2 mL
Minced green pepper	3 tbsp.	50 mL
Roasted red pepper, chopped (or chopped pimiento)	1 tbsp.	15 mL
Large hard-boiled egg, finely chopped	1	1
Saltine cracker crumbs	½ cup	125 mL
Sesame seeds	¼ cup	60 mL

Mix first 5 ingredients well in medium bowl.

Add next 4 ingredients. Mix well. Shape into roll, 1½ inches (3.8 cm) in diameter and about 9 inches (22 cm) long. Wrap in waxed paper. Chill for at least 1 hour to firm.

Spread sesame seeds over bottom of ungreased 9 x 13 inch (22 x 33 cm) pan. Toast in 350°F (175°C) oven for 5 to 10 minutes until lightly toasted. Set cheese log at end. Roll over warm seeds to coat. Wrap in waxed paper. Chill until ready to serve. Makes 1 log, about 2 cups (500 mL). Cuts into 36 slices.

1 slice: 50 Calories; 3.9 g Total Fat; 90 mg Sodium; 2 g Protein; 2 g Carbohydrate; trace Dietary Fiber

SHRIMP MOUSSE

A real party attraction. Surround with a variety of crackers or cocktail-size dark bread squares.

Envelopes unflavored gelatin	2 x ¼ oz.	2 x 7 g
Water	½ cup	125 mL
Cream cheese, softened	8 oz.	250 g
Condensed tomato soup	10 oz.	284 mL
Salad dressing (or mayonnaise)	½ cup	125 mL
Lemon juice	2 tbsp.	30 mL
Salt	½ tsp.	2 mL
Onion powder	½ tsp.	2 mL
Worcestershire sauce	¼ tsp.	1 mL
Finely chopped celery	1 cup	250 mL
Finely chopped green pepper	⅓ cup	75 mL
Canned small (or broken) shrimp, drained, rinsed and chopped	2 x 4 oz.	2 x 113 g

Sprinkle gelatin over water in small saucepan. Let stand for 1 minute. Heat and stir until gelatin is dissolved. Remove from heat.

Beat cream cheese and tomato soup in small bowl until smooth. Beat in salad dressing, lemon juice, salt, onion powder and Worcestershire sauce. Add gelatin mixture. Stir well.

Fold in remaining 3 ingredients. Turn into 6 cup (1.5 L) mold. Chill. Makes 5½ cups (1.4 L).

1 tbsp. (15 mL): 42 Calories; 3.2 g Total Fat; 117 mg Sodium; 2 g Protein; 2 g Carbohydrate; trace Dietary Fiber

APRICOT CHEESE SPREAD

One of the quickest, easiest and best. Serve with Party Crackers, page 117. Needs a cocktail spreader.

Cream cheese	8 oz.	250 g
Apricot jam	⅓ cup	75 mL
Dry mustard	1½ tsp.	7 mL
Apple cider vinegar	½ tsp.	2 mL

(continued on next page)

Set cream cheese block on serving plate.

Mix jam, mustard and vinegar in small bowl. Makes ⅓ cup (75 mL). Spoon over cream cheese, allowing some to run down sides. Makes about 16 servings.

1 serving: 75 Calories; 5.6 g Total Fat; 47 mg Sodium; 1 g Protein; 5 g Carbohydrate; trace Dietary Fiber

Pictured on page 53.

SALMON MOUSSE

A star attraction that will disappear quickly. Serve with Toast Cups, page 14, or an assortment of crackers.

Envelope unflavored gelatin	1 × ¼ oz.	1 × 7 g
Water	½ cup	125 mL
Salad dressing (or mayonnaise)	½ cup	125 mL
Sour cream	¼ cup	60 mL
Lemon juice	1 tbsp.	15 mL
Dill weed	2 tsp.	10 mL
Onion powder	1 tsp.	5 mL
Paprika	1 tsp.	5 mL
Hot pepper sauce	½ tsp.	2 mL
Salt	¼ tsp.	1 mL
Canned red salmon, drained, skin and bones removed, flaked	7½ oz.	213 g
Envelope dessert topping, prepared according to package directions	1	1

Sprinkle gelatin over water in small saucepan. Let stand for 1 minute. Heat and stir until gelatin is dissolved. Remove from heat. Cool.

Add next 8 ingredients. Whisk until well mixed. Chill, stirring often, until mixture starts to thicken.

Fold in salmon.

Fold dessert topping into salmon mixture. Turn into 4 cup (1 L) mold. Chill. Makes 4 cups (1 L).

2 tbsp. (30 mL): 40 Calories; 3.2 g Total Fat; 73 mg Sodium; 1 g Protein; 1 g Carbohydrate; trace Dietary Fiber

We should be like pianos, either upright or grand.

BRUSCHETTA BRIE

Wonderful basil and garlic flavor that everyone enjoys. Needs a cocktail spreader.

Small tomato, seeded and finely chopped	1	1
Garlic clove, crushed	1	1
Olive oil	1 tsp.	5 mL
Dried sweet basil, crushed	1½ tsp.	7 mL
Salt	¼ tsp.	1 mL
Pepper, sprinkle		
Brie cheese round, with rind	4 oz.	125 g
Baguette slices, toasted or plain	12	12

Combine first 6 ingredients in small bowl. Stir. Let stand at room temperature for 1 hour.

Set cheese round in ungreased small shallow casserole. Using slotted spoon, and allowing most liquid to drain off, transfer tomato mixture over top of cheese. Discard remaining liquid. Bake, uncovered, in 375°F (190°C) oven for 8 to 10 minutes until cheese is soft inside rind. Transfer with pancake lifter to serving plate.

Surround with baguette slices. Makes 12 appetizer servings.

1 serving: *151 Calories; 4.1 g Total Fat; 343 mg Sodium; 6 g Protein; 22 g Carbohydrate; 1 g Dietary Fiber*

Pictured on page 53.

1 Lettuce Wraps, page 110
2. Beef Buns, page 28
3. Hot And Sour Soup, page 150
4. Oriental Chicken Rolls, page 98
5. Crab Rangoon, page 58
6. Spring Rolls, page 109
7. Simple Sweet And Sour Sauce, page 41
8. Sprout Salad, page 140
9. Salad Rolls, page 96

Props Courtesy Of: Eaton's
Kitchen Treasures
Scona Clayworks
The Bay

Spreads

Write it down…

Keep a record of your guest list, menu and recipes, grocery list, theme and decorations, and any ideas or suggestions you may have for your next gathering. When you plan another party, you'll have all this helpful information at your fingertips!

SAVORY CHEESECAKE

Serve a slightly larger wedge for a sit-down starter, or surround the smaller appetizer wedges with raw vegetables and taco chips on a platter.

CRUST

Hard margarine (or butter)	½ cup	125 mL
Soda cracker crumbs	1½ cups	375 mL
Grated Parmesan cheese	¼ cup	60 mL

FILLING

Cream cheese, softened	2 x 8 oz.	2 x 250 g
Grated Monterey Jack cheese	1 cup	250 mL
Grated sharp Cheddar cheese	1 cup	250 mL
Sour cream	1 cup	250 mL
Onion powder	½ tsp.	2 mL
Salt	¼ tsp.	1 mL
Pepper	⅛ tsp.	0.5 mL
Large eggs	3	3
Canned diced green chilies, drained	4 oz.	114 mL

TOPPING

Salsa	½ cup	125 mL

Crust: Melt margarine in medium saucepan. Add cracker crumbs and Parmesan cheese. Mix. Press in bottom of ungreased 9 inch (22 cm) springform pan. Bake in 350°F (175°C) oven for 10 minutes. Cool.

Filling: Combine first 7 ingredients in large bowl. Beat until smooth and creamy.

Slowly beat in 1 egg at a time, beating after each addition until just mixed. Add green chilies. Stir. Pour over crust. Bake for 50 minutes until center is barely firm. Remove from oven. Immediately run paring knife around top edge so cheesecake settles evenly. Cool. Refrigerate overnight.

Topping: Spread salsa over top of chilled cheesecake. Cuts into 20 wedges.

1 wedge: 246 Calories; 21.1 g Total Fat; 475 mg Sodium; 8 g Protein; 7 g Carbohydrate; trace Dietary Fiber

CHEESY CHILI BALL

Surround this full-flavored spread with your favorite crackers. Has a wee bit of a bite to it.

Cream cheese, softened	8 oz.	250 g
Process cheese loaf (such as Velveeta), room temperature	8 oz.	250 g
Grated medium Cheddar cheese	2 cups	500 mL
Chili powder	1½ tsp.	7 mL
Garlic powder	¼ tsp.	1 mL
Onion salt	¹⁄₁₆ tsp.	0.5 mL
Chopped pecans (or walnuts)	½ cup	125 mL

Mix first 6 ingredients well in medium bowl. Chill until firm enough to roll. Shape into ball.

Roll in pecans to coat. Cover with plastic wrap. Makes 3¼ cups (800 mL).

1 tbsp. (15 mL): 57 Calories; 5 g Total Fat; 117 mg Sodium; 2 g Protein; 1 g Carbohydrate; trace Dietary Fiber

BLUE CHEESE BALL

Just enough blue cheese to give a bit of a nip. Looks terrific either alone or surrounded with crackers.

Cream cheese, softened	8 oz.	250 g
Blue cheese, softened	4 oz.	125 g
Grated medium Cheddar cheese	2 cups	500 mL
Chopped pecans (or walnuts)	½ cup	125 mL
Parsley flakes	1 tbsp.	15 mL
Worcestershire sauce	1 tsp.	5 mL
Onion powder	½ tsp.	2 mL
Chopped pecans (or walnuts)	½ cup	125 mL

Combine first 7 ingredients in large bowl. Mix thoroughly. Shape into ball.

Put second amount of pecans onto working surface. Roll cheese ball in pecans to coat. Chill. Bring to room temperature just before serving for best flavor. Makes about 3 cups (750 mL).

1 tbsp. (15 mL): 62 Calories; 5.7 g Total Fat; 81 mg Sodium; 2 g Protein; 1 g Carbohydrate; trace Dietary Fiber

Individual salads on a lettuce bed look so neat.

Envelopes unflavored gelatin	2 x ¼ oz.	2 x 7 g
Water	½ cup	125 mL
Condensed tomato soup	10 oz.	284 mL
Cream cheese, cut up	8 oz.	250 g
Salad dressing (or mayonnaise)	¾ cup	175 mL
Sour cream	¼ cup	60 mL
Chopped pimiento-stuffed green olives	¼ cup	60 mL
Chopped celery	½ cup	125 mL
Onion powder	¼ tsp.	1 mL
Salt	¼ tsp.	1 mL
Granulated sugar	1 tsp.	5 mL
Shredded iceberg lettuce	5 cups	1.25 L
Thin slices peeled cucumber	10	10
Sour cream (or mayonnaise)	2 tbsp.	30 mL

Sprinkle gelatin over water in medium saucepan. Let stand for 1 minute. Heat and stir until gelatin is dissolved.

Add tomato soup. Mix well. Add cream cheese. Heat, stirring often, until cream cheese is melted. Use whisk or beater if necessary.

Whisk in salad dressing and first amount of sour cream. Add olives, celery, onion powder, salt and sugar. Stir well. Pour into 10 individual ⅓ cup (75 mL) salad molds. Chill for 20 minutes. Stir gently to distribute contents. Chill until firm.

Let stand at room temperature for 30 to 45 minutes for easy unmolding. Divide lettuce among 10 salad plates. Unmold aspic onto lettuce. Garnish each with cucumber slice. Place a dab of sour cream on top of each cucumber slice. Makes 10.

1 mold: 218 Calories; 19 g Total Fat; 554 mg Sodium; 4 g Protein; 9 g Carbohydrate; 1 g Dietary Fiber

What a noise. Ever since their cat ate their canary, it thinks it can sing.

SHRIMP PAPAYA SALAD

Just an incredible mixture of flavors. Very showy and so very good.

DILL SAUCE

Sour cream	¼ cup	60 mL
Salad dressing (or mayonnaise)	¼ cup	60 mL
Lemon juice	1 tsp.	5 mL
Dill weed	½ tsp.	2 mL
Granulated sugar	½ tsp.	2 mL
Lettuce cups	4	4
Papayas, peeled, seeded and diced	2	2
Cooked medium shrimp, peeled and deveined	1 cup	250 mL

Dill Sauce: Mix sour cream, salad dressing, lemon juice, dill weed and sugar in small bowl. This can be prepared ahead and chilled.

Lay 1 lettuce cup on each of 4 salad plates. Place ¼ of diced papaya on each lettuce leaf. Divide shrimp over papaya. Drizzle sauce over shrimp. Serves 4.

1 serving: 199 Calories; 10.4 g Total Fat; 185 mg Sodium; 9 g Protein; 19 g Carbohydrate; 3 g Dietary Fiber

Pictured on page 143.

PISTACHIO SALAD

A dramatic contrast is created with the dark green spinach leaves and the white cottage cheese. Very showy.

Canned fruit cocktail, drained	14 oz.	398 mL
Canned crushed pineapple, well drained	8 oz.	227 mL
Instant pistachio pudding powder, 4 serving size (add dry)	1	1
Creamed cottage cheese	2 cups	500 mL
Miniature marshmallows	1 cup	250 mL
Envelope dessert topping, prepared according to package directions	1	1
Shredded fresh spinach, packed	4 cups	1 L
Maraschino cherries, patted dry	8	8
Chopped pistachios (optional)	1 tbsp.	15 mL

(continued on next page)

Stir first 3 ingredients together well in large bowl.

Add cottage cheese and marshmallows. Stir. Fold in dessert topping.

Divide spinach among 8 salad plates. Use ice-cream scoop to place salad on spinach.

Top each with cherry. Add sprinkle of chopped pistachios. Serves 8.

1 serving: 196 Calories; 3.5 g Total Fat; 355 mg Sodium; 10 g Protein; 33 g Carbohydrate; 2 g Dietary Fiber

FRESH FRUIT SALAD

A festive-looking salad to pass around the table for a first course. Dressing is very tasty and clings well to the fruit.

APRICOT DRESSING		
Dried apricots	8	8
Boiling water, to cover		
Vanilla yogurt	**¾ cup**	**175 mL**
SALAD		
Whole fresh strawberries, halved	6	6
Kiwifruit, peeled and cut lengthwise into 6 wedges	4	4
Seedless red grapes, halved	18	18
Cantaloupe balls or pieces	24	24
Fresh blueberries	**½ cup**	**125 mL**
Thin red apple wedges, with peel, dipped into lemon juice	12	12

Apricot Dressing: Soak apricots in boiling water to cover for about 20 minutes. Drain. Transfer to blender.

Add yogurt. Process until smooth. Makes ¾ cup (175 mL) dressing.

Salad: Arrange assorted fruit on large plate, beginning with strawberries in center. Add rings of other fruit. Stand apple slices, skin side up, around top of fruit. Drizzle with dressing. Serves 6.

1 serving: 129 Calories; 1.3 g Total Fat; 35 mg Sodium; 4 g Protein; 29 g Carbohydrate; 4 g Dietary Fiber

BLUEBERRY STARTER

This is so good you could almost serve it for dessert.

Packages raspberry-flavored gelatin (jelly powder)	2 × 3 oz.	2 × 85 g
Boiling water	2 cups	500 mL
Reserved juice from blueberries and pineapple, plus water if needed to make	1 cup	250 mL
Canned blueberries, drained and juice reserved	14 oz.	398 mL
Canned crushed pineapple, drained and juice reserved	14 oz.	398 mL
CREAM CHEESE DRESSING		
Light cream cheese, softened	8 oz.	250 g
Granulated sugar	½ cup	125 mL
Light sour cream	1 cup	250 mL
Vanilla	1 tsp.	5 mL
Chopped pecans (or walnuts)	½ cup	125 mL
Lettuce cups	9	9

Combine gelatin and boiling water in medium bowl. Stir until gelatin is dissolved.

Add reserved juices. Stir. Chill, stirring and scraping down sides occasionally, until syrupy consistency.

Add blueberries and pineapple. Stir. Pour into ungreased 9 × 9 inch (22 × 22 cm) square pan. Chill until firm.

Cream Cheese Dressing: Beat cream cheese, sugar, sour cream and vanilla in medium bowl until smooth. Spread over jelled layer, or drizzle dressing over individual servings.

Sprinkle with pecans.

Set lettuce cup on each of 9 plates. Cut salad into 9 pieces. Set piece of salad in center of lettuce. Serves 9.

1 serving: 310 Calories; 10.9 g Total Fat; 306 mg Sodium; 6 g Protein; 50 g Carbohydrate; 2 g Dietary Fiber

Color, flavor, crunch and more flavor. This is the one.

NOODLES		
Hard margarine (or butter)	1½ tbsp.	25 mL
Worcestershire sauce	1½ tsp.	7 mL
Seasoned salt	¼ tsp.	1 mL
Garlic salt	⅛ tsp.	0.5 mL
Onion powder	⅛ tsp.	0.5 mL
Curry powder	¼ tsp.	1 mL
Chow mein noodles	1 cup	250 mL

SALAD		
Head of romaine lettuce, cut up	1	1
Green pepper slivers, 1-1½ inches (2.5-3.8 cm) long	⅔ cup	150 mL
Medium tomatoes, halved, seeded and cut into thin wedges	2	2

DRESSING		
Salad dressing (or mayonnaise)	⅓ cup	75 mL
French dressing (red)	2 tbsp.	30 mL
Milk	2 tbsp.	30 mL
Granulated sugar	½ tsp.	2 mL

Noodles: Put first 6 ingredients into medium saucepan. Heat and stir until margarine is melted.

Add noodles. Stir well to coat. Spread on ungreased baking sheet. Bake in 250°F (120°C) oven for 15 minutes. Cool.

Salad: Toss all 3 ingredients together in large bowl.

Dressing: Measure all 4 ingredients into small bowl. Stir. Add to salad along with noodles. Toss. Makes 8 cups (2 L).

1 cup (250 mL): 141 Calories; 11.2 g Total Fat; 266 mg Sodium; 2 g Protein; 9 g Carbohydrate; 2 g Dietary Fiber

What colorful weather. The sun rose and the wind blew.

PINK SALAD MOLDS

Small salads with a creamy raspberry flavor. Lots of crunchy pecans. Mousse consistency.

Package raspberry-flavored gelatin (jelly powder)	1 × 3 oz.	1 × 85 g
Boiling water	1 cup	250 mL
Cream cheese, softened	4 oz.	125 g
Canned crushed pineapple, well drained	8 oz.	227 mL
Envelope dessert topping, prepared according to package directions	1	1
Chopped pecans (or walnuts)	½ cup	125 mL
Lettuce cups	8	8

Stir gelatin and boiling water in medium bowl until gelatin is dissolved. Chill, stirring and scraping down sides occasionally, until syrupy consistency.

Mash cream cheese with fork in medium bowl until very soft. Add pineapple. Mix. Stir into thickened jelly.

Fold in dessert topping and pecans. This makes 4½ cups (1.1 L) jelly. Fill 8 individual molds, each holding about ½ cup (125 mL). Chill until set.

Set lettuce cup on each of 8 salad plates. Unmold salads onto lettuce cups. Serves 8.

1 serving: 191 Calories; 12.8 g Total Fat; 87 mg Sodium; 4 g Protein; 17 g Carbohydrate; 1 g Dietary Fiber

What else would invisible parents feed their baby but evaporated milk?

An artistic arrangement makes for a conversational presentation. These are almost too pretty to disturb.

POPPY SEED DRESSING

Granulated sugar	⅓ cup	75 mL
White vinegar	¼ cup	60 mL
Prepared mustard	1½ tsp.	7 mL
Prepared horseradish	¼ tsp.	1 mL
Salt	¼ tsp.	1 mL
Pepper, just a pinch		
Cooking oil	⅓ cup	75 mL
Poppy seeds	1½ tsp.	7 mL

SALAD

Chinese cabbage inner leaves	18	18
Paper-thin lengthwise slices of small English cucumber	18	18
Cantaloupe center ring slices, peeled	6	6
Red pepper ring slices	6	6
Strawberries (or cherry tomatoes), cut into fans, for garnish	18	18

Poppy Seed Dressing: Measure first 6 ingredients into blender. Process until smooth.

With blender running, add cooking oil in a slow steady stream until mixture has thickened.

Pour into container. Stir in poppy seeds. Chill until needed. Makes ⅔ cup (150 mL) dressing.

Salad: Arrange 3 cabbage leaves on each of 6 salad plates, placing leaves in spoke fashion out from center equal distance apart. Lay cucumber slice on each leaf, rounding ends that are visible. Set ring of cantaloupe in center. Place red pepper ring on top of cantaloupe.

Cut strawberries in slices from top almost to, but not through, bottom. Press gently to fan out. Set 1 in center of each red pepper ring. Place 1 between each pair of cabbage leaves. Drizzle about 2 tbsp. (30 mL) dressing over each salad. Serves 6.

1 serving: 190 Calories; 13.4 g Total Fat; 141 mg Sodium; 1 g Protein; 18 g Carbohydrate; 1 g Dietary Fiber

Pictured on page 143.

WHITE SALAD

A white salad nestled inside a green border.

Shredded dark green lettuce (such as romaine), packed	3 cups	750 mL
Sliced fresh white mushrooms	1½ cups	375 mL
Sliced center white ribs of celery	1½ cups	375 mL
Peeled and sliced radishes	½ cup	125 mL
Grated Monterey Jack cheese	¾ cup	175 mL
HONEY DRESSING		
Liquid honey	⅓ cup	75 mL
White vinegar	¼ cup	60 mL
Cooking oil	3 tbsp.	50 mL
Pepper, just a pinch		

Make outer ring of lettuce on each of 6 salad plates.

Divide mushrooms, celery and radish inside lettuce rings, leaving a border of green all around. Pile cheese in center.

Honey Dressing: Mix all 4 ingredients well in small bowl. Makes ⅔ cup (150 mL). Drizzle about 2 tbsp. (30 mL) over each salad. Serves 6.

1 serving: 194 Calories; 11.7 g Total Fat; 114 mg Sodium; 5 g Protein; 20 g Carbohydrate; 1 g Dietary Fiber

AVOCADO SALAD

Smooth creamy avocado takes center stage. Delicious.

Chili sauce	¼ cup	60 mL
Lemon juice	1 tbsp.	15 mL
Granulated sugar	4 tsp.	20 mL
Onion powder	¼ tsp.	1 mL
Worcestershire sauce	½ tsp.	2 mL
Salt	½ tsp.	2 mL
Celery salt	¼ tsp.	1 mL
Garlic powder	¼ tsp.	1 mL
Avocados, peeled and sliced	2	2
Salad greens, cut up	2 cups	500 mL

(continued on next page)

Stir first 8 ingredients together well in medium bowl.

Add avocado. Stir to coat well. Cover. Let stand in refrigerator for several hours or overnight, stirring gently once or twice.

Divide salad greens among each of 4 salad plates. Gently spoon avocado with dressing over greens. Serves 4.

1 serving: 205 Calories; 15.6 g Total Fat; 693 mg Sodium; 3 g Protein; 18 g Carbohydrate; 4 g Dietary Fiber

PARFAIT SALAD

Layers of crabmeat, lettuce and assorted vegetables. Topped with cheese, this is a novel presentation.

Salad dressing (or mayonnaise)	1/4 cup	60 mL
Sweet pickle relish	2 tsp.	10 mL
Finely chopped celery	2 tsp.	10 mL
Parsley flakes	1 tsp.	5 mL
Onion powder	1/8 tsp.	0.5 mL
Sour cream	3 tbsp.	50 mL
Salt	1/4 tsp.	1 mL
Milk	1 tbsp.	15 mL
Canned crabmeat, drained and cartilage removed	41/4 oz.	120 g
Large hard-boiled eggs, chopped	2	2
Chopped lettuce, packed	1 cup	250 mL
Green onions, thinly sliced	2	2
Cooked peas, cooled	1/2 cup	125 mL
Grated medium Cheddar cheese	1/4 cup	60 mL

Combine first 10 ingredients in medium bowl. Stir together.

Divide lettuce among 4 stemmed large wine or water goblets or other glassware. Even an old-fashioned glass will work.

Divide crab mixture over top, being careful not to smear edge of glass. Divide and layer green onion and peas over crabmeat.

Sprinkle 1 tbsp. (15 mL) cheese over each. Chill until serving time. Serves 4.

1 serving: 211 Calories; 15.1 g Total Fat; 565 mg Sodium; 11 g Protein; 8 g Carbohydrate; 1 g Dietary Fiber

SALAD HORNS

These little horns of plenty are impressive with a fruit and chicken filling and a curry dressing.

PASTRY HORNS

Frozen puff pastry (see Note), thawed according to package directions	$\frac{1}{2}$ x 14.1 oz.	$\frac{1}{2}$ x 397 g
Large egg, fork-beaten	1	1

SALAD

Cooked chicken, cut bite size	1 cup	250 mL
Diced celery	$\frac{1}{4}$ cup	60 mL
Canned pineapple tidbits, drained and cut smaller (reserve remaining whole pieces for garnish)	$\frac{1}{4}$ cup	60 mL
Seedless green grapes, quartered	$\frac{1}{2}$ cup	125 mL
Sliced almonds, toasted and chopped	$\frac{1}{4}$ cup	60 mL
Salt, sprinkle		
Pepper, sprinkle		

CURRY DRESSING

Salad dressing (or mayonnaise)	$\frac{1}{4}$ cup	60 mL
Lemon juice	$\frac{3}{4}$ tsp.	4 mL
Soy sauce	$\frac{3}{4}$ tsp.	4 mL
Curry powder, scant measure	$\frac{1}{2}$ tsp.	2 mL
Milk	1 tbsp.	15 mL

GARNISH

Seedless green grapes	12	12
Pimiento strips	12	12
Reserved pineapple tidbits, cut up		

Pastry Horns: Roll out pastry on lightly floured surface to 12 x 12 inch (30 x 30 cm) square. Cut into long strips about $\frac{3}{4}$ to 1 inch (2 to 2.5 cm) wide.

Brush 1 strip with egg. Turn strip over. ❶ Place pointed end of metal form at lower end of strip. ❷ Wind strip around form, overlapping edges slightly, working up towards open end. Place on greased baking sheet. Repeat with remaining strips. Bake in 425°F (220°C) oven for 15 to 20 minutes until golden brown. Let stand for 10 minutes. Gently push horns off metal forms.

(continued on next page)

Starter Salads

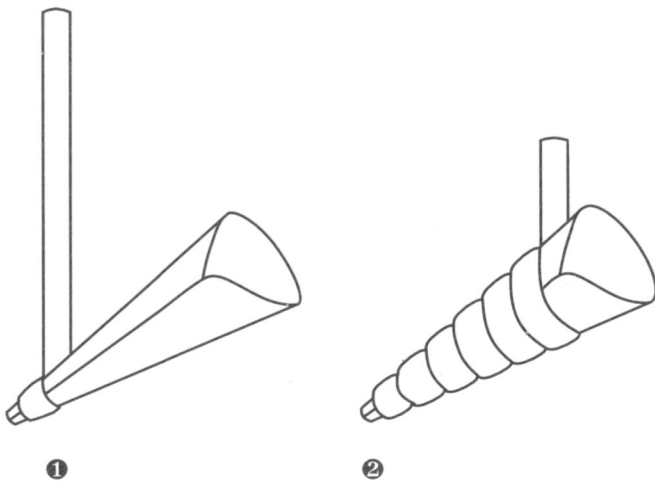

❶　　　　　　❷

Salad: Combine all 7 ingredients in medium bowl. Toss. Chill until needed.

Curry Dressing: Stir all 5 ingredients together in small bowl. Chill until needed. Set 1 pastry horn on each of 8 salad plates. Combine salad and dressing. Toss well. Gently spoon small amount into each horn. Spoon remaining salad spilling from horn.

Garnish: Place 2 grapes on 1 side of horn. Set 2 pimiento strips on salad. Divide remaining pineapple pieces alongside. Serves 8.

1 serving: 336 Calories; 22.2 g Total Fat; 392 mg Sodium; 10 g Protein; 24 g Carbohydrate; 1 g Dietary Fiber

Pictured on page 53.

Note: This much puff pastry will make 12 horns. Salad fills 8. Freeze remaining horns.

When a beautiful girl offers you a date and you would prefer a fig— you are beyond help.

SPROUT SALAD

Tangy dressing, crunchy sprouts, colorful red pepper slivers and more. As fresh as they come.

Chopped fresh bean sprouts	3 cups	750 mL
Green onion, chopped	1	1
Chopped fresh mushrooms	$2/3$ cup	150 mL
Paper-thin slivers of red pepper, 1 inch (2.5 cm) long	$1/4$ cup	60 mL
Apple cider vinegar	1 tbsp.	15 mL
Soy sauce	1 tbsp.	15 mL
Granulated sugar	$1/2$ tsp.	2 mL
Cooking oil	2 tsp.	10 mL
Lettuce cups (or shredded lettuce)	4	4

Combine bean sprouts, green onion, mushrooms and red pepper in medium bowl.

Mix vinegar, soy sauce, sugar and cooking oil in small cup. Stir well. Add to sprout mixture. Toss.

Set lettuce cup on each of 4 salad plates. Divide sprout mixture among them. Serves 4.

1 serving: 57 Calories; 2.5 g Total Fat; 267 mg Sodium; 3 g Protein; 7 g Carbohydrate; 1 g Dietary Fiber

Pictured on page 125.

CORN CHOWDER

Flavorful bacon is the star in this chowder. Great taste. Nice and chunky.

Bacon slices, diced	5	5
Chopped onion	$1/2$ cup	125 mL
Medium potatoes, peeled and diced	2	2
Water	1 cup	250 mL
Canned cream-style corn	2 × 14 oz.	2 × 398 mL
Salt	$1/2$ tsp.	2 mL
Pepper	$1/4$ tsp.	1 mL
Parsley flakes	2 tsp.	10 mL
Milk	3 cups	750 mL

(continued on next page)

Cook bacon in frying pan for 5 to 8 minutes. Drain. Add onion. Sauté until onion is soft.

Cook potato in water in large saucepan until tender. Do not drain.

Add remaining 5 ingredients. Add bacon and onion. Stir. Heat through. Makes 8³/₄ cups (2.2 L). Serves 8.

1 serving: 167 Calories; 3.5 g Total Fat; 590 mg Sodium; 7 g Protein; 30 g Carbohydrate; 2 g Dietary Fiber

VEGETABLE CREAM SOUP

A thick creamy soup with tiny bits of green showing through. Yum!

Chopped onion	¹/₂ cup	125 mL
Diced carrot	1 cup	250 mL
Frozen green beans	²/₃ cup	150 mL
Frozen kernel corn	¹/₂ cup	125 mL
Diced parsnip (or yellow turnip)	1 cup	250 mL
Water	1 cup	250 mL
Frozen peas	¹/₂ cup	125 mL
Celery salt	¹/₈ tsp.	0.5 mL
Salt	¹/₂ tsp.	2 mL
Pepper	¹/₈ tsp.	0.5 mL
Chicken bouillon powder	2 tsp.	10 mL
Milk	2 cups	500 mL

Place first 6 ingredients in medium saucepan. Bring to a boil. Cover. Simmer until vegetables are cooked. Transfer to blender, including any liquid left in saucepan.

Add peas, celery salt, salt, pepper and bouillon powder. Process until smooth. Pour back into saucepan. Heat, stirring often, until simmering. Simmer for 1 minute.

Add milk. Heat, stirring often, until almost boiling. Makes 5 cups (1.25 L). Serves 4.

1 serving: 147 Calories; 2.1 g Total Fat; 807 mg Sodium; 8 g Protein; 26 g Carbohydrate; 4 g Dietary Fiber

When a bee is on a bluebell you have a humdinger.

GOUDA SOUP

A thick chowder texture. A small serving is sufficient.

Skim evaporated milk	13½ oz.	385 mL
All-purpose flour	¼ cup	60 mL
Milk	2 cups	500 mL
Salt	½ tsp.	2 mL
Pepper (white is best), sprinkle		
Worcestershire sauce	¾ tsp.	4 mL
Grated Gouda (or Edam) cheese	2 cups	500 mL
Dried chopped chives, for garnish	2 tbsp.	30 mL
Grated Gouda (or Edam) cheese, for garnish	2 tbsp.	30 mL

Whisk evaporated milk into flour in large saucepan until no lumps remain.

Add next 4 ingredients. Heat, stirring continually, until boiling and slightly thickened.

Add first amount of cheese. Whisk until melted.

Sprinkle each bowl of soup with chives and second amount of cheese. Serve very hot. Makes 4½ cups (1.1 L). Serves 6.

1 serving: 256 Calories; 12.3 g Total Fat; 692 mg Sodium; 19 g Protein; 17 g Carbohydrate; trace Dietary Fiber

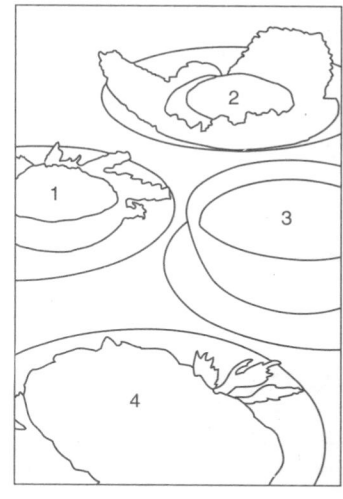

1. Prize Mushrooms, page 80
2. Picture Book Salad, page 135
3. Peach Soup, page 147
4. Shrimp Papaya Salad, page 130

Starter Soups

First course starters…

First course starters are usually served on a small plate at the dining table. Keep in mind: the heavier the meal, the lighter the starter. Also, be sure to provide contrast to the main course, such as a seafood appetizer with a meat entrée.

Vary the color by varying the beans. Serve with a dollop of sour cream or yogurt. Good soup.

Hard margarine (or butter)	2 tsp.	10 mL
Finely chopped onion	¼ cup	60 mL
Grated carrot	½ cup	125 mL
Garlic clove, minced (or ¼ tsp., 1 mL, garlic powder)	1	1
Water	2½ cups	625 mL
Chicken bouillon powder	1 tbsp.	15 mL
Canned lima beans, drained	14 oz.	398 mL
Sherry (or alcohol-free sherry)	1 tbsp.	15 mL

Heat margarine in large saucepan. Add onion, carrot and garlic. Sauté until onion is soft.

Add water and bouillon powder. Simmer for 15 minutes.

Add beans. Simmer for 15 minutes. Process in blender until puréed. Return to saucepan. Heat through.

Stir in sherry. Makes 3 cups (750 mL). Serves 4.

1 serving: 107 Calories; 2.6 g Total Fat; 658 mg Sodium; 5 g Protein; 16 g Carbohydrate; 1 g Dietary Fiber

Variation: Substitute a 19 oz. (540 mL) can of drained black beans for the lima beans. Soup will be darker in color.

When a goat eats a dictionary you can take the words right out of his mouth.

CREAM OF SHRIMP SOUP

Simply doctor a can of soup to get this end result.

Hard margarine (or butter)	2 tsp.	10 mL
Chopped celery	3 tbsp.	50 mL
Green onions, chopped	3	3
Condensed cream of asparagus soup	2 × 10 oz.	2 × 284 mL
Milk	1½ cups	375 mL
Garlic powder	¼ tsp.	1 mL
Worcestershire sauce	1 tsp.	5 mL
Cayenne pepper	¹⁄₁₆ tsp.	0.5 mL
Skim evaporated milk	½ cup	125 mL
Cooked small fresh (or frozen, thawed) shrimp	½ lb.	225 g
Salt	½ tsp.	2 mL
Pepper	¼ tsp.	1 mL
Sherry (or alcohol-free sherry or white wine)	1 tbsp.	15 mL

Melt margarine in large saucepan. Add celery and green onion. Sauté until celery has softened a bit.

Add next 6 ingredients. Stir together well. Bring to a boil.

Add remaining 4 ingredients. Return just to a boil. Serve immediately. Makes 5½ cups (1.4 L). Serves 6.

1 serving: 167 Calories; 5.7 g Total Fat; 1183 mg Sodium; 14 g Protein; 15 g Carbohydrate; trace Dietary Fiber

BEEF WINE CONSOMMÉ

A clear rich rusty brown color. Easy to double.

Water	3 cups	750 mL
Onion slivers	1 tbsp.	15 mL
Carrot slivers	1 tbsp.	15 mL
Celery slivers	1 tbsp.	15 mL
Yellow turnip (or parsnip) slivers	1 tbsp.	15 mL
Chopped green onion	1 tbsp.	15 mL
Beef bouillon powder	1 tbsp.	15 mL
Granulated sugar	1½ tsp.	7 mL
Lemon juice	½ tsp.	2 mL
Salt	¼ tsp.	1 mL
Red (or alcohol-free red) wine	¼ cup	60 mL

(continued on next page)

Place first 6 ingredients in medium saucepan. Bring to a boil. Cover. Simmer for about 5 minutes until vegetables are cooked.

Add remaining 5 ingredients. Stir. Simmer for about 1 minute. Makes 3 cups (750 mL). Serves 4.

1 serving: 28 Calories; 0.3 g Total Fat; 619 mg Sodium; 1 g Protein; 4 g Carbohydrate; trace Dietary Fiber

PEACH SOUP

Bright cheery-looking chilled soup.

Hard margarine (or butter)	1 tbsp.	15 mL
Small onion, chopped	1	1
Granulated sugar	1½ tbsp.	25 mL
Curry powder	½ tsp.	2 mL
Turmeric	⅛ tsp.	0.5 mL
Chili powder, just a pinch		
Citric acid (available at drug store)	½ tsp.	2 mL
Salt	⅛ tsp.	0.5 mL
All-purpose flour	1 tbsp.	15 mL
Canned sliced peaches, with juice	14 oz.	398 mL
Water	2 cups	500 mL
Lemon juice	1 tsp.	5 mL
Cooking apples (McIntosh is good), peeled and chopped	2	2
Skim evaporated milk (or light cream)	⅓ cup	75 mL

Heat margarine in medium saucepan. Add onion, sugar, spices, citric acid and salt. Sauté until onion is soft.

Mix in flour.

Add peaches with juice, water, lemon juice and apple. Sauté until apple is cooked. Transfer to blender. Process until smooth.

Stir in evaporated milk. Chill. Makes 5⅓ cups (1.35 L). Serves 6.

1 serving: 107 Calories; 2.2 g Total Fat; 102 mg Sodium; 2 g Protein; 22 g Carbohydrate; 2 g Dietary Fiber

Pictured on page 143.

PUMPKIN SOUP

Golden orange with a thick texture. Make your own design with the sour cream garnish.

Skim evaporated milk	13^1/$_2$ oz.	385 mL
Canned pumpkin (without added spices)	14 oz.	398 mL
Milk	^{1}/$_2$ cup	125 mL
Salt	^{3}/$_4$ tsp.	4 mL
Ground nutmeg	^{1}/$_{16}$ tsp.	0.5 mL
Maple (or maple-flavored) syrup	1^1/$_2$ tbsp.	25 mL
Sour cream, for garnish (optional)		

Combine first 5 ingredients in large saucepan. Stir. Heat, stirring often, until almost boiling. Remove from heat.

Stir in maple syrup. Divide among 4 bowls.

Add swirl of sour cream to each. Makes scant 4 cups (1 L). Serves 4.

*1 **serving:** 150 Calories; 0.9 g Total Fat; 651 mg Sodium; 10 g Protein; 27 g Carbohydrate; 2 g Dietary Fiber*

ALMOND SOUP

An interesting texture. Serve hot or chilled.

Condensed chicken broth	2 × 10 oz.	2 × 284 mL
Ground blanched almonds	3^1/$_2$ oz.	100 g
Small bay leaf	1	1
Milk	1 cup	250 mL
All-purpose flour	2 tbsp.	30 mL
Hard margarine (or butter)	2 tsp.	10 mL
Skim evaporated milk (or light cream)	1 cup	250 mL
Lemon pepper	^{1}/$_8$ tsp.	0.5 mL
Chopped sliced almonds, toasted in 350°F (175°C) oven for 5 to 10 minutes	1 tbsp.	15 mL

(continued on next page)

Heat first 3 ingredients in medium saucepan until simmering. Cover. Simmer for 20 minutes. Discard bay leaf.

Whisk milk into flour in small bowl until smooth. Stir into simmering broth until boiling and thickened.

Stir in margarine, evaporated milk and lemon pepper. Heat through. Cool. Chill overnight for flavors to blend.

Serve chilled or hot. Sprinkle with toasted almonds just before serving. Makes 4 cups (1 L). Serves 6.

1 serving: 209 Calories; 12.2 g Total Fat; 719 mg Sodium; 13 g Protein; 13 g Carbohydrate; 1 g Dietary Fiber

Variation: Stir in $1/4$ cup (60 mL) white wine just before serving.

LOBSTER BISQUE

Serve when price is no object. Recipe may be halved if desired. Rich flavor.

Condensed cream of mushroom soup	2 × 10 oz.	2 × 284 mL
Milk	$2^2/3$ cups	650 mL
Skim evaporated milk	$13^1/2$ oz.	385 mL
All-purpose flour	2 tbsp.	30 mL
Sherry (or alcohol-free sherry)	$1/4$ cup	60 mL
Hot pepper sauce	$1/4$ tsp.	1 mL
Chili sauce	$1/4$ cup	60 mL
Canned frozen lobster meat, thawed (or imitation lobster), broken up	11.3 oz.	320 g
Paprika, sprinkle		

Whisk first 7 ingredients in large saucepan until smooth. Heat, stirring occasionally, until almost boiling.

Add lobster meat. Stir. Process in blender to purée if desired. Return to saucepan. Heat through.

Sprinkle with paprika to serve. Makes 8 cups (2 L). Serves 12.

1 serving: 144 Calories; 4.7 g Total Fat; 658 mg Sodium; 11 g Protein; 13 g Carbohydrate; 1 g Dietary Fiber

CRAB BISQUE: Omit lobster. Add canned crabmeat, drained and cartilage removed.

HOT AND SOUR SOUP

You may not have this uncommon vinegar on hand but if you have always wanted to try this soup, you may want to get some.

Condensed chicken broth	2 × 10 oz.	2 × 284 mL
Water	2 cups	500 mL
Tomato juice	10 oz.	284 mL
Rice (or white wine) vinegar	¼ cup	60 mL
Soy sauce	2 tbsp.	30 mL
Canned bamboo shoots, drained and cut julienne	8 oz.	227 mL
Chopped fresh mushrooms	½ cup	125 mL
Slivers red or yellow pepper, 1½ inches (3.8 cm) long	½ cup	125 mL
Hot pepper sauce	½ tsp.	2 mL
Dried crushed chilies	¼-½ tsp.	1-2 mL
Diagonally sliced green onion	¼ cup	60 mL
Cooked chicken (or ham or beef), cut julienne	½ cup	125 mL
Cornstarch	1½ tbsp.	25 mL
Water	¼ cup	60 mL
Large egg, fork-beaten	1	1

Combine first 10 ingredients in large saucepan. Bring to a boil. Simmer, uncovered, for 10 minutes.

Add green onion and chicken. Cook for 1 minute.

Stir cornstarch into water in small cup. Stir into soup until mixture is boiling and slightly thickened.

Slowly add beaten egg in a continuous stream while soup is boiling. Stir until threads form in the soup from the egg. Makes 7¾ cups (1.9 L). Serves 8.

1 serving: 71 Calories; 1.9 g Total Fat; 879 mg Sodium; 8 g Protein; 6 g Carbohydrate; 1 g Dietary Fiber

Pictured on page 125.

MEASUREMENT TABLES

Throughout this book measurements are given in Conventional and Metric measure. To compensate for differences between the two measurements due to rounding, a full metric measure is not always used. The cup used is the standard 8 fluid ounce. Temperature is given in degrees Fahrenheit and Celsius. Baking pan measurements are in inches and centimetres as well as quarts and litres. An exact metric conversion is given below as well as the working equivalent (Standard Measure).

OVEN TEMPERATURES

Fahrenheit (°F)	Celsius (°C)
175°	80°
200°	95°
225°	110°
250°	120°
275°	140°
300°	150°
325°	160°
350°	175°
375°	190°
400°	205°
425°	220°
450°	230°
475°	240°
500°	260°

SPOONS

Conventional Measure	Metric Exact Conversion Millilitre (mL)	Metric Standard Measure Millilitre (mL)
1/8 teaspoon (tsp.)	0.6 mL	0.5 mL
1/4 teaspoon (tsp.)	1.2 mL	1 mL
1/2 teaspoon (tsp.)	2.4 mL	2 mL
1 teaspoon (tsp.)	4.7 mL	5 mL
2 teaspoons (tsp.)	9.4 mL	10 mL
1 tablespoon (tbsp.)	14.2 mL	15 mL

CUPS

	Metric Exact Conversion	Metric Standard Measure
1/4 cup (4 tbsp.)	56.8 mL	60 mL
1/3 cup (5 1/3 tbsp.)	75.6 mL	75 mL
1/2 cup (8 tbsp.)	113.7 mL	125 mL
2/3 cup (10 2/3 tbsp.)	151.2 mL	150 mL
3/4 cup (12 tbsp.)	170.5 mL	175 mL
1 cup (16 tbsp.)	227.3 mL	250 mL
4 1/2 cups	1022.9 mL	1000 mL (1 L)

PANS

Conventional Inches	Metric Centimetres
8x8 inch	20x20 cm
9x9 inch	22x22 cm
9x13 inch	22x33 cm
10x15 inch	25x38 cm
11x17 inch	28x43 cm
8x2 inch round	20x5 cm
9x2 inch round	22x5 cm
10x4 1/2 inch tube	25x11 cm
8x4x3 inch loaf	20x10x7.5 cm
9x5x3 inch loaf	22x12.5x7.5 cm

DRY MEASUREMENTS

Conventional Measure Ounces (oz.)	Metric Exact Conversion Grams (g)	Metric Standard Measure Grams (g)
1 oz.	28.3 g	28 g
2 oz.	56.7 g	57 g
3 oz.	85.0 g	85 g
4 oz.	113.4 g	125 g
5 oz.	141.7 g	140 g
6 oz.	170.1 g	170 g
7 oz.	198.4 g	200 g
8 oz.	226.8 g	250 g
16 oz.	453.6 g	500 g
32 oz.	907.2 g	1000 g (1 kg)

CASSEROLES (Canada & Britain)

Standard Size Casserole	Exact Metric Measure
1 qt. (5 cups)	1.13 L
1 1/2 qts. (7 1/2 cups)	1.69 L
2 qts. (10 cups)	2.25 L
2 1/2 qts. (12 1/2 cups)	2.81 L
3 qts. (15 cups)	3.38 L
4 qts. (20 cups)	4.5 L
5 qts. (25 cups)	5.63 L

CASSEROLES (United States)

Standard Size Casserole	Exact Metric Measure
1 qt. (4 cups)	900 mL
1 1/2 qts. (6 cups)	1.35 L
2 qts. (8 cups)	1.8 L
2 1/2 qts. (10 cups)	2.25 L
3 qts. (12 cups)	2.7 L
4 qts. (16 cups)	3.6 L
5 qts. (20 cups)	4.5 L

INDEX

152

153

154

155

156

Recipe Notes

Recipe Notes

Sweet Cravings

Jean Paré

companyscoming.com
visit our website

Divider Photo

1. Instant Maple Walnut Fudge, page 42
2. Marshmallow Brownie Dreams, page 138
3. Tropical Rumba Cheesecake, page 68
4. Raspberry Turkish Jellies, page 30

Props Courtesy Of:
Anchor Hocking Canada
Cornell Trading Ltd.
La Cache
Pfaltzgraff Canada

We gratefully acknowledge the following suppliers for their generous support of our Test Kitchen and Photo Studio:

Broil King Barbecues
Corelle®
Hamilton Beach® Canada
Lagostina®
Proctor Silex® Canada
Tupperware®

Cooking tonight?

A selection of
feature recipes
is only a
click away—
absolutely **FREE!**

Visit us at ➘
www.companyscoming.com

Table of Contents

Beverages

Cakes

Confections

Cookies

Pastries

Foreword

I love sweets! In fact, dessert is the course that I most look forward to. The most memorable meals I've ever had were those that were followed by just the right dessert. It's true that the last thing eaten is the first thing remembered.

And my love of sweets doesn't end with desserts. I also enjoy having a batch of squares on hand for friends who drop by or a dish of candied nuts on the coffee table to nibble during the game. On lazy weekend mornings, I love sticky buns, warm from the oven, drizzled with icing. And on chilly winter evenings, I enjoy a rich, frothy mug of hot chocolate. And then there are those times when I just feel like a little something to satisfy that sweet tooth craving!

My particular weakness is chocolate! There is something so irresistible about the smooth, creamy rich texture and taste of chocolate. It's the ultimate comfort food—equally at home in puddings and sauces, cakes and pies, and squares and pastries. Its versatility and popularity make it an ideal treat or dessert ingredient.

Many of us lead such busy lives that dessert is often the one course to be dropped from the menu when planning a meal. What a shame, whenso many of us enjoy a sweet ending! But dessert preparation doesn't have to be time-consuming and labour intensive. *Sweet Cravings* has many simple recipes for desserts and treats that are quick and easy to prepare.

I have always thought that sweets are best enjoyed in the company of family and friends. But why not make a batch of something sweet and surprise your neighbour, your child's classmates or your office colleagues? Let the kids help prepare the treat of their choice. Or have a friend or two drop by for an afternoon of candy making.

Sweet Cravings was fun to write— and even more fun to test! I know that many of these recipes will be prepared over and over again in your own home—and many a sweet craving will be satisfied!

Jean Paré

Fluffy Duck

A thick, creamy, sun-tinted beverage with a delicate orange flavour.
A perfect sipping beverage to be savoured slowly.

Crushed ice	2 tbsp.	30 mL
Advocaat liqueur	2 tbsp.	30 mL
White rum	1 tbsp.	15 mL
Orange-flavoured liqueur (such as Grand Marnier)	1 tbsp.	15 mL
Prepared orange juice	1/4 cup	60 mL
Half-and-half cream	1/4 cup	60 mL
Orange twist, for garnish	1	1
Maraschino cherries, for garnish	2	2

Put ice into 6 oz. (170 mL) glass. Pour next 5 ingredients over ice. Stir. Makes 3/4 cup (175 mL).

Garnish with orange twist and cherries. Serves 1.

1 serving: 467 Calories; 14.3 g Total Fat; 116 mg Sodium; 4 g Protein; 55 g Carbohydrate; trace Dietary Fibre

Pictured on page 17.

Mai Tai

A summer classic! The perfectly blended flavours of orange, pineapple and lime laced with rum! Close your eyes and imagine the sand, the surf and the palms without ever leaving home.

White (or amber) rum	1 oz.	30 mL
Dark rum	1 oz.	30 mL
Bitter orange-flavoured liqueur (such as Curaçao)	1/4 oz.	8 mL
Lime juice	2 tsp.	10 mL
Simple Cocktail Syrup, page 10	2 tsp.	10 mL
Crushed ice	1 cup	250 mL

(continued on next page)

| Crushed ice | 3 tbsp. | 50 mL |
| Pineapple juice | 1/2 cup | 125 mL |

Combine first 6 ingredients in cocktail shaker or jar with tight-fitting lid. Shake well.

Strain through sieve over second amount of ice in 12 oz. (341 mL) glass. Discard crushed ice in shaker.

Stir in pineapple juice. Makes 1 cup (250 mL). Serves 1.

1 serving: 272 Calories; 0.1 g Total Fat; 3 mg Sodium; trace Protein; 31 g Carbohydrate; trace Dietary Fibre

Pictured on page 17.

Planter's Punch

Perfect for a hot summer afternoon. This rosy pink beverage is tart and refreshing. Put a paper umbrella in the crushed ice and imagine the tropics.

Crushed ice	1 cup	250 mL
Lime juice	2 tbsp.	30 mL
White rum	1 1/2 oz.	45 mL
Simple Cocktail Syrup, page 10	2 tsp.	10 mL
Grenadine syrup	1 tsp.	5 mL

Pineapple slice, for garnish
Lime slice, cut into quarters, for garnish

Combine first 5 ingredients in cocktail shaker or jar with tight-fitting lid. Shake well. Makes 3/4 cup (175 mL). Pour into 8 oz. (227 mL) glass.

Garnish with fruit. Serves 1.

1 serving: 159 Calories; trace Total Fat; 6 mg Sodium; trace Protein; 17 g Carbohydrate; trace Dietary Fibre

Pictured on page 17.

Strawberry Slush

A slushy summer favourite! The sweet juiciness of ripe strawberries with a tang of lime.

Lemon lime soft drink	1 1/2 cups	375 mL
Frozen whole strawberries, cut up (about 15)	1 1/2 cups	375 mL
Crushed ice	1 cup	250 mL
Granulated sugar	1/4 cup	60 mL
Fresh whole strawberries, for garnish		

Measure first 4 ingredients into blender. Process until smooth. Makes 2 2/3 cups (650 mL).

Garnish individual servings with strawberries. Serves 2.

1 serving: 242 Calories; 0.2 g Total Fat; 25 mg Sodium; 1 g Protein; 63 g Carbohydrate; 3 g Dietary Fibre

Pictured on page 17.

Simple Cocktail Syrup

A versatile syrup used for sweet cocktails such as Mai Tai, page 8, Planter's Punch, page 9, or Singapore Sling, page 11.

Water	1/2 cup	125 mL
Granulated sugar	1 cup	250 mL

Heat and stir water and sugar in small saucepan on medium-high until sugar is dissolved. Bring to a boil. Reduce heat to medium-low. Simmer, uncovered, for 5 minutes. Cool. Store in jar with tight-fitting lid in refrigerator for up to 6 months. Makes 1 cup (250 mL).

2 tsp. (10 mL): 33 Calories; 0 g Total Fat; trace Sodium; 0 g Protein; 8 g Carbohydrate; 0 g Dietary Fibre

Singapore Sling

I've been told that the first sling was created for Somerset Maugham in Raffles in Singapore. This refreshing variation has a lime undertone and a sweet cherry aftertaste.

Crushed ice, to fill glass half full		
Lime juice	2 tsp.	10 mL
Simple Cocktail Syrup, page 10	1 tbsp.	15 mL
Grenadine syrup	1 tbsp.	15 mL
Gin	1 1/2 oz.	45 mL
Cherry whiskey	1/2 oz.	15 mL
Ginger ale	3/4 cup	175 mL

Put crushed ice into 16 oz. (500 mL) glass. Pour lime juice, Simple Cocktail Syrup, grenadine, gin and whiskey over ice.

Add ginger ale. Stir. Serve with swizzle stick and straw. Makes 9 oz. (255 mL). Serves 1.

1 serving: 310 Calories; trace Total Fat; 29 mg Sodium; trace Protein; 47 g Carbohydrate; trace Dietary Fibre

VIRGIN SLING: Omit gin and cherry whiskey.

 *To be able to make the most common cocktails, this is a basic list for stocking your cabinet. Start with some basics and add as you experiment with different drinks.*

Bourbon
Brandy
Gin
Peach Schnapps
Rum
Scotch
Tequila
Vodka
Whiskey
Liqueurs (such as Amaretto,Crème de Cacao, Kahlúa, Baileys, Irish Cream and Grand Marnier)

Indian Chai

The fragrant harmony of eastern spices makes this hot beverage captivating. The warm scents of cardamom, ginger and cinnamon will delight your nose and your taste buds.

Orange pekoe tea bag	1	1
Milk	2 cups	500 mL
Water	1/2 cup	125 mL
Granulated sugar	4 tsp.	20 mL
Whole green cardamom, bruised (see Note)	6	6
Chopped gingerroot (or 3/4 tsp., 4 mL, ground ginger)	1 tbsp.	15 mL
Cinnamon stick (4 inch, 10 cm, length), crushed	1	1
Dried mint leaves	1/4 tsp.	1 mL
Tea Masala	1/4 – 1/2 tsp.	1 – 2 mL

Combine all 9 ingredients in medium saucepan. Heat on medium for about 10 minutes, stirring occasionally, until beginning to boil. Remove from heat. Strain through fine sieve into 2 mugs. Discard solids. Makes 2 cups (500 mL). Serves 2.

1 serving: 155 Calories; 3 g Total Fat; 138 mg Sodium; 9 g Protein; 24 g Carbohydrate; trace Dietary Fibre

Pictured on page 18.

Note: To bruise cardamom, hit cardamom pods with a mallet or the flat side of a wide knife to "bruise" or crack them open slightly.

 *To keep winter drinks warm at a party, serve in a slow cooker on Low setting.*

Beverages

Hazelnut Hot Chocolate

The decadent richness of chocolate with an elegant hint of hazelnut.
This frothy beverage is a dessert in itself.

Milk	2 cups	500 mL
Milk chocolate candy bar, chopped	3 1/2 oz.	100 g
Hazelnut-flavoured liqueur (such as Frangelico)	1/4 cup	60 mL
Whipped cream	1/3 cup	75 mL
Chopped hazelnuts (filberts), toasted (see Tip, page 79)	1 1/2 tbsp.	25 mL
Chocolate sauce	1 tsp.	5 mL

Heat milk in medium saucepan on medium-high for about 3 minutes until small bubbles form around edge and milk is hot. Do not boil. Remove from heat.

Add chocolate and liqueur. Stir until chocolate is melted. Makes 2 1/2 cups (625 mL). Pour into 2 mugs.

Dollop whipped cream onto milk mixture.

Sprinkle with hazelnuts. Drizzle chocolate sauce over top. Serves 2.

1 serving: 584 Calories; 28.4 g Total Fat; 184 mg Sodium; 13 g Protein; 57 g Carbohydrate; 2 g Dietary Fibre

Pictured on page 18.

Paré Pointer

They wanted to go waterskiing but they couldn't find a lake with a slope.

Bistro Milk

A steamed milk beverage similar to what you find in trendy coffee shops—no steam machine required! Perfect for soothing the nerves before bed.

Skim milk	1 1/3 cups	325 mL
White corn syrup	3 tbsp.	50 mL
Clear vanilla	1 1/2 – 2 tsp.	7 – 10 mL
Ground cinnamon, sprinkle (optional)		

Heat milk and corn syrup in small saucepan until hot. Do not boil. Remove from heat.

Add vanilla. Whisk until frothy or use milk frother. Pour into mug.

Sprinkle with cinnamon. Serves 1.

1 serving: 331 Calories; 0.6 g Total Fat; 221 mg Sodium; 12 g Protein; 68 g Carbohydrate; 0 g Dietary Fibre

ALMOND BISTRO MILK: Omit vanilla. Add 1/8 to 1/4 tsp. (0.5 to 1 mL) almond flavouring.

Maple Milk

Warm your soul with this hot, comforting beverage.
A subtle maple flavour with a hint of cloves to ebb your cares away.

Milk	2 cups	500 mL
Maple syrup	1/4 cup	60 mL
Cinnamon stick (4 inch, 10 cm, length)	1	1
Whole cloves	4	4
Granulated sugar	2 tsp.	10 mL

Combine all 5 ingredients in medium saucepan. Heat and stir on medium for 5 minutes. Remove from heat. Let stand for 10 minutes. Strain. Discard solids. Return to same pan. Heat and stir milk mixture for 2 to 3 minutes until hot. Makes about 2 1/4 cups (550 mL). Pour into 2 mugs. Serves 2.

1 serving: 234 Calories; 2.8 g Total Fat; 133 mg Sodium; 8 g Protein; 45 g Carbohydrate; 0 g Dietary Fibre

Sweet Pineapple Tea

The complementary flavours of pineapple and honey will tingle your taste buds and awaken your senses. Serve hot to soothe a sore throat. Also delicious over ice and topped with a maraschino cherry.

Boiling water	2 cups	500 mL
Orange pekoe tea bag	1	1
Pineapple juice, warmed	1/2 cup	125 mL
Liquid honey	1 – 2 tbsp.	15 – 30 mL
Lemon juice (optional)	1/2 tsp.	2 mL
Cinnamon sticks (4 inch, 10 cm, lengths)	2	2

Pour boiling water over tea bag in small teapot. Let steep for 10 minutes. Squeeze and discard tea bag.

Add pineapple juice, honey and lemon juice. Stir. Pour into 2 mugs.

Add 1 cinnamon stick to each for stirring. Makes 2 1/2 cups (625 mL). Serves 2.

1 serving: 72 Calories; 0.1 g Total Fat; 9 mg Sodium; trace Protein; 19 g Carbohydrate; trace Dietary Fibre

Pictured on page 18.

COLD PINEAPPLE TEA: Prepare as above but in 4 cup (1 L) glass liquid measure. Add cinnamon sticks. Chill. Remove cinnamon sticks. Pour over ice cubes in glasses. Add 1 cinnamon stick to each, if desired.

Paré Pointer

They hoped their plane didn't travel faster than sound. They wanted to have a visit while flying.

Bartender's Iced Tea

A tall and delicious "tea-less" iced tea. This citrusy beverage is refreshing and summery. Enjoy beside the pool or on your shaded deck.

Ice cubes	3	3
Vodka	1 tbsp.	15 mL
Gin	1 tbsp.	15 mL
White rum	1 tbsp.	15 mL
Orange-flavoured liqueur (such as Grand Marnier)	1 tbsp.	15 mL
Lemonade	1 cup	250 mL
Cola beverage	2 tbsp.	30 mL

Put ice cubes into tall 16 oz. (500 mL) glass. Pour vodka, gin, rum and liqueur over ice cubes.

Add lemonade and cola. Stir. Makes 1 1/2 cups (375 mL). Serves 1.

1 serving: 279 Calories; 0.1 g Total Fat; 11 mg Sodium; trace Protein; 38 g Carbohydrate; 0 g Dietary Fibre

1. Planter's Punch, page 9
2. Fluffy Duck, page 8
3. Strawberry Slush, page 10
4. Mai Tai, page 8

Cherry Tea Float

A summer drink that is full of cherry fun! This frothy, fruity beverage is both rich and refreshing. It's like a dressed-up float!

Boiling water	3/4 cup	175 mL
Orange pekoe tea bag	1	1
Chilled maraschino cherry syrup	1/4 cup	60 mL
Chilled lemon lime soft drink	1/2 cup	125 mL
Maraschino cherries	2	2
Scoop of vanilla ice cream (about 1/2 cup, 125 mL)	1	1

Pour boiling water over tea bag in small teapot. Let steep for 10 minutes. Squeeze and discard tea bag. Pour tea into 2 cup (500 mL) liquid measure. Chill.

Add cherry syrup and soft drink. Stir well.

Put cherries into tall 16 oz. (500 mL) glass. Add ice cream. Slowly pour tea mixture over ice cream. Foam will form. Serve with long spoon and straw. Makes about 1 1/2 cups (375 mL). Serves 1.

1 serving: 274 Calories; 7.8 g Total Fat; 76 mg Sodium; 3 g Protein; 51 g Carbohydrate; 1 g Dietary Fibre

1. Hazelnut Hot Chocolate, page 13
2. Indian Chai, page 12
3. Sweet Pineapple Tea, page 15

Props Courtesy Of: Anchor Hocking Canada

Oatmeal Cake

A mildly spiced oatmeal cake with a chewy, nutty topping. A perfect snacking cake.

Rolled oats (not instant)	1 cup	250 mL
Boiling water	1 cup	250 mL
Large eggs	2	2
Granulated sugar	1 cup	250 mL
Cooking oil	1/2 cup	125 mL
Vanilla	1 tsp.	5 mL
All-purpose flour	1 1/3 cups	325 mL
Baking soda	1 1/2 tsp.	7 mL
Ground cinnamon	1 tsp.	5 mL
Salt	1/2 tsp.	2 mL
TOPPING		
Hard margarine (or butter)	1/4 cup	60 mL
Brown sugar, packed	2/3 cup	150 mL
Half-and-half cream (or milk)	2 tbsp.	30 mL
Chopped pecans (or walnuts)	1/2 cup	125 mL
Medium coconut	1/2 cup	125 mL

Measure rolled oats into small bowl. Pour boiling water over top. Stir. Let stand, uncovered, for 20 minutes.

Beat eggs in large bowl until frothy. Add sugar. Beat. Add cooking oil and vanilla. Beat until well combined.

Combine flour, baking soda, cinnamon and salt in separate small bowl. Add flour mixture to egg mixture in 3 additions, alternating with oatmeal mixture in 2 additions, beginning and ending with flour mixture. Turn into greased 9 x 9 inch (22 x 22 cm) pan. Spread evenly. Bake in 350°F (175°C) oven for about 30 minutes until wooden pick inserted in centre comes out clean.

Topping: Mix all 5 ingredients in small saucepan. Heat and stir on medium-low until margarine is melted and brown sugar is dissolved. Do not boil. Spread over cake. Bake for 5 to 7 minutes until top bubbles all over. Cuts into 16 pieces.

1 piece: 302 Calories; 16.2 g Total Fat; 244 mg Sodium; 3 g Protein; 37 g Carbohydrate; 1 g Dietary Fibre

Pictured on page 35.

Cakes

Pineapple Mini-Cakes

Cinnamon-flecked pineapple dresses up a simple white cake recipe. A perfect, light dessert.

Can of crushed pineapple, drained	14 oz.	398 mL
Hard margarine (or butter), softened	1/4 cup	60 mL
Brown sugar, packed	1/2 cup	125 mL
Ground cinnamon	1 tsp.	5 mL
Large egg	1	1
Granulated sugar	2 tbsp.	30 mL
Hard margarine (or butter), softened	1/4 cup	60 mL
Milk	1 cup	250 mL
All-purpose flour	2 cups	500 mL
Baking powder	1 tbsp.	15 mL
Salt	1/2 tsp.	2 mL

Combine first 4 ingredients in medium bowl. Divide evenly and spoon into 12 greased muffin cups.

Beat egg, granulated sugar and second amount of margarine in small bowl. Add milk. Mix.

Combine flour, baking powder and salt in large bowl. Make a well in centre. Pour milk mixture into well. Stir until just moistened. Divide evenly and spoon onto pineapple mixture. Bake in 400°F (205°C) oven for about 18 minutes until wooden pick inserted in centre comes out clean. Invert immediately onto wire rack to cool. There will be some stickiness on bottom. Makes 12 mini-cakes.

1 mini-cake: 224 Calories; 9 g Total Fat; 307 mg Sodium; 4 g Protein; 33 g Carbohydrate; 1 g Dietary Fibre

Chocolate Snack Cake

A rich chocolate cake from mixing bowl to dessert plate in less than 30 minutes! The most difficult part is limiting yourself to one piece! Delicious with a scoop of ice cream and a drizzle of caramel or hot fudge sauce.

Hard margarine (or butter), softened	2 tbsp.	30 mL
Granulated sugar	1/2 cup	125 mL
Large egg	1	1
Milk	1/3 cup	75 mL
Vanilla	1/2 tsp.	2 mL
All-purpose flour	2/3 cup	150 mL
Cocoa, sifted if lumpy	2 tbsp.	30 mL
Baking powder	1/2 tsp.	2 mL
Baking soda	1/2 tsp.	2 mL
Salt	1/4 tsp.	1 mL

Beat first 5 ingredients together in medium bowl.

Add flour, cocoa, baking powder, baking soda and salt. Beat until smooth. Turn into greased 9 × 9 inch (22 × 22 cm) pan. Bake in 350°F (175°C) oven for about 14 minutes until wooden pick inserted in centre comes out clean. Cool. Cuts into 9 pieces as a dessert or 12 pieces as a snack.

1 piece: 120 Calories; 3.5 g Total Fat; 200 mg Sodium; 2 g Protein; 20 g Carbohydrate; 1 g Dietary Fibre

Cola Zucchini Cake

This unlikely combination of ingredients makes a surprisingly rich and chocolatey cake. It is deliciously moist and speckled with chocolate chips throughout. Drizzle with White Chocolate Sauce, page 111, for a special occasion.

Devil's food cake mix (2 layer size)	1	1
Cola beverage	1/2 cup	125 mL
Large eggs	3	3
Cooking oil	1/3 cup	75 mL

(continued on next page)

Grated zucchini, with peel	1 1/2 cups	375 mL
Semi-sweet chocolate chips	1 cup	250 mL

Empty cake mix into large bowl. Add cola, eggs and cooking oil. Beat on low until just moistened. Beat on medium for 2 minutes.

Add zucchini. Stir. Turn into greased 9 x 13 inch (22 x 33 cm) pan.

Sprinkle with chocolate chips. Bake in 350°F (175°C) oven for 35 to 40 minutes until wooden pick inserted in centre comes out clean. Cool. Cuts into 24 pieces.

1 piece: 170 Calories; 9.5 g Total Fat; 189 mg Sodium; 2 g Protein; 21 g Carbohydrate; 1 g Dietary Fibre

Pictured on page 107.

White Snack Cake

This versatile snacking cake is so easy to prepare and can be enjoyed in so many ways. Serve with a scoop of ice cream, a spoonful of your favourite pie filling or with hot caramel or fudge sauce. Use your imagination to create other dessert sensations.

Hard margarine (or butter), softened	1 tbsp.	15 mL
Granulated sugar	1/3 cup	75 mL
Large egg	1	1
Vanilla	1/2 tsp.	2 mL
Milk	1/4 cup	60 mL
All-purpose flour	1/2 cup	125 mL
Baking powder	1/2 tsp.	2 mL
Salt	1/8 tsp.	0.5 mL

Beat first 5 ingredients together in medium bowl.

Add flour, baking powder and salt. Beat until smooth. Turn into greased 8 x 8 inch (20 x 20 cm) pan. Bake in 350°F (175°C) oven for about 12 minutes until wooden pick inserted in centre comes out clean. Cool. Cuts into 9 pieces as a dessert or 12 pieces as a snack.

1 piece: 81 Calories; 2 g Total Fat; 81 mg Sodium; 2 g Protein; 14 g Carbohydrate; trace Dietary Fibre

Lemon Poppy Loaf

This moist, lemony loaf has a melt-in-your-mouth, creamy icing that will have your guests lining up for seconds. Enjoy with a nice cup of tea or coffee.

Granulated sugar	3/4 cup	175 mL
Hard margarine (or butter), softened	6 tbsp.	100 mL
Finely grated lemon zest	1 tbsp.	15 mL
Large eggs	3	3
All-purpose flour	1 1/2 cups	375 mL
Baking powder	2 tsp.	10 mL
Medium coconut	3/4 cup	175 mL
Poppy seeds	6 tbsp.	100 mL
Sour cream	6 tbsp.	100 mL
Milk	6 tbsp.	100 mL
LEMON CREAM CHEESE ICING		
Block of cream cheese, softened	4 oz.	125 g
Finely grated lemon zest	2 tsp.	10 mL
Icing (confectioner's) sugar	1 1/2 cups	375 mL
Long thread coconut, toasted (see Tip, page 79)	1/4 cup	60 mL

Beat first 4 ingredients in medium bowl until light and fluffy. Mixture may look curdled.

Stir flour and baking powder into margarine mixture.

Add next 4 ingredients. Mix well. Spread in greased 8 x 4 x 3 inch (20 x 10 x 7.5 cm) loaf pan. Bake in 350°F (175°C) oven for about 1 hour until wooden pick inserted in centre comes out clean. Let stand in pan for 10 minutes before turning out onto wire rack to cool.

Lemon Cream Cheese Icing: Beat cream cheese, lemon zest and icing sugar in medium bowl until light and fluffy. Makes about 1 cup (250 mL) icing. Spread over top of loaf.

Sprinkle with coconut. Cuts into 16 slices.

1 slice: 278 Calories; 14.3 g Total Fat; 141 mg Sodium; 4 g Protein; 35 g Carbohydrate; 1 g Dietary Fibre

Pictured on page 108.

Cakes

Cherry Snack Cake

This fun, rosy-coloured cake makes a fabulous child's birthday cake—especially with the cherries and chocolate chips throughout. Who found the only whole cherry?

Ingredient		
Hard margarine (or butter), softened	1/2 cup	125 mL
Granulated sugar	1 cup	250 mL
Large eggs	2	2
Vanilla	1 tsp.	5 mL
Semi-sweet chocolate baking square, grated	1 oz.	28 g
Chopped maraschino cherries	1/4 cup	60 mL
Whole maraschino cherry	1	1
All-purpose flour	1 1/2 cups	375 mL
Baking powder	1 1/2 tsp.	7 mL
Salt	1/4 tsp.	1 mL
Maraschino cherry syrup	1/4 cup	60 mL
Icing (confectioner's) sugar, for dusting		

Cream margarine and granulated sugar in large bowl. Beat in eggs, 1 at a time, beating well after each addition.

Add vanilla, chocolate and cherries. Stir.

Mix flour, baking powder and salt in small bowl.

Add flour mixture to margarine mixture in 3 additions, alternating with cherry syrup in 2 additions, beginning and ending with flour mixture. Spread in greased 9 x 9 inch (22 x 22 cm) pan. Bake in 350°F (175°C) oven for about 35 minutes until wooden pick inserted in centre comes out clean. Cool.

Dust individual servings with icing sugar. Cuts into 9 pieces as a dessert or 12 pieces as a snack.

1 piece: 318 Calories; 13 g Total Fat; 269 mg Sodium; 4 g Protein; 47 g Carbohydrate; 1 g Dietary Fibre

Pictured on page 36.

Cakes

25

Raisin Cake

Enjoy bursts of natural sweetness from the raisins in this simple spice cake. And who can resist the velvety smooth cream cheese icing?

All-purpose flour	2 1/2 cups	625 mL
Brown sugar, packed	2/3 cup	150 mL
Baking powder	1 tbsp.	15 mL
Baking soda	1 tsp.	5 mL
Ground cinnamon	1 tsp.	5 mL
Ground ginger	1/2 tsp.	2 mL
Ground nutmeg	1/4 tsp.	1 mL
Hard margarine (or butter), softened	1/2 cup	125 mL
Large eggs	2	2
Can of raisin pie filling	19 oz.	540 mL
Vanilla	1 1/2 tsp.	7 mL
CREAM CHEESE ICING		
Spreadable cream cheese	1/4 cup	60 mL
Hard margarine (or butter), softened	1 tbsp.	15 mL
Vanilla	1/2 tsp.	2 mL
Icing (confectioner's) sugar	2 cups	500 mL
Milk	8 tsp.	40 mL

Measure first 7 ingredients into large bowl. Stir. Make a well in centre.

Add margarine, eggs, pie filling and vanilla to well. Beat on low until just moistened. Beat on medium for 3 minutes. Spread in greased 9 x 13 inch (22 x 33 cm) pan. Bake in 350°F (175°C) oven for 35 to 40 minutes until wooden pick inserted in centre comes out clean. Cool in pan on wire rack.

Cream Cheese Icing: Beat cream cheese, margarine and vanilla until light and fluffy.

Add icing sugar, 1/2 cup (125 mL) at a time, beating well after each addition. Beat in milk, 1 tsp. (5 mL) at a time, until spreadable consistency. Spread over top of cooled cake. Cuts into 24 pieces.

1 piece: 202 Calories; 6.1 g Total Fat; 172 mg Sodium; 2 g Protein; 35 g Carbohydrate; 1 g Dietary Fibre

Pictured on page 35.

Almond Peach Little Cakes

These buttery, little, almond-flavoured cakes are delicious with the sweet, summery taste of peaches. Or try with fresh blueberries or raspberries in season. Individually freeze and thaw as needed.

Almond meal (ground almonds)	1 cup	250 mL
Hard margarine (or butter), melted	3/4 cup	175 mL
Egg whites (large), fork-beaten	6	6
Icing (confectioner's) sugar	1 1/2 cups	375 mL
All-purpose flour	1/2 cup	125 mL
Finely chopped peaches (about 1/2 of 14 oz., 398 mL, can, drained)	1/2 cup	125 mL

Icing (confectioner's) sugar, for dusting

Stir first 5 ingredients in large bowl until just combined. Divide evenly and spoon into 12 well-greased muffin cups 1/2 full.

Divide and scatter peaches onto batter. Bake in 375°F (190°C) oven for about 25 minutes until wooden pick inserted in centre comes out clean. Let stand in pan for 10 minutes before turning out onto wire rack to cool.

Dust with icing sugar. Makes 12 little cakes.

1 little cake: 236 Calories; 15.1 g Total Fat; 170 mg Sodium; 4 g Protein; 23 g Carbohydrate; trace Dietary Fibre

Pictured on page 35.

Paré Pointer

The real reason climbers are tied together with rope is so no one can decide to go home.

Cakes

27

Cherry Mini-Cakes

Moist, cherry-flavoured tea cakes with crunchy pecans and chewy cherries.

Hard margarine (or butter), softened	1/2 cup	125 mL
Brown sugar, packed	1 cup	250 mL
Granulated sugar	1/4 cup	60 mL
Large eggs, fork-beaten	2	2
Almond flavouring	1/2 tsp.	2 mL
Apple juice	1/4 cup	60 mL
All-purpose flour	1 2/3 cups	400 mL
Baking powder	1 tsp.	5 mL
Salt	1/2 tsp.	2 mL
Chopped pecans (or walnuts)	1/3 cup	75 mL
Chopped glazed cherries	1/2 cup	125 mL

Icing (confectioner's) sugar, for dusting

Beat first 6 ingredients together in large bowl until well combined.

Combine flour, baking powder and salt in medium bowl. Add to margarine mixture. Mix until no dry flour remains.

Sprinkle 1 tsp. (5 mL) pecans and 2 tsp. (10 mL) cherries each into bottom of 12 greased muffin cups. Divide evenly and spoon batter over top. Bake in 400°F (205°C) oven for 18 to 20 minutes until wooden pick inserted in centre comes out clean. Let stand in pan for 5 minutes before turning out onto wire rack to cool.

Dust with icing sugar. Makes 12 mini-cakes.

1 mini-cake: 293 Calories; 11.4 g Total Fat; 243 mg Sodium; 3 g Protein; 46 g Carbohydrate; 1 g Dietary Fibre

Cakes

Candies & Confections

Candy-Making Tips:

- Use a candy thermometer to take the guesswork out of candy making. Test your candy thermometer before each use. Bring cold water to a boil. Candy thermometer should read 212°F (100°C) in boiling water at sea level. Adjust recipe temperature up or down based on test results. For example, if your thermometer reads 206°F (97°C), subtract 6°F (3°C) from each temperature called for in recipe. Double check with the cold water test.

- Do not alter any ingredient amounts or double or halve candy recipes.

- Use a good quality mixing spoon and be prepared to use your muscles for stirring.

Candy Thermometer Chart

Stage	Temperature	Until small amount dropped into cold water...
Thread	223° to 234°F 106° to 112°C	forms a soft 2 inch (5 cm) thread.
Soft ball	234° to 240°F 112° to 116°C	forms a soft ball that flattens on its own accord when removed.
Firm ball	242° to 248°F 117° to 120°C	forms a pliable ball.
Hard ball	250° to 265°F 120° to 129°C	forms a rigid ball that is still somewhat pliable.
Soft crack	270° to 290°F 132° to 143°C	separates into hard, but pliable, threads.
Hard crack	300° to 310°F 150° to 154°C	separates into hard, brittle threads.

Raspberry Turkish Jellies

A fruity variation on the ever-popular Turkish Delight.
These deep red jellies are ideal for satisfying after-dinner sweet cravings.
As beautiful as they are delicious.

Water	1 cup	250 mL
Granulated sugar	1 3/4 cups	425 mL
Sweetened powdered raspberry-flavoured	1/4 cup	60 mL
drink crystals (see Note)		
Lemon juice	1 tbsp.	15 mL
Cold water	3/4 cup	175 mL
Envelopes of unflavoured gelatin	5	5
(1/4 oz., 7 g, each)		
Fine granulated sugar	3 tbsp.	50 mL

Stir water, first amount of sugar, drink crystals and lemon juice in large saucepan. Bring to a boil on medium. Boil for 3 to 4 minutes, stirring occasionally, until sugar is dissolved.

Stir cold water and gelatin in small bowl. Let stand for 1 minute. Add to boiling syrup mixture. Heat and stir for about 1 minute until gelatin is dissolved. Reduce heat to medium-low or just enough to keep syrup at a steady boil. Boil slowly, uncovered, without stirring, for about 40 minutes until mixture reaches soft ball stage (about 235°F, 113°C, on candy thermometer) or until small amount dropped into very cold water forms a soft ball that flattens on its own accord when removed. Dampen 8 x 8 inch (20 x 20 cm) or 9 x 9 inch (22 x 22 cm) pan with cold water. Immediately pour syrup mixture into pan. Let stand, uncovered, at room temperature for at least 24 hours until very firm.

Put second amount of sugar in separate small bowl. To remove jellies from pan, coat long sharp knife with sugar and cut along sides of pan. Cut into 4 more-manageable portions, coating edge of knife before each cut. Pull jelly sections from pan, 1 at a time, and place on work surface coated with sugar. Sprinkle sugar as needed to prevent sticking. Cut jellies into 1 inch (2.5 cm) pieces with edge of knife coated in sugar and press straight down to cut through. Coat individual jellies on all sides with sugar. Store for up to 4 weeks with sugar in between layers in airtight container. Makes about 1 1/4 lbs. (560 g). Cuts into about 80 jellies.

(continued on next page)

Candies & Confections

Note: Any flavour of sweetened powdered drink crystals, such as passion fruit, kiwifruit, cranberry, grape, orange or lemonade, can be used.

Variation: Omit second amount of sugar. Use icing sugar to coat individual jellies.

Candied Peanuts And Dates

These candied peanuts and dates have something to satisfy a variety of cravings—they are sweet, chewy, crunchy and chocolatey.

Butter (not margarine)	6 tbsp.	100 mL
Brown sugar, packed	3 tbsp.	50 mL
Corn syrup	2 tbsp.	30 mL
Unsalted peanuts	1 cup	250 mL
Finely chopped dates	1/2 cup	125 mL
Box of candy-coated chocolate candies (such as Smarties)	2 oz.	56 g

Heat butter, brown sugar and corn syrup in large saucepan on medium until bubbly.

Add peanuts and dates. Heat and stir for about 3 minutes until peanuts are coated and mixture is slightly thickened. Remove from heat. Let stand for 15 to 20 minutes to cool. If mixture cools too much, it will be difficult to mix in candies.

Stir in candies. Press in greased foil-lined 8 x 8 inch (20 x 20 cm) pan. Cool completely. Cuts into 24 triangles.

Pictured on page 126.

Candy Fruit Balls

These chewy fruit and nut balls are so delicious you won't notice how healthy they are! Excellent packed into the kids' lunches or as a snack while hiking.

Hard margarine (or butter)	2/3 cup	150 mL
Granulated sugar	1 cup	250 mL
Chopped dried apricots	1/2 cup	125 mL
Chopped dates	1/2 cup	125 mL
Vanilla	1/2 tsp.	2 mL
Crisp rice cereal	2 cups	500 mL
Chopped walnuts (or pecans)	1/2 cup	125 mL
Granulated (or icing, confectioner's) sugar	1/4 cup	60 mL

Combine first 4 ingredients in large saucepan. Heat and stir on medium for 5 minutes until fruit is soft. Remove from heat.

Add vanilla, cereal and walnuts. Stir well. Cool until able to handle. Shape into 1 inch (2.5 cm) balls.

Put second amount of sugar into resealable plastic bag. Drop, a few balls at a time, into sugar. Shake until well coated. Makes about 40 fruit balls.

1 fruit ball: 79 Calories; 4.2 g Total Fat; 53 mg Sodium; 1 g Protein; 10 g Carbohydrate; trace Dietary Fibre

Pictured on page 143.

 *Most candies will store for 2 to 3 weeks in an airtight container in a cool, dry place. Be sure to store only one kind of candy in each container or the texture and flavour might change. Protect individual candies by covering with plastic wrap or store in between layers of waxed paper. If you want to freeze candies, store in a resealable freezer bag or airtight container.*

Spiced Candied Almonds

*The delicious taste of toasted almonds, candied and spiced
with nutmeg and allspice. It's hard to stop once you start!*

GLAZE		
Granulated sugar	1 1/2 cups	375 mL
Water	1/4 cup	60 mL
Ground nutmeg	1/2 tsp.	2 mL
Ground allspice	1/4 tsp.	1 mL
Salt	3/4 tsp.	4 mL
Whole almonds (see Note), toasted (see Tip, page 79)	1 cup	250 mL

Glaze: Heat and stir sugar and water in large heavy saucepan or frying pan on medium. Brush side of saucepan with damp pastry brush to prevent any sugar crystals from forming. Boil slowly, uncovered, without stirring, until sugar is melted and mixture is light caramel colour. Remove from heat.

Stir in nutmeg, allspice and salt. Mixture will foam a bit. Drizzle over almonds on lightly greased 11 x 17 inch (28 x 43 cm) baking sheet being sure to get some on each one. Candy will not fill pan. Cool completely. Break into bite-size pieces. Makes about 14 oz. (395 g).

1 oz. (28 g): 151 Calories; 5.6 g Total Fat; 129 mg Sodium; 2 g Protein; 25 g Carbohydrate; 1 g Dietary Fibre

Note: Almonds with or without the skins work fine. You may even want to use a mix of both.

Paré Pointer

Her eyes have never been checked. They have always been brown.

Macadamia Nut Toffee

A crunchy, nutty, oven-baked toffee that doesn't require a candy thermometer.
For a more economical, but equally delicious, variation, try with peanuts.

Butter (not margarine)	2/3 cup	150 mL
Brown sugar, packed	1 cup	250 mL
Coarsely chopped macadamia nuts	1 cup	250 mL
Semi-sweet chocolate chips	1/2 cup	125 mL
Finely chopped macadamia nuts	1/4 cup	60 mL

Stir butter and brown sugar in small saucepan on medium until boiling and sugar is dissolved.

Stir in first amount of nuts. Pour into greased 9 × 9 inch (22 × 22 cm) pan. Bake in 375°F (190°C) oven for about 15 minutes until caramel coloured and entire surface is covered with small bubbles. Let stand in pan on wire rack for 5 minutes to cool slightly.

Sprinkle with chocolate chips. Let stand for about 5 minutes until chocolate chips are melted. Spread evenly.

Sprinkle with second amount of nuts while chocolate is still warm. Cool completely. Makes 1 lb., 2 oz. (511 g). Breaks into about 64 pieces.

1 piece: 55 Calories; 4.1 g Total Fat; 23 mg Sodium; trace Protein; 5 g Carbohydrate; trace Dietary Fibre

1. Butter Pecan Pudding Fudge, page 41
2. Raisin Cake, page 26
3. Almond Peach Little Cakes, page 27
4. Oatmeal Cake, page 20

Props Courtesy Of: Wiltshire®

Candies & Confections

Seed And Honey Fruit Plums

This no-bake sweet treat is so easy and so healthy. A perfect blend of dried fruit, honey and coconut. A popular after-school snack for kids.

Small navel orange, with peel	1	1
Dried figs, stems removed, packed	1/4 cup	60 mL
Whole dates, packed	1/4 cup	60 mL
Dried apricots, packed	1/4 cup	60 mL
Seedless raisins	1/4 cup	60 mL
Liquid honey	2 tbsp.	30 mL
Roasted sunflower seeds	1/4 cup	60 mL
Long thread coconut, toasted (see Tip, page 79)	1/2 cup	125 mL

Cut off and discard 1/2 inch (12 mm) from top and bottom of orange. Cut remainder of orange into quarters.

Put orange into food processor fitted with chopping blade. Add next 6 ingredients. Pulse with on/off motion in 3 to 4 second bursts until coarsely chopped. Process for 30 seconds until finely chopped. Food grinder may also be used. Shape into balls, using 2 tsp. (10 mL) for each ball.

Place coconut in shallow dish or on waxed paper. Roll balls to coat well. Makes about 28 balls.

1 ball: 41 Calories; 1.8 g Total Fat; 1 mg Sodium; 1 g Protein; 7 g Carbohydrate; 1 g Dietary Fibre

Pictured on page 53.

1. Spiced Palmiers, page 87
2. Cherry Snack Cake, page 25
3. A Touch Of Danish, page 94

Props Courtesy Of: Pfaltzgraff Canada

Chocolate Fudge

Who can resist a rich, creamy, dark, melt-in-your-mouth fudge?
Your guests will ask for a small piece, but they'll be back for another.

Brown sugar, packed	1 1/2 cups	375 mL
Granulated sugar	1 1/2 cups	375 mL
Milk	1 cup	250 mL
Corn syrup	3 tbsp.	50 mL
Unsweetened chocolate baking squares	3	3
(1 oz., 28 g, each), cut up		
Salt	1/8 tsp.	0.5 mL
Hard margarine (or butter)	2 tbsp.	30 mL
Vanilla	1 tsp.	5 mL

Combine first 6 ingredients in large heavy saucepan. Heat and stir on medium until chocolate is melted and mixture begins to boil. Reduce heat to medium-low. Brush side of saucepan with damp pastry brush to allow any sugar crystals on side of saucepan to dissolve. Boil slowly, uncovered, without stirring, until mixture reaches soft ball stage (about 238°F, 114°C, on candy thermometer) or until small amount dropped into very cold water forms a soft ball that flattens on its own accord when removed. Remove from heat. Chocolate will mix in when beaten later.

Add margarine and vanilla. Stir. Let stand for 20 minutes. Beat for about 2 minutes until just beginning to thicken, glossy look disappears and looks creamy. Turn quickly into greased 8 x 8 inch (20 x 20 cm) pan. Spread evenly. Cut while barely warm. Keep well covered to prevent drying. Makes about 1 1/2 lbs. (680 g). Cuts into 64 pieces.

1 piece: 55 Calories; 1.1 g Total Fat; 14 mg Sodium; trace Protein; 12 g Carbohydrate; trace Dietary Fibre

CHOCOLATE NUT FUDGE: Stir in 1/2 cup (125 mL) finely chopped walnuts (or pecans) just prior to turning into pan.

Peanut Butter Fudge

A peanut butter lover's delight. This creamy and peanutty fudge looks and smells as delicious as it tastes.

Granulated sugar	2 cups	500 mL
Hard margarine (or butter)	3 tbsp.	50 mL
Milk	1/2 cup	125 mL
Salt, just a pinch		
Smooth peanut butter	1/2 cup	125 mL
Marshmallow creme	1/2 cup	125 mL
Vanilla	1/2 tsp.	2 mL

Combine sugar, margarine, milk and salt in large heavy saucepan. Heat and stir on medium until sugar is dissolved and mixture begins to boil. Reduce heat to medium-low. Boil slowly, uncovered, for about 8 minutes, stirring twice, until mixture reaches soft ball stage (about 235°F, 113°C, on candy thermometer) or until small amount dropped into very cold water forms a soft ball that flattens on its own accord when removed. Remove from heat. Let stand for 10 minutes.

Stir in peanut butter, marshmallow creme and vanilla. Pour into greased 8 x 8 inch (20 x 20 cm) pan. Spread evenly. Cool. Makes about 1 1/2 lbs. (680 g). Cuts into 64 pieces.

1 piece: 50 Calories; 1.7 g Total Fat; 18 mg Sodium; 1 g Protein; 9 g Carbohydrate; trace Dietary Fibre

Paré Pointer

Tennis is such a noisy game. You have to raise a "racket" to play.

Burnt Sugar Fudge

Smooth and creamy with a subtle burnt sugar caramel flavour.
Keep this recipe handy—there will be requests for repeats!

Granulated sugar	1 cup	250 mL
Water	1/4 cup	60 mL
Half-and-half cream (or evaporated milk)	1 cup	250 mL
Granulated sugar	2 cups	500 mL
Hard margarine (or butter)	3 tbsp.	50 mL
Vanilla	1 tsp.	5 mL
Chopped pecans (or walnuts)	3/4 cup	175 mL

Grease side of large heavy saucepan. Place first amount of sugar in saucepan. Heat and stir on medium until sugar is melted and rich brown in colour. Remove from heat.

Gradually, and very carefully, stir in water. Mixture will sputter furiously and sugar may start to solidify. Return to heat. Add cream, second amount of sugar and margarine. Heat and stir on medium until boiling and caramelized sugar is dissolved. Reduce heat to medium-low. Brush side of saucepan with damp pastry brush to allow any sugar crystals on side of saucepan to dissolve. Boil slowly, uncovered, for about 30 minutes, stirring frequently, until mixture reaches soft ball stage (about 240°F, 116°C, on candy thermometer) or until small amount dropped into very cold water forms a soft ball that flattens on its own accord when removed. Remove from heat. Let stand for 20 minutes.

Stir in vanilla and pecans. Beat on low until very thick and difficult to beat further. Turn into greased 9 x 9 inch (22 x 22 cm) pan. Spread evenly. Cool. Makes about 1 3/4 lbs. (790 g). Cuts into 64 pieces.

1 piece: 58 Calories; 1.9 g Total Fat; 8 mg Sodium; trace Protein; 10 g Carbohydrate; trace Dietary Fibre

Butter Pecan Pudding Fudge

The classic flavour of butter pecan makes this rich, creamy fudge extraordinary! This simple microwave fudge recipe requires no candy thermometer and is prepared in just a few minutes. Store this soft fudge in the refrigerator.

Chopped pecans	1/2 cup	125 mL
Butter (not margarine)	2 tsp.	10 mL
Milk	1/3 cup	75 mL
Vanilla	1 tsp.	5 mL
Butterscotch pudding powder (not instant), 6 serving size	1	1
Butter (not margarine)	3 tbsp.	50 mL
Icing (confectioner's) sugar	2 1/2 cups	625 mL

Fry pecans in first amount of butter in small frying pan until browned. Set aside.

Whisk milk, vanilla and pudding powder in large microwave-safe bowl until smooth. Add second amount of butter. Microwave, uncovered, on high (100%) for 1 minute. Whisk until smooth. Microwave on high (100%) for 30 seconds. Whisk. Microwave on high (100%) for 50 to 60 seconds until just beginning to bubble on side of bowl. Whisk. Do not overcook.

Immediately whisk in icing sugar until thickened. Stir in pecan mixture. Pack into greased foil-lined 9 x 5 x 3 inch (22 x 12.5 x 7.5 cm) loaf pan. Cover with plastic wrap. Chill for 1 hour before serving. Makes about 1 lb. (454 g). Cuts into 40 pieces.

1 piece: 67 Calories; 2.2 g Total Fat; 27 mg Sodium; trace Protein; 12 g Carbohydrate; trace Dietary Fibre

Pictured on page 35.

Instant Maple Walnut Fudge

A rich fudge that is quick and easy to make.

Butterscotch chips	1 1/2 cups	375 mL
Semi-sweet chocolate chips	1/2 cup	125 mL
Container of vanilla frosting	16 oz.	450 g
Maple flavouring	1/4 tsp.	1 mL
Chopped walnuts	1 cup	250 mL

Heat butterscotch and chocolate chips in medium saucepan on lowest heat until almost melted. Do not overheat. Remove from heat. Stir until smooth.

Stir in frosting, flavouring and walnuts. Pour into greased foil-lined 8 × 8 inch (20 × 20 cm) pan. Spread evenly. Chill, uncovered, for about 45 minutes until firm. Remove fudge and foil from pan. Remove and discard foil. Makes about 1 1/2 lbs. (680 g). Cuts into 64 pieces.

1 piece: 63 Calories; 2.9 g Total Fat; 9 mg Sodium; 1 g Protein; 9 g Carbohydrate; trace Dietary Fibre

 *To reduce frustration when making candy, be sure to read the entire recipe before you begin. Collect the ingredients and tools you will need (such as candy thermometer and a cup for cold water) and make sure you have the exact measurements. Keep everything close by and handy.*

English Toffee

A smooth, hard toffee with a delicious caramel flavour.
Suck on it slowly and savour its richness.

Brown sugar, packed	1 cup	250 mL
Granulated sugar	1 cup	250 mL
Half-and-half cream	1/2 cup	125 mL
Butter (not margarine)	1/4 cup	60 mL
Corn syrup	1/4 cup	60 mL
Cream of tartar	1/2 tsp.	2 mL
Salt	1/8 tsp.	0.5 mL
Vanilla	1 tsp.	5 mL

Grease side of large heavy saucepan. Combine first 7 ingredients in saucepan. Heat and stir on medium-low to dissolve sugar slowly. Bring to a boil. Brush side of saucepan with damp pastry brush to allow any sugar crystals on side of saucepan to dissolve. Boil slowly, uncovered, without stirring, for about 30 minutes until mixture reaches hard crack stage (about 310°F, 154°C on candy thermometer) or until small amount dropped into very cold water separates into hard, brittle threads. Remove from heat.

Stir in vanilla. Pour into greased 8 x 8 inch (20 x 20 cm) pan. Let stand for 25 minutes. Mark into squares with sharp knife, pressing straight down but not quite through toffee. Break apart once cooled completely. Makes 1 1/4 lbs. (560 g). Breaks into about 64 pieces.

1 piece: 40 Calories; 1 g Total Fat; 16 mg Sodium; trace Protein; 8 g Carbohydrate; 0 g Dietary Fibre

Pictured on page 53.

Paré Pointer

One good turn deserves another.
Actually, one good turn gives you most of the blankets.

Homemade Chocolate Marshmallows

Kids and adults alike love this fun, fluffy treat! These melt-in-your-mouth mallows taste like hot chocolate and marshmallows in one. The ultimate comfort food.

Icing (confectioner's) sugar	1/2 cup	125 mL
Cocoa, sifted if lumpy	1 tbsp.	15 mL
Cornstarch	1/2 cup	125 mL
Cold water	1/3 cup	75 mL
Envelopes of unflavoured gelatin	2	2
(1/4 oz., 7 g, each)		
Granulated sugar	1 1/2 cups	375 mL
White corn syrup	1/2 cup	125 mL
Cocoa, sifted if lumpy	3 tbsp.	50 mL
Instant coffee granules	1/4 tsp.	1 mL
Water	1/3 cup	75 mL
Vanilla	1/2 tsp.	2 mL

Combine icing sugar, first amount of cocoa and cornstarch in small dish. Line 8 x 8 inch (20 x 20 cm) or 9 x 9 inch (22 x 22 cm) pan with lightly greased foil. Thickly coat bottom and sides of foil with about 2 tbsp. (30 mL) icing sugar mixture. Reserve remaining icing sugar mixture.

Combine cold water and gelatin in large bowl. Set aside.

Heat and stir next 5 ingredients in large saucepan on medium-low until sugar is dissolved. Brush side of saucepan with damp pastry brush to allow any sugar crystals on side of saucepan to dissolve. Increase heat to medium. Boil vigorously, uncovered, for about 4 minutes, without stirring, until mixture reaches soft ball stage (about 240°F, 116°C, on candy thermometer) or until small amount dropped into very cold water forms a soft ball that flattens on its own accord when removed. Do not overcook. Immediately remove from heat. Slowly pour hot syrup into gelatin mixture while beating on medium. Increase speed to high. Beat for about 15 minutes, scraping down side of bowl 2 to 3 times.

(continued on next page)

Add vanilla during last few minutes of beating, until mixture is thick and fluffy. Scrape into prepared pan. Spread evenly. Sprinkle with about 2 tbsp. (30 mL) reserved icing sugar mixture. Let stand at room temperature for several hours or overnight until set. Turn out onto work surface. Remove and discard foil. Cut with long greased sharp knife, pushing straight down into marshmallow mixture with full length of blade. Re-grease knife as necessary to make cutting easier. Put remaining icing sugar mixture into shallow dish or on waxed paper. Roll marshmallows to coat completely. Store in airtight container for up to 2 weeks. To serve, tap off excess icing sugar mixture or shake gently in sieve. Makes about 2 dozen marshmallows.

1 marshmallow: 95 Calories; 0.1 g Total Fat; 6 mg Sodium; trace Protein; 24 g Carbohydrate; trace Dietary Fibre

Mints

These delectable little mints are the perfect finale to a special meal. Bite-sized mints with a creamy, melt-in-your-mouth texture. Different shapes can be made by using 1/2 inch (12 mm) pastry or canapé cutters.

Hard margarine (or butter), softened	2 tbsp.	30 mL
Egg white (large)	1	1
Peppermint flavouring	1/2 tsp.	2 mL
Drops of green food colouring	3	3
Icing (confectioner's) sugar, more if needed	2 1/2 cups	625 mL

Beat margarine, egg white, flavouring and food colouring in small bowl.

Slowly beat in icing sugar. Shape into 1/2 inch (12 mm) balls or roll out into 1/4 inch (6 mm) thick rope. Cut into 1/2 inch (12 mm) pieces. Arrange on waxed paper-lined baking sheet. Let stand overnight until dry. Store in airtight container. Makes 13 oz. (370 g). Makes 7 1/2 to 8 dozen mints.

5 mints: 81 Calories; 1.3 g Total Fat; 18 mg Sodium; trace Protein; 18 g Carbohydrate; 0 g Dietary Fibre

Coconut Marshmallow Creams

A surprisingly easy and unusual sweet treat. These tender mallows have a delicious, crispy, sweet coconut coating. Excellent as lunch box treats.

Long thread coconut, toasted (see Tip, page 79)	1 1/2 cups	375 mL
Envelopes of unflavoured gelatin (1/4 oz., 7 g, each)	2	2
Cold water	1/3 cup	75 mL
Granulated sugar	1 1/3 cups	325 mL
White corn syrup	1/2 cup	125 mL
Water	1/3 cup	75 mL
Salt, just a pinch		
Vanilla	1 tsp.	5 mL

Line 8 × 8 inch (20 × 20 cm) pan with lightly greased foil. Sprinkle 1/2 cup (125 mL) coconut over bottom of pan. Reserve remaining coconut.

Sprinkle gelatin over cold water in large bowl. Set aside.

Heat and stir next 4 ingredients in large saucepan on medium until sugar is dissolved. Brush side of saucepan with damp pastry brush to allow any sugar crystals on side of saucepan to dissolve. Increase heat to medium-high. Boil vigorously, uncovered, for about 4 minutes, without stirring, until mixture reaches soft ball stage (about 240°F, 116°C, on candy thermometer) or until small amount dropped into very cold water forms a soft ball that flattens on its own accord when removed. Do not overcook. Immediately remove from heat. Slowly pour hot syrup into gelatin mixture while beating on medium. Increase speed to high. Beat for about 15 minutes, scraping down side of bowl 2 to 3 times.

(continued on next page)

Add vanilla during last few minutes of beating, until mixture is thick and fluffy. Scrape into prepared pan. Spread evenly. Sprinkle with 1/2 cup (125 mL) reserved coconut. Let stand at room temperature for several hours or overnight until set. Turn out onto work surface. Remove and discard foil. Cut with long greased sharp knife, pushing straight down into marshmallow mixture with full length of blade. Re-grease knife as necessary to make cutting easier. Put remaining coconut into shallow dish or on waxed paper. Roll marshmallows to coat completely. Store in airtight container for up to 2 weeks. Makes about 2 dozen marshmallows.

1 marshmallow: 96 Calories; 2 g Total Fat; 21 mg Sodium; 1 g Protein; 20 g Carbohydrate; 1 g Dietary Fibre

---

Broken Glass

A rose-coloured, glass-like candy with a tangy berry flavour. Break into pieces and display in a candy dish.

Granulated sugar	3 3/4 cups	925 mL
Water	1 1/4 cups	300 mL
White corn syrup	1 1/2 cups	375 mL
Cherry (or strawberry) candy flavouring	1/4 tsp.	1 mL
Drops of red food colouring	9	9

Heat and stir sugar, water and corn syrup in large saucepan on medium until boiling and sugar is dissolved. Reduce heat to medium-low. Brush side of saucepan with damp pastry brush to allow any sugar crystals on side of saucepan to dissolve. Boil slowly, without stirring, for 60 to 75 minutes until mixture reaches hard crack stage (about 300°F, 150°C, on candy thermometer) or until small amount dropped into very cold water separates into hard, brittle threads. Remove from heat.

Add candy flavouring and food colouring. Stir. Pour into greased 11 x 17 inch (28 x 43 cm) baking sheet with sides. Let stand for about 45 minutes until cool. Turn out onto cutting board. Break into bite-size pieces. Makes 2 1/2 lbs. (1.1 kg).

1/2 oz. (14 g): 59 Calories; 0 g Total Fat; 5 mg Sodium; 0 g Protein; 15 g Carbohydrate; 0 g Dietary Fibre

Pictured on page 53.

Apricot Pecan Bark

A swirly white and milk chocolate bark with chewy apricots and crunchy pecans. This snack is such fun to make and your guests will marvel at how pretty it is.

Milk chocolate candy bars (3 1/2 oz., 100 g, each), chopped	2	2
Finely chopped dried apricots	1/2 cup	125 mL
White chocolate candy bars (3 1/2 oz., 100 g, each), chopped	2	2
Finely chopped pecans	1/2 cup	125 mL

Heat milk chocolate in heavy medium saucepan on lowest heat for about 5 minutes, stirring often, until almost melted. Do not overheat. Remove from heat. Stir until smooth. Add apricots. Stir.

Heat white chocolate in heavy medium saucepan on lowest heat for about 5 minutes, stirring often, until almost melted. Do not overheat. Remove from heat. Stir until smooth.

Add pecans. Stir. Alternately spoon milk chocolate mixture and white chocolate mixture onto parchment paper-lined 10 x 15 inch (25 x 38 cm) baking sheet. Swirl both mixtures together using wooden skewer. Smooth top. Chill for about 2 hours until set. Break into bite-size pieces. Makes about 1/2 lb. (225 g). Makes about 35 pieces.

1 piece: 76 Calories; 4.7 g Total Fat; 10 mg Sodium; 1 g Protein; 8 g Carbohydrate; trace Dietary Fibre

Pictured on page 72.

Paré Pointer

Disgusted ant to another: "Life is just one big picnic to you."

Mandarin Truffles

A definite must for your holiday baking list! These rich, chocolatey balls have a festive orange flavour and mild nutty crunch.

Dark chocolate candy bar, chopped	3 1/2 oz.	100 g
Whipping cream	3 tbsp.	50 mL
Orange-flavoured liqueur (such as Grand Marnier)	1 tbsp.	15 mL
Finely chopped pistachios	1/3 cup	75 mL
Finely grated mandarin (or any orange) zest	1 1/2 tsp.	7 mL
Cocoa, sifted if lumpy	2 tbsp.	30 mL

Heat chocolate, whipping cream and liqueur in medium saucepan on lowest heat for about 3 minutes, stirring often, until almost melted. Do not overheat. Remove from heat. Stir until smooth.

Add pistachios and mandarin zest. Mix well. Chill for about 1 hour, stirring occasionally, until firm enough to roll into balls.

Shape rounded teaspoonfuls into balls. Place on foil-lined baking sheet. Chill for 30 minutes. Place cocoa in shallow dish or on waxed paper. Roll each ball in cocoa to coat lightly. Chill for 1 to 3 hours until firm. Store in airtight container for up to 2 weeks. Makes about 18 truffles.

1 truffle: 57 Calories; 4 g Total Fat; 2 mg Sodium; 1 g Protein; 5 g Carbohydrate; 1 g Dietary Fibre

Variation: Omit orange-flavoured liqueur and pistachios. Use same amounts of coffee-flavoured liqueur (such as Kahlúa) and pecans.

 *Store chocolate in a cool, dry place for up to one year. Chocolate absorbs odours easily, so store in airtight container away from strong-smelling food.*

Crispy Sandwich Cookies

These buttery, crispy oatmeal wafers are scrumptious, both on their own and with the chocolate filling. Serve them filled for a simple, yet rich and elegant, treat.

Hard margarine (or butter), softened	1 cup	250 mL
Granulated sugar	3/4 cup	175 mL
Brown sugar, packed	3/4 cup	175 mL
Large egg	1	1
Vanilla	1 tsp.	5 mL
All-purpose flour	1 1/3 cups	325 mL
Baking soda	3/4 tsp.	4 mL
Salt	1/4 tsp.	1 mL
Coarsely crushed corn flakes cereal	1 1/4 cups	300 mL
Rolled oats (not instant)	1 1/4 cups	300 mL
Medium coconut	2/3 cup	150 mL
CHOCOLATE FILLING		
Semi-sweet chocolate chips	1 cup	250 mL
Icing (confectioner's) sugar	1/2 cup	125 mL
Water	1 tbsp.	15 mL
Block of light cream cheese, softened and cut into pieces	4 oz.	125 g

Cream margarine and both sugars in medium bowl. Beat in egg and vanilla.

Combine flour, baking soda and salt in small bowl. Add to margarine mixture. Mix well.

Add cereal, rolled oats and coconut. Mix. Shape into 1 inch (2.5 cm) balls. Arrange 2 inches (5 cm) apart on greased cookie sheets. Press with fork. Bake in 350°F (175°C) oven for about 15 minutes until golden. Remove to wire racks to cool. Makes about 5 1/2 dozen cookies.

(continued on next page)

Cookies

Chocolate Filling: Heat chocolate chips in small saucepan on lowest heat, stirring often, until almost melted. Do not overheat. Remove from heat. Stir until smooth.

Stir in icing sugar and water. Add cream cheese. Beat on low until smooth. Makes 1 1/4 cups (300 mL) filling. Sandwich cookies together, rough sides facing out, with 2 tsp. (10 mL) filling. Makes about 2 1/2 dozen cookies.

1 cookie: 217 Calories; 10.9 g Total Fat; 203 mg Sodium; 3 g Protein; 29 g Carbohydrate; 1 g Dietary Fibre

Cherry Coconut Macaroons

Wonderfully blended flavours of almond, coconut and cherry in a sweet, chewy macaroon! Almost too pretty to eat—but not quite!

Flake coconut	2 cups	500 mL
Sliced almonds, toasted (see Tip, page 79)	1/2 cup	125 mL
Maraschino cherries, chopped and blotted dry	3/4 cup	175 mL
All-purpose flour	1/2 cup	125 mL
Salt	1/4 tsp.	1 mL
Egg whites (large), room temperature	4	4
Almond flavouring	1/2 tsp.	2 mL
Granulated sugar	1/2 cup	125 mL

Combine first 5 ingredients in medium bowl.

Beat egg whites and flavouring in large bowl on medium until frothy. Add sugar, 1 tbsp. (15 mL) at a time, until soft peaks form. Fold in cherry mixture until just moistened. Drop by spoonfuls, using about 2 tbsp. (30 mL) for each, about 2 inches (5 cm) apart onto greased cookie sheets. Bake in 325°F (160°C) oven for about 15 minutes until edges are golden. Remove to wire racks to cool. Makes about 2 1/2 dozen macaroons.

1 macaroon: 64 Calories; 2.7 g Total Fat; 41 mg Sodium; 1 g Protein; 9 g Carbohydrate; 1 g Dietary Fibre

Pictured on page 54.

Soft Apricot Cashew Chews

The mixture of apricots and nuts gives a wonderful flavour and texture to these golden macaroon-like treats.

Coarsely crushed corn flakes cereal	2 cups	500 mL
Salted cashews, toasted (see Tip, page 79), chopped	3/4 cup	175 mL
Dried apricots, finely chopped	1/2 cup	125 mL
Egg whites (large), room temperature	4	4
Vanilla	1/2 tsp.	2 mL
Icing (confectioner's) sugar	1 cup	250 mL

Combine cereal, cashews and apricots in medium bowl.

Beat egg whites and vanilla in large bowl on high until almost stiff. Add icing sugar, 1/4 cup (60 mL) at a time, until glossy and very soft peaks form. Fold in cereal mixture. Drop by rounded tablespoonfuls about 2 inches (5 cm) apart onto greased cookie sheets. Bake in 325°F (160°C) oven for about 15 minutes until lightly golden. Remove to wire racks to cool. Makes about 2 1/2 dozen cookies.

1 cookie: 67 Calories; 1.4 g Total Fat; 73 mg Sodium; 1 g Protein; 12 g Carbohydrate; trace Dietary Fibre

1. English Toffee, page 43
2. Broken Glass, page 47
3. Spiced Toffee Nuts, page 131
4. Seed And Honey Fruit Plums, page 37

Props Courtesy Of: Wal-Mart Canada Inc.

Cookies

Orange And Carrot Cookies

Like a fruit and nut health bar in cookie form. A chewy cookie with the pleasing crunch of nuts and hint of zesty orange.

Large egg	1	1
Cooking oil	1/3 cup	75 mL
Brown sugar, packed	1/3 cup	75 mL
Grated carrot	1/2 cup	125 mL
Finely chopped dates	1/3 cup	75 mL
Finely chopped pecans	1/3 cup	75 mL
Freshly squeezed orange juice	1 tbsp.	15 mL
Finely grated orange zest	1 tsp.	5 mL
All-purpose flour	1 cup	250 mL
Baking powder	1 tsp.	5 mL
Salt	1/4 tsp.	1 mL

Combine egg, cooking oil and brown sugar in large bowl.

Add next 5 ingredients. Mix well.

Stir flour, baking powder and salt into carrot mixture. Mix well. Drop by rounded tablespoonfuls about 2 inches (5 cm) apart onto greased cookie sheets. Bake in 350°F (175°C) oven for about 15 minutes until golden. Let stand on cookie sheets for 10 minutes before removing to wire racks to cool. Makes about 1 1/2 dozen cookies.

1 cookie: 111 Calories; 6.2 g Total Fat; 60 mg Sodium; 1 g Protein; 13 g Carbohydrate; 1 g Dietary Fibre

1. Cranberry Chocolate Cookies, page 61
2. Cherry Coconut Macaroons, page 51
3. Pecan Caramel Kisses, page 57

Cookies

Coffee Meringues

These fancy little meringues are perfect with your after-dinner coffee.
Elegantly dipped in chocolate and delicately flavoured with coffee.

Egg whites (large), room temperature	2	2
Cream of tartar	1/2 tsp.	2 mL
Granulated sugar	1/3 cup	75 mL
Icing (confectioner's) sugar, sifted	1/3 cup	75 mL
Instant coffee granules	1 tbsp.	15 mL
Warm water	1 tbsp.	15 mL
Semi-sweet chocolate baking squares (1 oz., 28 g, each), chopped	4	4

Beat egg whites and cream of tartar in medium bowl on medium until soft peaks form.

Add granulated sugar, 1 tbsp. (15 mL) at a time, until stiff peaks form and sugar is dissolved.

Fold in icing sugar.

Stir coffee granules into warm water in small bowl until dissolved. Fold into meringue. Spoon meringue into piping bag fitted with plain 1 1/2 inch (3.8 cm) nozzle. Pipe about 40 small pointed mounds (about 1/2 inch, 1.2 cm, high and 1 inch, 2.5 cm, in diameter) about 2 inches (5 cm) apart onto greased cookie sheets. Bake on lowest rack in 225°F (110°C) oven for 35 to 40 minutes until dry. Turn oven off. Let meringues stand in oven until cool.

Heat chocolate in medium saucepan on lowest heat, stirring often, until almost melted. Do not overheat. Remove from heat. Stir until smooth. Dip 1/2 of each meringue into chocolate, allowing excess to drip back into saucepan. Place on foil or waxed paper-lined cookie sheets. Let stand in cool place until chocolate is set. Do not chill. Makes about 3 1/2 dozen meringues.

1 meringue: 24 Calories; 0.8 g Total Fat; 3 mg Sodium; trace Protein; 4 g Carbohydrate; trace Dietary Fibre

Pictured on page 107.

Pecan Caramel Kisses

Light and crispy meringues drizzled with a sticky caramel sauce.
Crunchy toasted pecans make this an immensely satisfying sweet treat.

Egg whites (large), room temperature	2	2
Cream of tartar	1/8 tsp.	0.5 mL
Maple flavouring	1/4 tsp.	1 mL
Icing (confectioner's) sugar	1 cup	250 mL
Whole pecans, toasted (see Tip, page 79), finely chopped	1/3 cup	75 mL
Caramels	10	10
Milk	2 tsp.	10 mL

Beat egg whites, cream of tartar and flavouring in medium bowl on medium until stiff peaks form. Beat in icing sugar, 2 tbsp. (30 mL) at a time, until very glossy and stiff.

Fold in pecans. Drop by level tablespoonfuls about 2 inches (5 cm) apart onto greased parchment paper-lined cookie sheets. Bake in 275°F (140°C) oven for about 30 minutes until dry and edges are golden. Remove from parchment paper to wire racks to cool.

Heat and stir caramels and milk in small saucepan on medium-low until smooth. Cool slightly. Spoon into bottom corner of small resealable freezer bag. Snip tiny piece off corner. Drizzle caramel over meringues. Makes about 2 1/2 dozen meringues.

1 meringue: 36 Calories; 1.1 g Total Fat; 10 mg Sodium; trace Protein; 7 g Carbohydrate; trace Dietary Fibre

Pictured on page 54 and on back cover.

Paré Pointer

The woman covered herself with vanishing cream.
Nobody knows where she went.

Giant Candy Bar Cookies

These cookies often don't make it from the cookie sheet to the cookie jar!
Irresistible when hot from the oven even if they are a little expensive to make.

Hard margarine (or butter), softened	1 cup	250 mL
Granulated sugar	1 cup	250 mL
Brown sugar, packed	1 cup	250 mL
Large eggs, fork-beaten	2	2
Vanilla	2 tsp.	10 mL
All-purpose flour	2 cups	500 mL
Baking powder	1 tsp.	5 mL
Baking soda	1 tsp.	5 mL
Salt	1/2 tsp.	2 mL
Rolled oats (not instant)	2 1/3 cups	575 mL
Chocolate-covered crispy toffee bars	8	8
(such as Skor or Heath), 1 1/2 oz. (39 g)		
each, chopped		
Granulated sugar	1/4 cup	60 mL

Cream margarine, first amount of granulated sugar and brown sugar in large bowl. Beat in eggs, 1 at a time, beating well after each addition. Add vanilla. Mix.

Add next 4 ingredients. Stir until just moistened.

Add rolled oats and chocolate bar pieces. Mix well. Shape into 2 inch (5 cm) balls. Arrange 4 or 5 balls on large greased cookie sheet.

Dip bottom of glass into second amount of granulated sugar. Flatten cookies to 1/2 inch (12 mm) thick, dipping glass in sugar as necessary. Bake in 375°F (190°C) oven for about 11 minutes until lightly golden. Let stand on cookie sheet for 5 minutes before removing to wire rack to cool. Repeat with remaining cookie dough. Makes about 3 dozen cookies.

1 cookie: 204 Calories; 9.2 g Total Fat; 168 mg Sodium; 3 g Protein; 29 g Carbohydrate; 1 g Dietary Fibre

Pictured on page 126.

(continued on next page)

Variation: For smaller cookies, shape into 1 1/2 inch (3.8 cm) balls. Arrange about 2 inches (5 cm) apart on greased cookie sheets. Flatten cookies slightly with bottom of glass dipped in second amount of granulated sugar. Bake in 375°F (190°C) oven for 8 to 10 minutes until lightly golden. Makes about 5 dozen cookies.

Anzac Cookies

A sweet treat favourite of the Australian And New Zealand Army Corps. A satisfying cookie of oats and coconut. Great for dunking in coffee, tea or milk.

Rolled oats (not instant)	1 cup	250 mL
All-purpose flour	1 cup	250 mL
Granulated sugar	1 cup	250 mL
Medium coconut	2/3 cup	150 mL
Hard margarine (or butter), chopped	1/2 cup	125 mL
Cane syrup (such as Rogers)	1 tbsp.	15 mL
Boiling water	2 tbsp.	30 mL
Baking soda	1 tsp.	5 mL

Combine first 4 ingredients in large bowl.

Heat and stir margarine and cane syrup in medium saucepan on medium-low until margarine is melted. Remove from heat.

Mix boiling water and baking soda in small cup. Add to margarine mixture. Mixture will foam a bit. Stir. Add to rolled oat mixture. Mix well. Shape into 1 1/4 inch (3 cm) balls. Arrange about 2 inches (5 cm) apart on greased cookie sheets. Flatten slightly using spatula. Bake in 325°F (160°C) oven for 15 to 20 minutes until golden. Let stand on cookie sheets for 10 minutes before removing to wire racks to cool. Makes about 2 1/2 dozen cookies.

1 cookie: 101 Calories; 4.9 g Total Fat; 82 mg Sodium; 1 g Protein; 14 g Carbohydrate; 1 g Dietary Fibre

Chocolate Malt Cookies

Moist, dark cookies with a rich chocolate flavour.
Give them a fancy look by drizzling with melted white chocolate.

Semi-sweet chocolate baking squares (1 oz., 28 g, each), chopped	8	8
Hard margarine (or butter), cut up	1/2 cup	125 mL
All-purpose flour	1 1/2 cups	375 mL
Baking powder	1/2 tsp.	2 mL
Cocoa, sifted if lumpy	1/2 cup	125 mL
Brown sugar, packed	1 cup	250 mL
Malted milk balls, coarsely chopped	1 cup	250 mL
Large eggs, fork-beaten	2	2

Melt chocolate and margarine in medium saucepan on lowest heat, stirring often, until almost melted. Do not overheat. Remove from heat. Stir until smooth. Cool slightly.

Stir flour, baking powder and cocoa in large bowl.

Add brown sugar and milk balls. Mix well.

Add eggs and chocolate mixture. Stir. Shape into 1 1/4 inch (3 cm) balls. Arrange about 2 inches (5 cm) apart on greased cookie sheets. Bake in 350°F (175°C) oven for about 15 minutes until cooked. Rearrange trays at halftime. Let stand on cookie sheets for 5 minutes before removing to wire racks to cool. Makes about 3 1/2 dozen cookies.

1 cookie: 111 Calories; 5.6 g Total Fat; 38 mg Sodium; 1 g Protein; 16 g Carbohydrate; 1 g Dietary Fibre

Paré Pointer
Fleas "itch hike" from dog to dog.

Cranberry Chocolate Cookies

Chunky, festive, flavourful cookies perfect for any sweet craving!
Great for a mid-afternoon snack or an energy boost after ball practice.

Large eggs	2	2
Brown sugar, packed	1 2/3 cups	400 mL
Vanilla	1 tsp.	5 mL
All-purpose flour	1 3/4 cups	425 mL
Baking powder	1 tsp.	5 mL
Baking soda	1/2 tsp.	2 mL
Cooking oil	1/2 cup	125 mL
Dried cranberries	1/2 cup	125 mL
Unsalted peanuts	1/2 cup	125 mL
White chocolate chips	1/2 cup	125 mL

Beat eggs, brown sugar and vanilla in large bowl for about 3 minutes until light and creamy.

Stir flour, baking powder and baking soda into egg mixture. Mix well.

Add remaining 4 ingredients. Mix well. Cover. Chill for 1 hour. Shape into balls, using 1 tbsp. (15 mL) for each. Arrange 2 inches (5 cm) apart on greased cookie sheets. Bake in 350°F (175°C) oven for about 15 minutes until golden. Let stand on cookie sheets for 5 minutes before removing to wire racks to cool. Makes about 3 1/2 dozen cookies.

1 cookie: 108 Calories; 4.6 g Total Fat; 33 mg Sodium; 1 g Protein; 16 g Carbohydrate; 1 g Dietary Fibre

Pictured on page 54.

 *To save time when baking cookies, you can get the next batch ready on large piece of parchment paper. When one batch comes out of oven, simply slip the parchment paper off the baking sheet and replace it with a new batch.*

Lemon Sugar Slices

Buttery sweet crisps with a tang of lemon. Perfect with a cup of tea.
Simplicity gives this treat its class.

Butter (not margarine), softened	1/2 cup	125 mL
Granulated sugar	1/2 cup	125 mL
Package of lemon-flavoured jelly powder (gelatin)	3 oz.	85 g
Finely grated lemon peel	2 tsp.	10 mL
Cold water	2 tbsp.	30 mL
All-purpose flour	1 1/2 cups	375 mL
Baking powder	1/2 tsp.	2 mL
Salt	1/4 tsp.	1 mL
Coarse sugar crystals (optional)	2 1/2 tbsp.	37 mL

Cream butter, granulated sugar, jelly powder, lemon peel and cold water in medium bowl.

Mix flour, baking powder and salt in small bowl. Gradually add to butter mixture. Mix until just moistened. Shape into rough log about 2 inches (5 cm) in diameter. Cover with plastic wrap. Roll out into smooth log. Freeze for 30 minutes. Cut into 1/4 inch (6 mm) slices. Lay slices flat, 2 inches (5 cm) apart, on greased cookie sheets.

Sprinkle about 1/8 tsp. (0.5 mL) coarse sugar on each slice. Bake in 350°F (175°C) oven for about 12 minutes until barely coloured on bottom. Remove to wire racks to cool. Makes about 5 dozen cookies.

1 cookie: 39 Calories; 1.7 g Total Fat; 33 mg Sodium; trace Protein; 6 g Carbohydrate; trace Dietary Fibre

Paré Pointer
Young little monsters like to play hide and shriek.

Famous Cookies

The ultimate oatmeal cookie with chocolate chips and nuts.
The perfect energy booster for your active family.

Hard margarine (or butter), softened	3/4 cup	175 mL
Brown sugar, packed	1/2 cup	125 mL
Granulated sugar	1/2 cup	125 mL
Large eggs	2	2
Vanilla	1/2 tsp.	2 mL
All-purpose flour	1 cup	250 mL
Quick-cooking rolled oats (not instant), processed in blender for 10 to 15 seconds	1 1/4 cups	300 mL
Baking powder	1/2 tsp.	2 mL
Baking soda	1/2 tsp.	2 mL
Salt	1/4 tsp.	1 mL
Semi-sweet chocolate chips	1 cup	250 mL
Sweet chocolate baking squares (1 oz., 28 g, each), grated	2	2
Chopped pecans	3/4 cup	175 mL

Cream margarine and both sugars in large bowl. Beat in eggs, 1 at a time, beating well after each addition. Add vanilla. Mix.

Stir next 5 ingredients together in medium bowl. Add to margarine mixture. Mix well.

Add chocolate chips, grated chocolate and pecans. Mix. Shape into 1 1/4 inch (3 cm) balls or drop by spoonfuls 2 inches (5 cm) apart onto well-greased cookie sheets. Bake in 375°F (190°C) oven for about 10 minutes until edges are golden. Remove to wire racks to cool. Makes about 5 dozen cookies.

1 cookie: 84 Calories; 5 g Total Fat; 56 mg Sodium; 1 g Protein; 10 g Carbohydrate; 1 g Dietary Fibre

Mocha Crinkles

These tantalizing cookies are the perfect blend of mocha and chocolate. Crunchy on the outside and chewy on the inside. One just isn't enough.

Hard margarine (or butter), softened	1/2 cup	125 mL
Brown sugar, packed	1 cup	250 mL
Granulated sugar	3/4 cup	175 mL
Large eggs	3	3
Vanilla	1 1/2 tsp.	7 mL
Unsweetened chocolate baking squares (1 oz., 28 g, each), cut up	2	2
Instant coffee granules, crushed to fine powder	1 tbsp.	15 mL
All-purpose flour	2 cups	500 mL
Baking powder	1 1/2 tsp.	7 mL
Salt	1/2 tsp.	2 mL
Granulated sugar	1/3 cup	75 mL

Cream margarine, brown sugar and first amount of granulated sugar in large bowl. Beat in eggs, 1 at a time, beating well after each addition. Add vanilla. Mix.

Heat chocolate and coffee granules in small saucepan on lowest heat, stirring often, until almost melted. Do not overheat. Remove from heat. Stir until smooth. Add to margarine mixture. Mix well.

Stir in flour, baking powder and salt. Cover. Chill for at least 2 hours or overnight. Shape into 1 1/4 inch (3 cm) balls.

Put second amount of granulated sugar into shallow dish or on waxed paper. Roll balls in sugar to coat completely. Arrange 2 inches (5 cm) apart on greased cookie sheets. Bake in 350°F (175°C) oven for 10 to 12 minutes until slightly puffy and have cracked appearance on top. Do not overbake. Cookies will be soft. Remove to wire racks to cool. Makes about 3 1/2 dozen cookies.

1 cookie: 98 Calories; 3.5 g Total Fat; 75 mg Sodium; 1 g Protein; 16 g Carbohydrate; trace Dietary Fibre

Crunch Cheesecake

Who ever said cheesecake had to be difficult to prepare? This chilled sweet treat is so rich, creamy and easy to make that you'll prepare it again and again.

Chocolate wafer crumbs	2 cups	500 mL
Hard margarine (or butter), melted	2/3 cup	150 mL
FILLING		
Envelope of unflavoured gelatin	1/4 oz.	7 g
Cold water	1/4 cup	60 mL
Blocks of cream cheese (8 oz., 250 g, each), softened	2	2
Granulated sugar	1/2 cup	125 mL
Vanilla	1 tsp.	5 mL
Whipping cream	1/2 cup	125 mL
Chocolate-covered sponge toffee candy bars (such as Crunchie), 1 1/2 oz. (44 g) each, chopped	5	5
Cocoa, for dusting		

Combine wafer crumbs and margarine in medium bowl until well mixed. Pack into bottom and up side of ungreased 9 inch (22 cm) springform pan. Chill for 1 hour.

Filling: Sprinkle gelatin over water in small saucepan. Let stand for 1 minute. Heat and stir on medium until gelatin is dissolved. Cool.

Beat next 4 ingredients in large bowl until smooth.

Fold in chopped candy bar and gelatin mixture. Turn into crust. Spread evenly. Cover. Chill overnight.

Dust with cocoa. Cuts into 12 wedges.

1 wedge: 486 Calories; 36.3 g Total Fat; 380 mg Sodium; 6 g Protein; 36 g Carbohydrate; trace Dietary Fibre

Cherry Oat Dessert

The golden brown crumble and the rich cherry red filling will delight your guests.
Makes a delicious dessert when served hot but is
also good as a cold small square.

CRUST

White cake mix (2 layer size)	1	1
Rolled oats (not instant)	1 cup	250 mL
Hard margarine (or butter), chilled	1/2 cup	125 mL
Large egg	1	1
Can of cherry pie filling	19 oz.	540 mL
Chopped pecans	3/4 cup	175 mL
Brown sugar, packed	1/3 cup	75 mL
Rolled oats (not instant)	1/4 cup	60 mL
Hard margarine (or butter)	2 tbsp.	30 mL

Crust: Stir cake mix and first amount of rolled oats together. Cut in first amount of margarine until coarse crumbs form. Reserve 1 2/3 cups (400 mL).

Add egg to remaining oat mixture. Stir. Pack into greased 9 x 13 inch (22 x 33 cm) pan using sheet of waxed paper to press down in even layer.

Spread pie filling over oat mixture.

Combine reserved oat mixture, pecans, brown sugar and second amount of rolled oats in medium bowl. Cut in second amount of margarine until coarse crumbs form. Sprinkle over pie filling. Bake in 350°F (175°C) oven for 50 to 60 minutes until golden. Let stand for 10 minutes to cool slightly. Cuts into 12 pieces.

1 piece: 456 Calories; 21.2 g Total Fat; 419 mg Sodium; 5 g Protein; 64 g Carbohydrate; 2 g Dietary Fibre

CHERRY OAT BITES: Chill. Cut into 54 squares.

Sweet Banana Packets

These unique treats are as much fun to prepare as they are to eat. Ideal for birthday parties. What kid doesn't love bananas, chocolate, marshmallows and ice cream?

Ripe medium bananas	2	2
Lemon juice	1 tbsp.	15 mL
Large flour tortillas (about 10 inches, 25 cm)	4	4
Miniature marshmallows	1/2 cup	125 mL
Milk chocolate candy bar, coarsely chopped	3 1/2 oz.	100 g
Brown sugar, packed	2 tbsp.	30 mL
Ground cinnamon	1/4 tsp.	1 mL
Hard margarine (or butter), melted	2 tbsp.	30 mL
Caramel ice cream topping	1/4 cup	60 mL
Scoops of vanilla ice cream (optional)	4	4

Cut each banana in half lengthwise and then crosswise, for a total of 8 pieces. Brush with lemon juice.

Place 2 banana pieces on each tortilla to 1 side of centre. Divide and sprinkle marshmallows and chocolate over each.

Combine brown sugar and cinnamon in small bowl. Sprinkle about 1 tsp. (5 mL) over chocolate on each tortilla. Reserve remaining brown sugar mixture. Roll up tortillas, while tucking in sides to enclose filling. Arrange, seam-side down, on greased baking sheet.

Brush packets with margarine. Sprinkle with reserved brown sugar mixture. Bake in 425°F (220°C) oven for about 10 minutes until lightly browned and crisp.

Drizzle individual packets with ice cream topping. Serve each with 1 scoop of ice cream. Makes 4 packets.

1 packet: 468 Calories; 16.8 g Total Fat; 368 mg Sodium; 6 g Protein; 78 g Carbohydrate; 3 g Dietary Fibre

Pictured on page 71.

Tropical Rumba Cheesecake

A medley of tropical flavours—coconut, pineapple, maraschino cherries and rum. Exotic-looking, but easy to prepare.

COCONUT COOKIE CRUST

Coconut cream-filled cookies	13	13
Hard margarine (or butter), melted	3 tbsp.	50 mL

PINEAPPLE FILLING

Can of crushed pineapple, with juice	14 oz.	398 mL
Instant banana cream pudding powder (4 serving size)	1	1
Icing (confectioner's) sugar	1/4 cup	60 mL
Blocks of light (or regular) cream cheese (8 oz., 250 g, each), softened and cut into 8 pieces each (see Note)	2	2
Whipping cream	1 cup	250 mL

PINEAPPLE RUM SYRUP

Reserved pineapple juice	1/4 cup	60 mL
Dark (or amber) rum (or 1 tsp., 5 mL, rum flavouring plus water)	1/4 cup	60 mL
Brown sugar, packed	2/3 cup	150 mL
Golden corn syrup	2/3 cup	150 mL
Hard margarine (or butter)	2 tbsp.	30 mL
Maraschino cherries	2/3 cup	150 mL
Can of pineapple tidbits, drained and juice reserved	8 oz.	227 mL

Coconut Cookie Crust: Process cookies in food processor until consistency of fine crumbs. Add margarine. Pulse with on/off motion until mixed. Pack into bottom of ungreased 9 inch (22 cm) springform pan.

Pineapple Filling: Put crushed pineapple with juice, pudding powder, icing sugar and cream cheese into same food processor. Pulse with on/off motion until just mixed. Process until cream cheese is smooth. Turn out into large bowl.

(continued on next page)

Beat whipping cream in small bowl until soft peaks form. Fold into cream cheese mixture. Turn out onto crust. Spread evenly. Chill for at least 8 hours or overnight before cutting. Cuts into 12 wedges.

Pineapple Rum Syrup: Combine reserved pineapple juice and rum in medium saucepan. Bring to a boil on medium. Add brown sugar and corn syrup. Heat and stir until brown sugar is dissolved. Boil for about 5 minutes, stirring occasionally, until syrupy. Remove from heat.

Stir in margarine, cherries and pineapple tidbits. Cool to room temperature. Stir. Makes 2 cups (500 mL) syrup. Spoon about 2 1/2 tbsp. (37 mL) over each wedge. Serves 12.

1 serving: 468 Calories; 22 g Total Fat; 615 mg Sodium; 5 g Protein; 63 g Carbohydrate; 1 g Dietary Fibre

Note: This dessert works well using light cream cheese, reducing the amount of fat in each serving!

Amaretto Strawberries

A very classy dessert prepared in just minutes. A smooth, creamy sauce over fresh, juicy strawberries. Serve in crystal dishes for an elegant light dessert.

Sliced fresh strawberries	1 1/2 cups	375 mL
Icing (confectioner's) sugar	1 1/2 tbsp.	25 mL
Sour cream	1/3 cup	75 mL
Almond-flavoured liqueur (such as Amaretto)	1 tbsp.	15 mL

Put strawberries and icing sugar into medium bowl. Stir. Let stand for about 1 hour until juices form. Drain juice into small bowl.

Add sour cream and liqueur to juice. Stir. Divide and spoon berries into 2 sherbet dishes or fruit nappies. Spoon juice mixture over top. Serves 2.

1 serving: 155 Calories; 6.2 g Total Fat; 19 mg Sodium; 2 g Protein; 20 g Carbohydrate; 3 g Dietary Fibre

Pictured on page 89.

Desserts

Bowl-O-Bananas

A decadent, hot chocolatey sauce spooned over bananas. Top with a dollop of whipped dessert topping or add a scoop of ice cream. Or both!

CHOCOLATE SAUCE

Brown sugar, packed	1 cup	250 mL
Cocoa, sifted if lumpy	2 tbsp.	30 mL
Hard margarine (or butter)	1 tbsp.	15 mL
Corn syrup	1 tbsp.	15 mL
Milk	2 tbsp.	30 mL
Vanilla	1/4 tsp.	1 mL
Medium bananas, sliced	4	4
Frozen whipped topping, thawed	1 cup	250 mL

Chocolate Sauce: Put first 6 ingredients into medium saucepan. Heat and stir on medium until boiling. Gently boil for about 3 minutes, stirring constantly, until slightly thickened. Makes 3/4 cup (175 mL) sauce.

Divide banana among 4 individual bowls. Divide and spoon sauce over each.

Top each with whipped topping. Serves 4.

1 serving: 439 Calories; 8.9 g Total Fat; 71 mg Sodium; 2 g Protein; 94 g Carbohydrate; 3 g Dietary Fibre

1. Sweet Banana Packets, page 67
2. Cream-Layered Pastries, page 91

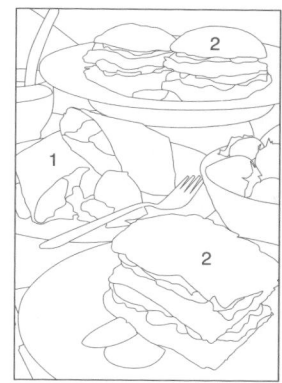

Gooey Banana Fix

When you need a sweet treat that is indulgent, decadent, sweet and fast, prepare this chocolatey, gooey, sticky, lip-smacking treat in just minutes.

Medium banana, sliced lengthwise	1	1
Milk chocolate candy bar (3 1/2 oz., 100 g, size), chopped	1/2	1/2
Caramel ice cream topping	2 tbsp.	30 mL
Miniature marshmallows	16	16

Form oval "dish" from foil, scrunching up sides slightly. Place on ungreased baking sheet. Arrange banana halves in foil, cut side up.

Sprinkle chocolate over banana halves. Drizzle with 1/2 of ice cream topping.

Randomly place marshmallows over top. Drizzle with remaining ice cream topping. Bake in 425°F (220°C) oven for 5 to 6 minutes until marshmallows are puffed and golden and chocolate is almost melted. Cut each piece into thirds. Serves 1 or 2.

1 serving: 485 Calories; 16 g Total Fat; 190 mg Sodium; 5 g Protein; 89 g Carbohydrate; 4 g Dietary Fibre

Variation: Instead of foil, use ovenproof oval dish.

Pictured on page 72.

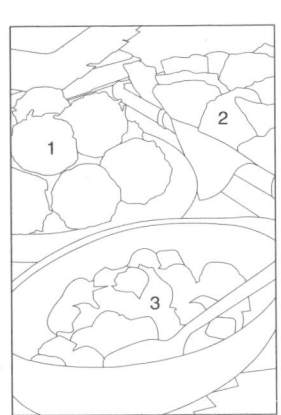

1. Chocolate Banana Snack, page 123
2. Apricot Pecan Bark, page 48
3. Gooey Banana Fix, above

Crown Jewel Dessert

As pretty as its name! This colourful and fun dessert is
perfect for special occasions such as a sweet 16 birthday party.

CRUST

Hard margarine (or butter)	1/3 cup	75 mL
Graham cracker crumbs	1 3/4 cups	425 mL
Cocoa, sifted if lumpy	1 tbsp.	15 mL
Package of raspberry-flavoured jelly powder (gelatin)	3 oz.	85 g
Package of orange-flavoured jelly powder (gelatin)	3 oz.	85 g
Package of lime-flavoured jelly powder (gelatin)	3 oz.	85 g
Boiling water	4 1/2 cups	1.1 L
Pineapple juice	1 cup	250 mL
Package of lemon-flavoured jelly powder (gelatin)	3 oz.	85 g
Cold water	1/4 cup	60 mL
Envelopes of dessert topping (prepared), see Note	2	2

Crust: Melt margarine in small saucepan. Stir in graham crumbs and cocoa until well combined. Pack in bottom of ungreased 9 x 13 inch (22 x 33 cm) pan. Bake in 350°F (175°C) oven for 10 minutes. Cool.

Dissolve first 3 amounts of jelly powder in 1 1/2 cups (375 mL) boiling water each in 3 separate bowls. Pour into 3 square pans. Chill until set. Cut into 1/2 inch (12 mm) cubes.

Bring pineapple juice to a boil in small saucepan. Stir in lemon jelly powder until dissolved. Stir in cold water. Chill for about 1 hour, stirring once or twice, until slightly thickened.

Fold lemon jelly powder mixture into dessert topping. Add cubed gelatin mixture using straight-edged lifter to remove from pan. Fold in. Turn into crust. Spread evenly. Chill overnight. Cuts into 18 squares.

1 square: 185 Calories; 6.8 g Total Fat; 155 mg Sodium; 3 g Protein; 29 g Carbohydrate; trace Dietary Fibre

Note: To use whipping cream, beat 2 cups (500 mL) whipping cream and 1/4 cup (60 mL) granulated sugar in medium bowl until soft peaks form.

 Desserts

Sweet Crêpe Roll-Ups

These delicate and easy-to-prepare crêpes are so versatile. Use with your favourite sweet filling and serve for brunch or evening dessert. Very European and very chic!

Large eggs	2	2
All-purpose flour	1/2 cup	125 mL
Granulated sugar	1 tsp.	5 mL
Salt	1/4 tsp.	1 mL
Milk	2/3 cup	150 mL
Hard margarine (or butter), melted	2 tbsp.	30 mL
Vanilla	1/2 tsp.	2 mL
Jam, your choice	1/3 cup	75 mL
Icing (confectioner's) sugar, for dusting	2 tsp.	10 mL

Measure first 7 ingredients into small bowl. Beat on low for 1 minute. Stir until air bubbles disappear and mixture is smooth. Heat 7 or 8 inch (18 or 20 cm) greased non-stick frying pan or crêpe pan on medium until hot. Add about 2 tbsp. (30 mL) batter, quickly tilting pan to coat bottom. Cook for 1 to 2 minutes until edges start to brown and top loses shine. Remove to waxed paper to cool. Repeat with remaining batter. Stack cooked crêpes on top of one another.

Spread 1 1/2 to 2 tsp. (7 to 10 mL) jam down centre on unbrowned side of each crêpe. Roll up tightly, jelly roll-style. Arrange in single layer, seam-side down, on serving plate.

Dust with icing sugar. Makes about 10 roll-ups.

1 roll-up: 96 Calories; 3.6 g Total Fat; 112 mg Sodium; 3 g Protein; 14 g Carbohydrate; trace Dietary Fibre

Variation: Omit jam. Use same amount of jelly, chocolate hazelnut spread, peanut butter or lemon spread.

Mango Macadamia Sandwich

Mango and macadamia nuts give this ice cream sandwich a wonderful, tropical taste. The satisfying crunch of nuts gives it a delightful texture. You'll have lots of offers to help you make these fun treats.

All-purpose flour	1 1/2 cups	375 mL
Icing (confectioner's) sugar	3/4 cup	175 mL
Ground cinnamon	3/4 tsp.	4 mL
Finely grated orange zest	2 tsp.	10 mL
Vanilla	1 tsp.	5 mL
Hard margarine (or butter)	1/2 cup	125 mL
Egg yolks (large)	2	2
Vanilla ice cream, softened	2 cups	500 mL
Can of mango slices, drained, chopped	14 oz.	398 mL
Macadamia nuts, toasted (see Tip, page 79), chopped	1/2 cup	125 mL

Put first 5 ingredients into large bowl. Cut in margarine until crumbly.

Add egg yolks. Process until mixture forms ball. Roll out on lightly floured surface (or on lightly floured parchment paper) to 1/4 inch (6 mm) thickness. Cut out using 3 inch (7.5 cm) round fluted cookie cutter. Arrange about 1 inch (2.5 cm) apart on lightly greased cookie sheets. Bake in 350°F (175°C) oven for 10 to 15 minutes until golden. Let stand on cookie sheets for 5 minutes before removing to wire racks to cool. Makes 16 cookies.

Combine ice cream, mango and macadamia nuts in medium bowl. Line 9 x 9 inch (22 x 22 cm) pan with waxed paper, ensuring paper comes up two opposite sides by 2 inches (5 cm). Turn ice cream mixture into pan. Spread evenly. Cover. Freeze for at least 1 hour until firm. Using extended paper on sides of pan, lift ice cream from pan. Cut out rounds, using 2 1/2 inch (6.4 cm) round cookie cutter, as close to each other as possible. Place 1 ice cream round on 1 cookie. Cover with another cookie. Repeat with remaining cookies and ice cream rounds. Return to freezer. Makes 8 sandwiches.

1 sandwich: 400 Calories; 22.9 g Total Fat; 173 mg Sodium; 5 g Protein; 45 g Carbohydrate; 2 g Dietary Fibre

Pictured on page 90.

Berry Ice Cream Cups

Few flavours combine as well as berries and vanilla ice cream.
Add a chocolatey crust and a berry juice sauce and you have perfection.
Keep these delectable little cups in your freezer to surprise guests
and family when their sweet cravings strike.

Chocolate wafers	12	12
Extra-large paper cupcake liners	12	12
Vanilla ice cream, slightly softened	4 cups	1 L
Chopped frozen whole strawberries (or raspberries), thawed, well drained and juice reserved	1 1/2 cups	375 mL
SAUCE		
White corn syrup	1 tbsp.	15 mL
Reserved strawberry juice	3 tbsp.	50 mL

Put wafers into bottom of paper liners set in muffin cups.

Mix ice cream and strawberries in large bowl. Makes 4 cups (1 L) ice cream mixture. Freeze for about 1 hour until slightly firm.

Sauce: Combine corn syrup and reserved juice in small bowl. Makes 1/4 cup (60 mL) sauce. Set aside. Scoop about 1/3 cup (75 mL) ice cream mixture onto each wafer. Spoon 1 tsp. (5 mL) sauce over ice cream in each cup. Swirl to make fancy design. Freeze until solid. Remove from freezer 10 minutes before serving. Makes 12 ice cream cups.

1 ice cream cup: 138 Calories; 6 g Total Fat; 74 mg Sodium; 2 g Protein; 20 g Carbohydrate; 1 g Dietary Fibre

Paré Pointer
A tired cow moos badly. An angry crowd boos madly.

Frozen Cheesecake Bites

A creamy lemon cheesecake on a buttery shortbread base. The hint of almond adds a touch of sophistication. Easy to eat by hand straight out of the freezer.

CRUST

All-purpose flour	1 1/2 cups	375 mL
Icing (confectioner's) sugar	2 tbsp.	30 mL
Sliced almonds	3/4 cup	175 mL
Hard margarine (or butter), chilled and cut into pieces	1/2 cup	125 mL
Blocks of cream cheese (8 oz., 250 g, each), softened	2	2
Granulated sugar	1/2 cup	125 mL
Large eggs	2	2
Finely grated lemon zest	1 tbsp.	15 mL
Container of lemon yogurt	6 oz.	175 mL
Cream of wheat	2 tbsp.	30 mL
Vanilla	1/2 tsp.	2 mL
Sliced almonds, toasted (see Tip, page 79), optional	1/4 cup	60 mL

Crust: Put first 3 ingredients into medium bowl. Cut in margarine until crumbly. Press firmly into greased 9 × 13 inch (22 × 33 cm) pan. Bake in 350°F (175°C) oven for 10 minutes.

Beat next 7 ingredients in medium bowl until smooth. Spread over crust.

Sprinkle with second amount of almonds. Bake in 350°F (175°C) oven for 25 to 30 minutes until firmly set and edges are slightly golden. Cool completely. Cut with wet knife into triangles. Arrange 1/2 inch (12 mm) apart on large baking sheet. Freeze for 2 to 3 hours until firm. Store in resealable freezer bags or tins, separating layers with waxed paper. Keep frozen. Cuts into 30 cheesecake bites.

1 cheesecake bite: 157 Calories; 11 g Total Fat; 90 mg Sodium; 3 g Protein; 12 g Carbohydrate; 1 g Dietary Fibre

Pictured on page 125.

Espresso Sundae

Satisfy your coffee, chocolate and ice cream cravings all at once!
Get your favourite spoon and enjoy.

CHOCOLATE DRIZZLE

Whipping cream	1/3 cup	75 mL
Prepared strong coffee	1 tbsp.	15 mL
Semi-sweet chocolate baking squares (1 oz., 28 g, each), chopped	5	5
Hard margarine (or butter)	1 tbsp.	15 mL
Scoops of chocolate ice cream (about 4 cups, 1 L)	16	16
Irish cream-flavoured liqueur (such as Baileys)	1/2 cup	125 mL
Pecans, toasted (see Tip, below), coarsely chopped	1/4 cup	60 mL

Chocolate Drizzle: Combine first 4 ingredients in small saucepan. Heat and stir on low for 3 to 4 minutes until chocolate is melted. Do not overheat. Remove from heat. Cool slightly. Makes about 1 cup (250 mL) Chocolate Drizzle.

Spoon 2 scoops of ice cream each into 8 individual sundae glasses.

Drizzle each with 1 tbsp. (15 mL) liqueur. Drizzle each with 2 tbsp. (30 mL) Chocolate Drizzle. Sprinkle with pecans. Serves 8.

1 serving: 284 Calories; 19.2 g Total Fat; 64 mg Sodium; 3 g Protein; 27 g Carbohydrate; 1 g Dietary Fibre

Pictured on page 107.

 *To toast almonds, cashews, coconut, hazelnuts, macadamia nuts and pecans, place in single layer in ungreased shallow pan. Bake in 350°F (175°C) oven for 5 to 10 minutes, stirring or shaking often, until desired doneness.*

Chocolate Raspberry Pie

A chocolate ice cream pie with two succulent layers of juicy red raspberries. Preparation requires a little patience, but tastes all the sweeter for the wait.

COOKIE CRUST

Hard margarine (or butter)	1/3 cup	75 mL
Vanilla wafer crumbs	1 1/4 cups	300 mL

FILLING

Frozen raspberries in syrup, thawed	15 oz.	425 g
Cornstarch	1 tbsp.	15 mL
Chocolate ice cream, softened	3 cups	750 mL
Whipped cream (or prepared dessert topping)	1 1/2 cups	375 mL
Chocolate sauce	1 tbsp.	15 mL

Cookie Crust: Melt margarine in medium saucepan. Add wafer crumbs. Stir until well mixed. Pack into bottom and up side of 9 inch (22 cm) pie plate. Freeze.

Filling: Drain raspberry syrup into small saucepan. Reserve raspberries. Stir cornstarch into syrup. Heat and stir on medium for 6 to 7 minutes until boiling and thickened. Remove from heat. Add reserved raspberries. Chill.

Spoon 1/2 of ice cream into crust. Spread evenly. Spread 1/2 of raspberry mixture over ice cream. Freeze until firm. Spoon remaining ice cream onto frozen raspberry mixture. Spread evenly. Spread remaining raspberry mixture over ice cream. Freeze until firm.

Top with whipped cream. Drizzle with chocolate sauce. Freeze for at least 8 hours or overnight. Cuts into 8 wedges.

1 wedge: 378 Calories; 23.5 g Total Fat; 186 mg Sodium; 4 g Protein; 42 g Carbohydrate; 2 g Dietary Fibre

Pictured on page 90.

Cran-Raspberry Ice

A creamy, iced treat with the summery sweet taste of raspberries and the crisp tartness of cranberries. Your guests will love the frosted rosy colour. A perfect way to beat the heat.

Boiling water	1/2 cup	125 mL
Package of raspberry-flavoured jelly powder (gelatin)	3 oz.	85 g
Frozen whole raspberries, partially thawed	2 1/4 cups	550 mL
Block of cream cheese, softened	4 oz.	125 g
Icing (confectioner's) sugar	1/4 cup	60 mL
Sour cream	1 cup	250 mL
Whole cranberry sauce	14 oz.	398 mL

Add boiling water to jelly powder in small bowl. Stir to dissolve. Stir in raspberries. Set aside.

Beat cream cheese and icing sugar in medium bowl until smooth. Add sour cream and cranberry sauce. Mix. Add raspberry mixture. Stir until well combined. Pour into 1/2 to 3/4 cup (125 to 175 mL) individual molds or 5 cup (1.25 L) freezing mold (see Tip, below). Freeze until firm. Cover. Keep frozen. Serves 10.

1 serving: 256 Calories; 7.9 g Total Fat; 83 mg Sodium; 3 g Protein; 46 g Carbohydrate; 3 g Dietary Fibre

Pictured on page 90.

 *Frozen desserts can be set in a variety of containers if you don't have a mold. Line a loaf pan or muffin cups with plastic wrap and fill. If using a mold, the plastic ones are the easiest from which to remove the dessert.*

Peanut Ice Cream Treat

Perfect in its simplicity. Vanilla ice cream drizzled with chocolate and caramel and topped with crunchy peanuts. The chocolate wafer crust oozes when cut.

Thick butterscotch (or caramel) ice cream topping	1/3 cup	75 mL
Thick chocolate (or fudge) ice cream topping	1/3 cup	75 mL
Commercial chocolate crumb crust (9 inch, 22 cm, size)	1	1
Vanilla (or butterscotch ripple) ice cream, softened	4 cups	1 L
Dry-roasted peanuts, chopped	1/2 cup	125 mL
Thick butterscotch (or caramel) ice cream topping, for garnish		
Thick chocolate (or fudge) ice cream topping, for garnish		

Spoon first amounts of butterscotch and chocolate toppings, in dabs, into bottom of crust. Freeze for 20 minutes.

Spoon ice cream into crust. Pack evenly to fill in all spaces.

Sprinkle with peanuts. Cover with plastic wrap. Freeze for several hours until firm.

Put second amounts of butterscotch and chocolate toppings into individual small resealable freezer bags. Snip tiny piece off corner. Drizzle over peanuts in lattice design. Freeze. Cuts into 8 wedges.

1 wedge: 413 Calories; 22.1 g Total Fat; 313 mg Sodium; 7 g Protein; 51 g Carbohydrate; 1 g Dietary Fibre

Pictured on page 89.

Pictured on page 89.

Jack Frost Lemon Pie

A refreshing chilled dessert that is both sweet and pleasingly tart. The lemony flavour is perfect for cleansing the palate after a rich meal. Very welcome on a hot summer day.

Granulated sugar	3/4 cup	175 mL
All-purpose flour	1 tsp.	5 mL
Large egg	1	1
Freshly squeezed lemon juice (about 1 medium lemon)	1/3 cup	75 mL
Finely grated lemon zest	1 tsp.	5 mL
Ground mace	3/4 tsp.	4 mL
Envelope of dessert topping (not prepared)	1	1
Cold milk	1/2 cup	125 mL
Graham cracker crust (9 inch, 22 cm, size)	1	1

Stir sugar and flour in small saucepan. Mix in egg, lemon juice and zest. Heat and stir on medium for about 5 minutes until boiling and thickened. Remove from heat. Cool completely.

Stir in mace.

Stir dessert topping and milk in small bowl. Beat until stiff peaks form. Fold into lemon mixture.

Turn into crust. Freeze until firm. Cuts into 8 wedges.

1 wedge: 276 Calories; 10.4 g Total Fat; 194 mg Sodium; 3 g Protein; 44 g Carbohydrate; trace Dietary Fibre

Paré Pointer

If you have a bad toothache in the rain, one is roaring with pain, the other is pouring with rain.

Peanut Butter Meringue Pie

A rich, sweet peanut buttery custard pie crowned with soft golden peaks of meringue. A peanut butter lover's delight.

Icing (confectioner's) sugar	2/3 cup	150 mL
Smooth peanut butter	1/3 cup	75 mL
Baked 9 inch (22 cm) pie shell	1	1
Milk	1 3/4 cups	425 mL
All-purpose flour	3 tbsp.	50 mL
Cornstarch	3 tbsp.	50 mL
Granulated sugar	1/2 cup	125 mL
Salt	1/2 tsp.	2 mL
Milk	1/2 cup	125 mL
Egg yolks (large)	3	3
Smooth peanut butter	1/4 cup	60 mL
Vanilla	1 1/2 tsp.	7 mL
MERINGUE		
Egg whites (large), room temperature	3	3
Cream of tartar	1/4 tsp.	1 mL
Cornstarch	1 tsp.	5 mL
Granulated sugar	6 tbsp.	100 mL
Finely chopped peanuts (optional)	1 tbsp.	15 mL

Mix icing sugar and first amount of peanut butter in medium bowl. Work with fingers until consistency of coarse crumbs.

Sprinkle over bottom of pie crust.

Heat first amount of milk in heavy medium saucepan on medium until hot. Do not boil.

Combine flour, cornstarch, granulated sugar and salt in small bowl. Add second amount of milk. Mix until smooth. Stir into hot milk in saucepan until boiling and thickened. Remove from heat.

Beat egg yolks with fork in separate small bowl. Add 1/2 cup (125 mL) hot milk mixture to egg yolks. Mix well. Stir into milk mixture. Heat and stir on medium-low for 2 to 3 minutes until mixture is thickened.

(continued on next page)

Add second amount of peanut butter and vanilla. Stir. Pour over icing sugar mixture in pie crust.

Meringue: Beat egg whites, cream of tartar and cornstarch in medium bowl until almost stiff. Add sugar, 1 tbsp. (15 mL) at a time, until stiff peaks form and sugar is dissolved. Spoon over top of hot filling, sealing edges to crust.

Sprinkle with peanuts. Bake in 350°F (175°C) oven for 10 to 15 minutes until golden. Cuts into 8 wedges.

1 wedge: 413 Calories; 18 g Total Fat; 404 mg Sodium; 11 g Protein; 54 g Carbohydrate; 1 g Dietary Fibre

Nutty Chocolate Pie

This incredible chocolate pie will draw breaths of amazement. So rich, nutty and chocolatey. A small slice will satisfy even the largest sweet craving.

Large eggs	2	2
Brown sugar, packed	1 cup	250 mL
Hard margarine (or butter), melted	3/4 cup	175 mL
Semi-sweet chocolate chips	1 cup	250 mL
Chopped walnuts (or pecans)	3/4 cup	175 mL
Unbaked 9 inch (22 cm) pie shell	1	1

Beat eggs until frothy. Add brown sugar and margarine. Beat until well mixed. Add chocolate chips and walnuts. Stir until well mixed.

Turn into pie shell. Bake on bottom rack in 325°F (160°C) oven for 50 to 60 minutes until wooden pick inserted in centre comes out clean. Cuts into 8 wedges.

1 wedge: 553 Calories; 38.3 g Total Fat; 345 mg Sodium; 6 g Protein; 52 g Carbohydrate; 2 g Dietary Fibre

Pastry Triangles With Pears

A sophisticated, yet easy-to-prepare dessert. Caramelized pears in spiced syrup and rum, nestled in a crispy, flaky puff pastry.

Package of frozen puff pastry (14 oz., 397 g, size), thawed according to package directions	1/2	1/2
Egg yolk (large), fork-beaten	1	1
Sliced almonds	1/4 cup	60 mL
CARAMELIZED PEARS		
Hard margarine (or butter)	1/3 cup	75 mL
Firm medium pears (about 1 1/2 lbs., 680 g), peeled, sliced 1/8 inch (3 mm) thick	4	4
Brown sugar, packed	1/4 cup	60 mL
Maple syrup	2 tbsp.	30 mL
Dark rum (or 1/2 tsp., 2 mL, rum flavouring plus water)	2 tbsp.	30 mL
Ground cinnamon	3/4 tsp.	4 mL
Icing (confectioner's) sugar, for garnish		
Whipped cream, for garnish		

Roll out pastry on lightly floured surface to about 8 x 8 inch (20 x 20 cm) square. Cut into quarters. Cut each quarter into 2 triangles. Arrange about 1/2 inch (12 mm) apart on ungreased baking sheet.

Brush with egg yolk. Sprinkle with almonds. Bake in 400°F (205°C) oven for about 15 minutes until golden. Let stand on baking sheet for 5 minutes before removing to wire rack to cool.

Caramelized Pears: Melt margarine in large frying pan on medium-low. Add next 5 ingredients. Heat and stir for 10 to 15 minutes until pears are soft and sauce is thickened. Split each triangle in half horizontally into 2 layers. Place bottom half of 1 triangle on individual serving plate. Top with 1/8 of pear mixture. Cover with top half of triangle. Repeat with remaining triangles and pear mixture.

Sprinkle with icing sugar. Serve with dollop of whipped cream. Serves 8.

1 serving: 308 Calories; 20 g Total Fat; 162 mg Sodium; 3 g Protein; 29 g Carbohydrate; 2 g Dietary Fibre

Pictured on page 108.

Spiced Palmiers

*Pronounced pahlm-YAY. No pastry lover can resist these crispy,
golden treats spiced with cinnamon, ginger and cloves.
The perfect treat to serve when unexpected guests arrive.*

Package of frozen puff pastry, thawed according to package directions	14 oz.	397 g
Hard margarine (or butter), melted	2 tbsp.	30 mL
Granulated sugar	1/4 cup	60 mL
Ground cinnamon	1/2 tsp.	2 mL
Ground ginger	1/2 tsp.	2 mL
Ground cloves	1/4 tsp.	1 mL

Roll out pastry on lightly floured surface to about 8 x 14 inch (20 x 35 cm) rectangle.

Brush pastry with margarine.

Combine next 4 ingredients in small bowl. Sprinkle 3 tbsp. (50 mL) over pastry. Fold long sides of pastry in to meet in centre. Brush with margarine. Sprinkle with remaining sugar mixture. Fold in half lengthwise. Press lightly. Cover. Chill for 30 minutes. Cut pastry into 1/2 inch (12 mm) slices. Arrange, cut side down, about 3 inches (7.5 cm) apart on lightly greased baking sheets. Bake in 375°F (190°C) oven for about 20 minutes, turning at halftime, until crisp and golden. Turn out onto wire racks to cool. Makes about 28 palmiers.

1 palmier: 93 Calories; 6.2 g Total Fat; 45 mg Sodium; 1 g Protein; 8 g Carbohydrate; trace Dietary Fibre

Pictured on page 36.

 *Pie crust dough freezes better in a ball than if rolled out, and a ball takes up little room in the freezer. Cover the dough tightly in plastic wrap. Thaw at room temperature, in plastic wrap to prevent drying out, until only slightly chilled.*

Upside-Down Treat

A light golden biscuit which, when inverted, is generously covered in warm pineapple, cherries and caramelized sugar. A classic comfort food.

Hard margarine (or butter)	2 tbsp.	30 mL
Brown sugar, packed	1/2 cup	125 mL
Can of crushed pineapple, drained	8 oz.	227 mL
Maraschino cherries, chopped	6	6
Tube of refrigerator country-style biscuits (10 biscuits per tube)	12 oz.	340 g

Coat 8 inch (20 cm) round pan with margarine. Sprinkle brown sugar over margarine. Scatter pineapple and cherries evenly over brown sugar.

Arrange biscuits close together over pineapple mixture. Bake in 425°F (220°C) oven for 15 minutes until lightly browned. Invert onto serving plate. Serve warm. Makes 10 biscuits.

1 biscuit: 163 Calories; 3.9 g Total Fat; 456 mg Sodium; 2 g Protein; 30 g Carbohydrate; trace Dietary Fibre

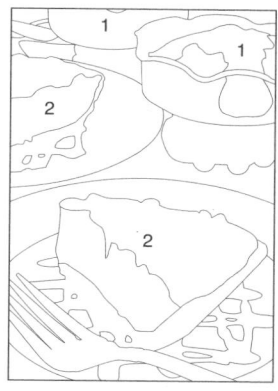

1. Amaretto Strawberries, page 69
2. Peanut Ice Cream Treat, page 82

Props Courtesy Of: Pfaltzgraff Canada

Cream-Layered Pastries

Layers of light puff pastry, strawberry jam and whipped cream.
Enjoy with a cup of coffee and imagine you are in a Parisian patisserie.

Package of frozen puff pastry (14 oz., 397 g, size), thawed according to package directions	1/2	1/2
Whipping cream	2/3 cup	150 mL
Strawberry jam, warmed	1/2 cup	125 mL
Icing (confectioner's) sugar, for dusting		

Roll out pastry on lightly floured surface to about 9 x 9 inch (22 x 22 cm) square. Place on ungreased baking sheet. Bake in 400°F (205°C) oven for 10 to 12 minutes until golden and puffed. Let baking sheet stand on wire rack to cool. Split pastry in half horizontally into 2 layers. Cut each half into 6 rectangles.

Beat whipping cream in small bowl until soft peaks form. Spread 1 tbsp. (15 mL) jam on 1 side of 1 pastry rectangle. Spread 3 tbsp. (50 mL) whipped cream over jam. Top with another pastry rectangle. Spread 1 tbsp. (15 mL) jam over pastry rectangle. Spread 3 tbsp. (50 mL) whipped cream over jam. Top with another pastry rectangle. Repeat with remaining pastry rectangles, jam and whipped cream.

Dust with icing sugar. Makes 4 pastries.

1 pastry: 503 Calories; 32.5 g Total Fat; 156 mg Sodium; 5 g Protein; 51 g Carbohydrate; 1 g Dietary Fibre

Pictured on page 71.

1. Mango Macadamia Sandwich, page 76
2. Chocolate Raspberry Pie, page 80
3. Cran-Raspberry Ice, page 81

Sweet Orange Rolls

A delectable variation of sticky buns. These sweet and gooey rolls have a tantalizing orange flavour and a citrusy, sticky glaze. A favourite brunch item that will have your guests licking their fingers.

Biscuit mix	2 cups	500 mL
Orange (or vanilla) yogurt	1/2 cup	125 mL
Milk	1/4 cup	60 mL
All-purpose flour, approximately	1/4 cup	60 mL
Hard margarine (or butter)	2 tbsp.	30 mL
Brown sugar, packed	1/2 cup	125 mL
Finely grated orange peel	1 tsp.	5 mL
Ground cinnamon	1/8 – 1/4 tsp.	0.5 – 1 mL
ORANGE GLAZE		
Prepared orange juice	1 1/2 tbsp.	25 mL
Icing (confectioner's) sugar	2/3 cup	150 mL
Finely chopped walnuts (or pecans), optional	1 tbsp.	15 mL

Combine biscuit mix, yogurt and milk in medium bowl until just moistened. Turn out dough onto well-floured surface. Knead gently 10 to 12 times, sprinkling surface with more flour as needed to keep from sticking. Pat or roll out to 12 x 12 inch (30 x 30 cm) square.

Combine margarine, brown sugar, orange peel and cinnamon in small bowl. Spread evenly over dough. Roll up tightly, jelly roll-style. Pinch edge closed. Cut into 9 slices. Arrange, cut side down, in greased 9 x 9 inch (22 x 22 cm) pan. Bake in 375°F (190°C) oven for about 30 minutes until golden.

Orange Glaze: Stir orange juice into icing sugar in separate small bowl until smooth, adding enough icing sugar until barely pourable consistency. Drizzle over warm rolls.

Sprinkle with walnuts. Makes 9 rolls.

1 roll: 269 Calories; 7.6 g Total Fat; 430 mg Sodium; 4 g Protein; 47 g Carbohydrate; trace Dietary Fibre

Jam And Nut Tart

A golden pastry that combines the flavours of apricot, cinnamon, pecans and honey. A versatile dessert perfect for all seasons. Slice and eat like pizza.

Package of pie crust mix for 2 crust 9 inch (22 cm) pie	9 1/2 oz.	270 g
Granulated sugar	3 tbsp.	50 mL
Cold water	4 – 5 tbsp.	60 – 75 mL
Apricot (or peach) jam	1/2 cup	125 mL
Ground cinnamon	1/4 tsp.	1 mL
Finely chopped pecans	3/4 cup	175 mL
HONEY GLAZE		
Liquid honey, warmed	1 tbsp.	15 mL
Icing (confectioner's) sugar	2 1/2 tbsp.	37 mL
Warm water		

Combine pie crust mix and granulated sugar in medium bowl. Add cold water, 1 tbsp. (15 mL) at a time, stirring with fork until dough forms a ball. Divide into 2 portions. Form each portion into disc. Cover with plastic wrap. Chill for 30 minutes. Roll 1 disc out on lightly floured surface to 9 inch (22 cm) circle. Place on ungreased baking sheet.

Spread jam on pastry to within 3/4 inch (2 cm) of edge. Sprinkle with cinnamon and pecans. Dampen edge of pastry with water. Roll second disc out on lightly floured surface to 9 inch (22 cm) circle. Place over jam mixture. Press edges together with fork tines. Poke several steam holes in top of pastry. Bake, uncovered, in 375°F (190°C) oven for 20 to 30 minutes until golden.

Honey Glaze: Stir honey into icing sugar in small bowl until smooth. Stir in warm water, 1 drop at a time, until barely pourable consistency. Drizzle over warm tart. Cuts into 12 wedges.

1 wedge: 226 Calories; 12.4 g Total Fat; 175 mg Sodium; 2 g Protein; 28 g Carbohydrate; 1 g Dietary Fibre

A Touch Of Danish

Warm, soft biscuits stuffed with a cream cheese filling and decorated with a sweet, sticky glaze. These are best served warm with coffee or tea. Enjoy with jam for a fruity variation.

Tube of refrigerator country-style biscuits (10 biscuits per tube)	12 oz.	340 g
FILLING		
Cream cheese, softened	2 oz.	62 g
Granulated sugar	1 tbsp.	15 mL
Milk	2 tsp.	10 mL
GLAZE		
Icing (confectioner's) sugar	6 tbsp.	100 mL
Milk	2 tsp.	10 mL
Vanilla	1/8 tsp.	0.5 mL

Arrange biscuits about 1 1/2 inches (3.8 cm) apart on ungreased baking sheet. Make deep indentation in centre of each biscuit.

Filling: Mash cream cheese, granulated sugar and milk together well in small bowl. Makes about 1/4 cup (60 mL) filling. Spoon about 1 tsp. (5 mL) into each indentation. Bake in 425°F (220°C) oven for 10 to 12 minutes until lightly golden.

Glaze: Mix icing sugar, milk and vanilla in separate small bowl. Drizzle over warm biscuits. Serve immediately. Makes 10 biscuits.

1 biscuit: 131 Calories; 3.5 g Total Fat; 442 mg Sodium; 3 g Protein; 22 g Carbohydrate; 0 g Dietary Fibre

Pictured on page 36.

Pictured on page 36.

Paré Pointer

The plastic surgeon stood so close to the fire that he melted.

Baklava

Pronounced BAHK-lah-vah. A classic dessert favourite of the Greek islands. Sweet, gooey syrup and walnut filling ooze out between layers of thin, flaky phyllo pastry. The only way to enjoy this sticky wonder is with your fingers.

Frozen phyllo pastry sheets, thawed according to package directions	12	12
Butter (not margarine), melted	1 cup	250 mL
Finely chopped walnuts (or pistachios)	2 cups	500 mL
SYRUP		
Granulated sugar	2 1/2 cups	625 mL
Water	1 1/2 cups	375 mL
Lemon juice	2 tbsp.	30 mL

Lay 1 pastry sheet on work surface. Keep remaining pastry sheets covered with damp tea towel to prevent drying out. Working quickly, brush pastry sheet with butter. Lay another pastry sheet over top. Brush with butter. Repeat with 4 more pastry sheets and butter. Cut pastry stack in half crosswise. Place 1/2 of stack in greased 9 x 13 inch (22 x 33 cm) dish. Top with remaining 1/2 of stack.

Sprinkle with walnuts. Repeat layering remaining pastry sheets and butter. Cut pastry in half crosswise. Place 1/2 of stack on top of walnuts. Top with remaining 1/2 of stack. Brush with butter. Make twelve 3 inch (7.5 cm) shallow square cuts into pastry sheets. Bake in 350°F (175°C) oven for about 50 minutes until golden. Cool.

Syrup: Combine sugar, water and lemon juice in medium saucepan. Heat and stir on medium until sugar is dissolved. Simmer, uncovered, without stirring, for about 15 minutes until slightly thickened. Makes 2 cups (500 mL) syrup. Pour hot syrup over cooled baklava. Cut each square into 2 triangles. Makes 24 triangles.

1 triangle: 252 Calories; 14.9 g Total Fat; 129 mg Sodium; 3 g Protein; 28 g Carbohydrate; 1 g Dietary Fibre

Pumpkin Tartlets

Warmly spiced pumpkin pie tartlets with a rich, creamy texture.
A heavenly aroma will fill your house while these treats are in the oven.

PASTRY

All-purpose flour	2 cups	500 mL
Brown sugar, packed	1 tbsp.	15 mL
Salt	1/2 tsp.	2 mL
Hard margarine (or butter), chilled, cut up	1 cup	250 mL
Water	1/3 cup	75 mL

FILLING

Can of pure pumpkin (without spices)	14 oz.	398 mL
Can of sweetened condensed milk	11 oz.	300 mL
All-purpose flour	2 tbsp.	30 mL
Large eggs	2	2
Ground cinnamon	3/4 tsp.	4 mL
Ground ginger	1/2 tsp.	2 mL
Ground nutmeg	1/4 tsp.	1 mL
Ground allspice	1/4 tsp.	1 mL
Salt	1/4 tsp.	1 mL
Whipped cream (or frozen whipped topping, thawed), for garnish		

Pastry: Combine flour, brown sugar and salt in large bowl. Cut in margarine until consistency of coarse crumbs.

Drizzle water over top. Stir with fork until dough forms a ball. Roll out on lightly floured surface to 1/8 inch (3 mm) thickness. Cut into 2 1/2 inch (6.4 cm) rounds. Line tartlet pans or mini-muffin cups.

Filling: Stir pumpkin and condensed milk in medium bowl. Sprinkle with flour. Mix well.

Add next 6 ingredients. Stir until smooth. Makes 3 1/4 cups (800 mL) filling. Spoon 1 1/2 tbsp. (25 mL) filling into each pastry shell. Bake in 375°F (190°C) oven for about 20 minutes until wooden pick inserted in centre of tartlet comes out clean.

(continued on next page)

Garnish with whipped cream. Makes 36 tartlets.

1 tartlet: 121 Calories; 6.7 g Total Fat; 130 mg Sodium; 2 g Protein; 13 g Carbohydrate; trace Dietary Fibre

PUMPKIN PIE: Line 9 inch (22 cm) pie plate with 1/2 of pastry. Freeze remaining pastry to use another time. Add filling. Bake in 425°F (220°C) oven for 10 minutes. Reduce heat to 325°F (160°C). Bake for about 1 hour until knife inserted near centre comes out clean. Cool. Garnish with whipped cream. Cuts into 8 wedges.

Lemon Pastries

Golden, flaky puff pastry with a sweet creamy filling and a sharp lemony tang.

Package of frozen puff pastry, thawed according to package directions	14 oz.	397 g
LEMON FILLING		
Finely grated lemon zest	2 tsp.	10 mL
Freshly squeezed lemon juice	1/4 cup	60 mL
Granulated sugar	1/2 cup	125 mL
Whipping cream	1/2 cup	125 mL
Large eggs	2	2
Icing (confectioner's) sugar, for dusting		

Roll pastry halves out to 1/8 inch (3 mm) thickness. Cut six 4 inch (10 cm) rounds from each pastry half. Press rounds into lightly greased muffin cups. Put scrunched up foil ball, about 1 1/4 inches (3 cm) in diameter, into each cup to fill. Bake in 400°F (205°C) oven for 10 to 15 minutes until lightly golden. Let stand in pan with foil balls in place until cool. Remove foil.

Lemon Filling: Whisk first 5 ingredients in 4 cup (1 L) liquid measure until well combined. Let stand for 5 minutes. Stir. Fill pastry cups 3/4 full. Bake in 325°F (160°C) oven for 20 to 25 minutes until almost set in centre. Let stand in pan for 30 minutes before removing to wire rack to cool. Chill.

Dust with icing sugar just before serving. Makes 12 pastries.

1 pastry: 262 Calories; 16.8 g Total Fat; 97 mg Sodium; 4 g Protein; 25 g Carbohydrate; trace Dietary Fibre

Creamy Banana Pie

Banana cream pie made easy! This pie is light and fluffy with a nice creamy texture. A delicious finale to any meal.

Brown sugar, packed	1/3 cup	75 mL
Cornstarch	3 tbsp.	50 mL
All-purpose flour	2 tbsp.	30 mL
Salt	1/4 tsp.	1 mL
Milk	2 cups	500 mL
Large eggs	2	2
Half-and-half cream	1/3 cup	75 mL
Hard margarine (or butter)	2 tsp.	10 mL
Vanilla	1 1/2 tsp.	7 mL
Medium bananas, diced	2	2
Baked 9 inch (22 cm) pie shell (or graham cracker crust)	1	1
Envelope of dessert topping (not prepared)	1	1
Milk	1/2 cup	125 mL
Vanilla	1/2 tsp.	2 mL

Sliced banana, for garnish

Combine brown sugar, cornstarch, flour and salt in medium saucepan. Stir in first amount of milk. Heat and stir on medium for about 6 minutes until boiling and thickened. Remove from heat.

Beat eggs and cream with fork in small bowl. Whisk into hot milk mixture. Heat and stir for about 3 minutes until beginning to boil. Remove from heat.

Stir in margarine, first amount of vanilla and diced banana.

Turn out into pie shell. Cover with plastic wrap directly on surface to prevent skin from forming. Chill for at least 2 hours until set.

Beat dessert topping and second amounts of milk and vanilla until stiff peaks form. Spread over filling.

Garnish with sliced banana just before serving. Cuts into 8 wedges.

*1 **wedge**: 270 Calories; 11.6 g Total Fat; 259 mg Sodium; 6 g Protein; 36 g Carbohydrate; 1 g Dietary Fibre*

Lemon Lime Pie

Indulgently sweet, yet tart enough to give your cheeks a little pucker.
This pie has a tantalizing lime green hue. It begs to be tasted.

Can of sweetened condensed milk	11 oz.	300 mL
Egg yolks (large)	4	4
Lime juice	1/4 cup	60 mL
Lemon juice	1/4 cup	60 mL
Egg white (large), room temperature	1	1
Drop of green food colouring (optional)	1	1
Finely grated lemon zest	1/2 tbsp.	7 mL
Baked 9 inch (22 cm) pie shell	1	1
Egg whites (large), room temperature	3	3
Cream of tartar	1/2 tsp.	2 mL
Granulated sugar	1/3 cup	75 mL

Combine condensed milk, egg yolks, lime juice and lemon juice in medium bowl. Mix well.

Beat first egg white in separate medium bowl until stiff peaks form. Fold into condensed milk mixture along with food colouring and lemon zest.

Pour into pie shell. Set aside.

Beat second amount of egg whites and cream of tartar in separate medium bowl until soft peaks form. Add sugar, 1 tbsp. (15 mL) at a time, until stiff peaks form and sugar is dissolved. Spoon over filling, sealing edges to crust. Bake in 350°F (175°C) oven for about 14 minutes until browned. Let stand on wire rack to cool to room temperature. Chill for at least 8 hours or overnight. Cuts into 8 wedges.

1 wedge: 313 Calories; 11.9 g Total Fat; 195 mg Sodium; 8 g Protein; 45 g Carbohydrate; trace Dietary Fibre

KEY LIME PIE: Omit lime juice and lemon juice. Use 1/2 cup (125 mL) key lime juice.

Rich Chocolate Pudding

This rich chocolate pudding is baked right in the pan.
A dusting of icing sugar gives a look of elegance. Serve in parfait glasses
with a cup of coffee or an after-dinner liqueur.

All-purpose flour	1 cup	250 mL
Baking powder	2 tsp.	10 mL
Cocoa, sifted if lumpy	3 tbsp.	50 mL
Salt	1/2 tsp.	2 mL
Granulated sugar	1 cup	250 mL
Milk	1/2 cup	125 mL
Hard margarine (or butter), melted	2 tbsp.	30 mL
Vanilla	1 tsp.	5 mL
Brown sugar, packed	3/4 cup	175 mL
Cocoa, sifted if lumpy	1/3 cup	75 mL
Hot water	1 3/4 cups	425 mL
Icing (confectioner's) sugar, for dusting		

Stir first 5 ingredients in large bowl.

Add milk, margarine and vanilla. Stir until smooth. Pour into greased 2 quart (2 L) shallow dish.

Stir brown sugar and second amount of cocoa in small bowl. Sprinkle evenly over pudding mixture.

Carefully pour hot water over top. Bake in 350°F (175°C) oven for 50 to 55 minutes until pudding is set.

Dust with icing sugar just before serving. Serves 8.

1 serving: 292 Calories; 4 g Total Fat; 293 mg Sodium; 3 g Protein; 65 g Carbohydrate; 2 g Dietary Fibre

Sticky Date Pudding

A sticky, cake-like pudding with a delicious buttery caramel sauce.
Based on the ever-popular English sticky toffee pudding. Serve warm.

Water	1 1/3 cups	325 mL
Seeded dates, coarsely chopped	1 1/3 cups	325 mL
Baking soda	1 tsp.	5 mL
Hard margarine (or butter), softened	1/3 cup	75 mL
Brown sugar, packed	3/4 cup	175 mL
Large eggs	2	2
All-purpose flour	1 cup	250 mL
Baking powder	2 tsp.	10 mL
Ground cinnamon	1 tsp.	5 mL
WARM CARAMEL SAUCE		
Whipping cream	1/2 cup	125 mL
Hard margarine (or butter)	1/2 cup	125 mL
Brown sugar, packed	1/2 cup	125 mL

Bring water to a boil in medium saucepan. Add dates. Stir. Remove from heat. Add baking soda. Stir. Let stand for 10 minutes. Stir. Pour into large bowl.

Add next 6 ingredients. Beat until well combined. Pour into greased and parchment paper-lined 8 inch (20 cm) springform pan. Bake in 350°F (175°C) oven for 50 to 55 minutes until wooden pick inserted in centre comes out clean. Let stand in pan for 10 minutes before turning out onto wire rack to cool. Cuts into 8 wedges.

Warm Caramel Sauce: Combine whipping cream, margarine and brown sugar in large saucepan. Heat and stir on medium for 3 to 5 minutes until margarine is melted. Bring to a boil. Boil, without stirring, for about 5 minutes until slightly thickened. Makes 1 cup (250 mL) sauce. Serve with pudding. Serves 8.

1 serving: 530 Calories; 26.8 g Total Fat; 508 mg Sodium; 4 g Protein; 72 g Carbohydrate; 3 g Dietary Fibre

Pictured on page 108.

Coconut Crunch Pudding

Rich, creamy coconut pudding layered with a cookie-type crumble.
Serve in individual parfait glasses with a dollop of whipped cream.

COCONUT CRUNCH

All-purpose flour	1/2 cup	125 mL
Brown sugar, packed	2 tbsp.	30 mL
Hard margarine (or butter), chilled	1/4 cup	60 mL
Flake coconut	1/2 cup	125 mL

COCONUT CUSTARD

Homogenized milk	1 1/3 cups	325 mL
All-purpose flour	2 tbsp.	30 mL
Cornstarch	2 tbsp.	30 mL
Granulated sugar	1/3 cup	75 mL
Salt	1/4 tsp.	1 mL
Half-and-half cream	2/3 cup	150 mL
Egg yolks (large), fork-beaten	2	2
Hard margarine (or butter)	2 tsp.	10 mL
Flake coconut	1/2 cup	125 mL
Coconut flavouring	2 tsp.	10 mL
Whipped cream (or dessert topping, prepared), optional	1 cup	250 mL

Coconut Crunch: Combine flour and brown sugar in medium bowl. Cut in margarine until crumbly.

Add coconut. Rub mixture between palms of hands until no lumps of margarine remain. Turn into ungreased 9 x 9 inch (22 x 22 cm) pan. Bake in 400°F (205°C) oven for about 20 minutes, stirring with fork every 5 minutes, until golden. Stir to break up large clumps. Cool. Makes 3 1/3 cups (825 mL) crunch.

Coconut Custard: Heat milk, uncovered, in medium saucepan on medium for about 5 minutes, stirring occasionally, until bubbles begin to form around side of pan. Do not boil.

Combine flour, cornstarch, sugar and salt in small bowl. Gradually stir in half-and-half cream until smooth. Slowly stir into milk. Heat and stir for about 2 minutes until boiling and thickened. Remove from heat.

(continued on next page)

Combine 1/4 cup (60 mL) milk mixture and egg yolks in small dish. Mix well. Stir into milk mixture. Heat and stir on medium for about 2 minutes until thickened. Remove from heat.

Stir in margarine, coconut and flavouring. Cover with plastic wrap directly on surface to prevent skin from forming. Makes 2 1/3 cups (575 mL) custard.

Layer crunch and custard, repeating layers several times, in clear serving bowl or in 4 individual parfait glasses, reserving 1/3 cup (75 mL) crunch. Top with whipped cream. Sprinkle reserved crunch over whipped cream. Serves 4.

1 serving: 535 Calories; 30.4 g Total Fat; 410 mg Sodium; 8 g Protein; 59 g Carbohydrate; 2 g Dietary Fibre

Pictured on page 125.

Cinnamon Bread Pudding

A unique variation of cinnamon bread. The sweet chunks of apples give this pudding a fruity tartness and the pecans add a satisfying crunch.

Large un-iced cinnamon buns, cut into 1 inch (2.5 cm) pieces (about 3 cups, 750 mL)	2	2
Dried apples, chopped	1/3 cup	75 mL
Milk	2 2/3 cups	650 mL
Large eggs	3	3
Brown sugar, packed	1/4 cup	60 mL
Pecans, chopped	1/3 cup	75 mL

Scatter cinnamon bun pieces and apples in greased 2 quart (2 L) shallow dish.

Whisk milk, eggs and brown sugar together in medium bowl or 4 cup (1 L) liquid measure until well combined. Carefully pour over cinnamon bun pieces.

Sprinkle with pecans. Let stand for 10 minutes. Bake, uncovered, in 350°F (175°C) oven for about 50 minutes until set and knife inserted in centre comes out clean. Let stand in pan for 15 minutes before serving. Serves 6.

1 serving: 292 Calories; 13.3 g Total Fat; 212 mg Sodium; 9 g Protein; 35 g Carbohydrate; 1 g Dietary Fibre

Old-Fashioned Apple Cobbler

Cinnamon-spiced apples with a golden brown biscuit topping.
A good old-fashioned comfort food. Serve hot with
a dollop of ice cream or whipped cream.

APPLE FILLING		
Medium cooking apples (such as McIntosh), peeled, cored, sliced	6	6
Granulated sugar	1/2 cup	125 mL
Ground cinnamon	1/2 tsp.	2 mL
Water	3/4 cup	175 mL
TOPPING		
All-purpose flour	1 cup	250 mL
Granulated sugar	1/4 cup	60 mL
Baking powder	2 tsp.	10 mL
Salt	1/2 tsp.	2 mL
Hard margarine (or butter), chilled	3 tbsp.	50 mL
Cold milk	1/2 cup	125 mL

Apple Filling: Put first 4 ingredients into large saucepan. Bring to a boil on medium-high. Reduce heat. Simmer, uncovered, for 5 to 7 minutes on medium until apple is tender. Turn into greased 1 1/2 quart (1.5 L) casserole. Keep warm in 400°F (205°C) oven while preparing topping.

Topping: Measure flour, sugar, baking powder and salt into medium bowl. Cut in margarine until crumbly.

Add milk. Mix until just moistened. Drop by spoonfuls over hot apple mixture. Bake, uncovered, for 20 to 25 minutes until wooden pick inserted in centre comes out clean. Serves 6 to 8.

1 serving: 318 Calories; 6.6 g Total Fat; 401 mg Sodium; 3 g Protein; 64 g Carbohydrate; 3 g Dietary Fibre

Peach Crumble

Tangy sweet peaches with a delicious rolled oat and brown sugar topping. As it bakes, the peachy syrup bubbles deliciously through the golden oat topping. Serve hot with ice cream or half-and-half cream.

Frozen sliced peaches, thawed	4 cups	1 L
Brown sugar, packed	1/4 cup	60 mL
Granulated sugar	1/4 cup	60 mL
Minute tapioca	1 tbsp.	15 mL
Ground cinnamon, sprinkle		
Quick-cooking rolled oats (not instant)	6 tbsp.	100 mL
All-purpose flour	1/4 cup	60 mL
Brown sugar, packed	1/4 cup	60 mL
Salt	1/8 tsp.	0.5 mL
Hard margarine (or butter)	3 tbsp.	50 mL

Turn peaches into greased 1 1/2 quart (1.5 L) shallow casserole.

Combine first amount of brown sugar, granulated sugar, tapioca and cinnamon in small bowl. Sprinkle over peaches.

Mix rolled oats, flour, second amount of brown sugar and salt in medium bowl. Cut in margarine until crumbly. Sprinkle over peaches. Pack down slightly with palm of hand. Bake, uncovered, in 350°F (175°C) oven for 50 to 55 minutes until golden and centre is bubbly. Serves 6.

1 serving: 292 Calories; 6.4 g Total Fat; 133 mg Sodium; 2 g Protein; 59 g Carbohydrate; 2 g Dietary Fibre

Mango Raspberry Trifles

A fun variation of the traditional trifle. Mango and fresh raspberries make this a very colourful dessert. Assemble in individual wine glasses and serve after a special meal.

Orange-flavoured liqueur (such as Grand Marnier)	2 tbsp.	30 mL
Prepared orange juice	1/4 cup	60 mL
Mascarpone cheese	1 1/3 cups	325 mL
Icing (confectioner's) sugar	1/3 cup	75 mL
Ladyfingers	8	8
Cans of sliced mango, with syrup (14 oz., 398 mL, each), drained, sliced diagonally	2	2
Fresh raspberries	1 1/3 cups	325 mL

Combine liqueur and orange juice in small bowl.

Mash or beat cheese and icing sugar in separate small bowl.

Break each ladyfinger in half. Dip each into orange juice mixture. Place 2 halves in bottom of each of 4 serving glasses. Divide 1/2 of mango over ladyfingers. Spoon or pipe 1/2 of cheese mixture over mango. Divide 1/2 of raspberries and sprinkle over cheese mixture. Repeat layers. Chill for 1 to 3 hours. Serves 4.

1 serving: 553 Calories; 31.3 g Total Fat; 277 mg Sodium; 10 g Protein; 58 g Carbohydrate; 6 g Dietary Fibre

Pictured on page 108.

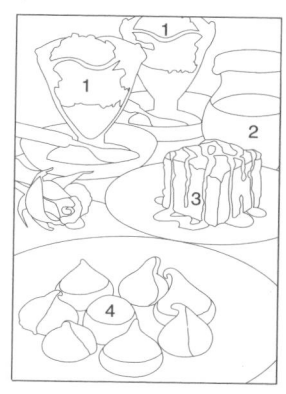

1. Espresso Sundae, page 79
2. White Chocolate Sauce, page 111
3. Cola Zucchini Cake, page 22
4. Coffee Meringues, page 56

Props Courtesy Of: Canhome Global

Chantilly Crumbs

This sweet, chewy, nutty dessert is so easy to prepare. Top with a dollop of whipped cream and garnish with nuts, cherries or shaved chocolate. Or all three!

Brown sugar, packed	1 cup	250 mL
All-purpose flour	1/3 cup	75 mL
Large egg, fork-beaten	1	1
Finely chopped mixed nuts	1/2 cup	125 mL
Baking soda	1/2 tsp.	2 mL
Whipping cream	1 cup	250 mL
Granulated sugar	1 tbsp.	15 mL
Vanilla	1/2 tsp.	2 mL

Measure first 5 ingredients into ungreased 8 x 8 inch (20 x 20 cm) pan. Stir until evenly mixed. Bake in 325°F (160°C) oven for 25 minutes. Cool. Turn into larger container. Break into small crumbly pieces.

Beat whipping cream, granulated sugar and vanilla in medium bowl until stiff peaks form. Fold crumb mixture into whipped cream mixture. Chill for 2 hours. To serve, divide and spoon into 6 sherbet dishes or champagne glasses. Serves 6.

1 serving: 388 Calories; 20.6 g Total Fat; 148 mg Sodium; 5 g Protein; 48 g Carbohydrate; 1 g Dietary Fibre

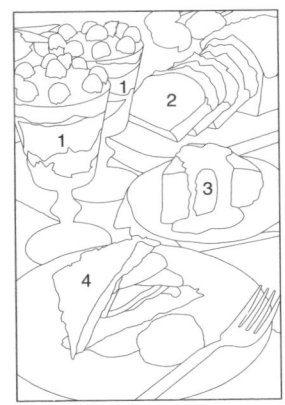

1. Mango Raspberry Trifles, page 106
2. Lemon Poppy Loaf, page 24
3. Sticky Date Pudding, page 101
4. Pastry Triangles With Pears, page 86

Props Courtesy Of: Cornell Trading Ltd.
La Cache

Coffee Custard Sauce

A creamy, coffee-flavoured sauce with a warming hint of brandy.
Delicious over ice cream or served with a rich chocolate cake.

Whipping cream	1 cup	250 mL
Instant coffee granules	1 tbsp.	15 mL
Egg yolks (large)	2	2
Granulated sugar	1/4 cup	60 mL
Brandy (or 1/4 tsp., 1 mL, brandy flavouring)	1 tbsp.	15 mL

Heat whipping cream, uncovered, in heavy medium saucepan on medium-high for about 5 minutes until bubbles begin to form around edge of saucepan. Remove from heat.

Add coffee granules. Stir until coffee is dissolved.

Beat egg yolks and sugar together in small bowl until light and fluffy. Add 1/4 of hot whipping cream mixture to egg yolk mixture. Mix well. Stir into whipping cream mixture. Heat and stir on low for about 10 minutes until thickened and mixture coats back of spoon. Remove from heat.

Add brandy. Stir. Makes about 1 2/3 cups (400 mL).

2 tbsp. (30 mL): 81 Calories; 6.6 g Total Fat; 8 mg Sodium; 1 g Protein; 5 g Carbohydrate; 0 g Dietary Fibre

Paré Pointer

Before spaghetti could be sold commercially,
it had to pasta taste test.

White Chocolate Sauce

The rich, sweet, creamy taste of white chocolate with a tempting hint of brandy. A white chocolate lover's dream come true! Excellent with Cola Zucchini Cake, page 22.

Granulated sugar	1/4 cup	60 mL
Whipping cream	1 cup	250 mL
Vanilla	1 tsp.	5 mL
Brandy (or 1/2 tsp., 2 mL, brandy flavouring)	2 tbsp.	30 mL
White chocolate baking squares (1 oz., 28 g, each), chopped	6	6

Combine sugar and whipping cream in heavy medium saucepan. Heat and stir on medium for 1 to 2 minutes until sugar is dissolved. Boil gently for 3 minutes.

Add vanilla and brandy. Stir. Remove from heat.

Stir in chocolate until melted and sauce is smooth. Cool. Makes about 1 2/3 cups (400 mL).

2 tbsp. (30 mL): 140 Calories; 9.5 g Total Fat; 17 mg Sodium; 1 g Protein; 12 g Carbohydrate; 0 g Dietary Fibre

Pictured on page 107.

 *The grayish-white film on chocolate is called bloom and is the result of cocoa butter or sugar crystals rising to the surface after exposure to varying temperatures. It does not affect flavour and after chocolate is melted, it will disappear.*

Maple Walnut Sauce

A delightfully rich and smooth caramel sauce with maple flavouring and crunchy walnuts. This sweet, gooey sauce is magical on ice cream or Christmas pudding.

Brown sugar, packed	1 cup	250 mL
All-purpose flour	3 tbsp.	50 mL
Water	1 1/2 cups	375 mL
Corn syrup	2 tbsp.	30 mL
Hard margarine (or butter)	2 tbsp.	30 mL
Maple flavouring	1 tsp.	5 mL
Chopped walnuts	1 cup	250 mL

Combine brown sugar and flour in 4 cup (1 L) liquid measure. Stir well.

Stir in water. Add remaining 4 ingredients. Stir. Microwave, uncovered, on high (100%) for about 5 minutes, stirring after each minute, until boiling and thickened. Makes 2 1/2 cups (625 mL).

2 tbsp. (30 mL): 101 Calories; 4.7 g Total Fat; 19 mg Sodium; 2 g Protein; 14 g Carbohydrate; trace Dietary Fibre

 *To quickly chop nuts, place in a resealable plastic bag and roll a rolling pin over top until desired consistency.*

Chocolate Fudge Sauce

This velvety smooth chocolate fudge sauce is rich and oh-so-decadent. Enjoy it over cake, ice cream, crêpes, fresh fruit or anything that needs a rich chocolate lift.

Semi-sweet chocolate chips	1 cup	250 mL
Hard margarine (or butter)	1/4 cup	60 mL
Corn syrup	2/3 cup	150 mL
Hot water	2/3 cup	150 mL
Instant coffee granules	1 1/2 tsp.	7 mL
Salt	1/16 tsp.	0.5 mL
Icing (confectioner's) sugar	1 cup	250 mL
Vanilla	1 1/2 tsp.	7 mL

Measure first 6 ingredients into medium saucepan. Heat on medium for about 10 minutes, stirring frequently, until margarine is melted and mixture is smooth. Remove from heat.

Gradually beat in icing sugar, 1/4 cup (60 mL) at a time, until consistency of medium-thick sauce. Beat in vanilla. Makes 2 1/3 cups (575 mL).

2 tbsp. (30 mL): 129 Calories; 5.3 g Total Fat; 47 mg Sodium; trace Protein; 22 g Carbohydrate; 1 g Dietary Fibre

Paré Pointer

Everyone knows a pediatrician is a doctor with very little patients.

Quick Caramel Fondue

Hot melted caramel with a tantalizing rum flavour! So creamy and rich.
Try as a dip for fresh fruit pieces or cubes of white snack cake.
And, of course, this is perfect over ice cream.

Caramels (about 11 oz., 310 g)	40	40
Milk	1/3 cup	75 mL
Rum flavouring	1 tsp.	5 mL

Heat and stir caramels, milk and flavouring in medium saucepan on medium-low for about 10 minutes until smooth. Carefully pour into fondue pot to no more than 2/3 full. Place over low heat. Makes about 1 cup (250 mL).

2 tbsp. (30 mL): 146 Calories; 3.1 g Total Fat; 96 mg Sodium; 2 g Protein; 29 g Carbohydrate; trace Dietary Fibre

Suggested Dippers: Apple and banana slices; Chocolate Snack Cake pieces, page 22; White Snack Cake pieces, page 23; cookie pieces; marshmallows. Serve with dish of chopped nuts to roll dipped food in.

 *Choose firm fruit and cakes for dipping in dessert fondues. Delicate fruit, such as watermelon or raspberries, and crumbly cakes or doughnuts may not stay on fondue forks and may get lost in the fondue pot.*

Sauces, Spreads & Dips

Orange Butter

This buttery orange spread is at home on the weekend brunch table.
Delicious on muffins, rolls, fresh bread, pancakes and crêpes.

Butter (or hard margarine), softened	1/2 cup	125 mL
Icing (confectioner's) sugar	6 tbsp.	100 mL
Orange marmalade	1/4 cup	60 mL

Beat butter, icing sugar and marmalade together in small bowl. Pack into small mold or airtight container. Makes 2/3 cup (150 mL).

2 tsp. (10 mL): 75 Calories; 5.8 g Total Fat; 62 mg Sodium; trace Protein; 6 g Carbohydrate; 0 g Dietary Fibre

Strawberry Spread

A fresh, fruity spread with the warm summery taste of strawberries.
Delicious on bagels or muffins.

Mashed fresh (or frozen whole, thawed to room temperature and drained) strawberries	2/3 cup	150 mL
Granulated sugar	2 tbsp.	30 mL
Icing (confectioner's) sugar	1/4 cup	60 mL
Hard margarine (or butter), softened	1/2 cup	125 mL

Beat all 4 ingredients together in small bowl for about 10 minutes until smooth. Pack into mold or shape into small balls. Cover. Chill. Makes 1 1/4 cups (300 mL).

1 tbsp. (15 mL): 54 Calories; 4.7 g Total Fat; 54 mg Sodium; trace Protein; 3 g Carbohydrate; trace Dietary Fibre

Pictured on page 144.

Peach Cream Cheese Spread

Cream cheese spread with the subtle fragrance and sweetness of peaches and the refreshing zing of ginger. Great spread on a toasted bagel or English muffin.

Block of cream cheese, softened	4 oz.	125 g
Brown sugar, packed	2 tbsp.	30 mL
Finely chopped (fresh or canned) peaches	1/4 cup	60 mL
Finely minced crystallized ginger	1 – 2 tbsp.	15 – 30 mL

Beat cream cheese and brown sugar together in medium bowl until smooth.

Add peaches and ginger. Beat until well combined. Cover. Chill for at least 1 hour to allow flavours to blend. Makes 1 cup (250 mL).

1 tbsp. (15 mL): 34 Calories; 2.6 g Total Fat; 23 mg Sodium; 1 g Protein; 2 g Carbohydrate; trace Dietary Fibre

Raspberry Spread

A rich, creamy spread with juicy sweet raspberries throughout. A very easy-to-prepare spread to dress up your toasted bagel, English muffin or toast.

Block of cream cheese, softened	4 oz.	125 g
Icing (confectioner's) sugar	1/3 cup	75 mL
Frozen (or fresh) raspberries, thawed and drained	1/3 cup	75 mL
Finely grated lemon zest	1/4 tsp.	1 mL

Beat cream cheese and icing sugar in medium bowl until smooth and light.

Add raspberries and lemon zest. Beat until well combined. Cover. Chill for at least 1 hour to allow flavours to blend. Makes 3/4 cup (175 mL).

1 tbsp. (15 mL): 55 Calories; 3.4 g Total Fat; 29 mg Sodium; 1 g Protein; 5 g Carbohydrate; trace Dietary Fibre

Pictured on page 144.

Ginger Cheese Spread

Creamy and smooth with zingy gingersnap crumbs throughout.
A melt-in-your-mouth spread that is unique and easy to prepare.
Delicious on bagels, English muffins or toast.

Block of cream cheese, softened	4 oz.	125 g
Hard margarine (or butter)	1/4 cup	60 mL
Gingersnaps, processed into fine crumbs (about 8)	1/3 cup	75 mL
Icing (confectioner's) sugar	1/3 cup	75 mL

Beat cream cheese and margarine until smooth and fluffy.

Add gingersnap crumbs and icing sugar. Beat until smooth. Cover. Chill for at least 1 hour to allow flavours to blend. Makes about 1 cup (250 mL).

1 tbsp. (15 mL): 76 Calories; 5.9 g Total Fat; 74 mg Sodium; 1 g Protein; 5 g Carbohydrate; trace Dietary Fibre

Pictured on page 144.

 *Too much heat cooks chocolate and makes it firm. Use lowest heat to melt, stirring often until melted. Do not overheat.*

Yogurt Fruit Dip

This dip works well with any flavour of yogurt. It is mild, creamy and fresh tasting. Use as a fruit dip or spoon over your favourite dessert. So quick and easy to prepare.

Strawberry yogurt (stir before measuring)	1/2 cup	125 mL
Icing (confectioner's) sugar	1 tbsp.	15 mL
Frozen whipped topping, thawed	1/2 cup	125 mL

Fold yogurt and icing sugar into whipped topping in small bowl. Makes 3/4 cup (175 mL).

2 tbsp. (30 mL): 46 Calories; 1.9 g Total Fat; 12 mg Sodium; 1 g Protein; 6 g Carbohydrate; 0 g Dietary Fibre

Pictured on page 144.

Hot Mocha Dip

Another sweet treat to delight the chocolate and coffee lovers. This dip is very rich, very flavourful and very decadent. Your guests would never believe how easy it is to prepare, so why tell them? Perfect for dunking fresh fruit and cookies or spooning over ice cream.

Semi-sweet chocolate chips	2 cups	500 mL
Whipping cream	1/3 cup	75 mL
Prepared very strong coffee (or 2 tbsp., 30 mL, coffee-flavoured liqueur, such as Kahlúa)	1/3 cup	75 mL
Vanilla	1/2 tsp.	2 mL

Combine all 4 ingredients in medium saucepan. Heat and stir on medium-low until smooth. Makes 1 1/2 cups (375 mL).

2 tbsp. (30 mL): 157 Calories; 10.7 g Total Fat; 6 mg Sodium; 1 g Protein; 18 g Carbohydrate; 2 g Dietary Fibre

Marshmallow Pudding Dip

A big hit with kids and easy enough for them to help you prepare. This sweet, sticky, creamy dip can be made with any pudding flavour. Perfect for dipping bananas or other fresh fruit.

Jar of marshmallow creme	7 oz.	198 g
Milk	2 1/2 cups	625 mL
Instant pudding powder (4 serving size), your choice	1	1
Vanilla	1 tsp.	5 mL

Beat marshmallow creme in large bowl, slowly adding milk until well combined.

Add pudding powder and vanilla. Beat on low for about 2 minutes until smooth. Let stand for 5 minutes to thicken slightly. Makes 3 1/2 cups (875 mL).

2 tbsp. (30 mL): 44 Calories; 0.3 g Total Fat; 65 mg Sodium; 1 g Protein; 10 g Carbohydrate; 0 g Dietary Fibre

 *To prevent commercial marshmallows from drying out, store in the freezer. Thawed or fresh, marshmallows are easily cut with scissors when ready to use.*

Peanut Munch

A variation of the crisp rice square classic. Peanuts add an enjoyable crunch to this sticky, chewy snack. Label for the kids' lunch boxes or afternoon snack.

Rice squares cereal	1 cup	250 mL
Crisp rice cereal	1 cup	250 mL
Unsalted peanuts	2/3 cup	150 mL
Hard margarine (or butter)	2 tbsp.	30 mL
White corn syrup	1/4 cup	60 mL
Smooth peanut butter	1/4 cup	60 mL
Vanilla	1/2 tsp.	2 mL
Granulated sugar	4 tsp.	20 mL

Combine both cereals and peanuts in large bowl.

Heat margarine, corn syrup and peanut butter in small saucepan on low until smooth and bubbly. Remove from heat.

Stir in vanilla. Pour over cereal mixture. Stir until well coated. Spread out on large greased baking sheet with sides.

Sprinkle with 2 tsp. (10 mL) sugar. Bake in 350°F (175°C) oven for 5 minutes. Stir. Sprinkle with remaining sugar. Bake for 5 minutes. Let baking sheet stand on wire rack, stirring once or twice, to cool. Makes 3 cups (750 mL).

1/3 cup (75 mL): 202 Calories; 12.2 g Total Fat; 144 mg Sodium; 5 g Protein; 20 g Carbohydrate; 2 g Dietary Fibre

Paré Pointer

A clever carpenter always nails down his agreements.

Crunchy Cereal Toss

A toss of cereal, nuts, seeds and dried fruit with an apricot candy coating. These delicious, crunchy, chewy pieces are perfect for snacking.

Hard margarine (or butter)	1/3 cup	75 mL
Granulated sugar	1/3 cup	75 mL
Apricot (or mango) jam, large pieces finely chopped	1/2 cup	125 mL
Rice squares cereal	3 cups	750 mL
Slivered almonds	1/3 cup	75 mL
Pecan halves	1/3 cup	75 mL
Dried apricots (or golden raisins), diced	1/2 cup	125 mL
Sunflower seeds	2 tbsp.	30 mL

Heat and stir margarine, sugar and jam in small saucepan on medium until sugar and jam are dissolved.

Combine remaining 5 ingredients in large bowl. Pour margarine mixture over top. Toss until well coated. Spread out on ungreased baking sheet. Bake in 325°F (160°C) oven for 25 minutes. Let baking sheet stand on wire rack to cool. Tap baking sheet on counter to loosen cereal mixture. Break into bite-size pieces. Makes 3 1/2 cups (875 mL).

1/3 cup (75 mL): 237 Calories; 11.7 g Total Fat; 177 mg Sodium; 3 g Protein; 33 g Carbohydrate; 1 g Dietary Fibre

 *To achieve even baking, be sure the baking sheets, cake pan or muffin pans do not touch the sides of the oven. This prevents the air from circulating properly.*

Peanut Butter Popcorn

A peanutty variation of caramel corn. This crunchy, sticky treat is the perfect companion to curl up with on movie night.

Unpopped corn	1/2 cup	125 mL
Golden corn syrup	3/4 cup	175 mL
Brown sugar, packed	1/2 cup	125 mL
Smooth peanut butter	3/4 cup	175 mL
Vanilla	1 tsp.	5 mL
Roasted salted peanuts	2 cups	500 mL

Pop corn, in hot air popper, into very large bowl or container.

Stir corn syrup and brown sugar together in medium saucepan on medium for 4 to 5 minutes until boiling and sugar is dissolved. Remove from heat.

Stir in peanut butter and vanilla until smooth. Stir in peanuts. Gradually pour over popped corn, while stirring, until coated. Spread out on large greased baking sheets or on waxed paper-covered surface. Let stand, uncovered, stirring once or twice, until cool. Makes 18 cups (4.5 L).

1/2 cup (125 mL): 131 Calories; 7.3 g Total Fat; 108 mg Sodium; 4 g Protein; 15 g Carbohydrate; 2 g Dietary Fibre

White Chocolate Popcorn

The ultimate snack for those who love white chocolate and caramel corn—the perfect "pick-me-up" snack.

White chocolate candy bars (3 1/2 oz., 100 g, each), chopped	3	3
Bag of caramel-coated popcorn and peanuts (about 5 cups, 1.25 L)	7 oz.	200 g
Slivered almonds, toasted (see Tip, page 79)	1/2 cup	125 mL

(continued on next page)

Heat chocolate in medium saucepan on lowest heat, stirring often, until almost melted. Do not overheat. Remove from heat. Stir until smooth.

Spread popcorn on foil-lined baking sheet. Drizzle chocolate evenly over popcorn. Stir. Sprinkle with almonds. Chill until set. Break into bite-size pieces. Makes about 5 1/2 cups (1.4 L).

1/2 cup (125 mL): 255 Calories; 13 g Total Fat; 79 mg Sodium; 4 g Protein; 33 g Carbohydrate; 1 g Dietary Fibre

Pictured on page 126.

Chocolate Banana Snack

Soft banana chunks with a firm coating of chocolate and toasted coconut. Kids enjoy making this treat as much as they enjoy making it disappear!

Milk chocolate candy bars (3 1/2 oz., 100 g, each), chopped	3	3
Medium bananas, cut into 1 inch (2.5 cm) slices	2	2
Flake coconut, toasted (see Tip, page 79)	1 1/2 cups	375 mL

Heat chocolate in medium saucepan on lowest heat for about 5 minutes, stirring often, until almost melted. Do not overheat. Remove from heat. Stir until smooth.

Dip banana into chocolate, allowing excess to drip back into saucepan.

Place coconut in shallow dish or on waxed paper. Roll banana in coconut to coat. Place on foil-lined baking sheet. Chill until set. Makes about 14 pieces.

1 piece: 178 Calories; 10.2 g Total Fat; 46 mg Sodium; 2 g Protein; 22 g Carbohydrate; 2 g Dietary Fibre

Pictured on page 72.

Hot Sauced Bananas

Sliced bananas topped with a golden sauce of orange, lemon and rum.
Serve with vanilla ice cream.

SAUCE

Brown sugar, packed	1/2 cup	125 mL
All-purpose flour	2 tbsp.	30 mL
Prepared orange juice	1 cup	250 mL
Lemon juice	1 tbsp.	15 mL
Rum flavouring	1/2 tsp.	2 mL
Large bananas, sliced	2	2
Scoops of vanilla ice cream (optional)	4	4

Sauce: Stir brown sugar and flour in small saucepan.

Gradually stir in orange juice, lemon juice and flavouring. Heat and stir on medium-high for about 3 minutes until boiling and thickened. Makes 1 cup (250 mL) sauce.

Divide and put banana into 4 individual bowls. Divide ice cream among banana. Spoon sauce over top. Serves 4.

1 serving: 218 Calories; 0.4 g Total Fat; 13 mg Sodium; 2 g Protein; 55 g Carbohydrate; 2 g Dietary Fibre

Pictured on page 125.

1. Coconut Crunch Pudding, page 102
2. Hot Sauced Bananas, above
3. Frozen Cheesecake Bites, page 78

Props Courtesy Of: Wiltshire®

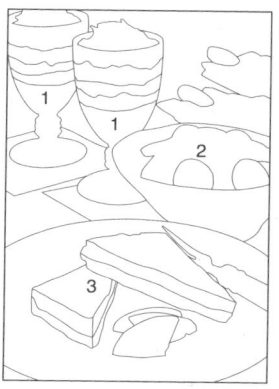

Snacks & Treats

Coffee Bean Clusters

These chocolate-covered coffee beans are sure to satisfy your sweet craving, as well as give you a little energy boost. Also very good with white or milk chocolate.

Dark chocolate candy bar, chopped	5 1/2 oz.	150 g
Roasted coffee beans (your choice)	2/3 cup	150 mL

Heat chocolate in medium saucepan on lowest heat for about 3 minutes, stirring often, until almost melted. Do not overheat. Remove from heat. Stir until smooth.

Add coffee beans. Stir until well coated. Drop by 1/2 tsp. (2 mL) onto foil-lined baking sheet. Let stand in cool place until chocolate is set. Do not chill. Makes about 70 clusters.

1 cluster: 12 Calories; 0.7 g Total Fat; 1 mg Sodium; trace Protein; 2 g Carbohydrate; trace Dietary Fibre

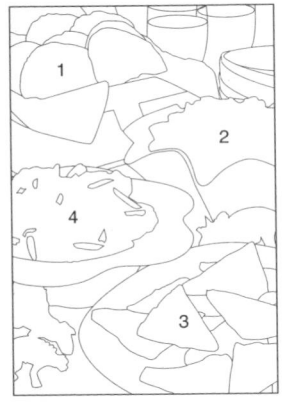

1. Giant Candy Bar Cookies, page 58
2. Sweet Sesame Snack, page 130
3. Candied Peanuts And Dates, page 31
4. White Chocolate Popcorn, page 122

Props Courtesy Of: Wal-Mart Canada Inc.

Caramelized Fresh Fruit

Golden, tender caramelized peaches served hot with a dollop of vanilla ice cream. A very simple yet elegant treat. Try over hot oatmeal for a breakfast treat.

Butter (not margarine)	2 tbsp.	30 mL
Sliced firm, ripe peaches (or pears or apples), peeled if desired, cut 1/2 inch (12 mm) thick (see Note)	1 cup	250 mL
Granulated sugar	3 tbsp.	50 mL
Brown sugar, packed	2 tbsp.	30 mL
Ice cream (or whipped cream), optional		

Heat butter in large frying pan on medium until sizzling.

Add peaches. Cook on medium for 2 to 3 minutes, stirring once or twice, until golden.

Sprinkle with granulated sugar and brown sugar. Stir carefully until both sugars are dissolved and peaches are glazed.

Serve with ice cream. Serves 2.

1 serving: 268 Calories; 11.8 g Total Fat; 125 mg Sodium; 1 g Protein; 43 g Carbohydrate; 2 g Dietary Fibre

Note: Cut peaches into thicker slices for firmer fruit in the finished product.

Paré Pointer

Do pet turtles wear people-neck sweaters?

Cinnamon Toast

*A classic on the list of comfort foods. Hot, buttery toast with a sweet,
slightly crunchy, cinnamon topping. A soothing snack treat
as well as a delicious breakfast choice.*

White bread slices	4	4
Hard margarine (or butter), melted	1/3 cup	75 mL
Granulated sugar	3 tbsp.	50 mL
Ground cinnamon	1 tsp.	5 mL

Place bread slices on ungreased baking sheet. Broil 4 inches (10 cm) from
heat for about 3 minutes until golden. Turn slices over.

Combine margarine, sugar and cinnamon in small bowl. Divide and spread
over untoasted side of bread. Broil for about 2 minutes until cinnamon
mixture is bubbly. Cool slightly. Cut each slice into 3 pieces, for a total of
12 pieces.

*1 piece: 83 Calories; 5.7 g Total Fat; 100 mg Sodium; 1 g Protein; 7 g Carbohydrate;
trace Dietary Fibre*

 *To keep dried fruit, marshmallows and other sticky foods from sticking
to your knife blade, dip the knife blade into cold water or spray with
nonstick cooking spray.*

Sweet Sesame Snack

Golden seeds, oats and almonds in a crunchy, buttery, caramel coating.
Great sweet nibblies for hiking, relaxing on the deck or watching the game.

Rolled oats (not instant)	2 cups	500 mL
Sesame seeds	1/2 cup	125 mL
Medium coconut	1/2 cup	125 mL
Sliced almonds, coarsely chopped	1/3 cup	75 mL
Brown sugar, packed	1/3 cup	75 mL
Cooking oil	1/4 cup	60 mL
Liquid honey	1/4 cup	60 mL
Golden corn syrup	1/4 cup	60 mL
Water	1/4 cup	60 mL
Vanilla	1 1/2 tsp.	7 mL
Salt	1/4 tsp.	1 mL

Combine first 4 ingredients in 2 quart (2 L) shallow microwave-safe baking dish.

Stir remaining 7 ingredients in medium microwave-safe bowl. Microwave, uncovered, on high (100%) for about 4 minutes until bubbly and syrupy. Pour over rolled oat mixture. Stir until well coated. Microwave, uncovered, on high (100%) for 4 minutes. Stir. Microwave on high (100%) for 6 to 7 minutes, stirring every 2 minutes, until toasted. Turn out and spread on large waxed paper-lined baking sheet. Cool. Makes about 5 cups (1.25 L).

1/2 cup (125 mL): 319 Calories; 16.5 g Total Fat; 79 mg Sodium; 6 g Protein; 40 g Carbohydrate; 3 g Dietary Fibre

Pictured on page 126.

Variation: For larger pieces, pack toasted rolled oat mixture into waxed paper-lined 9 x 13 inch (22 x 33 cm) pan. Cool. Turn out. Remove and discard waxed paper. Break into bite-size pieces.

Spiced Toffee Nuts

A deliciously spiced mix of nuts in a crunchy toffee coating.
A tempting nut brittle that won't stay around for long.

Egg white (large)	1	1
Whole almonds, toasted (see Tip, page 79)	1 cup	250 mL
Pecans, toasted (see Tip, page 79)	1 cup	250 mL
Hazelnuts (filberts), toasted (see Tip, page 79)	1 cup	250 mL
Granulated sugar	2/3 cup	150 mL
Liquid honey	1/2 cup	125 mL
Ground cinnamon	1 tsp.	5 mL
Ground ginger	1 tsp.	5 mL
Ground nutmeg	1 tsp.	5 mL
Salt	3/4 tsp.	4 mL

Beat egg white in medium bowl until frothy.

Add remaining 9 ingredients. Mix well. Spread on greased baking sheet. Bake in 350°F (175°C) oven for about 20 minutes, stirring 2 to 3 times, until browned. Spread out so nuts are in single layer. Cool completely. Break into bite-size pieces. Makes 3 1/3 cups (825 mL).

1/3 cup (75 mL): 375 Calories; 24.2 g Total Fat; 187 mg Sodium; 6 g Protein; 40 g Carbohydrate; 4 g Dietary Fibre

Pictured on page 53.

Paré Pointer

When credit cards were first available,
a good many got a real charge out of it.

Cinnamon-Sugared Pecans

Toasted pecans with a crunchy coating and warm cinnamon taste.
Delicious finger snacks and card-night nibblies.

Egg white (large), room temperature	1	1
Ground cinnamon	2 tsp.	10 mL
Granulated sugar	1/3 cup	75 mL
Hard margarine (or butter), melted and cooled	1/4 cup	60 mL
Pecan halves, toasted (see Tip, page 79), cooled slightly	2 cups	500 mL
Salt	1/2 tsp.	2 mL

Beat egg white in medium bowl until soft peaks form. Gradually beat in cinnamon and sugar until stiff peaks form.

Fold in margarine. Fold in pecans until coated. Turn into 9 x 9 inch (22 x 22 cm) pan. Bake in 325°F (160°C) oven for 25 to 30 minutes, stirring occasionally, until coating begins to look granular and nuts are loose. Remove from oven.

Immediately sprinkle with salt. Stir. Cool completely. Makes 2 cups (500 mL).

1/3 cup (75 mL): 338 Calories; 30.5 g Total Fat; 262 mg Sodium; 3 g Protein; 17 g Carbohydrate; 2 g Dietary Fibre

Paré Pointer
Even elevator companies have their ups and downs.

Date And Nut Bars

A moist, light cake with chewy dates and crunchy walnuts. The coconut topping is sticky and chewy. Perfect snacking squares for the bridge group.

Large eggs	2	2
Brown sugar, packed	1 cup	250 mL
Cooking oil	3 tbsp.	50 mL
Vanilla	1 tsp.	5 mL
All-purpose flour	2/3 cup	150 mL
Baking powder	1 tsp.	5 mL
Salt	1/2 tsp.	2 mL
Chopped dates	1 1/4 cups	300 mL
Chopped walnuts	1/2 cup	125 mL
TOPPING		
Hard margarine (or butter)	2 tbsp.	30 mL
Brown sugar, packed	3 tbsp.	50 mL
Half-and-half cream (or evaporated milk)	1 tbsp.	15 mL
Medium coconut	1/4 cup	60 mL

Beat eggs in medium bowl until thickened and light coloured.

Add brown sugar, cooking oil and vanilla. Beat well.

Stir in flour, baking powder and salt until just moistened. Stir in dates and walnuts. Turn into greased foil-lined 9 x 9 inch (22 x 22 cm) pan. Bake in 350°F (175°C) oven for 20 to 25 minutes until set and browned. Remove from oven.

Topping: Heat and stir margarine and brown sugar in small saucepan on medium until melted. Remove from heat. Stir in cream until smooth. Pour over bars. Spread evenly.

Sprinkle evenly with coconut. Broil 4 to 5 inches (10 to 12.5 cm) from heat for 30 seconds until coconut is lightly browned. Cool. Cuts into 32 bars.

1 bar: 104 Calories; 4.1 g Total Fat; 65 mg Sodium; 1 g Protein; 16 g Carbohydrate; 1 g Dietary Fibre

Cheery Cherry Brownies

Rich, creamy, no-frosting brownies with a chocolatey fudge base.
The cheesecake-like topping is full of maraschino cherries and chocolate chips.
A favourite with the kids' ball team.

Hard margarine (or butter)	6 tbsp.	100 mL
Cocoa, sifted if lumpy	1/4 cup	60 mL
Granulated sugar	1 cup	250 mL
Large eggs	2	2
All-purpose flour	3/4 cup	175 mL
Salt	1/4 tsp.	1 mL
Block of cream cheese, softened	4 oz.	125 g
Maraschino cherry syrup	1/4 cup	60 mL
Icing (confectioner's) sugar	1/4 cup	60 mL
Large egg	1	1
Mini semi-sweet chocolate chips (optional)	1/4 cup	60 mL
Chopped maraschino cherries	1/2 cup	125 mL

Heat margarine and cocoa in medium saucepan on medium-low until melted.

Add granulated sugar and first amount of eggs. Stir. Add flour and salt. Stir. Spread in greased 9 x 9 inch (22 x 22 cm) pan. Set aside.

Beat cream cheese, cherry syrup and icing sugar together in medium bowl until smooth. Beat in remaining egg. Stir in chocolate chips and cherries. Pour over cocoa mixture. Bake in 350°F (175°C) oven for 35 to 40 minutes until wooden pick inserted in centre comes out moist but not wet with batter. Do not overbake. Cool. Cuts into 36 squares.

1 square: 78 Calories; 3.7 g Total Fat; 55 mg Sodium; 1 g Protein; 10 g Carbohydrate; trace Dietary Fibre

Pictured on front cover and on page 143.

Chewy Chocolate Squares

A hearty and chewy square full of raisins, nuts and coconut.
The cereal adds a satisfying crispiness.

Miniature marshmallows	3 cups	750 mL
Semi-sweet chocolate chips	1/2 cup	125 mL
Hard margarine (or butter)	1/4 cup	60 mL
Cocoa, sifted if lumpy	2 tbsp.	30 mL
Vanilla	1 tsp.	5 mL
Quick-cooking rolled oats (not instant)	1 cup	250 mL
Raisins	1/2 cup	125 mL
Chopped walnuts	1/2 cup	125 mL
Medium coconut	1/2 cup	125 mL
Crisp rice cereal	1/2 cup	125 mL

Combine first 5 ingredients in large saucepan. Heat on medium for about 5 minutes, stirring often, until marshmallows and chocolate chips are melted.

Mix in remaining 5 ingredients. Press evenly in greased 9 x 9 inch (22 x 22 cm) pan. Cuts into 36 squares.

1 square: 78 Calories; 4.2 g Total Fat; 23 mg Sodium; 1 g Protein; 10 g Carbohydrate; 1 g Dietary Fibre

Paré Pointer

Who cornered the spice market? Some guy named Herb.

Lemon Meringue Squares

Creamy lemon filling over a crispy base with a topping of sweet, fluffy meringue. A delightful summery dessert.

BOTTOM LAYER		
Hard margarine (or butter), softened	1/2 cup	125 mL
Granulated sugar	1/4 cup	60 mL
All-purpose flour	3/4 cup	175 mL
Cornstarch	1/3 cup	75 mL
Milk	1 tbsp.	15 mL
MIDDLE LAYER		
Can of sweetened condensed milk	11 oz.	300 mL
Egg yolks (large)	2	2
Finely grated lemon zest	1 tbsp.	15 mL
Freshly squeezed lemon juice	1/2 cup	125 mL
TOP LAYER		
Egg whites (large)	2	2
Granulated sugar	1/4 cup	60 mL
Medium coconut	1/2 cup	125 mL
Flake coconut	1/3 cup	75 mL

Bottom Layer: Cream margarine and sugar in medium bowl.

Gradually beat in flour, cornstarch and milk until well mixed. Press dough in greased 7 x 11 inch (18 x 28 cm) or 9 x 9 inch (22 x 22 cm) pan. Bake in 350°F (175°C) oven for about 25 minutes until lightly browned.

Middle Layer: Combine next 4 ingredients in separate medium bowl. Pour over bottom layer. Bake in 350°F (175°C) oven for 12 to 15 minutes until just set.

Top Layer: Beat egg whites in small bowl until soft peaks form. Add sugar, 1 tbsp. (15 mL) at a time, until sugar is dissolved. Fold in medium coconut. Spread over middle layer.

Sprinkle with flake coconut. Bake in 350°F (175°C) oven for 12 to 15 minutes until golden brown. Cool. Cover. Chill for at least 8 hours or overnight. Cuts into 24 squares.

1 square: 153 Calories; 7.6 g Total Fat; 71 mg Sodium; 2 g Protein; 20 g Carbohydrate; trace Dietary Fibre

Pictured on front cover and on page 143.

Chocolate Oat Squares

Like a date square but a lot more decadent. A sweet, nutty, chewy treat with an oozy, rich filling and a subtle crispiness. Lots of chocolate and caramel flavour.

Caramels (about 11 oz., 310 g)	40	40
Milk	1/2 cup	125 mL
Quick-cooking rolled oats (not instant)	2 cups	500 mL
All-purpose flour	2 cups	500 mL
Brown sugar, packed	1 1/2 cups	375 mL
Baking soda	1 tbsp.	15 mL
Salt	1/2 tsp.	2 mL
Hard margarine (or butter), melted	1 cup	250 mL
Semi-sweet chocolate chips	2 cups	500 mL
Chopped pecans	1 cup	250 mL

Heat and stir caramels and milk in heavy medium saucepan on medium-low for about 10 minutes until smooth.

Combine next 5 ingredients in large bowl. Pour margarine over top. Stir until crumbly. Reserve 1/3 of crumb mixture. Press remaining crumb mixture in greased 9 x 13 inch (22 x 33 cm) pan. Bake in 350°F (175°C) oven for 10 minutes. Remove from oven.

Sprinkle with chocolate chips. Sprinkle with pecans. Drizzle caramel mixture over top. Sprinkle with reserved crumb mixture. Press down slightly. Bake for about 20 minutes until golden. Cool. Cuts into 54 squares.

1 square: 159 Calories; 7.9 g Total Fat; 154 mg Sodium; 2 g Protein; 22 g Carbohydrate; 1 g Dietary Fibre

Paré Pointer
Little Johnny said he couldn't stand on his head because it was too high.

Marshmallow Brownie Dreams

A creamy, sticky peanut butter filling with a fudge base. Add a crispy, chocolate peanut butter topping and you have an irresistible dessert square.

BOTTOM LAYER

Hard margarine (or butter), softened	2/3 cup	150 mL
Granulated sugar	1 cup	250 mL
Large eggs	2	2
Vanilla	1 tsp.	5 mL
All-purpose flour	1 cup	250 mL
Cocoa, sifted if lumpy	1/4 cup	60 mL
Baking powder	1/2 tsp.	2 mL
Salt	1/2 tsp.	2 mL
Chopped roasted peanuts	1/3 cup	75 mL

MIDDLE LAYER

Smooth peanut butter	1/3 cup	75 mL
Miniature marshmallows	4 cups	1 L

TOP LAYER

Hard margarine (or butter)	2 tbsp.	30 mL
Smooth peanut butter	1/2 cup	125 mL
Semi-sweet chocolate chips	1 cup	250 mL
Crisp rice cereal	1 cup	250 mL

Bottom Layer: Cream margarine and sugar in medium bowl. Add eggs, 1 at a time, beating well after each addition. Add vanilla. Beat well.

Combine flour, cocoa, baking powder and salt in small bowl. Add to margarine mixture. Beat on low until just moistened.

Stir in peanuts. Spread evenly in greased 9 x 13 inch (22 x 33 cm) pan. Bake in 350°F (175°C) oven for about 15 minutes until wooden pick inserted in centre comes out clean and edges are starting to pull away from sides of pan. Remove from oven.

Middle Layer: Spoon small dabs of peanut butter over bottom layer. Let stand for 3 to 4 minutes to soften. Carefully spread in thin layer.

(continued on next page)

Arrange marshmallows evenly over peanut butter. Bake for about 4 minutes until marshmallows are slightly puffed. Remove from oven. Pat marshmallows down in even layer with greased spatula. Cool for about 15 minutes until marshmallows are firm and no longer tacky on top.

Top Layer: Heat margarine and peanut butter in large saucepan on medium-low until melted. Add chocolate chips. Heat and stir until smooth.

Add cereal. Stir until coated. Pour over middle layer. Spread evenly. Chill for about 1 hour until set. Cut using hot, wet knife. Cuts into 54 squares.

1 square: 107 Calories; 6.3 g Total Fat; 84.3 mg Sodium; 1.7 g Protein; 12 g Carbohydrate; 1 g Dietary Fibre

Toffee Bars

These chewy toffee bars are ready in just minutes.
A delicious reward for very little effort.

Soda crackers, unsalted	40	40
Brown sugar, packed	1 cup	250 mL
Hard margarine (or butter)	1 cup	250 mL
Semi-sweet chocolate chips	1 1/3 cups	325 mL

Layer crackers in ungreased 10 x 15 inch (25 x 38 cm) jelly roll pan.

Heat and stir brown sugar and margarine in medium saucepan on medium-high until sugar is dissolved. Boil for 3 minutes. Pour over crackers. Bake in 350°F (175°C) oven for 5 minutes. Remove from oven. Let stand for 3 minutes.

Sprinkle with chocolate chips. Let stand for 5 minutes until chocolate chips begin to melt. Spread evenly. Cool. Cut while slightly warm. Cuts into 30 squares.

1 square: 142 Calories; 9.3 g Total Fat; 110 mg Sodium; 1 g Protein; 15 g Carbohydrate; 1 g Dietary Fibre

Caramel Chocolate Layers

Dark chocolate wafers layered with a rich, creamy caramel sauce.
Slather on an oh-so-gooey caramel frosting and chase those sweet cravings away.
These squares are very sweet and very rich. One is usually plenty.

Can of sweetened condensed milk	11 oz.	300 mL
Half-and-half cream	1/2 cup	125 mL
Caramels (about 7 1/2 oz., 214 g)	30	30
Boxes of whole chocolate wafers (7 oz., 200 g, each)	2	2
CARAMEL FROSTING		
Hard margarine (or butter)	2 tbsp.	30 mL
Brown sugar, packed	1/3 cup	75 mL
Half-and-half cream (or evaporated milk)	1 tbsp.	15 mL
Icing (confectioner's) sugar	3/4 cup	175 mL

Heat and stir condensed milk, cream and caramels in large heavy saucepan on medium-low for about 10 minutes until smooth.

Line 9 x 9 inch (22 x 22 cm) pan with waxed paper. Arrange about 16 wafers on bottom, filling spaces with broken pieces as best you can. Pour about 1/3 of caramel mixture over wafers. Carefully spread to cover completely. Cover with about 16 wafers, filling spaces with broken pieces as best you can. Repeat with 2 more layers of caramel mixture and wafers, ending with wafers.

Caramel Frosting: Heat margarine in small saucepan on medium until melted. Stir in brown sugar until bubbly. Margarine may separate but when the cream is added, it will come back together. Stir in cream until smooth and well combined. Remove from heat. Let stand for about 10 minutes until warm room temperature.

Beat in icing sugar on low until spreadable consistency. Makes about 1/2 cup (125 mL) frosting. Spread over top layer of wafers in thin layer. Cover with plastic wrap. Let stand at room temperature overnight to soften. Cuts into 36 squares.

1 square: 137 Calories; 4.1 g Total Fat; 105 mg Sodium; 2 g Protein; 24 g Carbohydrate; trace Dietary Fibre

Tropical Marshmallow Squares

A fluffy, sweet cherry and banana square on a crunchy shortbread base.
A sprinkle of coconut adds to the decorative tropical look and taste.
These pretty rose-coloured squares are a hit!

BOTTOM LAYER

All-purpose flour	1 1/4 cups	300 mL
Brown sugar, packed	1/3 cup	75 mL
Hard margarine (or butter)	1/2 cup	125 mL

TOP LAYER

Miniature marshmallows	4 cups	1 L
Maraschino cherry syrup	2 tbsp.	30 mL
Coarsely chopped maraschino cherries	3/4 cup	175 mL
Ripe large banana, mashed	1	1
Flake coconut	1/3 cup	75 mL

Bottom Layer: Combine flour and brown sugar in medium bowl. Cut in margarine until crumbly. Press in ungreased 9 x 9 inch (22 x 22 cm) pan. Bake in 350°F (175°C) oven for about 15 minutes until lightly golden.

Top Layer: Put marshmallows, cherry syrup and cherries into large heavy saucepan. Heat on medium-low, stirring frequently, until marshmallows are melted. Stir in banana. Pour over bottom layer.

Sprinkle with coconut. Press down slightly. Cool. Cuts into 36 squares.

1 square: 79 Calories; 3 g Total Fat; 37 mg Sodium; 1 g Protein; 13 g Carbohydrate; trace Dietary Fibre

 *To melt 30 to 40 caramels in the microwave, put caramels into medium microwave-safe bowl. Microwave, uncovered, on medium (50%) for 3 minutes. Stir to combine. Microwave, uncovered, on medium (50%) for 3 minutes. Stir. Repeat microwaving and stirring for another 6 minutes, stirring after each minute, until caramels are melted and smooth.*

Oatmeal Teas

A very easy-to-prepare tea-time treat. These buttery oat squares are delicious either warm or cooled, but are much easier to cut when warm.

Hard margarine (or butter)	3/4 cup	175 mL
Brown sugar, packed	1 cup	250 mL
Vanilla	1 tsp.	5 mL
Baking soda	1/2 tsp.	2 mL
Rolled oats (not instant)	3 cups	750 mL

Heat and stir margarine and brown sugar in large saucepan on medium until sugar is dissolved. Reduce heat to medium-low. Simmer, uncovered, for about 2 minutes until bubbly and syrupy. Remove from heat.

Stir in vanilla, baking soda and rolled oats. Press in greased 9 x 13 inch (22 x 33 cm) pan. Bake in 350°F (175°C) oven for about 15 minutes until golden. Let stand for 10 minutes. Cuts into 54 squares.

1 square: 63 Calories; 3.1 g Total Fat; 45 mg Sodium; 1 g Protein; 8 g Carbohydrate; 1 g Dietary Fibre

1. Pecan Brownies, page 146
2. Candy Fruit Balls, page 32
3. Lemon Meringue Squares, page 136
4. Cheery Cherry Brownies, page 134

Props Courtesy Of: Cherison Enterprises Inc.
Island Pottery Inc.

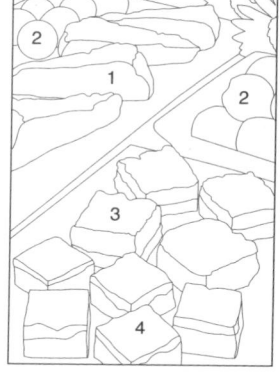

Squares

Chewy P.B. Squares

A sticky, sweet square of peanut butter, chocolate and butterscotch.
Very easy to prepare and makes an ideal take-along snack for any occasion.

Granulated sugar	1 cup	250 mL
Corn syrup	1 cup	250 mL
Smooth peanut butter	1 cup	250 mL
Crisp rice cereal	5 1/2 cups	1.4 L
TOPPING		
Semi-sweet chocolate chips	1 cup	250 mL
Butterscotch chips	1 cup	250 mL

Heat sugar and corn syrup in large pot or Dutch oven on medium, stirring occasionally, until boiling. Remove from heat.

Add peanut butter. Stir until thoroughly mixed.

Add cereal. Stir until well coated. Quickly press in greased 9 x 13 inch (22 x 33 cm) pan.

Topping: Heat chocolate and butterscotch chips in medium saucepan on lowest heat, stirring often, until smooth. Do not overheat. Pour over cereal mixture. Spread evenly. Let stand for at least 2 hours before cutting. Cuts into 54 squares.

1 square: 103 Calories; 3.7 g Total Fat; 60 mg Sodium; 2 g Protein; 17 g Carbohydrate; 1 g Dietary Fibre

1. Ginger Cheese Spread, page 117
2. Strawberry Spread, page 115
3. Yogurt Fruit Dip, page 118
4. Raspberry Spread, page 116

Props Courtesy Of: Anchor Hocking Canada

Squares

Pecan Brownies

A dense, fudgy brownie with a gooey caramel pecan topping that oozes down into the brownie once it is inverted. These squares are amazingly rich and sticky.

Hard margarine (or butter)	1/2 cup	125 mL
Unsweetened chocolate baking squares	3	3
(1 oz., 28 g, each), chopped		
Hard margarine (or butter)	3 tbsp.	50 mL
Brown sugar, packed	1/3 cup	75 mL
Evaporated milk (not skim)	1 tbsp.	15 mL
Pecans, coarsely chopped	1/2 cup	125 mL
Granulated sugar	3/4 cup	175 mL
Brown sugar, packed	3/4 cup	175 mL
Vanilla	1 1/2 tsp.	7 mL
Large eggs	2	2
All-purpose flour	1 cup	250 mL
Baking powder	1/2 tsp.	2 mL
Salt	1/2 tsp.	2 mL

Heat first amount of margarine and chocolate in small saucepan on lowest heat, stirring often, until smooth. Do not overheat. Remove from heat. Pour into small bowl. Cool to room temperature.

Heat second amount of margarine in same saucepan until melted. Stir in first amount of brown sugar. Add evaporated milk. Heat and stir on low until smooth. Pour into greased foil-lined 9 inch (22 cm) round pan. Tilt pan to coat evenly.

Sprinkle evenly with pecans.

Beat granulated sugar, second amount of brown sugar, vanilla and eggs together in medium bowl. Add chocolate mixture. Beat well.

(continued on next page)

Squares

Add flour, baking powder and salt. Stir until just moistened. Spoon over pecans. Carefully spread in even layer. Bake in 350°F (175°C) oven for 30 to 35 minutes until wooden pick inserted in centre comes out moist but not wet with batter and brownies are risen evenly across pan. Do not overbake. Immediately invert onto plate. Remove and discard foil. Let stand for 20 minutes before cutting into thin wedges. Cuts into 16 wedges.

1 wedge: 266 Calories; 14.5 g Total Fat; 198 mg Sodium; 3 g Protein; 34 g Carbohydrate; 1 g Dietary Fibre

Pictured on page 143.

Candy Bar Squares

Caramel, chocolate and chunky peanuts together in a delicious snack-time square. Substitute with white chocolate chips or different nuts for variation.

Hard margarine (or butter), softened	1/4 cup	60 mL
Brown sugar, packed	1 cup	250 mL
Large egg	1	1
Vanilla	1 tsp.	5 mL
All-purpose flour	1 cup	250 mL
Baking powder	1/2 tsp.	2 mL
Semi-sweet chocolate chips	1/2 cup	125 mL
Butterscotch chips	1/2 cup	125 mL
Coarsely chopped peanuts	1/2 cup	125 mL

Mix first 4 ingredients well in medium bowl.

Add remaining 5 ingredients. Stir. Turn into greased 8 x 8 inch (20 x 20 cm) pan. Bake in 350°F (175°C) oven for about 25 minutes until lightly golden. Cut while still warm into 25 squares.

1 square: 118 Calories; 4.6 g Total Fat; 38 mg Sodium; 2 g Protein; 19 g Carbohydrate; 1 g Dietary Fibre

Apricot Ginger Squares

Chewy ginger, apricots and coconut with crunchy pecans make these squares difficult to resist. The sweet, mildly flavoured icing adds a creamy texture. Wonderful lunch box squares.

Graham cracker crumbs	1 cup	250 mL
Finely chopped dried apricots	1 cup	250 mL
Minced crystallized ginger	1/2 – 2/3 cup	125 – 150 mL
Finely chopped pecans	1 cup	250 mL
Medium coconut	1/2 cup	125 mL
Can of sweetened condensed milk	11 oz.	300 mL
ICING		
Hard margarine (or butter)	2 tbsp.	30 mL
Vanilla	1 tsp.	5 mL
Sour cream	2 tbsp.	30 mL
Icing (confectioner's) sugar	1 cup	250 mL
Medium coconut	3 tbsp.	50 mL

Combine first 6 ingredients in large bowl. Mix well. Press in greased foil-lined 9 x 9 inch (22 x 22 cm) pan.

Icing: Beat margarine, vanilla and sour cream in medium bowl until creamy.

Add icing sugar. Stir until well combined. Makes about 1/2 cup (125 mL) icing. Spread over apricot mixture.

Sprinkle with coconut. Cover. Chill until set. Cuts into 48 squares.

1 square: 85 Calories; 4.1 g Total Fat; 29 mg Sodium; 1 g Protein; 12 g Carbohydrate; 1 g Dietary Fibre

---

Paré Pointer

There is a whole world of difference between the North Pole and South Pole.

Sweet Nutty Squares

These chewy and nutty squares have a creamy, rich topping of chocolate and peanut butter. Make ahead and store in the freezer for unexpected guests.

Brown sugar, packed	1 cup	250 mL
Corn syrup	1 cup	250 mL
Smooth peanut butter	1 cup	250 mL
Crisp rice cereal	4 cups	1 L
Finely chopped walnuts	1 cup	250 mL
TOPPING		
Semi-sweet chocolate chips	1 cup	250 mL
Smooth peanut butter	3 tbsp.	50 mL

Combine brown sugar, corn syrup and peanut butter in large saucepan. Heat and stir on medium until sugar is dissolved and mixture comes to a boil. Boil for 1 minute. Remove from heat.

Add cereal and walnuts. Mix well. Press into greased foil-lined 9 × 13 inch (22 × 33 cm) pan.

Topping: Heat chocolate chips and peanut butter in small saucepan on lowest heat, stirring often, until smooth. Do not overheat. Remove from heat. Spread evenly over cereal mixture. Cool. Cuts into 54 squares.

1 square: 110 Calories; 5.4 g Total Fat; 56 mg Sodium; 2 g Protein; 15 g Carbohydrate; 1 g Dietary Fibre

 *To cut uniform-sized squares and bars, line pan with foil. When cold, lift out of pan by holding edges of foil. Set on cutting surface. Use a long sharp knife to press straight down to cut in half. Clean knife between each cut. Cut in half again so you can work with one quarter at a time.*

Measurement Tables

Spoons

Conventional Measure	Metric Exact Conversion Millilitre (mL)	Metric Standard Measure Millilitre (mL)
1/8 teaspoon (tsp.)	0.6 mL	0.5 mL
1/4 teaspoon (tsp.)	1.2 mL	1 mL
1/2 teaspoon (tsp.)	2.4 mL	2 mL
1 teaspoon (tsp.)	4.7 mL	5 mL
2 teaspoons (tsp.)	9.4 mL	10 mL
1 tablespoon (tbsp.)	14.2 mL	15 mL

Cups

Conventional Measure	Metric Exact Conversion Millilitre (mL)	Metric Standard Measure Millilitre (mL)
1/4 cup (4 tbsp.)	56.8 mL	60 mL
1/3 cup (5 1/3 tbsp.)	75.6 mL	75 mL
1/2 cup (8 tbsp.)	113.7 mL	125 mL
2/3 cup (10 2/3 tbsp.)	151.2 mL	150 mL
3/4 cup (12 tbsp.)	170.5 mL	175 mL
1 cup (16 tbsp.)	227.3 mL	250 mL
4 1/2 cups	1022.9 mL	1000 mL (1 L)

Oven Temperatures

Fahrenheit (°F)	Celsius (°C)
175°	80°
200°	95°
225°	110°
250°	120°
275°	140°
300°	150°
325°	160°
350°	175°
375°	190°
400°	205°
425°	220°
450°	230°
475°	240°
500°	260°

Dry Measurements

Conventional Measure Ounces (oz.)	Metric Exact Conversion Grams (g)	Metric Standard Measure Grams (g)
1 oz.	28.3 g	28 g
2 oz.	56.7 g	57 g
3 oz.	85.0 g	85 g
4 oz.	113.4 g	125 g
5 oz.	141.7 g	140 g
6 oz.	170.1 g	170 g
7 oz.	198.4 g	200 g
8 oz.	226.8 g	250 g
16 oz.	453.6 g	500 g
32 oz.	907.2 g	1000 g (1 kg)

Pans

Conventional Inches	Metric Centimetres
8x8 inch	20x20 cm
9x9 inch	22x22 cm
9x13 inch	22x33 cm
10x15 inch	25x38 cm
11x17 inch	28x43 cm
8x2 inch round	20x5 cm
9x2 inch round	22x5 cm
10x4 1/2 inch tube	25x11 cm
8x4x3 inch loaf	20x10x7.5 cm
9x5x3 inch loaf	22x12.5x7.5 cm

Casseroles

CANADA & BRITAIN Standard Size Casserole	Exact Metric Measure	UNITED STATES Standard Size Casserole	Exact Metric Measure
1 qt. (5 cups)	1.13 L	1 qt. (4 cups)	900 mL
1 1/2 qts. (7 1/2 cups)	1.69 L	1 1/2 qts. (6 cups)	1.35 L
2 qts. (10 cups)	2.25 L	2 qts. (8 cups)	1.8 L
2 1/2 qts. (12 1/2 cups)	2.81 L	2 1/2 qts. (10 cups)	2.25 L
3 qts. (15 cups)	3.38 L	3 qts. (12 cups)	2.7 L
4 qts. (20 cups)	4.5 L	4 qts. (16 cups)	3.6 L
5 qts. (25 cups)	5.63 L	5 qts. (20 cups)	4.5 L

Tip Index

151

Recipe Index

153

154